엄마
UMMA

A Korean Mom's Kitchen Wisdom
& 100 Family Recipes

by Sarah Ahn & Nam Soon Ahn

AMERICA'S TEST KITCHEN

Family photos courtesy of the Ahn family

Photo of Korea during the Korean War on page 124:
CPA Media Pte Ltd/Alamy Stock Photo

Photo of jangdok (traditional Korean pots) on page 124:
VittoriaChe/Shutterstock

Photo of gamani (traditional sacks made from straw) on page 287:
Johnathan21/Shutterstock

Photo of South Korean President Park Chung-Hee on page 287:
World History Archive/Alamy Stock Photo

Photo of rice harvest on page 287: Bernhard Schmid/Alamy Stock Photo

Photo of rice and grains on page 287: Johnathan21/Shutterstock

Library of Congress Cataloging-in-Publication Data is available upon request.

ISBN 978-1-954210-56-1

AMERICA'S TEST KITCHEN
21 Drydock Avenue, Boston, MA 02210

Printed in Canada
10 9 8 7 6 5 4 3 2 1

Distributed by Penguin Random House Publisher Services
Tel: 800.733.3000

PICTURED ON FRONT COVER Kongnamul Muchim (Seasoned Soybean Sprouts; page 51), Broccoli Dubu Muchim (Seasoned Broccoli Tofu; page 52), Green Salad (page 72), Mat Kimchi (Cut Napa Cabbage Kimchi; page 115), Seoul-Sik Bulgogi (Seoul-Style Bulgogi; page 185), Baekmibap (Steamed White Rice; page 284)

PICTURED ON BACK COVER Dakgogi Ganjang Jorim (Soy Sauce–Braised Chicken; page 196)

Front Cover Food Styling: **Chantal Lambeth**
Cover Photography: **Kritsada Panichgul**

Book Design & Art Direction by **Katie Barranger**

Photography by **Kritsada Panichgul**

Image Processing by **Amanda Yong**

Editorial Director, Books: **Adam Kowit**

Executive Food Editor: **Dan Zuccarello**

Deputy Food Editor: **Stephanie Pixley**

Executive Managing Editor: **Debra Hudak**

Project Editor: **Valerie Cimino**

Test Cooks: **Carmen Dongo, José Maldonado, and Stephanie Winter**

Kitchen Intern: **Brooke Calhoun**

Assistant Editor: **Julia Arwine**

Design Director: **Lindsey Timko Chandler**

Art Director: **Katie Barranger**

Photography Director: **Julie Bozzo Cote**

Senior Photography Producer: **Meredith Mulcahy**

Featured Photographer: **Kritsada Panichgul**

Contributing Photographers: **Steve Klise and Kevin White**

Food Styling: **Chantal Lambeth, Monica Mariano, Ashley Moore, Elle Simone Scott, Kendra Smith, and Christine Tobin**

Project Manager, Books: **Kelly Gauthier**

Senior Print Production Specialist: **Lauren Robbins**

Production and Imaging Specialists: **Tricia Neumyer and Amanda Yong**

Production and Imaging Assistant: **Chloe Petraske**

Copy Editor: **Elizabeth Wray Emery**

Proofreader: **Karen Wise**

Language Consultant: **Lindsay Schaffer**

Indexer: **Elizabeth Parson**

Chief Executive Officer: **Dan Suratt**

Chief Content Officer: **Dan Souza**

Senior Content Adviser: **Jack Bishop**

Executive Editorial Directors: **Julia Collin Davison and Bridget Lancaster**

Senior Director, Book Sales: **Emily Logan**

About the Authors

SARAH AHN is the social media manager at America's Test Kitchen and the creator of the website Ahnest Kitchen. On Instagram and TikTok (@ahnestkitchen) she brings her digital storytelling prowess to recording her experiences living at home with her Korean immigrant parents, chronicling her mother's cooking, grocery shopping trips, and other everyday moments accompanied by Sarah's personal reflections that are by turns touching, funny, and deeply moving. She has been featured on NBC News, ABC News, Yahoo News, and *Good Morning America*.

NAM SOON AHN immigrated to America in the 1990s with the hope of providing a better life for herself and her family. After finding her footing through various challenges and successes, she purchased a restaurant specializing in Asian noodle dishes in 2008 and successfully operated it for nearly a decade. Her philosophy on cooking and eating foods is to make them as delicious as possible, asserting that there are no inherently "bad" ingredients or foods— they are all meant to be enjoyed. So cook without fear, and enjoy food with excitement, love, and the same feelings of returning to your childhood favorite restaurant.

CONTENTS

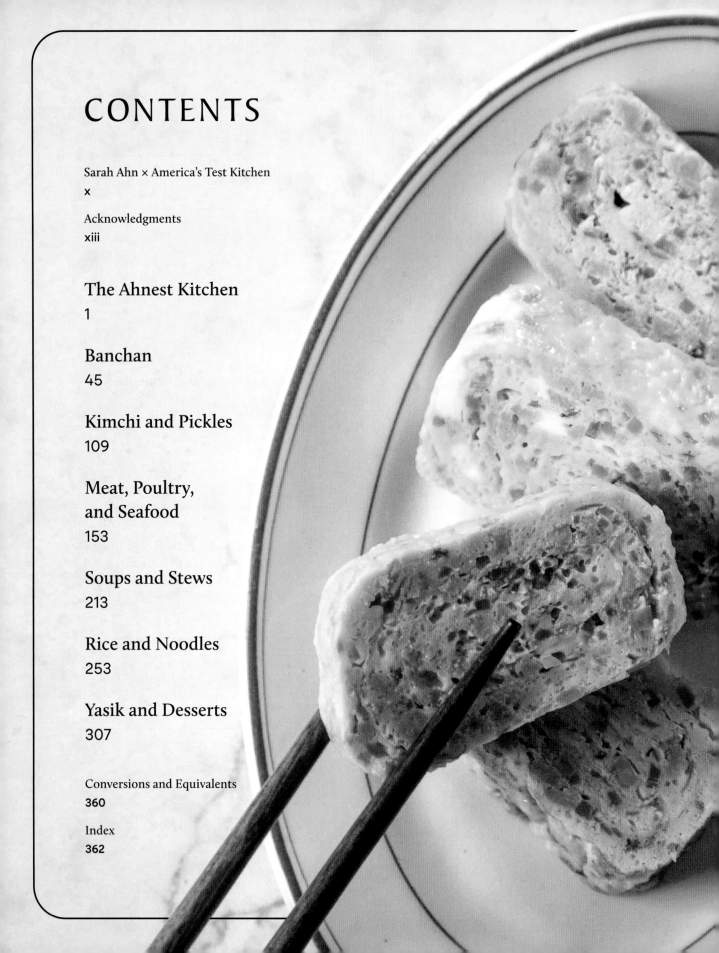

BANCHAN

KIMCHI AND PICKLES

Sarah Ahn × America's Test Kitchen

This book was written and all the recipes were developed by Sarah Ahn and her mother, Nam Soon Ahn. It was edited, tested, photographed, and designed by the team at America's Test Kitchen, a food media company founded in Boston, Massachusetts, in 1993. Located in the historic Innovation and Design Building, America's Test Kitchen is the workday destination for test cooks, editors, and cookware specialists whose mission is to empower and inspire confidence, community, and creativity in the kitchen.

Sarah joined the America's Test Kitchen social media team in 2021, taking her Instagram and TikTok followers behind the scenes in our 15,000-square-foot test kitchen—and crafting many of the videos and posts that ATK fans see on our social media channels.

In creating *Umma*, Sarah and her mom collaborated with a team of more than a dozen cooks and editors at ATK to transform the work that started on Sarah's website, Ahnest Kitchen, preserving the flavors, traditions, and stories behind Nam Soon's recipes into the 384-page cookbook that you now hold.

To get more inspiration and instruction from Sarah—and dozens of other cooking experts—download the America's Test Kitchen app, visit us on the Web, subscribe to our newsletters, or follow us on social. Learn more at americastestkitchen.com/Umma.

A word about the approach to translation: The characters are in Hangul, the official writing system used in both North Korea and South Korea. The romanized words follow the Revised Romanization system, which is the official system used by the Korean government and is the most commonly used system in nonacademic texts. Where pronunciation guides have been provided, the goal is to demonstrate how to pronounce the words at hand, which is why you may sometimes see variance among similar syllables in different words. Special thanks to Lindsay Schaffer, a Korean language instructor at Harvard University, who was the language expert and consultant for this book.

Acknowledgments

Valerie Cimino, while this book is the result of a collective effort by a talented team, we can't imagine having gone through this process without you. From sitting through countless meetings and photo shoots to traveling between Boston and our home in California, you were there to ensure that every detail of Umma's cooking was captured perfectly. Your remarkable attention to detail, talent for writing, and ability to condense Sarah's (often long-winded) stories into something poignant and moving made this book what it is. You were the driving force behind making it meaningful and beautiful. Thank you for going beyond bringing this book to life and shaping every sentence, story, and photo.

Dan Zuccarello, thank you for your incredibly thorough oversight of all the recipes in this book. Your ability to transform rough, home-cooked instructions into polished, professional recipes everyone can enjoy at home is extraordinary. Your sharp eye, unwavering competence, and can-do attitude ensured that every challenge was met with a thoughtful solution. The cookbook team is so lucky to have you at the helm, and we are endlessly grateful for your guidance and expertise.

Carmen Dongo and José Maldonado, this book wouldn't have been possible without your stellar work as test cooks. Your steadfast support, curiosity, and dedication to perfecting Umma's recipes is evident in your meticulous testing of the recipes and in the stunning photos. One of our greatest hopes for this book was to make it feel like Umma herself had made each dish presented in the photo. You achieved that and more. Thank you for your talent, professionalism, and passion. We are so grateful to have had you both on this journey.

Katie Barranger, where do we even begin? Through your book design, you perfectly captured the warmth of Umma's kitchen, the essence of our family, and the love poured into every dish. What made this experience even more special was your sincere connection to our family's story, as though it were your own. Your creative vision, art direction, and design talent gave this cookbook its soul and beauty. Thank you for bringing our story to these pages so beautifully.

Lindsey Chandler, thank you for bringing your exceptional design talent and guidance to this book. Your calmness, positivity, and remarkable artistic eye made every step of the process seamless and enjoyable. Whenever you were on set, everything felt complete! We feel so fortunate to have had you helping to shape this project.

Kritsada Panichgul! You brought life, warmth, and joy to every page through your incredible photography. Your talent for capturing the perfect moments—those fleeting, beautiful glimpses of connection and emotion—is truly unmatched. Your joyful energy instantly lit up every room and made this experience special and unforgettable for us. You captured the soul of our family and this entire journey. For that, we will always be deeply grateful.

To our remarkable food stylists—Chantal Lambeth, Monica Mariano, Ashley Moore, Elle Simone Scott, Kendra Smith, and Christine Tobin—thank you for transforming Umma's recipes into true works of art. It was a joy connecting with each of you on set, sharing our love for Korean cuisine, and collaborating to bring these dishes to life.

To the production and image specialists, Lauren Robbins and Amanda Yong, thank you for enhancing every photo with such skill and care. The few cherished photos we have of Halmeoni hold immense meaning to us, and you gave them grace and dignity. Your talent and dedication elevated all the images in a way that honors the meaningful stories behind them.

Special thanks to Lindsay Schaffer for meticulously reviewing the Korean translations, usage, and pronunciations and for patiently answering endless queries regarding accuracy.

Special thanks to Emily Logan, Adam Kowit, Jack Bishop, and Dan Souza for your excitement and passion for this project from its inception, and for your unconditional support.

Copyeditor Elizabeth Wray Emery, proofreader Karen Wise, and indexer Elizabeth Parson all have keen eyes for detail, for which we are so thankful. The top-notch project management skills of Katie Kimmerer, Kelly Gauthier, and Debra Hudak helped keep the book's schedule on track.

A special thanks goes to Hannam Chain Supermarket in Buena Park, California, for graciously allowing us to use their space for all the grocery store photos. This store has always been a significant part of our life and a cornerstone of Umma's incredible cooking.

– SARAH AND NAM SOON

To the social media team at ATK: Charlotte Errity, you were the first person to see potential in me when I joined the social media team. You instilled belief in me when I needed it most. You are my friend, mentor, and greatest advocate, and I wouldn't be where I am today without your encouragement. Kathryn Przybyla, Norma Tentori, Karen Tran, and Maritza Hayes, thank you for your unconditional love and support throughout this journey. You made it possible for me to manage this book and my full-time job, always ensuring I had the help I needed when the weight of everything felt overwhelming. You were all there to provide support so I wouldn't fall. I feel so fortunate to work with such incredible women every day.

To my close friends and loved ones, thank you for your endless patience during this chaotic yet fulfilling year. I'm so grateful for your constant encouragement, willingness to taste-test recipes before submission, and understanding when I disappeared to focus on work. I promise to make up for the lost time by cooking all of Umma's dishes for you, now that I've learned to re-create them! A special thank you to Ali Bushra and Sophia Chun for helping me navigate the most challenging parts of this project and for always standing by my side and sharing constructive criticism when I needed it the most.

Thank you to all my Ahnest Kitchen fans and "day-ones" who have followed my family's journey. I truly wouldn't be here without you. It means the world to me that our stories, recipes, and traditions resonate with you in some way. Whether you keep up with our daily stories on Instagram or found a connection through a single post, your love and support inspire me daily. It's an honor to share these stories and recipes with you and to have you cook alongside us. Thank you for being such an important part of this journey.

– SARAH

THE AHNEST KITCHEN

그 옛날 엄마와 함께 했던 모든 추억들과
기억들이 이젠 희미해지고 아렴해집니다.

어린시절 그녀가 해 주었던 음식의 맛을 기억하며
그녀에 대한 그리움을 달래봅니다.

세월이 지나 나의 아이들도 나에 대한 그리움을
갖게 될 때 이 한권의 책이 그들에게,
혹은 나와 비슷한 누군가에게 위로가 되기를
바랍니다.

- 엄마가 -

The memories of the moments I shared with my mother are slowly fading,
becoming soft and distant.

I find comfort in remembering the taste of her meals from my childhood,
easing the ache I feel for her absence.

As time passes, I hope that when my children miss me,
this book will offer them comfort,
just as it might for anyone who understands this kind of love.

— Umma

No words or actions could ever repay
the love Umma has given me, the love
that lives in every page of this book.

I know that only when she's no longer
here will the full weight of my
gratitude truly settle in — a weight
I can't bear to imagine. How I wish
I could hold that gratitude in my
heart now, while I still have the
gift of her presence.

I feel deeply indebted and grateful—
for each recipe, all the memories,
and every ounce of love she poured
into this book.

And when the day comes that I long
for Umma, I'll know exactly where to
find her.　　　　—Sarah—

Every morning, Umma (Mom) wakes up at 4:30 a.m. and prepares a black coffee to enjoy in our Southern California backyard. She grips her mug to keep warm and slowly breathes in the cool, crisp morning air. On some mornings, I have watched her standing in our fruit and vegetable garden, taking in the peace and calm before the day's hustle and bustle begins.

As soon as the clock strikes 5:00 a.m., I can hear Umma walking briskly throughout the house in her worn-out house slippers. I hear the sound of silverware and dishes being washed, pots and utensils clanging, and the refrigerator door swinging open and closed as the sounds of a busy kitchen permeate our home. She meticulously prepares Appa's (Dad's) breakfast: a nutritious meal consisting of multigrain rice, a protein-rich soup, several banchan, sliced avocado with cherry tomatoes, and, of course, a serving of kimchi that varies with the seasons. She then prepares and packs a hearty lunch that will fuel Appa's long and laborious day as a painter.

At 7:00 a.m., she completes her morning ritual and says goodbye to Appa as he heads out for work. Our kitchen, which had been so busy earlier, is now quiet and clean, as though no one had set foot in it all morning. Not long after, though, Umma returns to the kitchen and begins preparing for the rest of the day's meals and, often, even preparing for meals to come in the weeks ahead.

Over the years that I have spent with Umma in the kitchen, learning her recipes and cooking secrets, I have come to understand and appreciate what Korean food means to her. The labor of cooking and the act of serving food to her loved ones are essential ways for her to express love and forgiveness, pay homage and tribute to Halmeoni (my grandma and her mother), and pass traditions from one generation to the next.

I started my website, Ahnest Kitchen, as a way to preserve Umma's recipes. Initially, I collected her recipes in my personal notebook, but it quickly grew into something bigger when I moved everything online. I wanted to capture the little tricks and tips that Korean ummas often use, which are hard to find elsewhere. As I shared these tips and recipes online and began to incorporate storytelling, more and more people connected with what I was sharing, and what started as a platform grew into a community.

Umma's incredible food resonated with viewers and readers, as did the stories I shared about my family and life experiences, and it has been gratifying to foster a space where people can come together over food and a bond that transcends the recipes themselves.

Creating this cookbook allows me to share not only Umma's recipes but also her passion for cooking and the invaluable life lessons she has passed down to me. Out of this collaboration with Umma has come two important things: First, it has deepened my connection with her. She was always there for me throughout the journey of writing this cookbook, and her unconditional love and support during this time have brought us closer than ever. Second, it has given me an even greater appreciation for Korean food, which I didn't think was possible. The greatest gift she's given me is this collection of her recipes, which she worked so hard to develop and perfect. These recipes will bring back memories of time spent with Umma and allow me to feel her presence, even when she's no longer by my side. For that, I am eternally grateful.

For me, Korean food embodies the same comforting feelings that one's home offers—a sense of belonging, safety, and warmth that is hard to encapsulate in simple terms. Korean food is so nourishing, healing, and, honestly, damn good, that it's no surprise that this cuisine is often described as a labor of love.

Growing up, I exclusively ate home-cooked Korean food made by Umma. As time has gone by, I have grown to appreciate the amount of effort and time this cuisine requires. While some Korean dishes are simple to make and come together quickly, others, as I have learned from watching Umma, are a true work of art requiring more care and attention. In this book, I celebrate these traditional and generational recipes from my Korean umma by sharing them with you in their most authentic form.

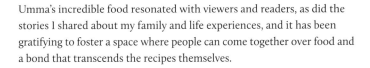

Welcome to Our Kitchen

Our family is from Southern California by way of South Korea by way of North Korea. As you might expect, we bring our own personal perspectives, life experiences, and food memories to our kitchen, and you'll see that reflected in our recipes. That said, there are some universal elements in Korean cooking, one of the most important being creation of a bold balance of spicy, sweet, salty, and umami flavors.

SPICY We think many Korean dishes occupy a middle ground in terms of spice level—in broad generalities, spicier than Japanese food, and maybe not as spicy as the spiciest Thai food. It all depends on how much gochugaru (ground dried red chiles) you use. In our recipes, you can adjust the gochugaru to your taste. Different brands will vary in spice level, so shop around to find one that suits your palate (see page 16 for shopping tips). As with the use of any kind of chile, it comes down to individual preference.

SWEET Many of our recipes use maesil cheong (plum extract syrup; see page 14), and some use corn syrup or sugar. Some degree of sweetness is a common flavor profile in Korean cooking. The intention is not to create a dessert-type sweetness. To Koreans, sugar is just another cooking ingredient to enhance flavors and create balance, much like salt. A great example is the sprinkle of sugar added to our Kimchi Grilled Cheese (page 313). Sugar also helps balance spiciness, especially in fermented foods. We achieve this balance in our kimchi recipes through the use of fresh Asian pear juice.

SALTY AND UMAMI Besides salt, we use soy sauce, fish sauce, gochujang (red chili paste), and doenjang (fermented soybean paste), all of which also contribute to umami flavors. A couple of other pantry items add what Umma (a former restaurant owner) likes to call "restaurant taste." It's a hard-to-describe combination of saltiness and umami that we find irresistible. One of these ingredients is miwon matsogeum (MSG seasoning salt; see page 17). The other is Dasida beef stock powder (see page 21).

Our Top Tips for Getting Started

START BUILDING YOUR KOREAN PANTRY
The top five essentials to buy first are gochugaru, gochujang, soy sauce, toasted sesame oil, and maesil cheong.

MINCE GARLIC IN BULK AND FREEZE IT
Korean cuisine uses a *lot* of garlic. See page 39 to learn how to prep it in a food processor and freeze it for convenience.

INVEST IN A SHARP KNIFE
Lots of attention is given to ingredient prep, both to achieve the right shape and size of vegetables and to cut them in an aesthetically pleasing way. You'll become a pro at cutting vegetable matchsticks (see page 40)!

FIND A GOOD INGREDIENT SOURCE
Though Korean food has become wildly popular and its ingredients more accessible in this country, for many staple items you'll need to find a good Korean or Asian grocery store in your area or order from H Mart, Amazon, or other online retailers. See page 15 for tips on sourcing ingredients.

ADJUST YOUR MINDSET
Making good, authentic Korean food isn't difficult, but it is a labor of love. Don't expect to find too many shortcuts for convenience (though we do take a few!). When you see a recipe that looks long, give it a read and you'll find that each step is actually simple.

MEAL-PREP YOUR BANCHAN
To ensure that we have a rotating selection of banchan in our refrigerator for weekday meals, Umma meal-preps her banchan whenever she has time throughout the week, making up to five or six in one go. As long as you have your pantry ingredients on hand, most of the banchan recipes that can be made ahead come together very quickly. If you're just getting started (either with Korean cooking or with meal prepping), preparing three or even two banchan is a great start. Try to balance your banchan selection with a mix of leafy vegetable–based banchan, starchier vegetable banchan, and protein-rich banchan. And we won't judge if you mix in some store-bought items to broaden your choices.

5 Easy Recipes to Get Started

Algamja Jorim
Braised Baby Potatoes
(page 90)

Dubu Jorim
Spicy Braised Tofu
(page 96)

Oi Kimchi
Cucumber Kimchi
(page 132)

Angel Hair Bibimguksu
*Angel Hair Mixed
Cold Noodles*
(page 291)

Kimchi Grilled Cheese
(page 313)

5 Most Popular Recipes on My Social Channels

Gosu Musaengchae
*Seasoned Cilantro
Radish Shreds*
(page 79)

LA Galbi
Korean BBQ Short Ribs
(page 162)

Galbi Jjim
Braised Beef Ribs
(page 187)

Korean Fried Chicken
(page 198)

Uyu Cream Doughnuts
Milk Cream Doughnuts
(page 345)

5 Impressive Occasion Recipes

Daepae Samgyeopsal
Yachae Jjim
*Steamed Thin Pork Belly
with Vegetables*
(page 168)

Galbitang
Beef Rib Soup
(page 232)

Gimbap
Seaweed Rice Rolls
(page 257)

Japchae
Stir-Fried Glass Noodles
(page 295)

Dosirak Cake
Lunchbox Cake
(page 351)

Elements of a Korean Meal

As with many cuisines, there are traditional rules for what and how to serve when it comes to Korean meals. Whether you choose to follow them or not is entirely up to you. If you want to prepare a traditional meal, go for it. If you want to just make one thing for dinner, such as the Dakgogi Ganjang Jorim (Soy Sauce–Braised Chicken; page 196), to serve with vegetables of your choice, that's fine too!

BAP One nonnegotiable for Korean meals is rice; everyone always gets individual bowls, and traditionally this bowl is placed on the left. Rice is so foundational to Korean meals that sometimes bap, the word for rice, is used interchangeably with the word for food. And the word for table setting, bapsang, includes the word for rice (bap = rice + sang = table).

GUK (SOUP) OR JJIGAE (STEW) Soups and stews are served in individual portions, although it was more common in the past to serve jjigae family-style. Depending on what else you're serving, you can choose a lighter soup such as Kongnamulguk (Soybean Sprout Soup; page 240) or a heartier stew like Sundubu Jjigae (Spicy Soft Tofu Stew; page 242).

KIMCHI As with rice, kimchi is another must-have on the table. Mat Kimchi (Cut Napa Cabbage Kimchi; page 115) is our go-to kimchi and the one we keep stocked in our refrigerator the most throughout the year. But we usually have others on hand as well, depending on the season. And kimchi doesn't always mean cabbage! We also offer recipes made from radish, cucumber, and fresh perilla leaves.

BANCHAN An assortment of these small plates or side dishes is always served. Banchan are traditionally served family-style, with various plates or bowls set out so that diners can use their chopsticks to enjoy directly or to transfer portions to their rice bowl as they eat. But a more modern approach is to serve everyone their own individual bowls of banchan. This makes for a lot of dishes, but it's just how everyone is doing it these days—coinciding with the turn of the 21st century and the rise of the internet. Umma likes to serve a balance of namul banchan (edible greens or seasoned herbal dishes) such as Sigeumchi Gochujang Muchim (Seasoned Spinach with Gochujang; page 54); non-namul vegetable banchan such as Algamja Jorim (Braised Baby Potatoes; page 90), and protein-rich banchan such as Jinmichae Muchim (Spicy Dried Squid; page 64) or Gyeran Jjim (Steamed Eggs; page 103).

JANG "Jang" refers both to seasoning pastes (used as ingredients to enhance dishes or to form the base for sauces) and to the sauces themselves. While we often recommend a particular sauce to pair with a specific recipe, others can be more versatile. See pages 34–37 for some of our favorite sauces for drizzling and dipping.

PROTEIN Dishes such as LA Galbi (Korean BBQ Short Ribs; page 162), Maeun Dwaejibulgogi (Spicy Pork Bulgogi; page 166), and Honey-Garlic Chicken (page 195) can be added as desired and are usually served family-style so that each diner can serve themselves.

NOODLE AND RICE DISHES Noodle dishes such as Kimchi Bibimguksu (Kimchi Mixed Cold Noodles; page 292) and rice dishes like Gyeranbap (Egg Rice with Avocado; page 274) are usually served on their own as a meal or snack and aren't typically added to this traditional meal setup.

UTENSILS Fun fact: Korea is the only country that uses metal chopsticks, although Korean chopsticks can be made of either metal or wood. Koreans use metal chopsticks that are flat rather than round and wooden chopsticks that are highly tapered at their ends. These are used to pick up banchan, as well as meat, poultry, or seafood dishes if those are added to the table (chopsticks are also used for noodle dishes). Spoons, which can also be made of metal or wood, are used for rice, soups, and stews. Korean spoons have long handles because in Korean dining, the rice bowl is never picked up. Traditionally, Koreans were raised to eat with their right hand, even if they were naturally left-handed, so spoons and chopsticks were always placed on the right. However, it's now more common to place utensils on either side to accommodate left-handed diners. One thing remains constant, though: The spoon should always be placed to the left of the chopsticks.

BANCHAN

BANCHAN

BANCHAN

JANG

BANCHAN

PROTEIN

KIMCHI

BAP

GUK OR JJIGAE

Counterclockwise from bottom left: Japgokbap (Multigrain Rice; page 288), Kongnamulguk (Soybean Sprout Soup; page 240), Mat Kimchi (Cut Napa Cabbage Kimchi; page 115), Buchu Yangnyeomjang (Chive Seasoning Sauce; page 35) with roasted gim, Algamja Jorim (Braised Baby Potatoes; page 90), Jinmichae Muchim (Spicy Dried Squid; page 64), Sigeumchi Gochujang Muchim (Seasoned Spinach with Gochujang; page 54), Honey-Garlic Chicken (page 195).

Top 10 Reasons Why Umma's Cooking Is Special

1 Umma spends a lot of time examining produce before purchase—I mean, a *lot*. Fresh seasonal produce is a foundation of Korean food, and getting the best for the money you spend is just smart shopping.

2 Umma has learned from experience that sometimes it's worth the time and money to source artisan ingredients at specialty stores. She also pays attention to when Korean grocery stores have a "drop" of imported Korean artisan brands (versus mass-market brands).

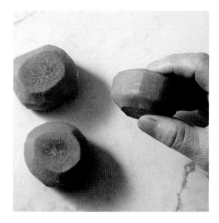

3 Umma never sacrifices flavor for convenience or shortcuts. For example, we use sesame seeds frequently in our recipes. You can buy toasted sesame seeds in a jar, but Umma always toasts her own sesame seeds, knowing they'll have a fresher, nuttier taste.

4 Umma also understands when convenience makes sense. She pays attention to modern approaches and isn't traditional just for the sake of it. A great example is the instant seafood broth tablets she sometimes uses for soups like Sundubu Gyerantang (Soft Tofu Egg Drop Soup; page 215) instead of making a from-scratch anchovy broth.

5 Umma pays great attention to detail when prepping, cutting, and shaping vegetables for various dishes, since how they are cut affects how they cook, which of course affects the outcome of the finished dish. You can learn about some of her most-used techniques starting on page 38.

6 Umma takes the time to pickle her own foods. Korean grocery stores sell prepared pickles, but banchan such as Gochu Jangajji Muchim Gochu (Spicy Green Chile Pickles; page 70) and pickles like Modeum Jangajji (Assorted Pickles; page 142) are so much better when made from scratch with balanced ingredients that don't skimp.

7 Umma always makes and strains fresh juices for cooking. Asian pear juice is integral to Mat Kimchi (Cut Napa Cabbage Kimchi; page 115) and Pogi Kimchi (Whole Napa Cabbage Kimchi; page 127), and Fuji apple juice and onion juice make their way into meat marinades. We offer store-bought substitutions, but fresh juice is easy to make from scratch (see page 41).

8 Umma takes the time to season ingredients individually, which is more of an effort but results in a far better dish in the end. For example, in Bibimbap (Mixed Rice; page 263), each vegetable is seasoned separately before being combined. This approach allows the unique flavors and textures of each ingredient to shine, ensuring that the final dish is harmonious and flavorful.

9 Umma is always very aware of achieving varying textures in a finished dish. For example, she turns off the heat before adding chopped green onions to finish a dish such as Sogogi Muguk (Beef and Radish Soup; page 225) so that the green onions remain crunchy and vibrant in color.

10 Umma has sonmat. This term translates literally as "hand taste," knowing how to make a recipe so well that you can feel, smell, and taste when it's right. More broadly, sonmat symbolizes a mother's love. It reflects an umma's deep knowledge of cooking through long experience, and it is at the heart of why it's so important to take the time to learn about your culture's food from the hands of its elders.

Building A Korean Pantry

Here's our guide to the ingredients we use, which you'll need to cook our recipes (and to prepare Korean food in general), along with our tips on sourcing and brands. We include both everyday items and more specialized ingredients that are used less often but you'll want to have on hand to make specific recipes.

Oils and Vinegars

NEUTRAL COOKING OIL

In our recipes, we specify "neutral cooking oil" because you really can use what you like without affecting the outcome of our recipes. We use avocado oil at home, but we recognize this can be more expensive than other oils. You can also use canola oil, corn oil, sunflower oil, vegetable oil, or light (not extra-virgin) olive oil whenever neutral cooking oil is called for.

TOASTED SESAME OIL

We use this rich, nutty oil in marinades or to add a drizzle of toasty flavor to finish dishes before serving. We like Ottogi brand, but any pure toasted sesame oil is fine.

DISTILLED WHITE VINEGAR

While Koreans often use rice vinegar or apple vinegar (which is not the same as apple cider vinegar) in their cooking, we usually use distilled white vinegar or apple cider vinegar. Any of these vinegars will work in our recipes. We don't have a particular brand loyalty.

Seasoning Pastes

DOENJANG

This thick, brown fermented soybean paste has a rich, sour, salty flavor profile and a pungent aroma and is a foundational ingredient for making soups, stews, and sauces. We use it in Baechu Mu Doenjangguk (Soybean Paste Soup with Cabbage and Radish; page 226) and Dwaeji Deunggalbi Kimchi Jjim (Braised Pork Back Ribs and Kimchi; page 174), among other dishes. Different brands will have different levels of saltiness; we use Sempio brand.

GOCHUJANG

Savory, sweet, and spicy, this fermented red chili paste is a fundamental ingredient in Korean cooking, used to add heat, color, and a balance of sweetness and saltiness with a hint of funk. Made from dried red chiles, glutinous rice, fermented soybean powder, barley malt powder, and salt, this paste is typically sold in tubs, and dollops of it are used to flavor a variety of dishes across Korean cuisine. This includes banchan such as Myeolchi Gochujang Bokkeum (Stir-Fried Anchovies with Gochujang; page 84) and stews like Spam Gochujang Jjigae (Spam Gochujang Stew; page 218), as well as noodle dishes, marinades for meats, and more. We also mix it with plum extract syrup and sesame seeds to make a sauce (see page 34) that's perfect for dipping raw vegetables or adding to vegetable wraps. We use Sempio brand.

Seasoning Liquids and Syrups

SOUP AND SAUCE BASE

Tsuyu is a highly versatile concentrated liquid that is often used in Korean and Japanese cooking. It's commonly used to create the base for dipping sauces, marinades, and soups, and it's also used as a flavor enhancer in savory dishes featuring rice, noodles, and even pan-fried vegetables such as Yachaejeon (Vegetable Pancakes; page 314). Hon Tsuyu is a proprietary version of tsuyu made by Kikkoman, and its ingredients include fish extract, soy sauce, mirin, and other seasonings. Umma likes the flavor of this product, but other brands of soup and sauce base can be substituted.

RICE WINE

We use seasoned cooking rice wine, commonly known as mirin (called mirim in Korean), in marinades and in other ways primarily to minimize any unpleasant odors from raw meat and seafood. Lotte is the most widely available brand, but other brands work fine.

SOY SAUCE

There are various types of Korean soy sauce (ganjang), each tailored for specific dishes, including soups, stir-fries, noodles, and no-heat dishes. We have found that it's easier and more affordable to buy one all-purpose soy sauce, and we don't notice much difference in the finished dish. For that reason, we buy Kikkoman regular soy sauce, made in the United States by a Japanese company.

FISH SAUCE

You might associate fish sauce (aekjeot) mainly with Southeast Asian cuisines, but it's used commonly throughout East Asia too. Made from fermented, strong-flavored fish and seafood, it's an umami powerhouse and a vital component of soups, stews, stir-fries, and kimchi. In addition to using it in our kimchi recipes, we use it to bring umami to dishes such as Eomukguk (Fish Cake Soup; page 237) and Doljaban Muchim (Seasoned Dried Seaweed; page 48). We usually buy Three Crabs brand, which is especially popular among Korean Americans.

TUNA EXTRACT SAUCE

Tuna extract sauce (chamchi aek) is used in a similar way as fish sauce, but it adds a more subtly smoky, umami element than fish sauce. We use this only in Angel Hair Bibimguksu (Angel Hair Mixed Cold Noodles; page 291), a recipe Umma and I were invited to develop in collaboration with the Korean food brand Sempio. We buy Dongwon brand tuna extract sauce. You can substitute fish sauce.

PLUM EXTRACT SYRUP

Maesil cheong is made from green plums and adds a mild, fresh, fruity sweetness to dishes and, as a bonus, aids in digestion since it's fermented. We use this in many recipes and there are multiple brands that range in quality. We recommend brands such as Ha Bong Jeong that contain minimal ingredients: plum and sugar. However, these can be expensive and harder to find. More affordable and widely accessible brands like Beksul and Ottogi offer their own versions, though they may contain additives.

CORN SYRUP

Koreans commonly use corn syrup to add a touch of sweetness to various dishes. It's not as sweet as granulated sugar and brings glossy viscosity to sauces in recipes such as Dubu Jorim (Spicy Braised Tofu; page 96) and Ueong Jorim (Braised Burdock Root; page 95). Buy regular corn syrup (which is no worse for you than granulated sugar), not the high-fructose kind, which is further processed. If you like, substitute rice syrup or malt syrup, though these may affect the color of the dish.

Tracking Down Korean Ingredients

Although Korean ingredients are readily found in supermarkets specializing in Asian ingredients, they are less common in American-style grocery stores than, say, Chinese or Thai ingredients. Still, sometimes there are items hiding in plain sight, labeled in different ways.

KOREAN GROCERY STORES H Mart is the biggest Korean grocery store chain in America, with locations primarily on the East and West coasts, as well as a few in the South (and they ship orders too). In areas with large Korean populations, you can also find other Korean grocery stores that offer a wider variety of brands and products catering specifically to Korean cooks like Umma. They include Hannam Chain Market / HanNam Mart (California and New Jersey), Zion Market (California, Georgia, and Texas), and others.

ASIAN GROCERY STORES If there are no Korean grocery stores in your area, the next best option is to find a Chinese, Japanese, or other Asian grocery store, such as 99 Ranch Market, Mitsuwa Marketplace, or J Mart. These stores typically don't carry as many Korean products and ingredients, but you can still find ingredients commonly used in various Asian cuisines, such as dried seaweed, noodles, soup and sauce base, and lotus and burdock roots, to name a few.

AMERICAN SUPERMARKETS Don't overlook American-style grocery stores. Costco and American-style grocery stores that specialize in natural and organic foods (such as Whole Foods) often carry premade Korean foods such as kimchi, specific cuts of meat that we use in our recipes, and produce including Asian pears and napa cabbage. Trader Joe's also carries Asian pears, though they are typically smaller in size than what we like to buy. Large chains such as Stop & Shop may carry jumbo carrots.

ONLINE SHOPPING You can also use online shops such as Mega Mart (megakfood.com), Wooltari (wooltariusa.com), and Weee! (sayweee.com) to order Korean ingredients and supplement any items that might be difficult to find locally. These retailers offer fresh ingredients, including thinly sliced meat, seafood, Korean vegetables, and high-quality artisan brands, delivered to your door. And Amazon is a good place to look for pantry items.

Herbs and Spices

GOCHUGARU

Gochugaru is ground dried red chiles. This key ingredient in Korean cooking is typically made from red chiles grown and sun-dried in Korea, following traditional practices for the best quality and flavor. It's essential for adding heat, color, and depth to so many dishes. If you shop at a Korean grocery store, you'll likely encounter a vast aisle of different gochugaru brands. It comes in two forms: powder and flakes. Flakes are more versatile and can be used in a variety of dishes such as banchan, kimchi, and stews, while the powdered form is much finer and is typically used for specific dishes that benefit from a smoother texture, such as homemade gochujang. Umma prefers flakes for their nearly all-purpose use, so all the recipes in this book that call for gochugaru use the flaked version. Be aware that labels can sometimes inaccurately describe the contents, so be sure to do a visual check. Here are some tips for buying high-quality gochugaru: It should be a vibrant, medium color, neither dull nor electric-looking. Ideally it should be a product of Korea. And it won't be cheap: Since we use a lot, we buy 1-kilogram bags seasonally imported from Korea, which cost upward of $30, and sometimes as much as $80. We store a small amount in the refrigerator for immediate use and freeze the rest in an airtight container for up to one year.

Flakes

Powder

SALT

We call for "fine salt" throughout this book, which is everyday table salt. Umma always cooks with fine pink Himalayan salt because of the many trace minerals it contains, although this is interchangeable with regular table salt. For her kimchi and pickle recipes, however, she uses Diamond Crystal Granulated Plain Salt, a fine salt (not to be confused with kosher salt) that contains no iodine or other additives that could darken the pickles, make the brine cloudy, or inhibit the growth of good microbes.

MSG SEASONING SALT

Known as miwon matsogeum, this seasoning blend of salt and monosodium glutamate is made by the Chung Jung One company, and it's been an iconic (and common) seasoning in Korea since the 1960s. It contributes what Umma calls "restaurant taste" to many dishes, including Gyeran Mari (Rolled Omelet; page 104), Dwaeji Deunggalbi Twigim (Fried Pork Ribs with Cumin Seasoning Salt; page 176), and Japchae (Stir-Fried Glass Noodles; page 295). Chung Jung One also makes pure MSG; don't purchase that product. If you're having trouble identifying the correct product, check for packaging that says "Miwon MSG Salt Seasoning," look for Chung Jung One or Daesung (the parent company) on the label, and make sure the ingredients, which should appear in English, include both salt and MSG.

NEW SUGAR

New sugar is made of 95% glucose and 5% sodium saccharin, which is the solid form of the artificial sweetener saccharin. Unlike in the United States, saccharin is widely accepted and not stigmatized in Korean cooking. We use new sugar in one recipe: Dongchimi (Radish Water Kimchi; page 120). It's important because it adds the right amount of sweetness while preventing the brine from turning syrupy as the kimchi ferments and helps keep the radishes crisper (don't substitute regular sugar, which will result in a syrupy brine).

GROUND PERILLA SEEDS

Ground perilla seeds (sometimes labeled as perilla seed powder or perilla seed flour) add their herbal, nutty flavor to Jeongigui Tongdak Yangbaechu Mari (Rotisserie Chicken Cabbage Rolls; page 191) and Deulgae Sauce (Perilla Seed Sauce; page 37). Ground perilla seeds are sometimes also used as a thickener in soups, and their nutty aroma minimizes any unpleasant odors traditionally associated with raw meat and seafood. In a pinch, you can substitute ground toasted sesame seeds, though the flavor will be quite different.

MSG Stigma Syndrome

While none of our recipes call for pure MSG, we do use ingredients such as Dasida beef stock powder and miwon matsogeum, both of which contain MSG. This flavor-enhancing ingredient deserves praise, but it is unfortunately often misunderstood. MSG is simply a compound made from glutamic acid, a naturally occurring amino acid found in umami-rich foods such as mushrooms and seaweed. Its origins can be traced back to Japanese chemist Dr. Kikunae Ikeda, who discovered how to extract glutamic acid from seaweed in 1908, leading to the creation of MSG. Today, MSG is created by fermenting other plant-based ingredients like molasses, sugarcane, and more.

Despite its natural roots and culinary benefits, MSG has been wrongly stigmatized, often due to outdated and racially prejudiced misconceptions. So-called "Chinese Restaurant Syndrome," which claims that MSG causes headaches, dizziness, and other symptoms, has been debunked numerous times through scientific studies. The FDA has long considered it safe. This stigma has unjustly maligned MSG, in the process casting doubt on the cuisines that use it. This negative discourse not only misrepresents the ingredient but also undermines the groundbreaking work of Dr. Ikeda, who revolutionized Asian cuisine with his discovery.

MSG doesn't add a distinct flavor of its own, as is commonly believed, but rather enhances the umami flavors already present in dishes. It's less salty than regular table salt, allowing for a rich, savory flavor profile that many associate with restaurant-quality food. It breaks my heart when Asian cuisines proudly market their products with a big "NO MSG" label. When used skillfully, it brings out the best in culinary creations.

Dried Vegetables and Fruits

ASTER SCABER

The leafy herb known as chwinamul is found in the mountains of Korea. It has an herbal, earthy, and pleasingly bitter (but not grassy) flavor. The fresh version is rarely available in the United States, so you'll need to purchase the dried version and rehydrate it in water to make Chwinamul Muchim (Seasoned Aster Scaber; page 58) and Chwinamulbap (Aster Scaber Rice; page 271).

DRIED RADISH

It wasn't too long ago that it was common for Koreans to sun-dry radishes on the roofs of their homes to preserve them. That tedious process is no longer necessary thanks to the commercial availability of mumallaengi, or dried Korean radish, which we use in Mumallaengi Muchim (Seasoned Dried Radish; page 61). When shopping for dried radish, look for lighter-colored strips with bits of green. Radish strips that are darker in color and look dried out are older and less desirable.

DRIED SMALL RED CHILES

For recipes like Ganjang Mu Jangajji (Soy Sauce Radish Pickles; page 144) and Dongchimi (Radish Water Kimchi; page 120), Umma buys packages of small dried red chiles at the Korean grocery store that are simply labeled "dried chiles" or "dried peppers." It's not the most informative labeling, but these are mildly flavored Korean chiles that resemble japones chiles. If you can't find them, use a red chile on the milder side, such as Aleppo.

JUJUBES

Jujubes are a fruit in the buckthorn family, also called Chinese dates or red dates (they're less sweet than Medjool dates). They're often used in Korean cooking to add sweetness and depth, as in Galbi Jjim (Braised Beef Ribs; page 187). We also simmer them in water to make Saenggang Daechucha (Ginger-Jujube Tea, page 354). You can find jujubes at any Korean grocery store or online. We're lucky enough to have jujube trees, cultivated by Umma, in our backyard, so our freezer is always stocked with Umma's own sun-dried fruit.

SEAWEED

Gim

This variety of dried seaweed (a close relative of nori) is available in various shapes and sizes, both roasted and unroasted, seasoned and unseasoned. Guun gim means "roasted gim" and is sold as large, unseasoned sheets, which are sometimes re-roasted at home, cut into smaller portions, and enjoyed as wraps, as in Guun Gimgwa Dubu (Roasted Gim with Tofu; page 76). Jomigim, roasted seasoned gim, is very popular in the United States, marketed as a healthy snack and sold in convenient snacking sizes. (Larger sheets are also available at Korean grocery stores.) Many Korean children grow up enjoying jomigim as a banchan. Gimbapgim is a thicker type of roasted unseasoned gim designed to hold its shape when rolled. It is specifically used for Gimbap (Seaweed Rice Rolls; page 257) and is often labeled as "sushi nori." Gimjaban is roasted gim sold pre-shredded with additional seasonings like sugar and sesame seeds to enhance its crispiness and flavor. Unseasoned versions are also available, usually labeled as "shredded nori." We use both of these as toppings for rice and noodle dishes (Korean ummas often use gimjaban to make seaweed rice balls, called jumeokbap, for their kids.) If you can't find gimjaban, you can shred jomigim as a substitute.

Doljaban

This is a type of unroasted, unseasoned seaweed that comes either shredded or as a large, compressed sheet. It's often used to make banchan such as Doljaban Muchim (Seasoned Dried Seaweed; page 48). Its name can vary—sometimes packages label it as paraejaban or gimjaban. Look for sheets that appear unseasoned and unprocessed, and are large and thick.

Miyeok

Also called sea mustard or wakame, miyeok is sold as large sheets or as cut strips. Each requires a different preparation before using in a recipe. For our Miyeokguk (Seaweed Soup, page 238) you'll want to purchase cut strips.

Dashima

Also known as dried kelp or kombu, dashima is primarily used to create a quick umami-rich broth that serves as the foundation for many soups and stews. It's even featured in some of our kimchi, rice, and banchan recipes, including Chadolbagi Mu Sotbap (Beef Brisket and Radish Pot Rice; page 282) and Yeongeun Jorim (Braised Lotus Root; page 92). The kelp is simmered in hot or boiling water to release its complex flavors, forming the foundation for a deeply flavorful dish.

MIYEOK

DASHIMA

DOLJABAN

GIMJABAN

GUUN GIM

GIMBAPGIM

JOMIGIM

Fermented Vegetables

KIMCHI

One area of cooking where Umma takes no shortcuts is with kimchi—she always makes her own. We do recommend that you make your own from scratch (it takes time but isn't hard) and have provided you with two different cabbage kimchi recipes as well as kimchi made from cucumbers, radishes, and perilla leaves. However, if you want to purchase prepared kimchi, look for a fresh to well-fermented kimchi (depending on your needs and preferences) in the refrigerated section of the grocery store. Labels will not always specify "fresh" or "well-fermented," so here are some clues to help figure it out: Fresh kimchi, which hasn't fermented much, will appear crisp and plump, with bright, vibrant colors from the seasoning. Its texture is firm and juicy, with the natural colors of the ingredients still visible. At this stage, it has a satisfying crunch and bright flavors, and there isn't a lot of exuded liquid present. We set fresh kimchi on our table along with various banchan to eat as is. You likely won't find very fresh kimchi unless you're able to purchase it at a mom-and-pop shop.

For use in recipes, such as Kimchi Jjigae (Kimchi Stew; page 216) and Kimchi Bokkeumbap (Kimchi Fried Rice; page 279), Umma prefers the flavor of her well-fermented Mat Kimchi (Cut Napa Cabbage Kimchi; page 115) that's been aged for at least 4 weeks. If you choose to purchase an aged kimchi, look for the opposite qualities of fresh kimchi. The jar should contain wilted-looking vegetables with muted, darkened color, surrounded by a thin juice. The texture will appear softer than fresh kimchi, and when you taste it, there will be a pronounced tangy sourness that comes from the longer fermentation. Because the taste of kimchi can vary greatly among brands, experiment to find one you like, and then adjust the seasonings to taste in any given recipe.

> ## *Tips for Buying Store-Bought Kimchi and Banchan*
>
> FIRST OPTION If you can, buy from a mom-and-pop shop that specializes in selling kimchi and banchan (some of these operations sell only kimchi). These stores are basically just stocked refrigerators of kimchi and banchan typically made by those who truly understand how to make good kimchi. They are often located in cities with a large Korean population.
>
> SECOND OPTION Look for a local Korean restaurant that sells containers of kimchi and banchan.
>
> THIRD OPTION Korean grocery stores like H Mart carry a selection of prepared banchan, as well as having a section dedicated to kimchi, with many different brands—some domestic, some imported from Korea. The level of fermentation typically varies from product to product. The kimchi that has fresh-looking, less pruney vegetables and is vibrant in color isn't as fermented. It will continue to develop in flavor as it ferments more. Kimchi that appears lighter in color, less vibrant, and more pruned is very fermented. It's often on sale, and it's great if you want to use it now, especially for dishes that call for well-fermented kimchi like Kimchi Jjigae (Kimchi Stew; page 216).
>
> FINAL OPTION We realize that American grocery stores such as Costco, Trader Joe's, or Whole Foods may be your only option for purchasing kimchi and banchan. Many Koreans purchase kimchi from Costco as well. The brand they carry, Jongga, is pretty good.

Just made

1 Week

4 Weeks

7 Weeks

Other Dry Ingredients

SEAFOOD BROTH TABLETS

These wondrous instant broth tablets are one of the great innovations of modern Korean cooking, in our opinion, and are often Umma's preferred way to make broth. Different brands have varying ingredients, but they typically include some combination of crab, anchovy, tuna, oysters, radish, cabbage, carrots, and more. There are numerous brands available, but Seoul Soup Secrets is one of the most accessible and the brand we used when developing our recipes. While they're similar in function to European-style bouillon products, the flavors are very different, so don't substitute a European-style instant broth product.

DASIDA BEEF STOCK POWDER

Dasida is essentially beef-flavored MSG salt seasoning and is used to enhance many savory dishes. Think of it as bouillon powder with a Korean flavor profile, adding an extra layer of umami. Its concentrated, savory boost makes it perfect for enhancing soups, stews, noodle and rice dishes, as well as yasik (late-night snacks) like Tteokbokki (Spicy Rice Cakes; page 319). Dasida is a proprietary name, trademarked by CJ Foods, and is the most widely available seasoning of this kind. When using it, be mindful of its saltiness—start with small amounts and adjust to taste.

KOREAN FRYING MIX

In a Korean grocery store, you'll likely find "frying mix" and "pancake mix" side by side. Both of these flour-based dry mixes have baking powder and added seasonings, making them more flavorful than plain all-purpose flour. When it comes to dishes like Sogogijeon (Beef Pancakes; page 178) and Kimchijeon (Kimchi Pancakes; page 316) and other pancakes, we choose frying mix over pancake mix, because it gives crispier results. Umma likes Beksul brand but buys other brands when they're on sale.

ACORN POWDER

Acorns have been used in cooking in Korea for centuries, thanks to the plentiful oak trees found in the country's mountainous regions. To make acorn powder, acorns are cracked open, the nuts are ground to a paste, and the starch is extracted and dried. Acorn powder is used in one recipe—Dotorimuk Muchim (Seasoned Acorn Jelly; page 62)—but it's the essential ingredient. It may be labeled "acorn powder," "acorn starch," or "acorn starch powder." Don't buy something labeled as acorn flour; this is a different product used to make noodles, among other dishes. A comparison might be that acorn powder is like cornstarch, whereas acorn flour is more like cornmeal.

MALTED BARLEY

Yeotgireum is a traditional ingredient that aids in the fermentation of various foods, including gochujang, rice syrups, and rice-based drinks. The enzymes in malted barley break down the starches in grains into sugars, creating a naturally sweet, malty flavor and driving the fermentation process for alcoholic beverages such as makgeolli (a rice liquor). The unique qualities of malted barley are highlighted in our Sikhye (Rice Punch; page 358).

GLUTINOUS RICE FLOUR

Also called sweet rice flour or sticky rice flour, glutinous rice flour is typically made from short-grain glutinous rice that becomes moist and sticky when cooked thanks to the particular starches it contains. The flour is sometimes used to make homemade rice cakes, as well as some baked goods. We make little glutinous rice balls to add texture and chew to Danpatjuk (Sweet Red Bean Porridge; page 247). Umma prefers to use Korean brands.

Rice, Rice Cakes, and Noodles

RICE

Short-grain sticky white rice is the most commonly enjoyed type of rice among Koreans, though other varieties, such as brown rice and purple rice, are also common. In our house, Umma typically buys whichever brand is on sale, often alternating between short-grain and medium-grain varieties. To accompany our recipes, any sticky white rice that you like will do just fine. For Gimbap (Seaweed Rice Rolls; page 257) and any stir-fried rice dishes such as Sigeumchi Bokkeumbap (Spinach Fried Rice; page 277), we particularly like Shirakiku brand Calrose rice, because this particular brand of Calrose cooks up a less moist and offers a lighter texture.

RICE CAKES

Tteok are made by pounding, steaming, and shaping short-grain or glutinous rice into various shapes (and there are dozens of different shapes and sizes of tteok). Although we often buy and recommend imported Korean products, tteok are one item where buying local is better. Umma prefers to buy rice cakes that are freshly made by a bakery and delivered to the Korean grocery stores where we shop. These rice cakes, which can be found in an unrefrigerated section devoted to rice cakes, are fresher and chewier than the refrigerated packaged varieties that have been imported. If all you can find are the refrigerated or frozen variety, by all means buy those. We use two kinds in this book: short cylindrical tteokbokki tteok in our Tteokbokki (Spicy Rice Cakes; page 319) and sliced oval tteok in our Tteok Manduguk (Rice Cake Soup with Dumplings; page 230).

DRIED WHEAT NOODLES

Somyeon are thin, delicate, off-white dried wheat noodles that serve as a cornerstone in many iconic Korean noodle dishes. They're featured in soups like Galbitang (Beef Rib Soup; page 232); in restaurants, diners are often asked to choose between somyeon and dangmyeon. Somyeon must be cooked in boiling water and then rinsed well in cold water to remove excess starch. These noodles appear in both hot and cold dishes such as Janchi Guksu (Banquet Noodles; page 302) and Kimchi Bibimguksu (Kimchi Mixed Cold Noodles; page 292). Umma likes to add a splash of water as these noodles cook in boiling water for a perfectly chewy, springy texture that's referred to as "jjolgit-jjolgit" (쫄깃쫄깃). Sempio and Ottogi are Umma's go-to brands. Sometimes we replace somyeon with angel hair pasta, as both are thin and delicate.

DUMPLING WRAPPERS

We save time when making dumplings by using store-bought mandu pi, or dumpling wrappers. We like Surasang brand, which are 4 to 4½ inches in diameter, the perfect size for making our Mandu (Dumplings; page 157). If you can only find the more common 3½-inch wrappers, don't worry; we give you instructions for adapting the recipe.

KNIFE-CUT WHEAT NOODLES

Kalguksu can be found in the refrigerated section of Korean grocery stores, often packed in bundles and visibly coated with a light layer of flour. While dried versions are available, we highly recommend the fresh variety for its tender texture. These noodles are typically used in hearty, comforting soups, such as Jeongigui Tongdak Kalguksu (Rotisserie Chicken Knife-Cut Noodle Soup; page 304). Their starchy composition not only helps create a rich, satisfying broth but also allows the noodles to absorb the flavors deeply.

UDON

Although these thick wheat noodles didn't originate in South Korea, they've become a well-loved ingredient in Korean cooking, especially in soups and stir-fries like Usamgyeop Bokkeum Udon (Stir-Fried Udon with Beef Belly; page 300). These noodles are available frozen, fresh, or dried. We prefer frozen because we think they have the most pleasingly chewy texture.

KOREAN VERMICELLI

Dangmyeon, often called Korean vermicelli, are dried cellophane noodles made from sweet potato starch. They're opaque in the package but turn translucent when cooked. It's important not to confuse them with cellophane noodles made from mung bean starch or with rice noodles, which are more common in Chinese and Vietnamese cuisines. These long, chewy noodles are a beloved Korean staple and are used in countless ways, including in signature dishes like Japchae (Stir-Fried Glass Noodles; page 295), where they absorb the other flavors beautifully. They're also used in soups such as Galbitang (Beef Rib Soup; page 232) and play a starring role in snacks like Gim Mari (Fried Seaweed Rolls; page 325), where the seasoned noodles are wrapped in seaweed and deep-fried to perfection. Ottogi and Wang are Umma's favorite brands, and she likes to cook them by bringing water to a boil, adding the noodles, and then turning off the heat to let them cook.

Pantry Proteins

DRIED ANCHOVIES

Different sizes of myeolchi are used in different ways. We use dried small anchovies to create Janmyeolchi Bokkeum (Stir-Fried Small Anchovies; page 83) and dried medium anchovies for Myeolchi Gochujang Bokkeum (Stir-Fried Anchovies with Gochujang; page 84). We also use dried large anchovies to create a broth used as the base for soups and stews including Baechu Mu Doenjangguk (Soybean Paste Soup with Cabbage and Radish; page 226) and in kimchi. Look for dried anchovies in the refrigerated and dried seafood sections of a Korean grocery store. Compare brands and you will notice that some products look more desiccated than others; this means they're old and should be avoided. Choose fresher, plumper-looking dried anchovies. Usually the boxed anchovies freshly imported from Korea have the best flavor (they are also the most expensive). Small anchovies can be used as is. Medium and large anchovies need to be cleaned before using (see page 43).

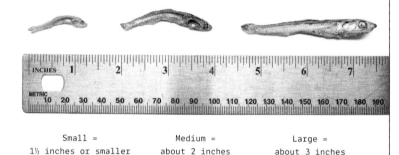

Small =
1½ inches or smaller

Medium =
about 2 inches

Large =
about 3 inches

DRIED LARGE-EYED HERRING

Dipori is an important traditional food and component of Mat Kimchi (Cut Napa Cabbage Kimchi; page 115) and Pogi Kimchi (Whole Napa Cabbage Kimchi; page 127). When paired with dried anchovies, this dried fish creates a rich, umami-packed broth that lends savory depth to soups and kimchi. Umma's mother always used large-eyed herring to make her kimchi, so Umma does the same. If you're unable to find it, you can omit it, although this will affect the flavors slightly.

DRIED SHREDDED SEASONED SQUID

Jinmichae is both a versatile ingredient and a snack. Made by drying, shredding, and seasoning fresh squid, it's a flavorful treat that's often enjoyed on its own or dipped in mayonnaise as a snack, paired with an alcoholic drink. Look for products that appear moist and not overly desiccated. We use jinmichae in Jinmichae Muchim (Spicy Dried Squid; page 64).

FERMENTED SALTED SHRIMP

Tiny saeujeot, or fermented salted "baby" shrimp, are used to add deep umami flavor to various dishes, including kimchi. Umma has tried making kimchi without these shrimp and found a significant flavor difference (not for the better!). You'll find this product, packed in brine and sold in jars, in the refrigerated section of Korean grocery stores. We put it directly into the freezer upon arriving home, where it will keep for about six months (you can scoop it out of the jar as needed). There's no need to thaw saeujeot before using it.

FISH CAKES

Made from ground white fish and seasonings and precooked by frying, eomuk are a great item to stock in your freezer. They come in many different shapes—flat sheets, circles, skewered onto sticks, and even in fun shapes such as stars and hearts. They have a savory, slightly sweet flavor, with a texture that's both soft and chewy. They're great as a snack, pan-fried with a squirt of sriracha. We also use them in Eomuk Bokkeum (Stir-Fried Fish Cakes; page 86), Eomukguk (Fish Cake Soup; page 237), and Gimbap (Seaweed Rice Rolls; page 257).

IMITATION CRAB

It may not be real crab, but it is real fish, most often made from pollack or other mild white fish. You might associate imitation crab with grocery store sushi, but it's a common ingredient in Korean cooking due to its light umami flavor, affordability, and high protein content. We use it in Gyeran Jjim (Steamed Eggs; page 103), Yachaejeon (Vegetable Pancakes; page 314), and more. Our favorite brand is Shirakiku Kani Kamaboko.

ROTISSERIE CHICKEN

We always keep frozen rotisserie chicken on hand to use in recipes such as Jeongigui Tongdak Yangbaechu Mari (Rotisserie Chicken Cabbage Rolls; page 191) and Jeongigui Tongdak Yachae Mussam Mari (Pickled Radish Chicken-Vegetable Wraps; page 311)—as well as in American-style dishes like barbecue chicken pizza! Umma also uses the carcass to make broth, as she does in Jeongigui Tongdak Kalguksu (Rotisserie Chicken Knife-Cut Noodle Soup; page 304). She freezes leftover rotisserie chicken by shredding it and placing it in a single layer in a zipper-lock bag (if there are a lot of leftovers, she freezes it on a tray first, covered, then transfers it to a zipper-lock bag). Once frozen, it's easy to break off portions as needed.

SALTED/SEASONED POLLACK ROE

Salty and deeply savory, myeongranjeot is typically available in the freezer section of Korean grocery stores. Be sure to buy seasoned pollock roe, as our recipes call for it rather than the unseasoned variety. You may have encountered myeongranjeot in Japanese sushi restaurants, where it's known as mentaiko; it also shares similarities with Italian bottarga, though bottarga is firmer. It's a great addition to one recipe in this book: our Avocado-Jang Myeongran Deopbap (Marinated Avocado and Pollack Roe Rice; page 266).

SPAM

To paraphrase Monty Python, Spam is wonderful. It gets a bad rap in the United States but became a valued and culturally significant food in Korea following the Korean War and remains popular today (see page 218 to learn more about Spam's place in Korean culture and cuisine).

TOFU

Called dubu in Korean, this high-protein ingredient appears regularly in Korean cuisine, featured in everything from banchan to soups and stews. Tofu comes in various textures, ranging from firm to soft, with its texture determined by how much water is pressed out (the more water removed, the firmer the tofu). In Korean cooking, both firm and soft tofu are commonly used. Firm tofu absorbs flavors well while holding its shape, making it perfect for dishes such as Dubu Jorim (Spicy Braised Tofu; page 96). It can also be sliced into planks and added to heartier dishes such as Kimchi Jjigae (Kimchi Stew; page 216) and Green Salad (page 72). In contrast, soft tofu, called sundubu in Korean, has a delicate, silky texture that's ideal for dishes like Sundubu Gyerantang (Soft Tofu Egg Drop Soup; page 215) and Sundubu Jjigae (Spicy Soft Tofu Stew; page 242). While there are subtle differences among Korean, Japanese, and Chinese varieties of tofu, you can use any type in our recipes. We typically buy Korean brands of tofu since they're readily available to us, with no particular brand preference.

Fresh Proteins

We buy our fresh meat, poultry, and seafood from either Korean grocery stores or Costco. Costco is convenient and affordable and has a wide selection. Korean grocery stores have an even broader variety, with the distinct advantage of offering cuts tailored specifically for particular Korean dishes.

For example, while pork belly is typically sold as whole slabs in American-style grocery stores, walk into any Korean grocery store and you'll find pork belly sliced to varying degrees of thickness, ready for use in Kimchi Bokkeumbap (Kimchi Fried Rice; page 279). You can even buy it sliced and rolled into small bundles for Daepae Samgyeopsal Yachae Jjim (Steamed Thin Pork Belly with Vegetables; page 168). At Costco, you can easily find thinly sliced sirloin for Sogogijeon (Beef Pancakes; page 178).

The same goes for fish. While you can buy whole mackerel pretty easily at most fish counters, if you tell the fishmonger at a Korean grocery store that you're making Godeungeo Jorim (Braised Mackerel; page 207), they'll cut it for you exactly how you need it.

A few cuts that we use may seem like specialty items if you're unfamiliar with Korean cooking. We use pork cushion, a shoulder cut, in our Maeun Dwaejibulgogi (Spicy Pork Bulgogi; page 166). Rich, tender pork neck, another cut from the shoulder area, goes into our Dwaeji Moksahl Yangnyeom Gui (Braised Marinated Pork Neck; page 170). We use beef plate in Usamgyeop Bokkeum Udon (Stir-Fried Udon with Beef Belly; page 300). You can special-order these cuts in American supermarkets, but they are always available in the meat case at Korean grocery stores. And you'll need to visit a Korean grocery store for salted dried croaker, a fish that we use in our Gulbi Gui (Pan-Fried Salted and Dried Croaker; page 210).

For the most part, we use cuts of meat and poultry that are available in most grocery stores, including flank steak, sirloin, brisket, steak tips, short ribs, pork ribs, ground beef and ground pork, and chicken wings and drumsticks.

Snack Attack, Korean Style

Whenever Umma and I go to our local Korean grocery store to buy produce, I can't resist making a detour to the snacks aisle to stock up on my favorite—and sometimes Umma's favorite—packaged Korean snacks. It's something I did as a child and will continue to do, no matter how old I get! (For some eye-opening information on the snacks Umma enjoyed as a child, see page 308.) Here are some of our top recommendations.

ORION GOSOMI SWEET & SALTY CRACKER
An OG snack that my parents grew up with and still buy today—it's loved by everyone in the family. Thin, buttery crackers seasoned with salt, sugar, and a hint of sesame, conveniently packed in small individual servings in yellow bags.

ORION SWEET CORN TURTLE CHIPS A newer snack to the snack scene, these chips became an instant hit with American Costco shoppers. Each corn-flour chip has four layers, shaped to resemble a turtle, and they feature a buttery, creamy corn flavor akin to corn chowder.

NONGSHIM SPICY FLAVOR SHRIMP CRACKERS
My all-time favorite snack is the spicy version of these baton-shaped crackers, which is different from the gochujang flavor and much better than the original flavor, in my opinion.

HAITAI HONEY BUTTER CHIPS These iconic chips swept across Korea in 2014, captivating potato chip lovers with their unique honey-butter flavor. Developed through a joint partnership between Korea's Haitai and Japan's Calbee companies, they became so popular that shortages soon followed. Today, they remain a well-loved staple on store shelves.

HAITAI MATDONGSAN PEANUT CRUNCH SNACK
A snack my parents have loved and enjoyed since the 1970s, this popular crunchy treat features sweet, savory, nutty flavors from peanuts.

ORION HOT & SPICY SQUID PEANUT BALLS A snack I can respect because the bag is mostly filled with the snack, not air! These are layered ball-shaped snacks that are sweet and spicy with an outer crust that has a hint of squid flavor and a peanut in the middle. Trust me, they're really good.

LOTTE PEPERO Korea's version of Japan's Pocky sticks, Pepero is a childhood snack that every Korean my age grew up with. The original flavor will always be a fave, but the unique flavors they offer, including snowy almond and choco cookie, are all delicious as well.

NONGSHIM SALT BREAD SNACK This treat is inspired by the famous Sogeumppang (Salt Bread; page 336). These small bites deliver buttery, salty, crispy flavor that's reminiscent of the real thing. They're made using real French Isigny butter and Guérande salt! Now, is it as good as actual salt bread? If I had to be real *ahnest*—no. But it's still a fun, unique snack that's worth trying!

NONGSHIM HONEY TWIST SNACK These bite-size, twist-shaped crackers with a honey flavor are one of Umma's favorite treats from her younger days in Korea.

OTTOGI MILD JIN RAMEN This is Umma's all-time favorite ramen, to which she remains ever loyal. She strongly prefers the mild version over the spicy one to enjoy a balanced pairing with kimchi.

BINGGRAE SAMANCO RED BEAN You'll have to detour to the frozen aisle for this sweet treat, but it's worth it to get these fish-shaped wafer ice cream sandwiches filled with vanilla ice cream and red bean syrup. Other flavors are available, but nothing beats this original classic, for both nostalgia and flavor.

HAITAI NOUGAT BAR Vanilla ice cream dipped in a sweet and savory chocolate nougat coating—this is an OG favorite loved by all generations. Classic snacks like these are timeless and unbeatable.

Umma's Guide to Choosing Produce

Although you can source many pantry ingredients online if necessary, you'll need to visit a grocery store for fresh produce. While a Korean grocery store will have the most options, other Asian-style stores should have a good selection. And when possible, we offer readily available substitutions that you can find at any supermarket.

ASIAN PEAR

These easily bruised fruits are often sold in individual netted covers or large compartmented boxes, presenting them like precious jewels and making them a popular choice for gifts. We buy Asian pears at the Korean grocery store because they are much larger and sweeter than the ones we find at American-style supermarkets. Umma prefers lighter-colored pears, since she thinks those tend to be juicier. Don't buy pears with any green tinge to the skin (they're not ripe). We use these pears to make fresh juice for marinades, to make kimchi, and to enjoy as a dessert. When it comes to juice for kimchi, fresh is best (see page 41 for how to make it), but you can substitute natural unsweetened pear juice.

BURDOCK ROOT

We use these long, skinny, dark-skinned roots in a banchan: Ueong Jorim (Braised Burdock Root; page 95). They're also a common filling for gimbap. Look for roots that are firm and not dried-out-looking. Medium-size ones are easier to cut than small roots (and since they spoil quickly, medium roots are preferable to large roots). Since they naturally taper, Umma looks for roots that don't taper that much, since the very skinny ends aren't usable. There's no need to peel burdock—just give it a good scrubbing before prepping for a recipe.

CARROTS

We prefer to use large, evenly cylindrical carrots, also known as jumbo carrots. In our recipes, carrots are often cut into matchsticks or chopped into large pieces for stews, and using these larger, evenly shaped carrots makes prep more convenient. If you can't find jumbo carrots, choose individual carrots from the loose bin rather than buying bagged carrots.

CHILES

Fresno Chile

Korean fresh red chiles, known as honggochu, are challenging to find in America and are not always in season. However, Fresno chiles are readily available year-round—and are sweet, flavorful, and refreshing!—so we prefer to use these. Umma highly recommends using them in dishes such as Dubu Jorim (Spicy Braised Tofu; page 96) and Yachaejeon (Vegetable Pancakes; page 314).

Jalapeño Chile

We use green jalapeños to add not only spice but also sweetness and crunch to dishes such as Myeolchi Gochujang Bokkeum (Stir-Fried Anchovies with Gochujang; page 84) and and Modeum Jangajji (Assorted Pickles; page 142).

Young Green Korean Chile

We use crunchy putgochu to add sweet, mild heat to dishes, to make pickles, and also to enjoy raw, dipped into sauces such as Yangnyeom Gochujang (Seasoned Gochujang; page 34). You can find fresh putgochu in Korean grocery stores. You can substitute Anaheim or another similar mild green chile with thin skin in cooked dishes such as Gim Mari (Fried Seaweed Rolls; page 325), but Umma doesn't recommend any substitute when making Gochu Jangajji (Green Chile Pickles; page 150). Choose firm, bright green, medium-size putgochu with a bit of elasticity. If they feel too thick or are dark green, that means the chile was ripened for too long and will be tough. Choose chiles that are more straight versus very curvy for easier preparation and more convenient eating.

EGGPLANT

Chinese eggplant is available year-round and what we usually buy. You can use Japanese eggplant, but this is a more seasonal ingredient. Straighter eggplants are easier to prep for our recipes than curved ones.

FUJI APPLES

Fuji apples are among the most popular apples in Korea, and we use them to make fresh juice for marinades and kimchi. We also enjoy these apples as a dessert. Fresh juice is best, but you can substitute natural unsweetened apple juice.

GARLIC

Because garlic is used so extensively in Korean cooking, buying fresh garlic bulbs involves too much tiresome prep. Umma prefers to buy peeled garlic cloves (if you do that, make sure they're blemish-free, creamy white, and neither very large nor very small). We wash the cloves with baking soda (which helps reduce bacteria during storage), process a big batch in a food processor to mince it, and then freeze the minced garlic in appropriate portions to use in cooking. See page 39 to learn how.

GARLIC CHIVES

Garlic chives, Chinese chives, and Korean chives are closely related (they are all flat, like grass) but are different varieties. These names are often used interchangeably in grocery stores, which can create confusion. We buy garlic chives (often called Chinese chives) because we find them to be sturdy and not too watery in texture, with a nice garlicky kick. They add their distinctive flavor to Buchu Yangnyeomjang (Chive Seasoning Sauce; page 35), Daepae Samgyeopsal Yachae Jjim (Steamed Thin Pork Belly with Vegetables; page 168), Yachaejeon (Vegetable Pancakes; page 314), and more. Don't buy the kind with flower buds on top. Umma doesn't recommend substituting American chives (which are tubular in shape) for garlic chives.

GREEN ONIONS

We use regular green onions (scallions) in many of our recipes. Sometimes we call for daepa, which are jumbo Korean green onions that are much larger than American green onions. They sort of resemble leeks but have hollow green parts, like regular green onions, and have a subtle appealing sweetness. If you can't find daepa, you can substitute an equal weight of regular green onions. Avoid substituting leeks for daepa.

KABOCHA SQUASH

This velvety-textured squash (sometimes called Korean pumpkin or Japanese pumpkin) tastes like sweet potatoes, pumpkin, and chestnuts combined. It's the key ingredient in Hobakjuk (Pumpkin Porridge; page 244). When choosing one, it's commonly recommended to look for heavy, dark green squash with lighter-colored vertical lines on the skin. Maybe it's a question of personal preference, but Umma chooses squashes that feel lighter and have more light green or gray skin pigment, as she finds these to be sweeter.

KOREAN CUCUMBERS

Although Korean cucumbers are available in Korean grocery stores during the summer, Umma thinks they're not that different from more readily available year-round cucumbers. She often uses Kirby or other similar pickling cucumbers to make Oi Kimchi (Cucumber Kimchi; page 132) and Oiji (Cucumber Pickles; page 149). Persian cucumbers are not a good substitute.

KOREAN RADISH

Korean radish is a white radish that's similar to daikon, but it's shorter, rounder, and often has a gradient green tint near the top. Try to select medium-size radishes that have as much of that vibrant green color as possible and are more rounded and oval shaped as opposed to long, skinny, and vertical. As with any radish, if it's soft, that means it's old. There's a lot of nutrition in the skin, so after washing it, only peel away any blemishes or discolorations. You may see this radish year-round, but its flavor is noticeably the best in the late fall and winter. There is a variety of Korean radish harvested young in the summertime, and this is known as yeolmu. The small root and all the tender leafy greens are used in Yeolmu Putbaechu Kimchi (Young Summer Radish and Napa Cabbage Kimchi; page 137).

KOREAN SUMMER SQUASH

We buy aehobak over other kinds of summer squash when it's in season during the warmer months. It's sweet and sturdy, with a dense texture, and is delicious in Gaji Aehobak Muchim (Seasoned Eggplant and Squash; page 57) and Janchi Guksu (Banquet Noodles; page 302). Look for medium-size squash with vibrant green color and fresh-looking stem and tip ends, with no browning. It is often sold in a plastic sleeve. You can substitute grey squash or zucchini.

LOTUS ROOT

Lotus root is in peak season during the fall, so it may be challenging to find in other seasons, especially summer. Look for cleaned and trimmed roots packaged in plastic in the produce section; choose those that are bright white with no brown spots or bruising. Presliced fresh lotus root, which typically comes in a plastic bag with water, is a convenient alternative at any time of year. Simply drain the water and rinse the lotus roots before cooking. Umma tries to buy roots that are 3 inches or smaller in diameter, which make a beautiful presentation in Yeongeun Jorim (Braised Lotus Root; page 92).

MUSHROOMS

We love the appearance and delicate flavor of enoki and oyster mushrooms and often use them in our cooking, from Bibimbap (Mixed Rice; page 263) to Seoul-Sik Bulgogi (Seoul-Style Bulgogi; page 185). In most of our recipes, you can substitute other varieties, including cremini and white mushrooms.

NAPA CABBAGE

Napa Cabbage
Called baechu in Korean, this is the cabbage most commonly used in Korean cooking, whether in kimchi, soups, stews, or meat dishes. Look for medium-size cabbages (about 4 pounds) with vibrant green and white leaves and a clean white stem end. Avoid cabbages with outer leaves that have very thick white ribs, as well as those with yellowing leaves or browned bottom cores—these are signs that the cabbage is old. Sometimes the leaves are yellowish and the bottom core appears white; this may indicate that the browned bottom core was trimmed to make the cabbage look fresher.

Young / Baby Napa Cabbage
Known as putbaechu in Korean, this cabbage is a cultivar of napa cabbage with a mildly sweet flavor. It looks like a skinnier, leafier version of napa cabbage, with thinner stalks. We use it in our Yeolmu Putbaechu Kimchi (Young Summer Radish and Napa Cabbage Kimchi; page 137) and our Kongbiji Jjigae (Ground Soybean Stew; page 221). Its name derives from its resemblance to a "young" version of napa cabbage. Baby napa cabbage is available year-round, with its peak season in summer, making it an excellent choice for summer kimchi. Umma looks for medium-size heads with bright green leaves and white stems.

PERILLA LEAVES

Fresh perilla leaves are a beloved staple in Korean cooking, used in kimchi, pickles, stir-fries, and more. They're also served with grilled or barbecued meats to make little wraps, much like lettuce leaves are used. We're fortunate to have a perilla plant in our garden, allowing us to enjoy its strong herbal aroma as well as its unique herbaceous flavor in Kkaennip Kimchi (Perilla Leaf Kimchi; page 134). When purchasing, look for leaves that are 3 to 4 inches in diameter; larger perilla leaves tend to be chewier and stiffer and are more challenging to eat. Avoid perilla leaves with browned stems.

SOYBEAN SPROUTS

Sprouts aren't just for salads! We use fresh soybean sprouts in banchan such as Kongnamul Muchim (Seasoned Soybean Sprouts; page 51), soups such as Kongnamulguk (Soybean Sprout Soup; page 240), and rice dishes such as Kongnamulbap (Soybean Sprout Rice; page 268). Sprouts of all types are very perishable, so look for plump, white sprouts, with no browning on either the sprouts or the stringy root ends. Speaking of those stringy root ends—like the rest of the sprout, they contain a lot of nutrients, so Umma doesn't trim them off before cooking. Their health benefits outweigh any aesthetic concerns!

SPINACH

Korean spinach is a seasonal winter vegetable, a bit sweeter than curly-leaf or flat-leaf spinach. Unlike its American counterparts, it's not available year-round. We use flat-leaf spinach, which is what we used in developing our recipes, for recipes like Sigeumchi Gochujang Muchim (Seasoned Spinach with Gochujang; page 54) and Sigeumchi Bokkeumbap (Spinach Fried Rice; page 277). Umma thinks smaller leaves of flat-leaf spinach are tastier and buys those when possible.

Why Umma Loves Costco

Umma does a lot of her shopping at Costco, and she likes it for two reasons. First, it's a convenient one-stop shop, for not only common ingredients such as meat, fruit, eggs, dairy products, and beans but also for all kinds of home necessities including common cooking appliances and kitchen goods. Second, it's much more affordable to shop at Costco in general, whether you're buying groceries, toiletries, or even pet supplies. Of course, shopping at Costco means buying in bulk, so you might be wondering what Umma does with all the large quantities of ingredients she buys, such as meat. She has a practical approach: Once she gets home, she portions the meat or other food items into smaller servings and freezes them. This method ensures that she always has ingredients ready to cook in the appropriate portions, while also saving money. Here are some staples used in this book that we buy at Costco:

- Avocados
- Beef: *flank steak, flap meat, sirloin, thinly sliced meat labeled "shabu-shabu"*
- Distilled white vinegar
- Dried beans
- Dried spices
- Eggs
- Fine salt (and fine pink Himalayan salt, which Umma uses as her regular salt)
- Oils
- Oyster sauce
- Pork: *loin back ribs*
- Poultry: *split party wings, rotisserie chicken*
- Quinoa

Our Favorite Sauces for Dipping, Drizzling, and Dolloping

SEASONED GOCHUJANG

Yangnyeom Gochujang 양념 고추장

yahng-nyuhm goh-choo-jahng

SARAH
세라

Umma started her restaurant when I was in middle school. She was incredibly busy during those years, so she would often leave cash so my brother and I could order take-out. On one particular day, I just wanted homemade Korean food. I found some prepped vegetables in the fridge, which we would usually dip into gochujang that was stored in a separate container. I couldn't find that container, but I did spot the big red tub of gochujang from the grocery store. I scooped out a few spoonfuls and dipped the prepped vegetables into the paste. My face immediately scrunched into a grimace from the intense flavor. Confused and dismayed, I packed everything away. When I told Umma that something was wrong with the gochujang, she laughed and explained that gochujang isn't served plain, but is mixed with other ingredients. The next morning, she prepped a batch of her seasoned gochujang. Serve this with sliced bell pepper, cucumber, celery, putgochu (young green chile), raw sweet onion, and cooked broccoli and cabbage.

MAKES about ¾ cup   TOTAL TIME 5 minutes

- 7 tablespoons (154 grams) gochujang
- 5 tablespoons maesil cheong (plum extract syrup)
- 1 tablespoon sesame seeds, toasted and coarsely ground (see page 38)
- 1½ teaspoons minced garlic

Combine all the ingredients in a medium bowl. Serve. (Refrigerate for up to 4 days.)

VINEGAR SOY SAUCE

Cho Ganjang 초간장

cho gahn-jahng

SARAH
세라

Yangnyeomjang is a ubiquitous seasoning sauce enjoyed with a wide variety of foods, including dumplings, pancakes, fried foods, salads, rice bowls, and noodle dishes. The variations are endless, typically featuring soy sauce combined with vinegar, sweeteners, or other ingredients such as sesame oil and umami-rich elements such as dried shrimp powder and anchovy broth. This simple blend, known as cho ganjang, is an essential condiment that brings a satisfying touch to many dishes. We particularly like this sauce with dishes like Mandu (Dumplings; page 157), Yachae Twigim (Fried Vegetables; page 322), and Gim Mari (Fried Seaweed Rolls; page 325).

MAKES ½ cup   TOTAL TIME 5 minutes

¼ cup soy sauce
¼ cup distilled white vinegar
   Gochugaru

Combine the soy sauce and vinegar in a small bowl. Sprinkle with gochugaru to taste. Serve. (Refrigerate for up to 2 weeks.)

CHIVE SEASONING SAUCE

Buchu Yangnyeomjang 부추 양념장

boo-choo yahng-nyuhm-jahng

UMMA
엄마

One variation of yangnyeomjang caught me by surprise when my cousin from Korea visited and was served yangnyeomjang alongside gim, rice, and fried tofu. He asked, "Do you have any chives on hand?" He chopped the chives and added a generous amount to the sauce, to the point where the liquid beneath wasn't visible anymore. When I topped my gim wrap, filled with a spoonful of rice, with this chive sauce, I was in awe of the added aromatics, sweetness, and subtle hints of garlic flavor from the chives. Since that moment, I've consistently added chives to this sauce. I use both garlic chives and yellow onion for a robust kick; however, if you don't have garlic chives, green onions or additional yellow onion make a great substitute! I often use one of those when I don't have garlic chives on hand.

MAKES about 1 cup   TOTAL TIME 5 minutes

¼ cup soy sauce
3 tablespoons maesil cheong (plum extract syrup)
2 tablespoons toasted sesame oil
3 tablespoons toasted sesame seeds, toasted and coarsely ground (see page 38)
2 tablespoons chopped yellow onion (optional)
3 ounces (85 grams) garlic chives, chopped

Combine all the ingredients in a medium bowl. Serve. (You can make this ahead and refrigerate for up to 4 days, but don't add the chives until just before serving.)

SEASONING SAUCE FOR KALGUKSU

Kalguksu Yangnyeomjang
칼국수 양념장

kal-gook-ssoo yahng-nyuhm-jahng

SARAH
세라

Here's Umma's thick and spicy version of yangnyeomjang, specially made for the noodle soup called kalguksu. Umma adds fresh chiles in addition to the usual gochugaru. We serve this with Jeongigui Tongdak Kalguksu (Rotisserie Chicken Knife-Cut Noodle Soup; page 304), but it also adds a delicious spicy kick when spooned onto other hearty noodle soups.

MAKES about ¾ cup   TOTAL TIME 10 minutes

  ¼ cup soy sauce
  3 tablespoons gochugaru
  1 tablespoon toasted sesame oil
  1 tablespoon minced garlic
1½ teaspoons maesil cheong (plum extract syrup)
  1 teaspoon sugar
  1 large Fresno chile (35 grams), stemmed, seeded, and chopped fine
  1 jalapeño chile, stemmed, seeded, and chopped fine
  2 green onions, chopped fine

Combine the soy sauce, gochugaru, oil, garlic, maesil cheong, and sugar in a medium bowl. Stir in the Fresno chile, jalapeño, and onions. Serve. (Refrigerate for up to 4 days.)

Honey-Mustard Sauce
허니 머스터드 소스

SARAH
세라

This creamy, tangy yellow sauce is reminiscent of honey mustard but richer thanks to the added creaminess of mayonnaise. The mustard provides a slight kick, balanced by the sweetness of honey and the tanginess of the vinegar. This sauce goes well with grain bowls, chicken tenders, and sandwiches. If serving this sauce with the Jeongigui Tongdak Yachae Mussam Mari (Pickled Radish Chicken-Vegetable Wraps (page 311), omit the vinegar.

MAKES about ½ cup   TOTAL TIME 5 minutes

  3 tablespoons yellow mustard
2½ tablespoons honey
2½ tablespoons mayonnaise
  1 tablespoon distilled white vinegar

Combine all the ingredients in a small bowl. Serve. (Refrigerate for up to 1 day.)

Gochujang-Mustard Sauce
고추장 머스터드 소스

SARAH
세라

This twist on our Honey-Mustard Sauce is sweetened with maesil cheong (plum extract syrup) and spiced with gochujang. Creamy and tangy, this orange-hued sauce delivers a unique flavor profile that is sweet, spicy, and nutty, with hints of pungent garlic and toasted sesame seeds. Enjoy this sauce with grain bowls, burgers, and chicken tenders—it pairs wonderfully with any fried or oily foods. If serving this sauce with the Jeongigui Tongdak Yachae Mussam Mari (Pickled Radish Chicken-Vegetable Wraps (page 311), omit the vinegar.

MAKES about ½ cup   TOTAL TIME 5 minutes

  2 tablespoons yellow mustard
  2 tablespoons honey
  2 tablespoons mayonnaise
  1 tablespoon distilled white vinegar
  1 tablespoon gochujang
  2 teaspoons maesil cheong (plum extract syrup)
  1 teaspoon sesame seeds, toasted
  ¼ teaspoon minced garlic

Combine all the ingredients in a small bowl. Serve. (Refrigerate for up to 1 day.)

Deulgae Sauce 들깨 소스
deul-gae sauce

SARAH
세라

Combining the umami depth of soy sauce and oyster sauce with the warm, nutty richness of toasted sesame oil and perilla seed powder creates a one-of-a-kind sauce that's sweet, salty, and harmoniously balanced. It's great for spooning over cabbage salads, roasted vegetables, and grain bowls.

MAKES about ½ cup   TOTAL TIME 5 minutes

  2 tablespoons soy sauce
  2 tablespoons toasted sesame oil
  2 tablespoons maesil cheong (plum extract syrup)
  2 tablespoons perilla seed powder
  1 tablespoon oyster sauce

Combine all the ingredients in a small bowl. Serve. (Refrigerate for up to 1 day.)

Toasting and Grinding Seeds

We use toasted sesame seeds frequently, so Umma toasts large quantities at once and stores them in an airtight container. She doesn't freeze them because she goes through them pretty quickly, but freezing will extend their life up to 6 months.

Place 1 cup sesame seeds in a dry 14-inch flat-bottomed wok or 12-inch nonstick skillet and cook over medium heat, stirring frequently, until fragrant. Remove the toasted seeds from the wok quickly to prevent scorching.

A mortar and pestle makes grinding sesame seeds by hand a breeze. To use the mortar and pestle efficiently, use a circular grinding motion, maintaining downward pressure at all times, instead of up-and-down pounding motions, until the seeds are coarsely ground.

Pitting Jujubes

While we add whole dried jujubes to Galbi Jjim (Braised Beef Ribs; page 187), we pit these antioxidant-rich fruits to garnish Hobakjuk (Pumpkin Porridge; page 244) and to make the concentrated base for Saenggang Daechucha (Ginger-Jujube Tea; page 354).

Cut the jujube lengthwise from top to bottom (end to end) until the knife reaches the seed.

Using your hands, carefully open the jujube and unravel it completely, discarding the seed.

Prepping Minced Garlic

Rinse 1 pound peeled garlic cloves under cold water in a colander; let drain briefly. Add ⅓ cup baking soda and massage the cloves with the paste that forms from the water and baking soda. Rinse the garlic until the water runs clear.

Trim the ends of the garlic cloves. Add the cloves to a food processor and process until minced, stopping to redistribute the garlic as needed, about 12 seconds.

Transfer the minced garlic to a quart-size zipper-lock bag, seal the bag, and flatten it out. Using a bench scraper, make 16 even square blocks. Freeze the bag.

Once frozen, snap the garlic into individual squares and store the squares in the zipper-lock bag for convenient use when needed.

Slicing Green Onions

Separate the white and light green section from the darker green section.

Halve the white and light green section (if the white section is very large, quarter it).

Bundle the green onion pieces and slice crosswise into the desired thickness.

Trimming Vegetable Edges for Korean Stews

A common practice in Korean cooking is to trim the sharp edges of cut carrots and Korean radish, and it's one we like to follow. This creates a smooth surface and more attractive appearance when the vegetables are cooked tender.

Cutting Carrots, Cucumber, and Burdock into Matchsticks

Slice the vegetable on the bias about ⅛ inch thick to create approximately 3-inch-long slices.

Stack the slices and cut them into thin matchsticks. For thicker matchsticks, start by slicing the vegetable slightly thicker on the bias.

Cutting Korean Radish and Potatoes into Matchsticks

Umma prefers to use a cleaver for large, sturdy vegetables like radishes. Cut the vegetable crosswise into 3-inch lengths, then halve these pieces lengthwise to create 2 half-moon-shaped pieces.

Place the half-moon pieces flat side down on the cutting board and cut them into ⅛-inch-thick planks.

Stack 3 or 4 planks and cut lengthwise into ⅛-inch-thick sticks. Repeat with the remaining planks. For thicker matchsticks, start by slicing the vegetable into slightly thicker planks.

Making Fresh Juices

To make fresh juice from Asian pears, Fuji apples, or yellow onions, use 1 peeled, cored, and roughly chopped Asian pear (457 grams); 1 peeled, cored, and roughly chopped Fuji apple (230 grams); or 1 peeled and roughly chopped yellow onion (442 grams). Process the chopped fruit or vegetable in a blender until very smooth.

Drain the blended mixture through a double layer of cheesecloth, allowing the liquid to collect in a measuring cup.

Squeeze the cheesecloth to extract as much liquid as possible. Discard the pulp in the cheesecloth. You should have approximately 1¼ cups pear juice, ½ cup apple juice, or ½ cup onion juice. You can easily double the batch and freeze extra juice in ice cube trays or bottles for convenient use later.

Making Egg Ribbons

Egg ribbons make a tasty, protein-rich garnish for Tteok Manduguk (Rice Cake Soup with Dumplings; page 230) and Galbitang (Beef Rib Soup; page 232), as well as rice or noodle bowls.

Heat 1 teaspoon neutral cooking oil in a 10-inch nonstick skillet over medium heat. Add 1 beaten egg, tilting the pan gently to evenly coat the bottom of the skillet with the egg. Cook until the egg is set but not browned, 1 to 1½ minutes.

Gently slide a spatula underneath the edge of the egg, grasp the edge with your fingertips, and flip the egg. Cook until the second side is set but not browned, about 15 seconds. Repeat to make a second egg.

Slide each egg onto a cutting board and roll up gently into a tight log.

Using a sharp knife, thinly slice each egg log crosswise. Unfurl the ribbons and use according to the recipe.

Cleaning Dried Anchovies

To prep medium or large dried anchovies, hold the anchovy with the thumb and forefinger of one hand near the head, just beneath the gills.

With your other hand, grip the body of the anchovy near the spine. Using a gentle twisting motion, separate the head and attached innards from the body and discard.

Preparing Beef and Pork Ribs

Back ribs have a papery membrane on the underside that can make it hard to pull the meat off the bone and can also interfere with proper marinating. Loosen this membrane with the tip of a paring knife.

With the aid of a paper towel (to help you get a better grip), pull off the membrane slowly, all in one piece.

BANCHAN

Once We Ran

SARAH
세라

As children, my older brother and I would run to the door like eager pups to greet Appa home from work. To us, Appa was both the warmth of the sun and the gentle shade of the trees. His daily homecoming, a mundane event for most adults, was always a celebration for us. In our family, Appa is the quiet, unsung hero whose presence and hard work inspire Umma to cook with such passion. It's her way of expressing gratitude and love.

"Make an airplane!" I'd exclaim gleefully while flailing a piece of paper in his direction. As I watched him fold the paper with his sun-leathered hands, covered in dried, faded paint from the day's labor, my naivete kept me from noticing the deep crevices and cracks carved into them. Every line told a story of hardship and toil unknown to me, but which Appa suffered through for his family.

Despite the difficult days that Appa toiled through to provide for Umma, my brother, and me, he would return home with a smile on his face, ready to enjoy Umma's bountiful banchan that she had prepared to accompany that evening's hard-earned meal. Umma rotated the banchan selection each day, so that Appa could look forward to the variety. To Appa, Umma's banchan was a healing balm that restored his strength and spirit.

One day, my brother stopped running to greet Appa home and, eventually, so did I. It wasn't from youthful rebellion, but rather from our growing recognition of the toll that years of physical labor had taken on his aging body. Unable to meet his sun-weary eyes with our own, we would instead gaze down with humility, as it hurt too much to see him smile through crow's feet wrinkles that betrayed the exhaustion we knew he felt.

As we matured, the endless summer days were overshadowed by the heartache of knowing that Appa was laboring through long hours in the unforgiving desert sun. Despite his daily burden, Appa never complained when he returned home to us, humming in the dark of the night. He would simply unload his van, wash up, and enjoy the meal prepared by Umma. He would then silently prepare for the next day ahead. Appa is a man of few words, but his silences speak volumes. Through his actions, I've learned invaluable lessons: to love unconditionally, to sacrifice oneself for others, and to practice empathy and respect for people from all walks of life.

Though I'm no longer the gleeful and naive young daughter waiting at the door each day, my heart still runs to greet him, as I silently ask him to forgive me. As a father who gives all he has, his hands, weathered by sacrifice, have allowed mine to remain unblemished.

Below: Celebrating Sarah's first birthday at her doljanchi (a traditional Korean first birthday celebration) in 1996 in a hanbok sent by Halmeoni. Below left: Sarah's 2nd birthday, with Umma and Appa.

The recipes in this chapter are dedicated to Appa, featuring all his favorite banchan that have been a part of my life from childhood into adulthood. These small side dishes, meant to be served as part of the meal alongside rice and other dishes, are Appa's favorite type of food. There are many types of banchan, ranging from various proteins and vegetables to a variety of greens and fermented foods, each adding a harmonious element to the meal. For us, dining as a family, as few as three banchan can be filling and comforting. When guests come over, it's typical to offer a wider variety of banchan, sometimes even numbering in the double digits. Almost all of these can be made ahead, and we enjoy them warm, at room temperature, or cold.

Below: Sarah, age 3, with Appa.

Doljaban Muchim 돌자반무침

dohl-jah-bahn moo-chim

SARAH
세라

My parents were never strict with my brother and me. They generally trusted the decisions we made for ourselves, and things turned out okay. Looking back at their hands-off approach, I wish they had provided more guidance when it came to balancing school with life. My brother and I were studious. My brother, who is two years older than me, took Advanced Placement (AP) classes and had no trouble excelling while participating in extracurricular activities; he got A's and B's without much studying. Following in his footsteps, I took the same AP classes and participated in my own extracurricular activities, but I struggled to get A's and B's without the help of caffeine, tutoring services, and all-nighters. I would often come home from school feeling stressed and pressured about my grades, college admissions, and my future. I would quickly eat lunch or a snack and go study. Sometimes I wish I had allowed myself more room to breathe and enjoy my teenage years, and sometimes I wish my parents had just said, "Sarah, you're only a kid once." I don't necessarily regret my decisions—they got me into the college I dreamed of attending (UC Irvine, Zot! Zot!), but when I remember my high school years, I think about what I would tell my own kids if they were in that situation. This banchan reminds me of the happier aspects of those times. Coming home from school, nothing excited me more than seeing a freshly packed container of Umma's doljaban muchim in our fridge. I would grab the container without hesitation and scarf it down with rice and whatever protein I was craving. I never knew what banchan I would come home to, but this one always made my day. It uses a type of dried large seaweed known as doljaban, gimjaban, or paraejaban. It's often sold in jumbo packs in one giant, compressed sheet or torn into pieces already.

SERVES 4 (makes 3 cups)   TOTAL TIME 30 minutes

- 2 ounces (57 grams) doljaban, layers separated and torn into bite-size pieces, divided
- 6 tablespoons water
- 2 tablespoons soy sauce
- 2 tablespoons corn syrup
- 1½ tablespoons fish sauce
- 1½ tablespoons maesil cheong (plum extract syrup)
- 1½ tablespoons toasted sesame oil
- 1 tablespoon mirin
- 1 tablespoon sugar
- 1½ teaspoons minced garlic
- 1 Fresno chile, stemmed, seeded, and minced
- 2 green onions, sliced ¾ inch thick
- ½ cup (71 grams) thinly sliced yellow onion
- 1½ teaspoons sesame seeds, toasted

1 Working in 3 batches, toast the doljaban in a 14-inch flat-bottomed wok or 12-inch nonstick skillet over medium-high heat, tossing constantly, until fragrant and crisp, 1 to 2 minutes. Transfer the doljaban to a large bowl and wipe the wok clean with paper towels after each batch.

2 Whisk the water, soy sauce, corn syrup, fish sauce, maesil cheong, oil, mirin, sugar, and garlic in a separate bowl until well combined. Pour the sauce over the doljaban and, using your gloved hands, massage vigorously until most of the sauce has been absorbed. Break up any large clumps of the doljaban. Add the Fresno chile, green onions, yellow onion, and sesame seeds and mix. Serve. (Refrigerate for up to 4 days.)

Tear the doljaban sheet
into bite-size pieces before
toasting it.

Kongnamul Muchim 콩나물무침

kohng-nah-mool moo-chim

SARAH
세라

Umma used to make a seasoned soybean sprout banchan all the time. After all, it's one of the classic and traditional side dishes that every Korean knows. However, every time she made it, it was the lone banchan that didn't get the usual praise of "Wow, Umma, this is really good!" One day, she decided to add imitation crab to this side dish. Ever since, these sprouts have always received high praise when served. The lightly sweet shredded crab works beautifully with the delicate crunchiness of the soybean sprouts. The gochugaru adds spice and the Dasida adds umami, but you can leave either out if you prefer. You can also substitute mung bean sprouts for the soybean sprouts, with no other recipe changes.

Umma's Kitchen Wisdom

Make sure to let the sprouts drain for at least 1 hour in the refrigerator in step 2. Shortening that time is an impatient rookie mistake that I made when I was younger, and I discovered that it leads to a watery dish with diluted seasoning. If you wish to prepare this ahead of time, I highly recommend draining overnight!

Soybean sprouts contain a lot of water that will leach out during storage, so I don't recommend saving leftovers. Instead, I like to prepare this recipe in smaller batches so we can enjoy it fresh every time. Here's how: Cook the full amount of sprouts as instructed, then toss half the cooked sprouts with half of the remaining ingredients. You can refrigerate the remaining sprouts (leave them in the colander to continue to drain) and use them to make the rest of this dish later in the week.

SERVES 4 to 6 (makes 3½ cups)
TOTAL TIME 30 minutes, plus 1 hour draining

- 12 ounces (340 grams) soybean sprouts
- 2 green onions, chopped
- 2 tablespoons sesame seeds, toasted and coarsely ground (see page 38)
- 1 tablespoon toasted sesame oil
- 2½ teaspoons fish sauce
- 2 teaspoons minced garlic
- 1 teaspoon sugar
- 1 teaspoon gochugaru (optional)
- ½ teaspoon fine salt
- ¼ teaspoon Dasida beef stock powder (optional)
- 2¼ ounces (64 grams) imitation crab, lightly squeezed and pulled apart into fine strands

1 Cook the soybean sprouts and ⅔ cup water in a covered large saucepan over high heat until steam begins to rise out of the saucepan, about 4 minutes. Reduce the heat to medium. Turn the sprouts once, cover, and continue to cook until steam rises out of the saucepan again. Remove the saucepan from the heat and let sit, covered, for 1 minute.

2 Immediately drain the sprouts in a colander, transfer to a large bowl, and submerge in cold running water. Gently run your hands through the sprouts to cool them. Drain the sprouts again and repeat covering with cold water until the sprouts are completely cooled. (This is to stop the sprouts from cooking so they maintain their crunch.) Drain the sprouts in the colander, then set the colander in an empty bowl. Cover with plastic wrap and let sit in the refrigerator for a minimum of 1 hour to continue draining.

3 Gently toss the sprouts; onions; sesame seeds; oil; fish sauce; garlic; sugar; gochugaru, if using; salt; and Dasida powder, if using, in a bowl until well combined. Add the crab and toss gently to combine. (Don't overmix, as this will break apart the delicate crab shreds.) Serve immediately.

Broccoli Dubu Muchim
브로콜리두부무침

broccoli doo-boo moo-chim

SARAH
세라

Umma occasionally buys convenient frozen broccoli florets to enjoy them dipped into Yangnyeom Gochujang (Seasoned Gochujang; page 34), to add to main dishes, or to make this simple banchan. The broccoli is massaged with crumbled tofu for protein and texture before a toasty seasoning mixture is added. The flavorful seasonings impart a balanced depth of sweetness and saltiness, that, when combined with the varied textures, makes this broccoli banchan extremely enjoyable.

SERVES 4 (makes 2 cups)   **TOTAL TIME** 40 minutes

½ teaspoon fine salt

4 ounces (113 grams) firm tofu

8 ounces (227 grams) frozen broccoli florets, thawed and cut into 1-inch pieces

5 teaspoons toasted sesame oil

3½ teaspoons fish sauce

1½ teaspoons sesame seeds, toasted and coarsely ground (see page 38)

½ teaspoon sugar

1 Bring 1 quart water and the salt to a boil in a large saucepan. Add the tofu and boil for 30 seconds. Drain the tofu, then wrap it in a clean dish towel or a triple layer of cheesecloth and gently squeeze out excess water. Transfer the tofu to a large bowl and break into fine crumbles.

2 Gently squeeze the broccoli by hand to release excess water; add the broccoli to the bowl with the tofu. Using your gloved hands, gently mix the tofu and broccoli together, spreading the tofu crumbles evenly throughout the broccoli. Add the oil, fish sauce, sesame seeds, and sugar and mix, gently massaging the seasoning mixture and tofu into the broccoli. Serve. (Refrigerate for up to 1 week.)

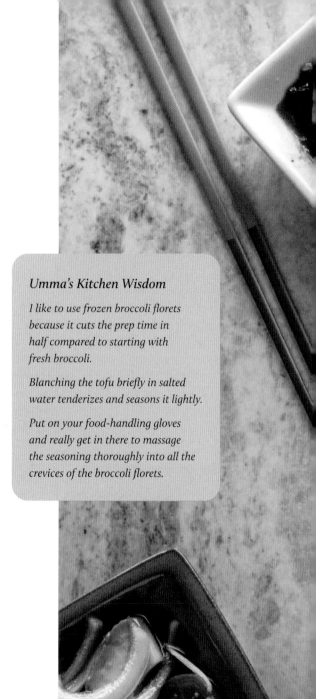

Umma's Kitchen Wisdom

I like to use frozen broccoli florets because it cuts the prep time in half compared to starting with fresh broccoli.

Blanching the tofu briefly in salted water tenderizes and seasons it lightly.

Put on your food-handling gloves and really get in there to massage the seasoning thoroughly into all the crevices of the broccoli florets.

Sigeumchi Gochujang Muchim
시금치고추장무침

shi-geum-chi goh-choo-jang moo-chim

UMMA
엄마

When my mother-in-law passed away, Appa and I attended her funeral on Yongjeong Island, near Incheon on the Korean mainland. Appa's family, made up mainly of farmers, had grown some Korean spinach and made a classic seasoned spinach banchan for us. This was the sweetest and most delicious spinach I'd ever tasted; I didn't know spinach could taste that good. It inspired me to create this recipe, which I think really highlights the flavor of fresh spinach, after I returned home.

SARAH
세라

You might be wondering why we included this particular recipe instead of the classic sigeumchi muchim (blanched spinach seasoned without gochujang). Simply put, my family isn't crazy about sigeumchi muchim, and we often have leftovers that go unfinished. Umma's trip to Yongjeong Island inspired her to adapt that recipe to create this one, where she adds gochujang for some spice that enhances the flavor of the spinach. Since Korean spinach isn't available year-round, we use flat-leaf spinach to make this so that we can enjoy it anytime.

SERVES 4 (makes 1½ cups)   TOTAL TIME 30 minutes

1 teaspoon fine salt
8 ounces (227 grams) flat-leaf spinach
1 tablespoon gochujang
1 tablespoon maesil cheong (plum extract syrup)
1 tablespoon toasted sesame oil
¼ teaspoon sugar
½ teaspoon minced garlic
1 tablespoon sesame seeds, toasted
1 green onion, white part only, sliced thin

1 Bring 1 quart water and the salt to a boil in a large, wide pot. Add the spinach and submerge completely. Blanch until the spinach is bright green but still has some bite, about 10 seconds. Immediately drain the spinach, transfer to a large bowl, and submerge in cold running water. Gently run your hands through the spinach to separate it. Drain the spinach again and repeat covering with cold water until the spinach is completely cooled.

2 Working in batches, squeeze the spinach by hand to remove excess water, then untangle the leaves. Using kitchen shears, cut the spinach into rough 2-inch lengths and transfer to a large bowl. (Be careful not to cut the spinach too short.)

3 Whisk the gochujang, maesil cheong, oil, sugar, and garlic in a separate bowl until well combined; add the sauce to the spinach. Using your gloved hands, lift and loosen individual pieces of spinach to separate them and mix gently until the spinach pieces are evenly coated with the sauce. Add the sesame seeds and onion and mix gently to combine. Serve. (Refrigerate for up to 4 days.)

Umma's Kitchen Wisdom

Korean spinach is sweeter in flavor, chewier, and thicker than the flat-leaf spinach you typically find in American supermarkets (and often in Korean grocery stores). If you can find Korean spinach, blanch it for about 30 seconds and adjust the seasonings to your taste.

Don't limit yourself to just spinach with this banchan! Dandelion greens, frozen broccoli, and crown daisies (chrysanthemum greens) are great substitutes. If you use frozen broccoli, thaw it first.

Gaji Aehobak Muchim 가지애호박무침

gah-ji ae-hoh-bahk moo-chim

SARAH
세라

Every summer night when I was a kid, after finishing tutoring homework and eating dinner, my family and I would gather to watch new episodes of the SBS (Seoul Broadcasting System) show *Animal Farm*. As we watched, my brother and I would enjoy a plate of different fruits that Umma and Appa had cut for us. This included pineapple, watermelon, honeydew, and peaches. I enjoyed all but one fruit: the terrifying peach. My family would ask why I avoided the cut-up pieces of peach, and I told them it was because the center and seed were covered in "blood" (in actuality, it's just red anthocyanin pigments, which are very high in antioxidants). No matter how much my family tried to convince me otherwise, I couldn't get over this fear. Similarly, I harbored a deep fear of another ingredient commonly found in Korean cuisine. Was it beondegi (a street food snack made from silkworm pupae)? Nope. Was it sundae (blood sausage made from intestines)? No—I enjoyed both of those snacks, so guess again! Oddly, it was eggplant, particularly cooked eggplant. My peculiar imagination got the best of me, and I found myself terrified of this grotesque-looking and slimy-textured vegetable. Thankfully, as I matured, I overcame these nonsensical fears. Today, I see peaches as nature's candy, full of health benefits. And I now perceive eggplants as plush, silky fruits capable of absorbing any sauce to create a flavorful banchan such as this one. The eggplant and squash cook to a tender texture, and the nutty, garlicky, spicy sauce adds bold flavor. You can use grey squash or zucchini if you can't find aehobak (see page 31).

Umma's Kitchen Wisdom

"Roasting" the eggplant on the stovetop (in a skillet with no added oil) removes excess moisture, intensifying its flavors. Adjust the heat as needed to make sure it doesn't get too dry or start to brown, which will make it leathery.

SERVES 4 (makes 1½ cups)   TOTAL TIME 45 minutes

- 1 tablespoon soy sauce
- 1 tablespoon maesil cheong (plum extract syrup)
- 1 tablespoon toasted sesame oil
- 2 teaspoons sugar
- 2 teaspoons minced garlic
- 1½ teaspoons fish sauce
- 1½ teaspoons gochugaru
- 1 Chinese eggplant (283 grams), trimmed and sliced into ⅛-inch-thick rounds
- 1 aehobak (Korean summer squash; 227 grams), trimmed and sliced into ⅛-inch-thick rounds
- 2 green onions, sliced thin
- ½ jalapeño chile, stemmed, seeded, and minced
- ½ Fresno chile, stemmed, seeded, and minced
- 1 tablespoon sesame seeds, toasted and coarsely ground (see page 38)

1 Whisk the soy sauce, maesil cheong, oil, sugar, garlic, fish sauce, and gochugaru in a small bowl until the sugar has dissolved. Set the sauce aside.

2 Working in batches, place a single layer of eggplant rounds in a 12-inch nonstick skillet over medium heat. Cook, turning as needed, until the eggplant is softened and pliable but not browned or dried out, 5 to 10 minutes. Transfer the eggplant to a medium bowl.

3 Working in batches, place a single layer of aehobak rounds in the now-empty skillet over medium heat. Cook, turning as needed, until the aehobak is softened and spotty brown, 4 to 7 minutes. Transfer the aehobak to the bowl with the eggplant.

4 Add the onions, jalapeño, Fresno chile, and sesame seeds to the bowl and toss gently to combine. Whisk the sauce to recombine, then add to the bowl and toss gently to coat. Serve. (Refrigerate for up to 4 days.)

Chwinamul Muchim 취나물무침

chwee-nah-mool moo-chim

SARAH
세라

Chwinamul (aster scaber) is a perennial herb commonly found in the mountains of Korea, as well as in China, Japan, and Russia. In Korean cuisine, these pleasantly bitter, aromatic leaves are widely used to create banchan such as this one, and they are also prominent in rice dishes like Chwinamulbap (Aster Scaber Rice; page 271) and sometimes bibimbap. Chwinamul is one of my favorite herbs—I love its unique flavor, which is earthy yet mellow and not overpowering. It's hard to find fresh chwinamul outside its native area, so we use the dried version, which is available in Korean grocery stores and online. It's important to rinse the dried aster scaber thoroughly after soaking it to remove any lingering acridness. Here's how to enjoy it as a banchan, where its herbaceous flavors meet a savory, toasty, umami-rich seasoning to create a balanced pairing. The Dasida adds a little extra umami, but it's optional.

SERVES 6 (makes 3½ cups)
TOTAL TIME 1½ hours, plus 8 hours soaking

2 ounces (57 grams) dried chwinamul (aster scaber)
2 green onions, sliced thin
2 tablespoons soy sauce
2 tablespoons toasted sesame oil
1 tablespoon sesame seeds, toasted and coarsely ground (see page 38)
2½ teaspoons sugar
1½ teaspoons minced garlic
½ teaspoon Dasida beef stock powder (optional)

1 Submerge the chwinamul in 3 quarts water in a large bowl or container. Let soak overnight (8 to 12 hours) to rehydrate.

2 Drain the chwinamul and rinse thoroughly in a bowl of water, using your hands to rub the chwinamul leaves against each other. Drain and rinse again in a bowl of water; repeat until the water runs clear.

3 Add the chwinamul and 3 quarts water to a large, wide pot and bring to a boil. Reduce the heat to a simmer and cook, flipping occasionally to push the chwinamul that has risen to the surface back under the water, until the stems are tender, about 45 minutes.

4 Drain the chwinamul, transfer to a large bowl, and submerge in cold running water. Drain the chiwanmul and submerge in cold water again. Using your hands, gently agitate the leaves to untangle any knotted sections. Drain the chiwanmul again and repeat covering with cold water, untangling, and draining until the chwinamul is completely cooled.

5 Working in batches, squeeze the chwinamul by hand to remove excess water, and transfer to a cutting board. (Don't over-squeeze; the chwinamul should remain slightly moist.) Lift and loosen individual leaves of chwinamul to untangle any knotted sections and arrange the strands in a single straight mound on the cutting board. Cut the mound crosswise into approximately 1-inch sections.

6 Transfer the chopped chwinamul to a large bowl and separate any clumps. Add the onions, soy sauce, oil, sesame seeds, sugar, garlic, and Dasida powder, if using. Using your gloved hands, lift and loosen individual pieces of chwinamul and mix gently until the pieces are evenly coated with the seasonings. Serve. (Refrigerate for up to 2 days.)

SEASONED DRIED RADISH

Mumallaengi Muchim 무말랭이무침

moo-mal-laeng-e moo-chim

UMMA 엄마

There is a Korean saying: "Radish in the fall is better than ginseng." Ginseng is highly regarded in traditional Korean medicine for its health benefits, so this phrase implies that radishes harvested in the fall are even more valuable. When I was growing up, Halmeoni would sun-dry Korean radish strips on the rooftop of our house in bamboo baskets to make this banchan. Sun-drying was her way of preserving the radish and concentrating its nutrients. Following Halmeoni's example, I began to sun-dry radish strips myself. Later, as an older umma, I bought a dehydrator to speed up the process. This method proved to be extremely convenient, as sun-drying foods can be challenging due to unpredictable weather, bugs, and mold. Even with the added convenience, though, it's still labor-intensive to dry fresh radish strips, so when developing this recipe I opted for store-bought dried radish strips, which you can find at Korean grocery stores. This is what Koreans typically use instead of drying the radish at home. I'm happy to report that this version tastes similar to what I grew up with from Halmeoni.

SARAH 세라

This banchan comes together quickly and delivers a bold and crunchy bite full of spice and tang. It's essential to wash the dried radish strips thoroughly to remove the odor associated with dehydrated radish (Umma washes them three times total) and to rehydrate the strips for 30 minutes. You can serve this right away, but for even better flavor, we like to let this prepared banchan rest for a day or so in the refrigerator before serving it. This allows the radish to absorb the sauce, resulting in a crunchier texture.

Umma's Kitchen Wisdom

When shopping for dried radish, look for lighter-colored strips with bits of green. Darker-colored, very dried-out-looking radish strips are older and less desirable. If the package carries an expiration date (they don't always), it can be a helpful guide.

SERVES 4 (makes 1¾ cups)
TOTAL TIME 20 minutes, plus 30 minutes soaking

- 2 ounces (57 grams) dried radish strips
- 2 green onions, chopped
- 2 tablespoons fish sauce
- 1½ tablespoons sugar
- 1½ tablespoons gochugaru
- 1 tablespoon soy sauce
- 1 tablespoon toasted sesame oil
- 1 tablespoon corn syrup
- 1 tablespoon minced garlic
- 1 tablespoon sesame seeds, toasted

1 Add the radish to a large bowl and cover with water by 1 inch. Using your hands, vigorously rub the strips against each other to eliminate the aroma of the dehydrated radish, then drain and cover with water again. Repeat the process until the water is no longer cloudy. Return the radish to the bowl, cover with water, and let sit until fully hydrated, about 30 minutes.

2 Working in batches, squeeze the radish by hand to remove excess water, and transfer to a large bowl. (Don't over-squeeze, as the radish should remain moist.) Add the onions, fish sauce, sugar, gochugaru, soy sauce, oil, corn syrup, garlic, and sesame seeds and toss until evenly coated. Serve. (Refrigerate for up to 4 days.)

Dotorimuk Muchim 도토리묵무침

doh-toh-ri-mook moo-chim

SARAH
세라

Every morning, you'll find Umma sipping on her 900-calorie drink that contains most of her daily nutritional needs. Yes, you read that right: her 900-calorie drink! And you'll always see a "chaser" next to this drink to make it a bit more tolerable. The chaser differs every day—most days it's kimchi but sometimes it's ramen, and on certain days it's this acorn jelly banchan. After she finishes her drink, she will enjoy this acorn jelly and tell me how good it is without fail. She has also served this at potlucks, arranging the jelly on top of a bed of chopped red leaf lettuce. It's always met first with curiosity, then with "Wow, this is good," followed by complete devour. Acorn jelly is extremely mild in flavor but has a hint of earthiness. Its texture is silky and delicate, and when paired with this vibrant sauce, crisp carrots, crunchy cucumbers, and herbaceous perilla leaves, it creates a surprising yet perfectly matched combination.

Umma's Kitchen Wisdom

Depending on what brand of acorn powder you buy, you might need to adjust the amount you use. I use a 1:6 ratio of acorn powder to water, but if the ratio stated on the acorn powder package you buy says something different, follow that ratio. Just be sure to start with 3 cups water.

It's important to prevent excess air bubbles from forming in the jelly. Whisking the acorn mixture in only one direction helps prevent this.

I like the neat squares created by using a rectangular dish as the jelly mold, but a bowl will work too.

If you have one, a crinkle-cut knife will give the jelly slices an attractive appearance.

SERVES 4 (makes 4 cups)
TOTAL TIME 45 minutes, plus 2 hours cooling

    3 cups water
 ½ cup (70 grams) acorn powder
 ¼ teaspoon fine salt
 1½ tablespoons toasted sesame oil, divided
    1 Persian cucumber (85 grams), halved lengthwise and sliced thin on bias
 ½ carrot (38 grams), peeled and cut into 3-inch matchsticks
    8 perilla leaves, stemmed and cut into thin strips
    4 teaspoons soy sauce
    1 tablespoon maesil cheong (plum extract syrup)
    1 tablespoon sesame seeds, toasted and coarsely ground (see page 38)
 1½ teaspoons gochugaru
 1½ teaspoons sugar
    1 teaspoon minced garlic

1 Whisk the water, acorn powder, and salt in a medium saucepan until thoroughly combined. Bring to a simmer over medium-high heat, whisking constantly in one direction, then cook until the mixture begins to thicken, 2 to 5 minutes.

2 Reduce the heat to medium and stir in 1½ teaspoons oil. Continue to cook, whisking constantly in one direction, until the mixture has darkened and thickened to the consistency of pudding, about 15 minutes, making sure to scrape the corners and bottom of the saucepan to prevent burning. Immediately pour the acorn mixture into a 2-cup rectangular casserole dish or storage container, smooth the top, and let cool to room temperature, about 2 hours. (You can cover and refrigerate for up to 1 day.)

3 Flip the acorn jelly onto a cutting board. Slice the jelly in thirds lengthwise, then cut each strip crosswise into ½-inch-thick pieces. Add the acorn jelly pieces, cucumber, carrot, perilla leaves, soy sauce, maesil cheong, sesame seeds, gochugaru, sugar, garlic, and remaining 1 tablespoon oil to a bowl and toss gently to combine. Serve immediately.

Jinmichae Muchim 진미채무침

jin-mi-chae moo-chim

SARAH
세라

One of the most comforting things I recall from my childhood was the certainty that "everything will be all right" because Umma and Appa were always there to fix any issue. Whatever I presented was met with an immediate solution that I didn't question. A question such as "Where does Santa get his toys?" was answered with "Santa gets his toys from Costco." I laugh at this now, because I realize that at the time my parents were unaware that Santa was supposed to make his toys in his workshop with the elves. If my brother or I broke our bikes, Appa was immediately ready to repair them with his tools. Any nervousness we experienced during major life events was met with reassurance and comfort. As I matured, I began to understand that my parents didn't have the answers to everything, and I started to question them. Sometimes these conversations were lighthearted, while at other times my doubt or refusal to trust in their wisdom caused my parents to feel hurt. Over the years, I have learned that sometimes it's best to leave certain doubts unspoken. These days, I tend to question only the lighthearted things, like whether it's *really* necessary to toast the dried squid in this spicy, sweet, and salty banchan.

Umma's Kitchen Wisdom

If you make this ahead, spread out the seasoned squid on a wide dish to prevent it from sticking together in clusters. Once it's completely cooled, transfer the squid to a storage container. You can eat this warm, at room temperature, or chilled.

SERVES 4 (makes 4 cups)   TOTAL TIME 20 minutes

3½ tablespoons gochujang
2 tablespoons mirin
2 tablespoons corn syrup
1 tablespoon maesil cheong (plum extract syrup)
1 tablespoon neutral cooking oil
1 tablespoon water
½ teaspoon soy sauce
½ teaspoon fish sauce
½ teaspoon sugar
7 ounces (198 grams) dried shredded squid, cut into rough 4-inch lengths
1 tablespoon toasted sesame oil
1½ tablespoons sesame seeds, toasted

1 Whisk the gochujang, mirin, corn syrup, maesil cheong, neutral oil, water, soy sauce, fish sauce, and sugar together in a small bowl. Set the sauce aside.

2 Cook the squid in a 14-inch flat-bottomed wok or 12-inch nonstick skillet over medium heat, tossing constantly, until lightly toasted and fragrant, 2 to 5 minutes. (Avoid over-cooking the squid; it should retain some moisture.) Transfer the squid to a separate bowl, leaving any crumbs behind. Wipe the wok clean with paper towels.

3 Add the sauce to the wok and bring to a brief simmer over medium heat. Turn off the heat but leave the wok on the burner. Add the squid and toss thoroughly to coat, separating any clusters of squid that cling together. Add the sesame oil and sesame seeds and toss to combine. Serve. (Refrigerate for up to 1 week.)

Kitchen Conversation

SARAH Is it really necessary to toast the squid in your recipe? Other recipes don't require it.

UMMA *It's not complicated to toast it, and yes, I think it's needed. It makes the squid more tender, it gets rid of the fishy aroma, and it makes the sauce cling better.*

SARAH Hmm. I'm not convinced.

[We proceed to make two batches—one with toasted squid and another one with untoasted squid. We take a bite of each.]

SARAH Oh, the untoasted batch feels like I'm chewing rubber bands. Sorry, you were right.

Ganjang Mu Jangajji Muchim
간장무장아찌무침

gahn-jahng moo jahng-ah-jji moo-chim

SARAH
세라

Though Ganjang Mu Jangajji (Soy Sauce Radish Pickles; page 144) are delicious on their own, Umma enhances them with additional seasonings to create this satisfyingly crunchy banchan full of rich, bold flavors. She starts with some of the soy sauce brine from the pickles, since it becomes fully infused and balanced in flavor from the Korean radish, maesil cheong, chiles, and sugar. Then she adds nutty sesame oil, pungent garlic, spicy gochugaru (you can leave it out for a mild version), and other seasonings. Finding other uses for the ultra-flavorful soy sauce brine ensures that it's used to its fullest potential and not wasted; see Avocado-Jang (Marinated Avocado; page 75) for another recipe that uses it.

Umma's Kitchen Wisdom

I think the best and most thorough way to combine the pickles with the seasoning—in this recipe and in the two seasoned pickle recipes that follow—is to put on a pair of food-handling gloves and mix everything together with your hands.

SERVES 4 (makes 2 cups)   **TOTAL TIME** 10 minutes

- 9 ounces (255 grams) Ganjang Mu Jangajji (Soy Sauce Radish Pickles; page 144), sliced crosswise ⅛ inch thick, plus 1 tablespoon seasoned soy sauce from pickles
- 1 green onion, sliced thin
- 1 tablespoon sesame seeds, toasted and coarsely ground (see page 38)
- 1 tablespoon toasted sesame oil
- 1 teaspoon minced garlic
- 1 teaspoon gochugaru (optional)
- ½ teaspoon sugar

Toss all the ingredients in a bowl until well combined. Serve. (Refrigerate for up to 2 weeks.)

Oiji Muchim 오이지무침

oh-e-ji moo-chim

SARAH
세라

As Umma massaged the ingredients together, ensuring every pickled cucumber slice was thoroughly coated and seasoned, she revealed to me, "This is my favorite banchan." Dumbfounded that I didn't know this, I realized there were many small details I didn't know about Umma, one of the people to whom I am closest. She then said, "Haven't you noticed? Whenever I make this, it disappears instantly because I eat it all up! I love it so much." *No, I never noticed that*, I silently thought to myself as Umma sampled pieces of the seasoned pickles. Perhaps I had become so preoccupied with my own life—work, new relationships, new hobbies, and growing independence—that I had unknowingly distanced myself from Umma. I stepped away with my notebook where I had jotted down the recipe, scratching my head: Knowing Umma's favorite banchan should have been as natural to me as knowing my partner's preferences. The following day, I noticed the empty LocknLock container in the sink from the batch that we had prepared together. It had been consumed entirely by Umma. Quickly, I made another batch of her favorite banchan with the remaining ingredients we had on hand for her to enjoy once more, and asked her if she wanted to get lunch at a quaint café nearby to catch up. In addition to being Umma's all-time favorite, this banchan is one of her most popular and cherished among our guests. These pickles achieve a sharp yet harmonious blend of sweet, spicy, and enchanting flavors that I hope you enjoy as much as Umma does.

SERVES 4 to 6 (makes 1½ cups)
TOTAL TIME 15 minutes

- 8 ounces (227 grams) Oiji (Cucumber Pickles; page 149), ends trimmed, sliced crosswise ⅛ inch thick
- 1 green onion, chopped
- 1½ tablespoons toasted sesame oil
- 4 teaspoons gochugaru
- 1 tablespoon sesame seeds, toasted and coarsely ground (see page 38), plus extra toasted seeds
- 2½ teaspoons sugar
- 2 teaspoons minced garlic

1 Submerge the cucumber pickle slices in a bowl of water. Using your hands, vigorously massage the slices to remove excess brine, then drain and rinse the cucumbers. Working in batches, squeeze the slices gently by hand to remove excess water, then transfer the slices to a medium bowl.

2 Add the onion, oil, gochugaru, sesame seeds, sugar, and garlic. Using your gloved hands, gently toss and massage the cucumbers until evenly coated in the seasonings. Sprinkle with extra sesame seeds and serve. (Refrigerate for up to 4 days.)

These pickles are also
delicious scooped up with
a spoonful of rice.

SPICY GREEN CHILE PICKLES

Gochu Jangajji Muchim 고추장아찌무침

goh-choo jahng-ah-jji moo-chim

UMMA
엄마

On our block, there used to be only one other Korean family, the Mins. The umma of this family, whom I called Justin Umma (after her son, Justin), was a talented home cook who had a bountiful fruit and vegetable garden. One summer's day, I tried Justin Umma's gochu jangajji muchim, which she had prepared using her homegrown chiles. It was a taste unlike anything I had experienced before. The chiles were wonderfully pickled, with a perfect balance of sweetness, tanginess, and crispiness. The additional spicy, sweet, and nutty flavors from the seasonings transformed these pickles into a banchan that I immediately wanted to learn how to make for my family. I went to the Korean grocery store and bought prepared green chile pickles. When I returned home and seasoned these pickles to re-create Justin Umma's banchan, the taste wasn't quite right. I could tell that the spicy seasoning was on target, but something about the pickles themselves seemed off. After several tries, I realized that the secret to good gochu jangajji muchim is to pickle the chiles yourself, just as Justin Umma did. Though it may seem daunting, truly good food requires a bit more effort, and shortcuts with premade ingredients simply won't deliver the same results. Fortunately, pickling the chiles is quite simple—you just need a little patience, and then you can enhance the pickles with additional seasonings to create a flavor-packed banchan like this. Once I figured out this recipe to my satisfaction, I served it to my family, and they promptly devoured it.

SARAH
세라

This banchan has a wow factor that is bold and quite memorable. It delivers a punch of flavors with its complexity—there's the tanginess and sweetness from the brine that has infused itself into the pickle, complemented by additional Korean seasonings that are both spicy and fiery yet comforting. I once packed a whole container of this banchan in my suitcase to bring to America's Test Kitchen from one coast to another. Everyone was floored by the multitude of flavors dancing together, and it was then that I realized that this banchan is truly a standout. To refrigerate leftovers, arrange a single layer of pickles in a container and add sauce on top. Repeat with the remaining pickles and sauce.

SERVES 4 to 6 (makes 2 cups)
TOTAL TIME 15 minutes

8 ounces (227 grams) Gochu Jangajji (Green Chile Pickles; page 150), drained, plus ¼ cup brine
3 tablespoons gochugaru
2 tablespoons sesame seeds, toasted and coarsely ground (see page 38)
1½ tablespoons fish sauce
3½ teaspoons sugar
1 tablespoon toasted sesame oil
1 tablespoon minced garlic
1½ teaspoons maesil cheong (plum extract syrup)
2 green onions, chopped

Whisk the pickle brine, gochugaru, sesame seeds, fish sauce, sugar, oil, garlic, and maesil cheong together in a medium bowl. Add the pickled chiles and the onions. Using your gloved hands, gently toss until the vegetables are evenly coated with the sauce. Serve. (Refrigerate for up to 4 days.)

Umma's Kitchen Wisdom

I like to use tongs to lift the pickles out of their container and allow the excess sauce to drain out through the pierced holes until they no longer drip.

For serving, you can either keep the chiles whole or use kitchen shears to cut them into bite-size pieces.

My family eats the entire pickle, including the stem end. While I've seen others not eat the stem, it's completely edible.

Green Salad
그린 샐러드

SARAH
세라

This is the one salad that my family never gets tired of—we consistently return to it because of its lightness and its ability to encapsulate Korean flavors in salad form. With just the right balance of spice, acidity, and sweetness from the gochugaru, vinegar, and plum extract, this salad never disappoints and always finds its way back to our dinner table. We often pair it with a protein such as a fried egg, sliced steak, or crispy tofu, and we like to add toppings such as cherry tomatoes, sliced perilla leaves, chickpeas, feta cheese, and more. It's great as is, but definitely consider this salad as a base to customize according to your preferences and imagination.

SERVES 4 to 6 (makes about 8 cups)
TOTAL TIME 15 minutes

- 4 teaspoons fish sauce
- 4 teaspoons maesil cheong (plum extract syrup)
- 4 teaspoons toasted sesame oil
- 1 tablespoon distilled white vinegar
- 2 teaspoons minced garlic
- 1 teaspoon sugar
- 7 ounces (198 grams) spring mix
- 2 ounces (57 grams) thinly sliced red onion
- 2 teaspoons gochugaru

Whisk the fish sauce, maesil cheong, oil, vinegar, garlic, and sugar in a liquid measuring cup or small bowl until the sugar has dissolved. Add the lettuce mix and onion to a large bowl. Pour the dressing over the salad, sprinkle with the gochugaru, and gently toss until well combined. Serve immediately.

Umma's Kitchen Wisdom

To mellow the spiciness and pungency of the raw red onion, I sometimes submerge the slices in an ice bath for about 10 minutes, then drain them well and add them to the salad.

I like to use spring mix for its varied texture and nutritional value, but you can use other greens. Garlic chives, green onions, green or purple cabbage, and romaine lettuce are also excellent options.

Avocado-Jang 아보카도장

avocado-jahng

UMMA
엄마

I remember being amazed the first time I tried avocados after moving to the United States. Although my initial reaction was a bit skeptical, it wasn't long before I started appreciating them and using them regularly in my cooking. I love this simple way of preparing them Korean-style.

SARAH
세라

In 2008, Samchon (Uncle) came to visit us from Korea for the first time. During his visit, we introduced him to avocados, a fruit that was not available in Korea at that time. He was amazed—if a little confused—by this buttery, savory fruit, and eventually fell in love with it when I prepared some guacamole for him. I remember Umma and Samchon's conversation at the dinner table, where Samchon was eating avocado by the spoonful like it was ice cream. When Samchon packed his bags to return to Korea, Umma gave him two bags of avocados to bring back home. He was excited to show his wife what they were missing out on, but both Umma and Samchon were unaware that TSA would not allow fresh produce on an international flight. Fast-forward to the present day, where avocados are one of the most popular fruits in Korea, loved by all generations for their nutritional value, taste, and trendy aesthetic. Here's how to enjoy avocados (and tomatoes) in a flavorful marinade from our seasoned soy sauce that's infused with Korean radish, maesil cheong, and chiles. In addition to serving this on its own, we also like to use it in Gyeranbap (Egg Rice with Avocado; page 274) in place of fresh avocados.

SERVES 4 TOTAL TIME 10 minutes, plus 3 hours marinating

- 2 avocados, halved, pitted, and sliced crosswise ¼ inch thick
- 4 ounces (113 grams) cherry or grape tomatoes, halved
- 1 ounce (28 grams) thinly sliced yellow onion
- 2 lemon slices, seeded
- 1 cup seasoned soy sauce from Ganjang Mu Jangajji (Soy Sauce Radish Pickles; page 144)

Shingle the avocados in a single layer in a 2-quart storage container. Arrange the tomatoes, onion, and lemon on top. Pour the seasoned soy sauce over the top, cover, and refrigerate for at least 1 hour or up to 3 hours. Serve.

Umma's Kitchen Wisdom

Look for avocados that are ripe but firm.

You can still make this dish even if you haven't made the Ganjang Mu Jangajji, by making my Instant Seasoned Soy Sauce. Mix together ½ cup maesil cheong (plum extract syrup), ¼ cup soy sauce, ¼ cup water, and 1 tablespoon sugar. Stir in 3 small dried red chiles, if you like. This instant seasoning sauce will have less richness and depth of flavor than the sauce from the radish pickles, but it will still be tasty!

ROASTED GIM WITH CRISPY TOFU

Guun Gimgwa Dubu 구운 김과 두부

goo-oon gim-gwa doo-boo

UMMA
엄마

This is really two banchan in one. The roasted gim and the crispy tofu are each great on their own as banchan, but when combined with rice, avocado, and garlic chive seasoning sauce, you get something that's much more than the sum of its parts. Yangnyeomjang is an ever-present condiment sauce on the Korean table that's typically made of soy sauce, a sweetener, toasted sesame oil, and other ingredients. Ever since my cousin from Korea visited and introduced me to a version of yangnyeomjang that includes garlic chives (buchu), I've made this version of the sauce to enjoy with this roasted gim and tofu banchan, as well as with rice bowls and more.

SARAH
세라

Jomigim, roasted salted seaweed pieces, is a familiar banchan in Korea and a popular snack in America, and packaged varieties are readily available. However, unseasoned gim sheets make a more substantial banchan (or a snack) when roasted on the stovetop and served with rice, crispy tofu, avocado, and our special chive seasoning sauce. The unique sauce recipe was passed down from Umma's cousin (whom I refer to as Samchon, or Uncle), who learned about this variation from his wife, who was born and raised in Jeolla-do, Korea—a region known for its gastronomic secrets. When the fillings are placed on the roasted gim and the gim is folded over to make a perfect little wrap, the multitude of flavors and textures will leave you wanting more. (Fun fact: When we finalized this recipe and gave it one last test, Umma ate the entire dish by herself!) Packaged gim sheets are usually about 7 x 8 inches or slightly larger, but the dimensions don't have to be exact. If you have a coil-burner electric stove or an induction stove, roast the gim sheets in a preheated dry skillet over medium heat.

SERVES 4   TOTAL TIME 45 minutes

  1 (14- to 16-ounce / 397- to 454-gram) block firm tofu
  ¼ teaspoon miwon matsogeum (MSG seasoning salt), divided
  2 tablespoons neutral cooking oil
 12 sheets unroasted, unseasoned gim (dried seaweed)
  1 recipe Baekmibap (Steamed White Rice; page 284)
  1 avocado, halved, pitted, and sliced thin
  1 recipe Buchu Yangnyeomjang (Chive Seasoning Sauce; page 35)

1 Rinse the tofu and pat dry with paper towels. Halve the tofu block lengthwise. Cut each half crosswise into ½-inch slices, then cut each slice into rough ½-inch-thick batons. Arrange the tofu in a single layer on a paper towel–lined plate. Pat the tops dry with additional paper towels, then sprinkle with ⅛ teaspoon seasoning salt.

2 Heat the oil in a 12-inch nonstick skillet over medium-high heat until shimmering. Arrange the tofu batons salted side down in the skillet. Sprinkle with the remaining ⅛ teaspoon seasoning salt and cook, turning as needed, until light golden brown on all sides, about 15 minutes. Transfer the tofu to a serving plate.

3 Grip 1 sheet gim with tongs and hold about 2 inches above the low flame of a gas burner, flipping and rotating the sheet every 1 to 2 seconds, until the entire sheet is toasted and fragrant. (The gim will shrivel slightly and change color from black/dark green to green, indicating it is properly toasted.) If using a glass-top electric stove, adjust the primary burner to medium heat and place the gim directly onto the surface of the burner. Transfer the gim to a plate and repeat with the remaining sheets.

4 Cut the toasted gim sheets into quarters. To serve, place platters of toasted gim, tofu, rice, and avocado on the table. Add a bowl of buchu yangnyeomjang and allow diners to create wraps to their taste.

Umma's Kitchen Wisdom

If your Korean grocery store only sells roasted unseasoned gim, that's perfectly fine. I recommend giving the roasted sheets another roast at home, as called for.

If the gim has holes in it, the sauce may drip right through. Purchasing gim that doesn't contain holes can be challenging due to its packaging, so if you find holes when you open the package, double up the pieces when building the wraps.

You might be wondering if gimbapgim, which is used for gimbap, is a good substitute, as this type is also unseasoned, but I don't recommend it. It's thicker and won't provide the right texture here.

Store any leftover roasted gim in an airtight container with a silica gel pack, which will help keep it crisp.

SEASONED CILANTRO RADISH SHREDS

Gosu Musaengchae 고수무생채

goh-soo moo-saeng-chae

SARAH
세라

This recipe holds a meaningful significance, as it originates from North Korea. Given that North Korea's culinary history is not widely known, this recipe offers a rare glimpse into the food culture of this secluded country. For Umma, this recipe is a cherished part of our family's heritage, passed down by Halmeoni, who was born and raised there. Halmeoni grew up with this dish and continued to make it whenever possible, instilling in us a deep appreciation for our culinary roots. Although the correct name is technically gosu musaengchae, Halmeoni always referred to this dish as gosu kimchi. Eat it like a salad—there's no fermentation involved, and it's best enjoyed during the fall and winter months, when Korean radish is in season. This dish is refreshing, punchy, and bursting with cilantro flavor that beautifully complements the Korean radish.

SERVES 8 (makes 8 cups)   TOTAL TIME 30 minutes

1½ pounds (680 grams) Korean radish, trimmed and
      cut into 3-inch matchsticks
2½ tablespoons sugar
2½ tablespoons gochugaru
 2   tablespoons distilled white vinegar
1½ tablespoons maesil cheong (plum extract syrup)
 1   tablespoon fish sauce
 1   tablespoon minced garlic
 2   teaspoons fine salt
 2   tablespoons sesame seeds, toasted
 6   ounces (170 grams) cilantro sprigs, ends trimmed,
      cut into 3-inch lengths

Toss the radish gently in a large bowl with the sugar, gochugaru, vinegar, maesil cheong, fish sauce, garlic, salt, and sesame seeds until evenly coated. Add half of the cilantro and toss to combine, separating strands of cilantro that stick together; repeat with the remaining cilantro. Serve. (Refrigerate for up to 2 days.)

Kitchen Conversation

UMMA *Smell this. Do you smell the cilantro?*

SARAH Yes, it's very strong and lively.

UMMA *That smell brings me back to the days when Halmeoni and neighborhood women made gimjang kimchi [the traditional seasonal gathering of people to make large batches of kimchi]. She would serve this banchan to the other women.*

SARAH Is cilantro a part of Korean cuisine?

UMMA *North Koreans are familiar with using cilantro in their food. It's a part of the cuisine. This is a North Korean dish that I learned from Halmeoni. When she visited us here in the United States years back, I remember her gasping when she saw cilantro at the grocery store. She said in amazement, "Unbelievable, America has cilantro too?"*

SARAH Why was she so shocked?

UMMA *Cilantro wasn't readily available in South Korea during Halmeoni's time, although it was abundant in North Korea while she was growing up. When she discovered how easily accessible cilantro was in America, it came as both a shock and a delight to her.*

Gul Musaengchae 굴무생채

gool moo-saeng-chae

UMMA
엄마

During gimjang days (see page 123), Halmeoni and the other women in our neighborhood would have leftover kimchi filling from making those big batches of pogi kimchi. While the actual kimchi filling is called baechu sog, this leftover filling was known as musaengchae. I recall this filling being a rich red color and the women packing and rolling extra brined cabbage with this filling to create a perfect bite for snacking. The woman hosting the gimjang would be responsible for feeding all the hardworking women who made the kimchi, and she would serve this leftover kimchi filling with multiple dishes. When Halmeoni hosted, she would serve this filling with Kongbiji Jjigae (Ground Soybean Stew; page 221) or Mandu (Dumplings; page 157) as the main meal. When we had oysters on hand, Halmeoni would add them to the musaengchae to create this banchan. I remember the oysters being stored in a large can, and I would drool at the sight of this can because we indulged in oysters only once a year, during the winter season—either with the women who made gimjang kimchi with us or with my family.

SARAH
세라

There is no requirement to make pogi kimchi and anticipate having leftover kimchi filling in order to prepare this banchan. In fact, our recipe for Pogi Kimchi (Whole Napa Cabbage Kimchi; page 127) has neither leftover filling nor a high enough proportion of Korean radish to create this dish. For this recipe, we deliberately make musaengchae with a balanced amount of radish to pair with the oysters. The result is an incredibly refreshing banchan that is sweet, spicy, and crunchy, with a hint of the sea. In addition to serving this with other banchan, we like to pair it with grilled pork.

> **Umma's Kitchen Wisdom**
>
> *I find it convenient and economical to keep frozen oysters always on hand, but you can substitute fresh shucked oysters in this dish, if you like.*

SERVES 6 (makes 6 cups) **TOTAL TIME** 30 minutes

- 1 teaspoon fine salt
- 8 ounces (227 grams) frozen oysters, thawed
- ¼ cup (71 grams) coarsely chopped yellow onion
- 1½ tablespoons maesil cheong (plum extract syrup)
- 1½ tablespoons saeujeot (salted shrimp)
- 1 pound (454 grams) Korean radish, trimmed and cut into 3-inch matchsticks
- 5 tablespoons (35 grams) gochugaru
- 2 tablespoons fish sauce
- 2 tablespoons minced garlic
- 1 tablespoon sesame seeds, toasted
- 1½ teaspoons distilled white vinegar
- 1½ teaspoons sugar
- 1 teaspoon grated fresh ginger
- 4 green onions (60 grams), white and light green parts halved lengthwise, cut into 1½-inch lengths

1 Dissolve the salt in 1 quart water in a large bowl. Add the oysters and mix thoroughly to rinse. Drain the oysters and repeat rinsing in fresh unsalted water; drain thoroughly.

2 Process the yellow onion, maesil cheong, and saeujeot in a blender until smooth, about 15 seconds. Toss the radish with the onion mixture, gochugaru, fish sauce, garlic, sesame seeds, vinegar, sugar, and ginger in a bowl until evenly coated. Add the oysters and green onions and mix gently until combined. Serve. (Refrigerate for up to 1 day.)

Janmyeolchi Bokkeum 잔멸치볶음

jahn-myuhl-chi boh-kkeum

SARAH
세라

When I was very young, I loved this banchan and ate it by the spoonful. With few exceptions, I had zero fear of eating anything—if it tasted good, I ate it. But things changed when I started elementary school; one day, I suddenly feared the little eyes of these anchovies and it felt foreign to eat them. I remember my brother being flustered by this sudden shift, because he knew how obsessed I was with this dish. Perhaps this was me becoming "Americanized" (and maybe it was the beginning of my identity crisis as a Korean American) because around that time, the store-bought cupcakes that my classmates brought to school—the very ones that I once found too sweet—suddenly tasted amazing to me. For years I didn't eat this banchan, despite the nostalgic aromas that filled our kitchen when Umma made it. My eyes would follow this banchan as it was packed and stored in Umma's LocknLock containers. Time passed, until one day in my late 20s I decided to try it again without much thought about the unexplainable fear I used to harbor. As I took a bite, I once again felt the various textures of each ingredient and the burst of flavors that danced harmoniously together in my mouth. I laughed in amazement as I celebrated this happy reunion. We use small anchovies here (look for those that are no more than 1 inch long), and this type of anchovy is eaten whole, with no cleaning needed.

Umma's Kitchen Wisdom

You can use any combination of nuts and pumpkin or sunflower seeds, as long as it's a total of ¼ cup.

In this recipe and in the Myeolchi Gochujang Bokkeum (Stir-Fried Anchovies with Gochujang; page 84), I shake the toasted anchovies over the wok so that the excess particles don't scatter everywhere.

If you make this ahead, spread out the seasoned anchovies on a wide dish to keep them from sticking together in clusters. Once they're completely cooled, transfer the anchovies to a storage container. Enjoy this warm, at room temperature, or chilled.

SERVES 4 (makes 1 cup)   **TOTAL TIME** 25 minutes

- 2 tablespoons corn syrup
- 1 tablespoon mirin
- 1½ teaspoons sugar
- 1 teaspoon minced garlic
- 1 teaspoon soy sauce
- ½ teaspoon oyster sauce
- ¾ cup (50 grams) dried small anchovies
- 1 tablespoon neutral cooking oil
- 2 tablespoons whole almonds, pecans, and/or walnuts, toasted
- 2 tablespoons pumpkin seeds or sunflower seeds, toasted
- 1 tablespoon toasted sesame oil
- 1 tablespoon sesame seeds, toasted
  Pinch black pepper

1 Whisk the corn syrup, mirin, sugar, garlic, soy sauce, and oyster sauce together in a small bowl. Set the sauce aside.

2 Cook the anchovies in a 14-inch flat-bottomed wok or 12-inch nonstick skillet over medium heat, tossing constantly, until lightly toasted and fragrant, 2 to 3 minutes. Transfer the anchovies to a fine-mesh strainer and vigorously shake over the now-empty wok to remove excess fish particles. (Massaging the anchovies while in the strainer will remove more particles too.) Wipe the wok clean with paper towels.

3 Heat the neutral oil in the wok over medium-high heat until shimmering. Add the anchovies and toss until fully coated in the oil, 10 to 15 seconds. Transfer the anchovies to a plate.

4 Add the sauce to the now-empty wok and bring to a vigorous simmer. Turn off the heat, quickly add the anchovies, almonds, and pumpkin seeds, and toss to coat. Add the sesame oil, sesame seeds, and pepper and gently toss until the sauce is absorbed, breaking up any clusters of anchovies. Serve. (Refrigerate for up to 4 days.)

Myeolchi Gochujang Bokkeum
멸치고추장볶음

myuhl-chi goh-choo-jahng boh-kkeum

SARAH
세라

Here's the bigger, bolder, spicier cousin to the classic preparation of Janmyeolchi Bokkeum (Stir-Fried Small Anchovies; page 83). This banchan completely transforms stir-fried anchovies through the magic of gochujang. The anchovies are cooked in the same oil that is used to fry the garlic slices, offering a sweet, spicy, garlicky stir-fry that is further intensified by additional heat from the jalapeño. It's just as delicious served at room temperature (or cold) as is it served hot. This recipe calls for dried medium anchovies (look for anchovies that are about 2 inches long), which you'll need to clean. This is easy to do, but it can be time-consuming if you're unfamiliar with the process. Small anchovies (about 1 inch long), which don't need to be cleaned, can be used too (although we do prefer the meatiness of the medium anchovies in this spicy dish). The rest of the preparation is extremely fast.

SERVES 4 (makes 1½ cups)   TOTAL TIME 1 hour

    4 teaspoons gochujang
    1 tablespoon maesil cheong (plum extract syrup)
    1 tablespoon water
    1 tablespoon mirin
    2 teaspoons sugar
    ½ teaspoon soy sauce
    ½ teaspoon fish sauce
    2 cups (85 grams) dried medium anchovies, gutted and heads removed (see page 43)
    2 tablespoons neutral cooking oil
    3 garlic cloves, thinly sliced lengthwise
    ½ jalapeño chile, stemmed, seeded, halved lengthwise, and cut into ½-inch pieces
    1 tablespoon corn syrup
    1 tablespoon sesame seeds, toasted
    1 teaspoon toasted sesame oil

1 Whisk the gochujang, maesil cheong, water, mirin, sugar, soy sauce, and fish sauce together in a small bowl. Set the sauce aside.

2 Cook the anchovies in a 14-inch flat-bottomed wok or 12-inch nonstick skillet over medium heat, tossing constantly, until lightly toasted and fragrant, 2 to 3 minutes. Transfer the anchovies to a fine-mesh strainer and vigorously shake over the now-empty wok to remove excess fish particles. (Massaging the anchovies while in the strainer will remove more particles too.) Wipe the wok clean with paper towels.

3 Add the neutral oil and garlic to the wok and cook over medium-high heat until the garlic just begins to turn golden brown around the edges and the oil becomes fragrant, about 2 minutes. Add the anchovies and cook, tossing constantly, until evenly coated in oil, 45 seconds to 1 minute. Transfer the anchovy mixture to a plate.

4 Add the sauce to the now-empty wok and bring to a vigorous simmer over medium-high heat. Turn off the heat, quickly add the anchovy mixture, and toss to coat. Add the jalapeño, corn syrup, sesame seeds, and sesame oil and toss to coat. Serve. (Refrigerate for up to 4 days.)

STIR-FRIED FISH CAKES

Eomuk Bokkeum 어묵볶음

uh-mook boh-kkeum

UMMA
엄마

I have loved fish cakes ever since I was a kid. When I was in middle school, I told Harabeoji (Grandpa) that I needed money to buy some school books, but that was a lie. In reality, I was buying eomuk (fish cakes sold on skewers) and tteokbokki (spicy rice cakes) from street food vendors. Since my family couldn't afford to buy snacks, that was the only way I could indulge in these foods. Looking back, it's quite funny telling this story, but I'm certainly not proud of lying to Harabeoji. I still love fish cakes to this day, though.

SARAH
세라

Fish cakes prepared by Umma are a mainstay on our family table, and I have regularly frequented the Korean grocery store freezer aisle to pick up this must-have ingredient for her. Fish cakes are such a convenient item to stock in your freezer. Typically made from a fried mixture of ground white fish, vegetables, and seasonings, they have a soft yet chewy texture, with a savory, slightly sweet flavor that's incredibly satisfying. You can enjoy them as a simple snack—just thaw, then pan-fry with a bit of oil, and squirt some sriracha on them. Umma enjoys sprucing them up as a stir-fried banchan like this one, adding carrots, onion, and seasonings. This banchan is equally good served warm, at room temperature, or cold. Fish cakes can be purchased as sheets, cut into smaller shapes such as circles, or even skewered on sticks like kebabs; for this recipe, we are working with fish cake sheets. To thaw them, let them sit either in the refrigerator for 24 hours or on the counter for 30 minutes to 1 hour. Rinsing the sliced fish cakes before stir-frying them removes any oil residue left from the manufacturing process.

SERVES 4 (makes 3½ cups)   **TOTAL TIME** 35 minutes

- ¼ cup water
- 1 tablespoon plus 2 teaspoons soy sauce
- 1½ tablespoons plus ¼ teaspoon sugar, divided
- 2 teaspoons fish sauce
- 2 teaspoons oyster sauce
- 1½ teaspoons minced garlic
- 7 ounces (198 grams) fish cake sheets, thawed
- 2½ tablespoons neutral cooking oil, divided
- 1 large carrot (100 grams), peeled and cut into 3-inch matchsticks
  Pinch fine salt
- ½ yellow onion (142 grams), sliced ¼ inch thick
- 2 green onions, quartered lengthwise and cut into 3-inch lengths
- 1 tablespoon toasted sesame oil
- 1 tablespoon sesame seeds, toasted
- ¼ teaspoon black pepper

1 Whisk the water, soy sauce, 1½ tablespoons sugar, fish sauce, oyster sauce, and garlic together in a small bowl. Set the sauce aside.

2 Slice the fish cake sheets crosswise into ¼-inch-thick strips. Place the strips in a strainer and thoroughly rinse under hot water. Drain the strips well and pat dry with paper towels; set aside.

3 Heat 1 tablespoon neutral oil in a 14-inch flat-bottomed wok or 12-inch nonstick skillet over medium-high heat until shimmering. Add the carrot, salt, and remaining ¼ teaspoon sugar and cook, tossing constantly, until nearly cooked through, about 2 minutes; transfer to a plate.

4 Add 1½ teaspoons neutral oil and the yellow onion to the now-empty wok and cook over medium-high heat, tossing constantly, until nearly cooked through, about 2 minutes; transfer to the plate with the carrot.

5 Heat the remaining 1 tablespoon neutral oil in the now-empty wok over medium-high heat until shimmering. Add the fish cake strips and cook, tossing constantly, until evenly coated in oil. Increase the heat to high and add the vegetables and sauce. Cook, tossing constantly, until the sauce has thickened slightly, about 1 minute. Turn off the heat, add the green onions, sesame oil, sesame seeds, and pepper, and toss to combine. Serve. (Refrigerate for up to 4 days.)

Gamja Bokkeum 감자볶음

gahm-jah boh-kkeum

UMMA 엄마

When I was in elementary school, Halmeoni dropped me off at Gomo's (aunt from paternal side) home for one month. I can't remember why, but there was one part of the visit I didn't forget. I think it was in the summertime, and Halmeoni came to pick me up after the visit. She prepped some banchan at Gomo's for everyone to enjoy as a thank-you. As she set the table with the different banchan and rice, I remember her placing the gamja bokkeum on the table, and it just stood out to me amongst all the other banchan. I snuck in many bites of the gamja bokkeum with my fingers when no one was looking. I couldn't wait for everyone to come and sit down. It tasted so incredibly good after not having had Halmeoni's home-cooked food for a month.

SARAH 세라

Like Umma, I find myself picking away at these stir-fried potatoes as if they were french fries whenever they're cooling down on our stovetop. The potatoes are savory and slightly sweet, with a harmonious blend of flavors, textures, and colors coming from the seasoning, carrots, and onions. We enjoy this banchan year-round—it's a go-to for many Korean households. Look for potatoes that are about 4 inches in length. Slicing the potatoes thin is crucial. You can do this by hand, or use a mandoline to cut evenly thin planks and then cut those planks into matchsticks by hand.

Umma's Kitchen Wisdom

As I cut the potatoes into matchsticks, I like to submerge them in a bowl of cold water to prevent them from browning and remove excess starch. I then drain them just before tossing them with the salt.

SERVES 4 (makes 3 cups)   **TOTAL TIME** 45 minutes

- 1 pound (454 grams) russet potatoes, peeled
- 1¾ teaspoons fine salt, divided
- 2 tablespoons neutral cooking oil
- 1 small carrot (50 grams), peeled and cut into 3-inch matchsticks
- 2 ounces (57 grams) yellow onion, sliced thin
- 2½ teaspoons fish sauce
- 1½ teaspoons sugar
- ¾ teaspoon Dasida beef stock powder
- 1 tablespoon corn syrup
- 2 green onions, quartered lengthwise and cut into 3-inch lengths
- 1 tablespoon sesame seeds, toasted and coarsely ground (see page 38), plus extra toasted seeds
- 1½ teaspoons toasted sesame oil

1 Slice the potatoes lengthwise into ⅛-inch planks, then cut the planks lengthwise into ⅛-inch matchsticks. Rinse and drain the potatoes, then toss with 1 teaspoon salt. Let sit for 5 minutes, tossing halfway through.

2 Rinse the potatoes thoroughly under running water to remove excess starch; drain well. Heat the neutral oil in a 14-inch flat-bottomed wok or 12-inch nonstick skillet over medium-high heat until shimmering. Add the potatoes and carrot (the oil will crackle) and cook, tossing constantly, until evenly coated in oil, about 1 minute. Reduce the heat to medium and continue to cook until the potatoes are nearly tender, about 5 minutes.

3 Add the yellow onion, fish sauce, sugar, Dasida powder, and remaining ¾ teaspoon salt. Increase the heat to medium-high and cook, tossing constantly, for 1 minute. Add the corn syrup and cook, tossing constantly, for 30 seconds. Turn off the heat, add the green onions, sesame seeds, and sesame oil, and toss to combine. Sprinkle with extra sesame seeds and serve. (Refrigerate for up to 1 day.)

Algamja Jorim 알감자조림

ahl-gahm-jah joh-rim

SARAH
세라

I always get excited when I see a bag of baby potatoes from our grocery haul waiting to be stored away, because it means that Umma is going to prepare algamja jorim very soon. These petite potatoes are boiled and then stir-fried and tossed with Umma's salty-sweet sauce and finished with sesame seeds, green onion, and gochugaru. The potatoes become extremely creamy and offer irresistible poppable bites. We like yellow potatoes best here, but you can buy baby potatoes of any color that are ¾ to 1 inch in diameter. If you can only find larger baby potatoes, you can cut them into 1-inch pieces.

Kitchen Conversation

SARAH When did you first try algamja jorim?

UMMA *When I came to the United States.*

SARAH Huh? You never had this in Korea?

UMMA *No, Halmeoni never prepared any banchan with this type of potato. I don't remember seeing them around our house. I wanted to try them when I first saw these little potatoes at the Korean grocery store here.*

SARAH I'm glad you finally tried it. It's really good, and it has always reminded me of baby dinosaur eggs since I was a kid, ha-ha.

UMMA *You're right, I can see a baby seeing it like that, ha-ha.*

SARAH The potatoes are so creamy and the sauce you add to them is just perfect. I love how you can also taste and feel the sesame seeds popping as you bite into the little whole potato.

UMMA *Yeah, I like it a lot. It's very different from the potatoes I grew up with.*

SERVES 4 (makes 3 cups)   TOTAL TIME 50 minutes

2 tablespoons plus ½ teaspoon soy sauce
1 tablespoon corn syrup
12 ounces (340 grams) baby yellow potatoes, unpeeled
1 teaspoon fine salt
1 tablespoon neutral cooking oil
1 tablespoon sugar
1½ teaspoons sesame seeds, toasted
1 green onion, sliced thin
½ teaspoon gochugaru

1 Whisk ⅔ cup water, the soy sauce, and corn syrup together in a small bowl. Set the sauce aside.

2 Add the potatoes and salt to a 14-inch flat-bottomed wok or 12-inch nonstick skillet and cover with water by 1 inch. Bring to a boil and cook for 5 minutes. Drain and pat dry with paper towels. Wipe the wok dry with paper towels.

3 Heat the oil in the wok over medium heat until shimmering. Add the potatoes and cook, tossing occasionally, until nearly tender, about 8 minutes. Add the sauce, toss to coat the potatoes, and bring to a simmer. Cover and cook for 1 minute. Uncover and continue to cook, tossing occasionally, until the potatoes are fully tender and well seasoned, about 6 minutes.

4 Increase the heat to medium-high and add the sugar. Cook, tossing constantly, until the sauce becomes thick and stringy, about 4 minutes. Remove from the heat and stir in the sesame seeds, green onion, and gochugaru. Serve. (Refrigerate for up to 4 days.)

BRAISED LOTUS ROOT

Yeongeun Jorim 연근조림

yuhn-geun joh-rim

UMMA 엄마

Root banchan are not only delicious to eat, but they're also incredibly healthy—it's a win-win. I remember buying lotus root for Appa to eat after learning about this root's health benefits, which include helping to alleviate acid reflux and indigestion. While cooking this, you might notice stringy parts of the root that resemble spiderwebs—these are completely normal and okay to eat and are a good source of dietary fiber. The longer you soak the dashima in water beyond 30 minutes here, the better. Granted, don't submerge it for days—but feel free to submerge it for several hours. It will slowly release an umami taste that gets better with time. You can use plain water instead, but I highly recommend the dashima water.

SARAH 세라

Seasoned with soy sauce, ginger, and brown sugar and braised in dashima-infused water, lotus root transforms into a sweet and savory banchan that's also quite beautiful to look at. Umma taught me three tips for selecting lotus root, which you can purchase at any Asian grocery store (not just at Korean grocery stores). First, pick a "pretty" lotus root with the least amount of discoloration and bruises. If there is discoloration, just make sure that it doesn't go beyond the skin (examine the cut ends of the root to determine this). Second, try to pick a root that has little to no dirt inside. Third, when possible, select a lotus root with a small circumference (less than 3 inches) so that you can cut it into perfect disks and show off the root's beautiful patterns inside. If your grocery store has only larger lotus roots (which is often the case for us), you will need to halve the root lengthwise so that you end up with half-moons.

SERVES 4 to 6 (makes 4 cups)
TOTAL TIME 1¼ hours, plus 30 minutes soaking

½ ounce (14 grams) dashima (dried kelp), rinsed and broken into 2-inch pieces
20 ounces (567 grams) lotus root, peeled, sliced crosswise ¼ inch thick, and rinsed
1 tablespoon distilled white vinegar
2 tablespoons neutral cooking oil
3 tablespoons packed dark brown sugar
¼ cup soy sauce
½ ounce (14 grams) thinly sliced peeled fresh ginger
¼ cup corn syrup
1 tablespoon toasted sesame oil
1½ teaspoons sesame seeds, toasted

1 Soak the dashima in 1 cup hot water for 30 minutes. Measure out and reserve ¾ cup water; discard the remaining water and solids. Bring 6 cups water to a boil in a 14-inch flat-bottomed wok or 12-inch nonstick skillet. Add the lotus root and vinegar and cook for 4 minutes. Drain the lotus root and rinse under cold water. Drain and pat dry with paper towels. Wipe the wok dry with paper towels.

2 Heat the neutral oil in the wok over medium-high heat until shimmering. Add the lotus root and cook, tossing constantly, until the oil is absorbed, 3 to 5 minutes. Reduce the heat to medium, add the sugar, and cook, tossing frequently, for 2 minutes. Add the reserved dashima water, soy sauce, and ginger and bring to a boil, stirring occasionally. Reduce the heat to medium, cover, and simmer, flipping the lotus root occasionally, until the liquid is reduced to about 2 tablespoons, 15 to 20 minutes.

3 Add the corn syrup and toss to coat the lotus root. Increase the heat to medium-high and cook, tossing constantly, until the sauce thickens and is almost completely absorbed, 6 to 10 minutes. (The lotus root will become stringy.) Remove from the heat, add the sesame oil and sesame seeds, and toss to coat. Serve. (Refrigerate for up to 1 week.)

If your lotus root is small enough, you can slice it into disks to show off its beautiful pattern. If the root is large, you'll want to slice it into half-moons.

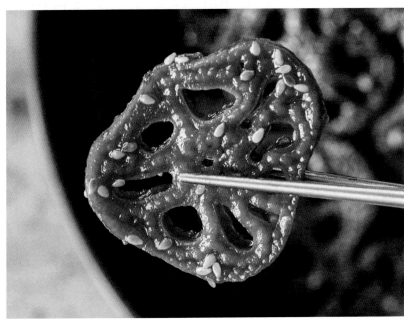

BRAISED BURDOCK ROOT

Ueong Jorim 우엉조림

oo-uhng joh-rim

SARAH
세라

I remember Umma buying burdock root from the Korean grocery store when I was a little kid. I could never remember the name of this root—Umma always told me it was ueong—but the word never stayed in my head. So I called it "skinny leg root" because that's what it looked like to me, and Umma just went with it. (Maybe this is why I'm not completely fluent in Korean, ha.) Anyhoo, I noticed that Umma rotated among buying three types of roots: this skinny leg root, aka ueong (burdock root); nagaimo (Japanese or Chinese yam), which I nicknamed "Umma's leg"; and yeongeun (lotus root). I asked her why she always bought these roots and she explained that it was primarily for Appa, who was treated for stomach cancer when I was two. They can help with digestion, so she made it a priority to buy and prepare them as banchan. The prep is simple but takes a little time, and I've always appreciated her labor of love to create this banchan for Appa's health. The braised root has a woodsy, earthy flavor, with a chewy and slightly crispy texture. Dashima water isn't necessary for this recipe, though Umma highly recommends it; you can substitute plain water instead. This banchan is also a common filling for Gimbap (Seaweed Rice Rolls; page 257).

Umma's Kitchen Wisdom

Burdock skin contains a lot of nutrition. I often scrub it clean rather than peeling it.

Slicing the burdock root into thin matchsticks is crucial. I use a knife, first cutting off a thin strip from the skinny root to create a flat, stable side. This will help you cut the burdock thinly and evenly. You can also use a mandoline to cut evenly thin planks, then cut those planks into matchsticks by hand.

SERVES 6 to 8 (makes 4 cups)
TOTAL TIME 1 hour, plus 30 minutes soaking

- ½ ounce (14 grams) dashima (dried kelp), rinsed and broken into 2-inch pieces
- 18 ounces (510 grams) burdock root, ends trimmed, scrubbed or peeled, and cut into 2½-inch lengths
- 2 tablespoons neutral cooking oil
- 3 tablespoons sugar
- 5 tablespoons soy sauce
- 2 tablespoons corn syrup
- 1 tablespoon sesame seeds, toasted

1 Soak the dashima in 1 cup hot water for 30 minutes. Measure out and reserve ½ cup water; discard the remaining water and solids.

2 Slice the burdock root pieces into ⅛-inch planks, then cut the planks into ⅛-inch matchsticks. Transfer the burdock root to a bowl, submerge in water, and swish with your hands to rinse. Drain the burdock root, then repeat rinsing with fresh water; drain well.

3 Heat the oil in a 14-inch flat-bottomed wok or 12-inch nonstick skillet over medium-high heat until shimmering. Add the burdock root and cook, tossing constantly until the oil is absorbed, about 2 minutes. Add the sugar and toss to coat.

4 Add the reserved dashima water and soy sauce and mix to coat the burdock. Bring to a simmer. Reduce the heat to medium, cover, and simmer, stirring occasionally, until the liquid is reduced to about 3 tablespoons, 20 to 25 minutes.

5 Add the corn syrup and increase the heat to medium-high. Cook, tossing constantly, until the sauce thickens and is almost completely absorbed, 3 to 5 minutes. Remove from the heat, add the sesame seeds, and toss to combine. Serve. (Refrigerate for up to 1 week.)

SPICY BRAISED TOFU

Dubu Jorim 두부조림

doo-boo joh-rim

SARAH
세라

This is one of a few banchan I have a hard time not eating completely all by myself. It truly is one of my favorites. Whenever Umma made this sweet and spicy dish, you would find me wandering into the kitchen and slowly nibbling away at it, piece by piece. Before I even realized it, there would be only two or three pieces remaining. Umma would always laugh and affectionately yell, "Ya! Did you eat this all yourself?" To which I would respond, "Yes, sorry, it was too good!" Too good is arguably an understatement, since this dish transforms mild tofu into a flavorful banchan full of irresistible contrasts: the light fried crust of the tofu set against its plush interior, with sweet, spicy, and umami flavors unfolding in your mouth. And, like most banchan, it also happens to taste great either hot or cold. In my family, we don't reheat this if serving leftovers. It tastes just as amazing, if not better, when cold, especially since the flavors have had a chance to be further absorbed by the tofu.

Umma's Kitchen Wisdom

It's very important to not overcook the tofu. If it's overcooked, the tofu will be tough to chew and won't taste good at all, especially as cold leftovers.

Some people prefer to leave the sauce thin so it can be mixed into their rice bowl, so feel free to reduce the sauce in step 4 to your desired thickness.

SERVES 4   TOTAL TIME 35 minutes

   2 tablespoons water
   2 tablespoons corn syrup
   2 tablespoons maesil cheong (plum extract syrup)
1½ tablespoons soy sauce
1½ tablespoons fish sauce
   1 tablespoon toasted sesame oil
1½ teaspoons minced garlic
1½ teaspoons gochugaru
   ½ Fresno chile, ribs and seeds removed, chopped fine
   ½ jalapeño chile, ribs and seeds removed, chopped fine
   2 tablespoons finely chopped yellow onion
   1 green onion, chopped fine, divided
   1 (14- to 16-ounce / 397- to 454-gram) block firm tofu
   ⅛ teaspoon fine salt, divided
   1 tablespoon neutral cooking oil
     Pinch black pepper

1 Whisk the water, corn syrup, maesil cheong, soy sauce, fish sauce, sesame oil, garlic, and gochugaru together in a bowl. Stir in the Fresno chile, jalapeño, yellow onion, and half of the green onion. Set the sauce aside.

2 Rinse the tofu and pat dry with paper towels. Halve the tofu block lengthwise, then cut crosswise into ½-inch slices. Arrange the tofu in a single layer on a paper towel–lined plate. Pat the tops dry with additional paper towels, then sprinkle with a pinch of salt.

3 Heat the neutral oil in a 12-inch nonstick skillet over medium-high heat until shimmering. Arrange the tofu salted side down in the skillet. Sprinkle with the remaining pinch of salt and cook until light golden brown, 3 to 5 minutes per side.

4 Add the sauce and cook, constantly spooning the sauce over the tofu, until the sauce has thickened and begins to coat the tofu, about 2 minutes. Remove the skillet from the heat and sprinkle with the remaining chopped green onion and pepper. Serve. (Refrigerate for up to 1 week.)

SOY-BRAISED BEEF

Jangjorim 장조림

jahng-joh-rim

SARAH
세라

Savory, sweet, garlicky, and infused with the salty depth of soy sauce, jangjorim is a beloved banchan for Korean kids as well as grownups. To serve it, ummas will typically shred the cooked beef and cut the boiled eggs into small pieces for their little ones to enjoy more easily. As a child, I remember waiting for Umma to finish shredding the meat with her hands, watching her as she quartered the soy-braised eggs with scissors. For me, there would always be four bite-size pieces of egg, all cut from a single egg, with the cooked yolk barely hanging on. She would say "ja" ("here") and arrange this banchan amongst the other dishes. I vividly remember hearing the glass plates clink against each other as she did this. This banchan usually features shishito peppers, which Umma adds toward the end to prevent them from becoming overly soft or soggy. The Dasida adds an umami boost, but it's optional. You'll need a 6- or 8-quart electric pressure cooker.

SERVES 8   TOTAL TIME 3 hours,
plus 30 minutes brining

   1 tablespoon granulated sugar
1½ pounds (680 grams) boneless beef eye-round
      roast, trimmed and halved with the grain
   8 large eggs
   1 ounce (28 grams) dashima (dried kelp),
      rinsed and broken into 2-inch pieces
  ½ cup soy sauce
   5 tablespoons (64 grams) packed brown sugar
   2 tablespoons mirin
   2 slices fresh ginger
   2 bay leaves
   3 tablespoons corn syrup
   3 ounces (85 grams) garlic cloves, peeled and
      root ends trimmed
   6 shishito peppers, stems trimmed
1½ teaspoons Dasida beef stock powder (optional)

1 Dissolve the granulated sugar in 5 cups cold water in a medium bowl. Submerge the beef in the liquid and refrigerate for 30 minutes.

2 Using the default sauté or browning function, bring 10 cups water to a boil in an electric pressure cooker. Gently lower the eggs into the water, cover without locking the lid, and cook for 15 minutes. Using tongs, transfer the eggs to a bowl of cold running water. Once cool enough to touch, peel the eggs and set aside.

3 Return the water to a boil in the pressure cooker using the default sauté function. Add the beef and blanch for 5 minutes. Transfer the beef to a colander and rinse under cold running water; discard the blanching liquid and clean the pressure cooker pot.

4 Bring 1 quart water to a boil in a small saucepan. Remove the saucepan from the heat and add the dashima. Cover and let steep for 15 minutes. Strain the liquid into the pressure cooker pot; discard the solids. Stir in the soy sauce, brown sugar, and mirin until the sugar has dissolved. Nestle the beef, eggs, ginger, and bay leaves into the pot. Lock the lid in place and close the pressure-release valve. Select the high pressure-cook function and cook for 20 minutes. Turn off the pressure cooker and quick-release the pressure. Carefully remove the lid, allowing the steam to escape away from you. Select the keep warm function and cover the pot without locking the lid.

5 Transfer the beef to a cutting board. Once cool enough to touch, shred the beef with your hands into strands about ½ inch thick.

6 Stir the corn syrup into the cooking liquid, then stir in the shredded beef and garlic. Select the default sauté function, cover without locking the lid, and simmer to season the beef with the sauce, about 20 minutes. Stir in the shishito peppers and Dasida powder, if using, and simmer until the peppers soften and turn olive green, about 10 minutes. To serve, transfer the eggs to a cutting board using a slotted spoon and halve or slice each egg. Serve the beef and peppers topped with a portion of the sauce and some of the eggs.

Umma's Kitchen Wisdom

Don't cut the raw beef into smaller pieces than directed. This will cause the beef to overcook and will make it difficult to shred.

When trimming the peppers, make sure you don't cut off so much of the stem that the seeds are exposed.

You can store leftovers for up to 4 days and serve them cold or reheated. Separate the solids from the sauce and let both cool to room temperature. Skim off the fat on top of the sauce before refrigerating it. If I know I'll be storing leftovers, I leave some of the boiled eggs whole, waiting to cut them until right before serving time.

Top: Halmeoni and Harabeoji with their first grandchild at his doljanchi in 1972.This is one of Umma's favorite pictures of her mother, and she remembers that the hanbok she is wearing was green.

Middle: Celebrating Sarah's first birthday at her doljanchi in 1996, in a hanbok sent by Halmeoni.

Bottom right: Umma, age 8, carrying a dosirak (lunchbox), with her two older sisters, likely on a rare trip to Seoul in 1967.

The Luxury of Eggs

UMMA
엄마

I was born in 1959, just six years after the Korean War ended. Korea wasn't the Korea that you see now; at that time, it was characterized as an impoverished country with one of the poorest economies in the world as a result of the devastating three-year war.

When I was growing up, my meals always consisted of two foods: rice and kimchi, sometimes with salted shrimp. And it wasn't just any rice; it was barley rice. Nowadays, people choose to buy barley rice because it is deemed as a "healthier" alternative to white rice, but back then, barley rice was our only option. And next to this rice would always be a side of kimchi. People often joke to me that that is the reason why I'm short, but this was the only meal my family could afford to eat every day, and I never questioned it.

Halmeoni was an incredibly hard-working woman, a seamstress who specialized in making hanbok (traditional Korean dresses), who also resold ice cream, brooches, and pins as a street vendor. When I was in middle school, Halmeoni was finally able to afford eggs, although only

for special occasions. On those occasions, Halmeoni would treat us to a meal with an egg. About once a month, our tinned lunchboxes would upgrade from just rice and kimchi to rice, kimchi, and eggs. On some occasions the eggs were fried, some days they were steamed to make Gyeran Jjim (Steamed Eggs; page 103), and other days they were pan-fried to make Gyeran Mari (Rolled Omelet; page 104). I distinctly remember the day she packed me 12 boiled eggs to enjoy for my once-a-year school field trip. Yes, all 12 of those eggs were for me! I can still feel the same excitement that I felt that day. It was the only time I could enjoy so many eggs.

I later found out that Halmeoni never allowed herself to indulge in eggs until after I had become a mother myself. When my children were young, Appa and I struggled with how to afford groceries and how we would pay our next bill. Whenever we ate out or were able to buy treats for the family, I didn't want to indulge in these special foods either. I wanted my kids to have them first. It was then I learned that Halmeoni did the same.

TURN FOR UMMA'S GYERAN JJIM RECIPE →

STEAMED EGGS

Gyeran Jjim 계란찜

gyeh-rahn jjim

SARAH
세라

Umma made this dish quite often when my brother and I were young because it's incredibly forgiving, convenient, and nutritious. Whenever we were running low on banchan, Umma would quickly whip this up in the morning and share it with the family. As my brother and I got older, Umma began adding a sprinkle of gochugaru for spice and color (leave it out if you want a mild version). This easy, tasty banchan is nostalgic for both Umma and me. We like to enjoy leftovers cold or at room temperature.

SERVES 4   TOTAL TIME 35 minutes

    3 large eggs
 ½ cup water
    1 teaspoon fish sauce
    1 teaspoon toasted sesame oil
 ¼ teaspoon sugar
 ¼ teaspoon fine salt
 1¼ ounces (35 grams) imitation crab,
       lightly squeezed and chopped
    1 green onion, chopped
 ¼ teaspoon gochugaru (optional)

1 Lightly beat the eggs, water, fish sauce, oil, sugar, and salt in a 12-ounce ramekin (4½ inches wide) until well combined. Stir in the crab and green onion, then sprinkle with the gochugaru, if using.

2 In a large, wide pot, add about 1 inch of water and a collapsible steamer basket (be sure to not add too much water; it should not hit the steamer basket) and bring to a boil. Place the ramekin in the steamer basket. Cover, reduce the heat to medium, and cook until no liquid egg remains, 12 to 16 minutes. (Insert a spoon or chopstick into the center to check if the egg is cooked completely. If there is still liquid egg in the middle, continue to cook, checking every 2 minutes.)

3 Remove the lid (try to avoid letting condensation drip onto the eggs in the ramekin). Transfer the ramekin to a trivet or folded dish towel and serve. (Refrigerate for up to 4 days.)

ROLLED OMELET

Gyeran Mari 계란말이

gyeh-rahn mah-ri

SARAH
세라

One thing I appreciate about Umma is that she has never pressured me to get married or have kids. She has told me of the happiness that kids and a partner could provide, but she has always reminded me that there are many ways to have a fulfilling life. Growing up, Umma was conditioned to believe that she must get married and have kids, and she accepted that notion without question. She didn't want this pressure to be passed down to my brother and me, so she never set expectations that she would one day become a mother-in-law or a halmeoni. As time passes, I ponder more and more whether I want kids. Whatever I decide, I'm grateful that Umma will always support my decision. One thing is for sure, though: If I do have kids, I won't be making American-style omelets for them but will instead opt for Korean-style rolled omelets like this one. I find gyeran mari to be much more delicate and purposeful, with a sense of "organization" that you can taste in every bite. Whenever Umma made this when I was a little girl, I would get so excited because it looked so fun and was so appealing to eat. I would want to share that same excitement of discovery with my kids.

SERVES 3 or 4   TOTAL TIME 45 minutes

    5 large eggs
    1 tablespoon milk
    ¼ teaspoon sugar
    ¼ teaspoon miwon matsogeum (MSG seasoning salt)
    2 green onions, minced
    5 tablespoons (50 grams) minced Spam
    3 tablespoons minced carrot
 2½ teaspoons neutral cooking oil, divided

1 Beat the eggs, milk, sugar, and seasoning salt in a 2-cup liquid measuring cup until the eggs are thoroughly combined and the mixture is pure yellow. Stir in the onions, Spam, and carrot.

2 Heat 1 teaspoon oil in an 8½ by 7½-inch nonstick omelet pan over medium-low heat until shimmering. Add ½ cup egg mixture, tilting and shaking the pan gently until the egg evenly covers the bottom of the pan. Using a small silicone spatula, distribute the vegetables and Spam evenly across the surface of the egg mixture. (If necessary, add extra egg mixture to fill in holes.) Cook, undisturbed, until the bottom of the omelet is just set but the top is still slightly wet, 1 to 3 minutes.

3 Using two small nonstick spatulas, gently lift and fold the lower one-quarter of the omelet away from you, like a letter, then repeat folding the lower one-quarter of the omelet once more. (The omelet is very delicate at this point and will most likely tear; this is okay. It will become sturdier with future folds.) Gently pull the partially rolled omelet toward you to the now-empty portion of the pan, creating an empty space at the upper end of the pan farthest from you. If the omelet begins to tear while sliding, loosen the edges with a spatula, wait 15 seconds, and try again.

4 Add ½ teaspoon oil to the empty space in the pan. Whisk the remaining egg mixture to recombine, then add one-third of the mixture to the empty space. Using a small silicone spatula, distribute the vegetables and Spam evenly across the surface of the freshly poured egg mixture. Position the pan so the upper half farthest from you is directly over the burner.

5 Lift and fold the lower one-quarter of the omelet away from you. Cook, without disturbing, until the bottom of the freshly poured portion is just set but the top is still slightly wet, 1 to 3 minutes. Lift and fold the lower one-third of the omelet. Gently pull the partially rolled omelet toward you to the now-empty portion of the pan, creating an empty space at the upper end of the pan farthest from you.

6 Add ½ teaspoon oil to the empty space in the pan. Whisk the remaining egg mixture to recombine, then add half of the mixture to the empty space and distribute the vegetables and Spam evenly across the surface of the freshly poured egg mixture. Lift and fold the lower one-third of the omelet away from you. Cook, without disturbing, until the bottom of the freshly poured portion is just set but the top is still slightly wet, 1 to 3 minutes. Gently pull the partially rolled omelet toward you to the now-empty portion of the pan, creating an empty space at the upper end of the pan farthest from you.

7 Add the remaining ½ teaspoon oil to the empty space in the pan. Add the remaining egg mixture to the empty space and distribute the vegetables and Spam evenly across the surface of the freshly poured egg mixture. Lift and fold the lower one-third of the omelet away from you. Cook, without disturbing, until the bottom of the freshly poured portion is just set but the top is still slightly wet, 1 to 3 minutes. Lift and fold the lower one-third of the omelet away from you to create a fully rolled omelet. Continue to cook, gently turning the omelet as needed, until fully sealed together on all sides, 1 to 3 minutes. Transfer the omelet to a cutting board and let rest for 5 minutes. Slice ½ inch thick and serve.

Umma's Kitchen Wisdom

I use an 8½ by 7½-inch nonstick Korean omelet pan. Square or rectangular omelet pans of a similar size (anything between 7 and 8½ inches will work). The most important thing is that your pan be in good condition and not scratched or worn.

Cooking a perfect rolled omelet takes lots of practice! But even a rolled omelet with cracks will be delicious.

TURN TO SEE HOW TO COOK GYERAN MARI →

Top left Add some egg mixture to the pan, tilting and shaking until the egg evenly covers the bottom. Distribute the vegetables and Spam evenly across the surface.

Top right Once the bottom has set, gently lift and fold the omelet away from you once, as though starting to fold a letter. Pull the folded portion down into the empty space.

Bottom Add more egg mixture to the newly empty space, again distributing the vegetables and Spam evenly. Continue to fold, pull, and cook.

Top The omelet will become sturdier and easier to fold as it gets larger and you add the remaining egg mixture.

Bottom left Continue to cook the fully rolled omelet, gently turning it as needed, until it's fully sealed together on all sides.

Bottom right Transfer the omelet to a cutting board and let rest, then slice and serve.

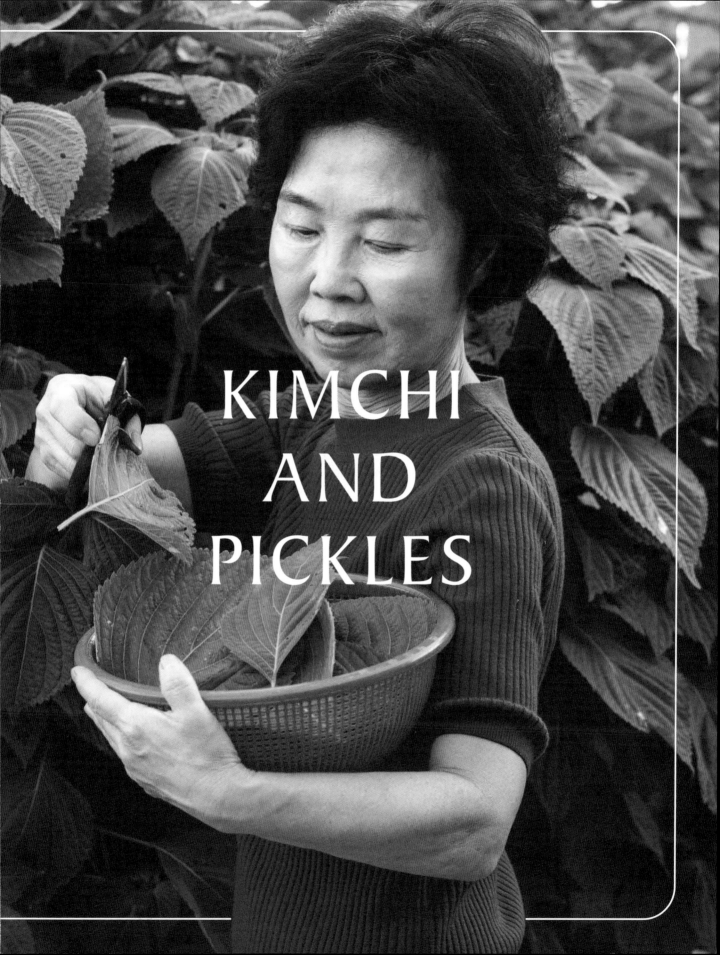

KIMCHI
AND
PICKLES

The Living Art of Kimchi

SARAH
세라

From a very young age, Korean children are fed kimchi by their umma, washed in water to gently introduce them to its bold flavors. Eating kimchi this way is one of my earliest memories and the way many Korean children are introduced to this dish, a staple of our cuisine, identity, and pride.

The beauty of making kimchi lies in its adaptability and the endless flavor combinations that you can discover through practice. The specific blend of ingredients Umma uses is the result of decades of her own practice, trial, and error. If you make it regularly, you'll find that kimchi offers limitless possibilities, and soon enough, you'll develop your own unique versions that reflect your preferences and wisdom.

What is kimchi?

Kimchi is a traditional dish made by fermenting vegetables with other ingredients. The most well-known version is made with napa cabbage, but there are more than 200 varieties of kimchi! It can also be made from radishes, cucumbers, perilla leaves, mustard greens, pumpkin, watermelon rind, and more. Other ingredients might include gochugaru, dried or fresh chiles, garlic, ginger, fresh fruit juices, fish sauce, and various seasonings. The mixture undergoes a transformative lactic acid fermentation process that not only preserves the vegetables but also develops a complex flavor that continues to evolve over time.

How do you eat kimchi?

Kimchi is enjoyed both as a side dish and as an ingredient in various main dishes, including stews, braises, noodles, savory pancakes—and even grilled cheese (see page 313)! Like bananas, which can be enjoyed at different stages of ripeness, kimchi can be enjoyed at different points during its fermentation. Some people prefer it fresh and crisp, while others enjoy it when it's well fermented or deeply aged. Each stage offers its unique character and can serve different purposes. For example, just as overly ripened bananas are ideal for banana bread, well-fermented kimchi is perfect for Kimchi Jjigae (Kimchi Stew; page 216), where its deeper flavors really shines.

When do you make kimchi?

A common practice in Korean households is to make different types of kimchi depending on the season. In our home, we loosely categorize kimchi in two ways: winter kimchi and summer kimchi. Winter kimchi is made with produce that's at its peak during colder months, such as napa cabbage and Korean radishes. We start preparing and stocking these kimchi in the fall, so that we can enjoy them from fall through spring. Summer kimchi is made with produce at its peak in the warmer months, including cucumbers and young summer radishes. They tend to have shorter fermenting times and arrive on our table along with the summer heat. While there are no strict rules, once you eat kimchi regularly, you may gravitate toward the best available seasonal variety without even realizing it.

CONTINUES

What ingredients do you need?

If you have your pantry stocked with the Korean staples we suggest (see page 13), you're well on your way to having what you need to make kimchi. While it's impossible to list every ingredient here because there are so many different types of kimchi, there are a few vital components to highlight.

SALT Salt plays a critical role, drawing moisture out of the vegetables to prevent the kimchi from becoming too watery, while also seasoning the vegetables and creating an ideal environment for the fermentation process to succeed. Salt reduces the activity of harmful microbes that would otherwise spoil the vegetables and allows beneficial microbes, primarily species of lactic acid bacteria (LAB), to flourish. The presence of LAB allows for proper fermentation and development of kimchi's signature flavors. While coarse sea salt (cheonilyeom) is a traditional choice for many Koreans, finer salts can be just as effective—and much more affordable. It's essential to choose salt that is free of iodine and anti-caking agents, as these additives can interfere with the fermentation process and inhibit the growth of beneficial microbes. Umma relies on Diamond Crystal Granulated Plain Salt (a fine salt) for her kimchi.

MAESIL CHEONG Plum extract syrup adds much more than just sweetness to kimchi. This syrup's organic acid component increases acidity, creating an environment conducive to healthy fermentation. Anthocyanins in the plums contribute vivid color, while the naturally derived sugars in the maesil cheong help preserve crispness, allowing kimchi to maintain its crunch to the very end of fermentation.

FRESH FRUIT JUICE Umma uses freshly made pear juice, and sometimes freshly made apple juice, to add deep, complex sweetness (see page 41 to learn how to make these juices). While Asian pear is often preferred because of its natural sugars and fermentation-friendly enzymes, overripe Hachiya persimmons make a great substitute. Simply discard the skin and use the fruit pulp as is.

SALTED FISH / FISH SAUCE Many kimchi recipes call for at least one type of jeotgal (salted seafood) or aekjeot (fish sauce) to deepen umami flavors. Depending on the kimchi, the seafood can be herring, anchovy, shrimp, or other fish. Some versions, though, including Dongchimi (Radish Water Kimchi; page 120), don't use any seafood.

What equipment do you need?

There are a few essential items needed to make kimchi: a couple of large bowls or basins, a large colander, and an airtight container. The large bowls and colander are key for salting, rinsing, and seasoning large volumes of vegetables with ease. An airtight container with at least 1-inch headspace between the lid and the kimchi is necessary for fermentation and storage. As kimchi ferments, it produces gases, primarily carbon dioxide, which cause the kimchi to expand. The headspace allows room for this gas buildup, reducing the risk of the container overflowing when opened. Additionally, the airtight seal prevents oxygen from getting in, which would inhibit the fermentation and cause spoilage. The seal also helps contain the strong odors of kimchi. You can buy dedicated fermentation containers, but other containers will work as long as they're airtight. Our recipes specify the container size you will need, ranging from 3 quarts for Kkaennip Kimchi (Perilla Leaf Kimchi; page 134) to 6 quarts for Pogi Kimchi (Whole Napa Cabbage Kimchi; page 127). Rubber gloves are optional—Halmeoni never used them to mix her kimchi by hand, but Umma strongly prefers to use them. If you want to take the traditional—and ergonomic—route as Umma does, you'll want a vinyl tablecloth. Lay it on the floor, squat with your feet flat, and mix everything by hand in the classic Asian squat position!

What does the fermentation process involve?

Essentially, there are two stages of kimchi fermentation. The first stage calls for letting the kimchi sit at room temperature to activate fermentation, while the second stage takes place in the refrigerator, where the kimchi continues to ferment more slowly for the remainder of the process.

Letting the kimchi sit at room temperature immediately after it's prepared allows good bacteria to multiply, kick-starting fermentation and the development of complex flavors. Traditionally, how long you leave kimchi at room temperature depends on the season and weather, because fermentation occurs faster in warmer temperatures. In our recipes, we specify a temperature range for this phase of fermentation. But keep in mind that even in a temperature-controlled environment, seasonal differences may still affect kimchi fermentation. The composition of vegetables changes throughout the year, including their sugar, mineral, and chemical content. These changes, as well as seasonal variations in LAB species and activity, will influence the fermentation process and the final flavor of the kimchi.

Once the kimchi enters the second stage of fermentation in the refrigerator, it will continue to ferment slowly for the rest of its shelf life. But even in a temperature-controlled refrigerator, seasonal shifts still affect fermentation rate. Kimchi made in warmer seasons continues to ferment faster, while kimchi made in colder seasons ferments more slowly. For example, in our Southern California conditions, our Mat Kimchi (Cut Napa Cabbage Kimchi; page 115) takes about 25 days to become well fermented in the summer, while in the winter, it takes about 40 days. Multiple factors contribute to this, including the temperature during the initial fermentation phase, natural variations in bacterial species, and seasonal changes in the composition of produce.

One often overlooked factor is the refrigerator itself. Conventional refrigerators use an indirect refrigerant system that circulates cooled air, leading to temperature fluctuations that are influenced by the surrounding environment. Minor temperature increases that occur with door openings can speed up fermentation, since LAB remains more active at higher temperatures. In contrast, dedicated kimchi refrigerators—a common sight in Korean households—use a direct refrigerant system with cooling coils, designed to maintain a consistent temperature and ensure optimal fermentation.

Countless small factors, shaped by the environment and ambient temperatures, affect kimchi fermentation. Whether or not you have a kimchi refrigerator (we don't), periodically tasting your kimchi as it ferments will give you the best sense of how far along it is in the process.

Does kimchi ever go bad?

Properly prepared kimchi doesn't technically "go bad"; it simply continues to ferment beyond its peak flavor. When properly fermented and stored, it's rare for kimchi to develop mold (of course, if this happens, discard it). Once kimchi passes its prime, it will develop an overly sour or bitter taste that will be less enjoyable.

CUT NAPA CABBAGE KIMCHI

Mat Kimchi 맛김치

maht ggim-chi

UMMA
엄마

This recipe goes by two names, and Sarah and I debated on which one to choose: mat kimchi or mak kimchi. "Mat" means taste and "mak" means carelessly, referring to the way the cabbage is coarsely chopped. I don't think this type of kimchi is carelessly made, and I feel like the latter name doesn't do this kimchi justice. Given how tasty this kimchi is right after it's made, I believe that mat kimchi is the more appropriate name.

SARAH
세라

We've included two types of napa cabbage kimchi: this mat kimchi, where the cabbage is cut into rough pieces, and Pogi Kimchi (Whole Napa Cabbage Kimchi; page 127), where the napa cabbage is quartered but otherwise kept whole. Whereas pogi kimchi undergoes a long fermentation and features a deep flavor and rich texture, mat kimchi comes together quickly and easily and offers a bright, fresh flavor profile. You can enjoy it as soon as the next day, making it a great "go-to" kimchi for everyday meals. Umma likes to use Fresno chiles in her mat kimchi to impart a refreshing flavor, making each bite feel revitalizing. It's her game-changing ingredient that makes her mat kimchi recipe unique! You'll need a large bowl or basin (at least 6 quarts) to comfortably salt and toss the cabbage, as well as a 4-quart storage container with a tight-fitting lid.

MAKES about 16 cups
TOTAL TIME 1¼ hours, plus 1 hour salting, 30 minutes draining, and 24 hours fermenting

- 3 cups water
- 1 yellow onion (283 grams), coarsely chopped, divided
- ½ ounce (14 grams) dried large anchovies, gutted and heads removed (see page 43)
- ½ ounce (14 grams) dashima (dried kelp), rinsed and broken into 2-inch pieces
- ¼ ounce (7 grams) dried large-eyed herring
- 6 pounds (2.7 kilograms) napa cabbage
- ¾ cup (216 grams) fine salt
- 3 tablespoons all-purpose flour
- ½ cup fresh Asian pear juice (see page 41)
- 5 tablespoons (94 grams) saeujeot (salted shrimp)
- 4 Fresno chiles (100 grams), stemmed and finely chopped
- 3 ounces (85 grams) green or red mustard greens, stemmed and coarsely chopped
- 5 green onions (75 grams), sliced ¾ inch thick
- ¾ cup (84 grams) gochugaru
- 7 tablespoons (102 grams) minced garlic
- 3 tablespoons maesil cheong (plum extract syrup)
- 2 tablespoons fish sauce
- 1½ teaspoons sugar
- 1½ teaspoons grated fresh ginger

RECIPE CONTINUES

1 Bring the water, half of the yellow onion, the anchovies, dashima, and herring to a boil in a small saucepan. Reduce the heat to a vigorous simmer and cook for 10 minutes. Strain the broth immediately through a fine-mesh strainer into a liquid measuring cup. Set aside 1 cup to cool completely. Discard the solids and the remaining broth (or reserve the broth for another use).

2 Peel away the outermost layer of leaves from each cabbage head and set aside. Starting halfway down the side of each head, cut the cabbage in half lengthwise through the core. Using your hands, pull the split section of the core apart to fully separate the cabbage into halves. Place each half cut side down on a cutting board and cut crosswise into 1½-inch-thick slices. Discard the core. Cut the larger pieces that contain mostly the white rib in half crosswise.

3 Submerge the cut cabbage and reserved outer layers in a large bowl or basin of water, separating the layers, then transfer to a large colander. (This is not to clean the cabbage, but rather to coat all the pieces with water so the salt sticks.) Discard the water.

4 Place a large handful of cut cabbage in the now-empty bowl to create a layer and sprinkle generously with some of the salt. Add the remaining cabbage and reserved outer leaves to the bowl in batches, sprinkling each batch with the remaining salt. Toss the cabbage to thoroughly distribute the salt, then spread it into an even layer. Cover and let sit for 1 hour, tossing the cabbage halfway through salting (set a timer so you don't forget!).

5 Meanwhile, transfer the reserved 1 cup broth to the now-empty saucepan. Whisk the flour into the broth until well combined, then bring to a boil, whisking constantly. Reduce the heat to a simmer and cook, whisking constantly, until thickened, about 1 minute. Remove from the heat and let cool completely.

6 Process the pear juice, saeujeot, and remaining yellow onion in a blender until smooth, about 20 seconds; set aside.

7 Transfer the cut cabbage and leaves to the colander; discard the liquid left in the bowl and rinse away any remaining salt from the bowl. Remove the cabbage from the colander and, working in batches, submerge the cabbage in cold water in the bowl, agitate gently to remove excess salt and dirt, and transfer back to the colander. Discard the water. Repeat rinsing the cabbage once more with fresh water. Let drain for 30 minutes. Wash and dry the bowl.

8 Using your gloved hands, gently mix the cabbage, cooled flour paste, pear juice mixture, Fresno chiles, mustard greens, green onions, gochugaru, garlic, maesil cheong, fish sauce, sugar, and ginger in the bowl until well combined. Pull out and reserve the outer cabbage leaves. Transfer the cut cabbage mixture to a 4-quart storage container and gently press into an even layer. Arrange the outer cabbage leaves evenly on top. Cover the container and place in a 50- to 70-degree location away from direct sunlight. Let the cabbage sit until liquid begins to pool around the edges of the container, up to 24 hours. (This will be temperature-dependent, so we suggest you start checking after 3 hours, especially if your location is on the warmer end of the range.) Serve. (Refrigerate for up to 2 months; the flavor will continue to develop over time.)

Umma's Kitchen Wisdom

Asian pear is my preferred choice for the fruit juice here, but very overripe Hachiya persimmons make a great substitute. You don't need to juice the persimmons—simply discard the skin and use the fruit pulp, which is like a thick liquid.

I save the remaining anchovy broth in step 1 to use for future kimchi or recipes that call for seafood or dashima broth, such as Sundubu Jjigae (Spicy Soft Tofu Stew; page 242—use this broth instead of the seafood broth), Ueong Jorim (Braised Burdock Root; page 95—use this broth instead of the dashima water), and Kimchi Jjigae (Kimchi Stew; page 216—use this broth as part of the 3 cups water in the stew). It can be refrigerated for up to 4 days or frozen for up to 3 months.

As Mat Kimchi continues to ferment over time, its color will become more muted and its texture will soften.

RADISH KIMCHI

Kkakdugi 깍두기

kkahk-doo-gi

SARAH
세라

Sometimes Umma and I visit the city where my brother and I were raised to pick up some Korean groceries that are harder to find near our home. Whenever we pass by this one liquor store, Umma always reminds me of the same story that highlights Appa's warm heart and mind. When I was just a baby and my brother, Kevin, was a toddler, Appa would always finish his day of painting by paying a visit to this liquor store. He would buy just one item: a king-size candy bar. He would arrive home with this candy bar gripped in one hand and the other hand gripping his cooler, excited to see his son run up to him in glee for both his return and the expected treat. When we became older, we frequented a seolleongtang restaurant adjacent to this liquor store. Appa knew I was obsessed with kkakdugi and how much I enjoyed this pungent kimchi alongside the rich beef bone soup, so he would always make sure to push the plate of kkakdugi toward me. To this day, whenever I sit with him as he eats dinner after returning home from a long work day, he will push all his banchan dishes toward me for us to share, despite knowing that I've already eaten. Whenever I drive through this area and Umma repeats the same story, I don't mention that I've heard it before, because I never get tired of being reminded of these cherished memories. To make our recipe, you'll need a large bowl or basin (at least 6 quarts) to comfortably toss the radish mixture, as well as a 4-quart storage container with a tight-fitting lid.

MAKES about 14 cups   TOTAL TIME 30 minutes, plus 30 minutes salting and 24 hours fermenting

     1 cup water
     3 tablespoons all-purpose flour
  4½ pounds (2 kilograms) Korean radish
     5 tablespoons (64 grams) sugar, divided
     2 tablespoons fine salt
  ½ yellow onion (142 grams), chopped coarse
     1 cup (140 grams) coarsely chopped peeled Asian pear
  ¼ cup (75 grams) saeujeot (salted shrimp)
  ¾ cup plus 1 tablespoon (91 grams) gochugaru
     5 green onions (75 grams), white and light green parts halved lengthwise, cut into 1-inch lengths
  ⅓ cup (78 grams) minced garlic
  ¼ cup maesil cheong (plum extract syrup)
     1 tablespoon fish sauce
     2 teaspoons grated fresh ginger

1 Whisk the water and flour together in a small saucepan until well combined. Bring to a boil, whisking constantly. Reduce the heat to a simmer and cook, whisking constantly, until thickened, about 1 minute. Remove from the heat and let cool completely.

2 Slice the radish crosswise ½ inch thick, then cut into rough 1-inch pieces. Rinse the radish under running water in a colander, drain briefly, then transfer to a large bowl. Add 3 tablespoons sugar and the salt and toss to coat. Let sit for 30 minutes, tossing the radish halfway through salting.

3 Meanwhile, process the yellow onion, pear, and saeujeot in a blender until smooth, about 15 seconds; set the pear mixture aside.

4 Drain the radish. Rinse the bowl, then return the radish to the bowl. Add the flour paste, onion mixture, gochugaru, green onions, garlic, maesil cheong, fish sauce, ginger, and remaining 2 tablespoons sugar. Using your gloved hands, mix gently until thoroughly combined; be careful not to overmix.

5 Transfer the radish mixture to a 4-quart storage container. Cover the container and place in a 50- to 70-degree location away from direct sunlight. Let the radish mixture ferment until liquid begins to pool around the edges of the container, up to 24 hours. (This will be temperature-dependent, so we suggest you start checking after 3 hours, especially if your location is on the warmer end of the range.) Serve. (Refrigerate for up to 1½ months; the flavor will continue to develop over time.)

RADISH WATER KIMCHI

Dongchimi 동치미

dohng-che-mi

UMMA
엄마

This is one of Appa's favorite kimchi. Whenever he eats this, you can catch him holding his bowl to his face, slurping up all of the kimchi juice and releasing the classic "ajeossi sigh" (older man sigh) of good food. Hearing a contented sigh, whether it is from Appa, my kids, or just anyone trying my food, never fails to make me happy. Besides serving this cold as is, along with its brine, I also like to use it in Dongchimi Guksu (Radish Water Kimchi Noodles; page 299). The time it takes for the kimchi brine to turn cloudy might vary based on the weather and the season, so be sure to check on the kimchi every day and make assessments.

SARAH
세라

Dongchimi translates as "winter water kimchi," and as its name suggests, this refreshing kimchi is best enjoyed in the winter, since Korean radishes are harvested in the fall and eaten throughout the winter. When the winter season comes around, you can find Umma regularly buying Korean radishes to make all sorts of different dishes and kimchi that feature this root. Of all of these, dongchimi stands out the most to me. It's unique in that it creates kimchi using a water brine, and though it contains some chiles, it's not spicy. It's one of my favorite kimchi and was also ranked as Korea's second favorite in a poll, just after Yeolmu Putbaechu Kimchi (Young Summer Radish and Napa Cabbage Kimchi; page 137). (This poll didn't include napa cabbage kimchi, as that is the most common type of kimchi, enjoyed on a daily basis.) New sugar (see page 17) is required for this kimchi; look for this ingredient, which is a blend of glucose and saccharin, at a Korean grocery store or online. If you substitute regular sugar, the kimchi juice will turn syrupy and will be too sweet. You'll need a large bowl or basin (at least 4 quarts) to comfortably strain the radish mixture, as well as a 4-quart storage container with a tight-fitting lid.

MAKES about 16 cups   TOTAL TIME 1 hour, plus 30 minutes salting and 1 month fermenting

  2 quarts plus 2½ cups water, divided
  2 tablespoons all-purpose flour
6½ pounds (2.9 kilograms) Korean radish, divided
  3 tablespoons fine salt, divided
  ½ teaspoon new sugar
  ½ Asian pear (400 grams) peeled, cored, and chopped coarse
  ½ yellow onion (142 grams), chopped coarse
  ½ Fuji apple (120 grams), peeled, cored, and chopped coarse
 18 garlic cloves, peeled (54 grams)
  2 tablespoons coarsely chopped peeled fresh ginger
  6 green onions (90 grams), white and light green parts only
  1 jalapeño chile, stemmed, seeded, and sliced lengthwise ¼ inch thick
8–10 dried small red chiles

1 Whisk 2½ cups water and the flour together in a small saucepan until well combined. Bring to a boil, whisking constantly. Reduce the heat to a simmer and cook, whisking constantly, until slightly thickened (it should sill be runny), about 1 minute. Remove from the heat and let cool completely.

2 Cut 1 pound radish into rough 1-inch pieces and reserve. Slice the remaining 5½ pounds radish crosswise ½ inch thick, then cut the slices into ⅜-inch-thick strips. Rinse the radish strips under running water in a colander, drain briefly, then transfer to a 4-quart storage container. Add 1 tablespoon salt and the new sugar and toss to coat. Let sit for 30 minutes, tossing halfway through salting.

3 Working in 2 batches, process the remaining 2 quarts water, reserved chopped radish, pear, yellow onion, apple, garlic, and ginger in a blender until smooth, about 20 seconds per batch. Strain each batch through a fine-mesh strainer into a large bowl, pressing on the solids to extract as much

liquid as possible; discard the solids. Rinse the strainer, then set over the bowl with the strained radish mixture. Pour the flour mixture into the strainer and let drain completely without disturbing; discard any solids. Stir the radish mixture to combine. Rinse the strainer again.

4 Cut the green onions into 3-inch lengths, then cut each piece almost in half lengthwise, leaving ½ inch intact at one end. Pour the strained radish mixture through the strainer into the container with the radish strips; discard any solids.

Add the remaining 2 tablespoons salt, green onions, jalapeño, and red chiles and stir to combine. Cover the container and place in a 50- to 70-degree location away from direct sunlight. Let the radish mixture ferment until the brine begins to turn cloudy, up to 48 hours. (This will be temperature-dependent, so we suggest you start checking after 3 hours, especially if your location is on the warmer end of the range.) Transfer the dongchimi to the refrigerator and let ferment for 1 month. Serve. (Refrigerate for up to 1 month longer; the flavor will continue to develop over time.)

A Conversation About Kimchi and Life

UMMA *Every November Halmeoni and her neighbors, particularly women, would host gimjang and make 150 to 200 pogi kimchi in a span of four to five days.*

SARAH What's gimjang?

UMMA *It's the traditional communal preparation and making of kimchi [also called gimjang kimchi] right before the winter season. Neighbors would take turns hosting gimjang, and we would all come together to make a lot of kimchi to share with one another.*

SARAH Why did you all make so much?

UMMA *During this time, kimchi was a necessity with our meals. There's a common saying in Korean, "If you have kimchi and rice, you have a meal." Kimchi is affordable and versatile. Halmeoni made so many dishes with this kimchi, such as kimchi stew, ground soybean stew with chopped kimchi, kimchi mandu, kimchi pancakes, and so much more. She and her neighbors would make a lot in one batch at the start of the winter months so that we all could eat the fermented kimchi until the next spring.*

SARAH Why did they have to make a lot in the winter, specifically?

UMMA *She had to make a lot for us to eat throughout the long, cold months that followed. Kimchi would take longer to ferment during the winter. Also, you couldn't buy napa cabbages from farmers during the peak of winter season. It was too cold to grow them. So that's why Halmeoni had to stock up at the start of winter. It's hard to believe, huh?*

SARAH It really is! Where did you store all that kimchi?

UMMA *We didn't have refrigerators. Remember, it was colder back then than it is now, so Halmeoni would store the kimchi in 4-foot Korean earthenware pots known as jangdok, and Harabeoji would dig 4 feet into the ground so that only a few inches of the lid would show when the pot was placed in the dirt. Then we waited for it to ferment.*

SARAH It's wild to think that this tradition of women gathering together to make kimchi has changed so much in just one generation. It's amazing and a little heartbreaking in a way because this tradition will become a thing of the past, especially for future generations and even myself. How was the kimchi?

UMMA *[sighs in amazement] Oh gosh, it was amazing. People would always ask Halmeoni how she made her kimchi dishes, but it's a taste you can't replicate. We don't have that weather anymore to ferment the kimchi like that now, and she made everything from scratch, even fermenting her own shrimp and fish. Those jangdok were filled with much more than kimchi. They also held Halmeoni's own soy sauce, doenjang, and gochujang. But most important, Halmeoni isn't around anymore.*

SARAH Did you try to get some sort of recipe from her, at least?

UMMA *I learned her recipes and techniques through my memories of watching her cook, but she was always hesitant to teach me directly. She told me she didn't want her daughters to live a hard life like hers.*

SARAH
세라

When I learned how to make pogi kimchi with Umma, she opened up and shared details about Halmeoni, someone I never got to know personally. Both Halmeoni and Harabeoji had thick North Korean accents, having lived there until the Korean War forced them to flee. To my shock, Umma revealed to me that Harabeoji was imprisoned in North Korea for nine years before escaping. During his captivity, Halmeoni was left alone with her children—a five-year-old daughter (Umma's oldest sister) and a baby son (Umma's older brother)—in a country engulfed in turmoil. One day, while Halmeoni was at the market, her in-laws fled to South Korea with her children. Returning home to find an empty house and a sense of abandonment from those she trusted the most, Halmeoni embarked on a desperate search, eventually crossing into South Korea, where she found her in-laws. Devastatingly, she learned that her son didn't survive the journey.

I asked Umma if she knew more about the baby boy who would have been her older brother, but she did not. She had tried asking Halmeoni about him, but Halmeoni's eyes immediately welled up with tears at the thought of her baby son. Umma eventually decided to stop inquiring further, as she didn't want to reopen old wounds for Halmeoni.

Halmeoni was eventually able to reunite with Harabeoji after he miraculously escaped from North Korea. Together, they went on to have two more daughters, and their new life began in South Korea. This story was recounted to us by their eldest daughter—Umma's sister—who, at just five years old, walked from North Korea to South Korea with Halmeoni's in-laws.

If I could have dinner with anyone in the world, it would undoubtedly be Halmeoni. Though I never had the chance to know her personally, my admiration and affection for her run deep. Her life was marked by countless tales of resilience and compassion, as she carried the weight of her family's burdens with unwavering strength. Despite facing so much adversity, Halmeoni found solace in tending to her rooftop garden. It wasn't just a garden; it was her sanctuary—a place where she could cultivate life and find comfort in watching something flourish. Her compassion extended beyond her plants to the stray animals she welcomed. She once took in a kitten, whom she affectionately named Nabi, seeking companionship in these small, unspoken bonds.

I wish Halmeoni had been given another chance at life or had been born at another time. She would have lived a beautiful life with fewer hardships.

Opposite page: Soldiers and civilians during the Korean War (left); jangdok, traditional earthenware pots for storing fermented foods (right).

This page: Umma mixing and storing her Pogi Kimchi (top). A beautiful way to present Pogi Kimchi is by cutting the wedges into smaller pieces (right).

TURN FOR UMMA'S POGI KIMCHI RECIPE →

Pogi Kimchi 포기김치

poh-gi gim-chi

SARAH
세라

Unlike Mat Kimchi (Cut Napa Cabbage Kimchi; page 115), which comes together easily from cut cabbage, pogi kimchi involves halving or quartering the heads and meticulously layering kimchi filling between each leaf. Initially, I contemplated choosing only one napa cabbage kimchi recipe, but I couldn't bring myself to follow through with this idea when I learned about the history and traditions of gimjang and the collective effort women such as Halmeoni put into making kimchi to get their families through the harsh winter months (see page 123). But most important, when Umma finalized her pogi kimchi recipe to her satisfaction and took her first bite once it had fully fermented, she was able to reminisce and recall the taste of Halmeoni's gimjang kimchi—a flavor she had craved for decades. Pogi kimchi embodies a traditional flavor that is fuller and richer than that of mat kimchi, reflecting the past and paying homage to those who endured the most for us to be here today. This kimchi carries on the traditions that have shaped Korean culture and culinary heritage for generations, and for these reasons, I decided to feature both recipes. While mat kimchi is ready to be enjoyed the day after you make it, pogi kimchi is best enjoyed after a longer fermentation time. To make this recipe, you'll need two large bowls or basins (at least 8 quarts) to comfortably salt the cabbage and combine the filling, as well as a 6-quart rectangular storage container with a tight-fitting lid. To serve, cut the desired amount of cabbage wedges into bite-size pieces (or to your preference).

MAKES about 24 cups   **TOTAL TIME** 1½ hours, plus 2½ hours salting and sitting and about 1 month fermenting

- 2 large heads napa cabbage (about 4 pounds / 1.8 kilograms each)
- 1⅓ cups (384 grams) fine salt
- 5 cups water
- 1 yellow onion (283 grams), chopped coarse, divided
- 1¼ ounces (35 grams) dried large anchovies, gutted and heads removed (see page 43)
- ¾ ounce (21 grams) dashima (dried kelp), rinsed and broken into 2-inch pieces
- ½ ounce (14 grams) dried large-eyed herring
- ¼ cup (35 grams) all-purpose flour
- 1½ cups fresh Asian pear juice (see page 41)
- ⅓ cup (100 grams) saeujeot (salted shrimp)
- 1½ pounds (680 grams) Korean radish, cut into 3-inch matchsticks
- 2½ cups (280 grams) gochugaru
- ⅔ cup (155 grams) minced garlic
- 4 ounces (113 grams) green or red mustard greens, stemmed and coarsely chopped
- 7 green onions (105 grams), sliced ¾ inch thick
- ⅓ cup maesil cheong (plum extract syrup)
- ¼ cup fish sauce
- 1 tablespoon sugar
- 1 tablespoon grated fresh ginger

1 Peel away the outermost layer of leaves from each cabbage head and set aside. If dirty or browned, trim the base of the cabbage heads, but make sure to leave most of the core and leaves intact. Starting from the core, cut the cabbage partially in half lengthwise through the core, cutting only halfway down the side of each head. Using your hands, pull the split section of the core apart to fully separate the cabbage into halves. Repeat the process with each cabbage half to create 8 cabbage quarters. Discard any loose cabbage pieces.

RECIPE CONTINUES

2 Submerge each cabbage quarter and outer layers in a large bowl or basin of water, gently agitate to loosen the layers, and transfer to a large colander. (This is not to clean the cabbage, but rather to coat it with water so the salt sticks.) Discard the water and any loose pieces of cabbage.

3 Working with one cabbage quarter at a time, sprinkle 2 rounded tablespoons salt evenly between the leaves, focusing most of the salt on the thicker white parts of the cabbage near the core. (There is no need to salt the green leaf part, as the cabbage will leach water, distributing the salt brine evenly.) Arrange the cabbage cut sides up in layers in the now-empty bowl, alternating core and leaf ends. Sprinkle the reserved outer leaves with the remaining salt and arrange on top of the cabbage quarters. Cover and let sit for 1½ hours, switching the layers from top to bottom halfway through salting. (Set a timer so you don't forget!)

4 Meanwhile, bring the water, half of the yellow onion, the anchovies, dashima, and herring to a boil in a large saucepan. Reduce the heat to a vigorous simmer and cook for 15 minutes. Immediately strain the broth through a fine-mesh strainer into a bowl; set aside to cool completely. Discard the solids. Transfer 1½ cups broth to the now-empty saucepan; discard the remaining broth or save it for another use. Whisk the flour into the broth until well combined, then bring to a boil, whisking constantly. Reduce the heat to a simmer and cook, whisking constantly, until thickened, about 1 minute. Remove from the heat and let cool completely.

5 Process the pear juice, saeujeot, and remaining yellow onion in a blender until smooth, about 20 seconds. Using your gloved hands, gently mix the cooled flour paste, pear juice mixture, radish, gochugaru, garlic, mustard greens, green onions, maesil cheong, fish sauce, sugar, and ginger in a large bowl until well combined. Cover and let the radish filling sit for 1 hour, mixing halfway through sitting to redistribute the liquid.

6 While the radish filling sits, transfer the cabbage quarters and leaves to a large colander; discard the liquid left in the bowl and rinse away any remaining salt in the bowl. Remove the cabbage from the colander, submerge each quarter in cold water in the bowl, agitate gently to remove excess salt and dirt between layers, and transfer back to the colander. Rinse the cabbage outer leaves and transfer to the colander.

Discard the water and any loose pieces of cabbage. Repeat rinsing the cabbage quarters and leaves once more with fresh water. Arrange the cabbage quarters cut sides down in the colander and top with the cabbage leaves. Let the cabbage drain for at least 30 minutes.

7 Stir the filling to recombine. Using your gloved hands, place one cabbage quarter in the bowl of radish filling and gently spread a thin layer of the filling between each leaf, making sure to coat both sides of the leaves. Coat the exterior of the cabbage quarter with additional filling, then use the outer leaves of each quarter to wrap the cabbage quarter so that it is tucked and "hugging itself" in an X shape. Arrange the cabbage cut side up in a 6-quart rectangular storage container. Repeat with the remaining quarters, alternating core and leaf ends for each layer. Coat the cabbage leaves with the remaining filling, then layer the leaves and remaining filling evenly over the cabbage quarters. Gently press into an even layer.

8 Cover the container and place in a 50- to 70-degree location away from direct sunlight. Let the cabbage sit until liquid begins to pool around the edges of the container, up to 24 hours. (This will be temperature-dependent, so we suggest you start checking after 3 hours, especially if your location is on the warmer end of the range.) Transfer the kimchi to the refrigerator and let ferment for 1 month. Serve. (Refrigerate for up to 2 months; the flavor will continue to develop over time.)

Umma's Kitchen Wisdom

Asian pear is my preferred choice for the fruit juice here, but very overripe Hachiya persimmons make a great substitute. You don't need to juice the persimmons—simply discard the skin and use the fruit pulp, which is like a thick liquid.

I save the remaining anchovy broth in step 4 to use for future kimchi or recipes that call for seafood or dashima broth such as Sundubu Jjigae (Spicy Soft Tofu Stew; page 242—use this broth instead of the seafood broth), Ueong Jorim (Braised Burdock Root; page 95—use this broth instead of the dashima water), and Kimchi Jjigae (Kimchi Stew; page 216—use this broth as part of the 3 cups water in the stew). It can be refrigerated for up to 4 days or frozen for up to 3 months.

Cut each cabbage head partially in half lengthwise, cutting through the core section. Then pull the split section of the core apart to fully separate the cabbage into halves.

Repeat this cutting and pulling process with each cabbage half to create cabbage quarters.

Sprinkle salt evenly between the leaves, focusing most of the salt on the thicker white parts of the cabbage near the core.

After the salting process, rinse and drain the cabbage quarters well.

TURN TO SEE HOW TO MAKE POGI KIMCHI →

Making Pogi Kimchi

Top Mix the flour paste, pear juice mixture, radish, gochugaru, garlic, mustard greens, green onions, maesil cheong, fish sauce, sugar, and ginger in a large bowl until well combined.

Bottom Place one cabbage quarter in the bowl of radish filling and gently spread a thin layer of the filling between each leaf, making sure to fully coat both sides of every leaf.

Top and bottom left Coat the exterior of the cabbage quarter with additional filling, then use the outer leaves to wrap the cabbage quarter so that it is swaddled and "hugging itself."

Bottom right Arrange the cabbage quarters cut side up in the storage container in layers, alternating core and leaf ends between layers.

CUCUMBER KIMCHI

Oi Kimchi 오이김치

oh-e gim-chi

UMMA
엄마

Cucumber kimchi was the first kimchi Sarah made on her own. When I taught Sarah how to make this, she was surprised at how quickly it came together, even with the prep and salting. She had no idea that kimchi with such bold flavor and crisp texture could be made so quickly.

SARAH
세라

Cucumber kimchi is a popular kimchi to enjoy in the summer because it's easy to prepare and offers a refreshing taste that can be enjoyed immediately. It requires just two simple steps. First, season the cucumber with salt (and sugar) to draw out its water. This prevents the kimchi from becoming too diluted. Then, add the remaining ingredients, toss together, and that's it! You'll have ready-to-eat kimchi that is vibrantly crisp and savory, with a hint of spiciness. Enjoy it as it ferments in the refrigerator, too, for a deeper yet still refreshing flavor. You'll need a 3-quart storage container with a tight-fitting lid.

Umma's Kitchen Wisdom

Look for smaller pickling cucumbers (Kirby cucumbers are perfect) that are 2 to 3 ounces (57 to 85 grams) each, as they will contain fewer seeds than larger cucumbers. Korean cucumbers also work well, but they have limited seasonal availability. I don't recommend Persian cucumbers here.

MAKES about 8 cups   **TOTAL TIME** 20 minutes, plus 2 hours 20 minutes salting

    3 pounds (1.4 kilograms) pickling cucumbers or oi (Korean cucumbers), trimmed, halved lengthwise, seeded, and sliced crosswise 1 inch thick
2½ tablespoons sugar, divided
    1 tablespoon fine salt
  ½ yellow onion (142 grams), cut into 1½-inch pieces, layers separated
    3 ounces (85 grams) garlic chives, cut into 1½-inch lengths
    1 Fresno chile, stemmed, halved lengthwise, and sliced thin crosswise
3½ tablespoons maesil cheong (plum extract syrup)
    3 tablespoons fish sauce
    3 tablespoons minced garlic
    2 tablespoons gochugaru
1½ teaspoons grated fresh ginger

1 Toss the cucumbers with 1 tablespoon sugar and the salt in a large bowl. Let sit for 20 minutes, tossing the cucumbers halfway through salting. Drain the cucumbers in a colander, shaking the colander to release any additional liquid. Rinse the now-empty bowl.

2 Using your gloved hands, toss the cucumbers with the onion, chives, Fresno chile, maesil cheong, fish sauce, garlic, gochugaru, ginger, and remaining 1½ tablespoons sugar in the bowl until evenly combined. Transfer the cucumber mixture to a 3-quart storage container, cover, and place in a 50- to 70-degree location away from direct sunlight for 2 hours. Serve. (Refrigerate for up to 1½ months; the flavor will continue to develop over time.)

PERILLA LEAF KIMCHI

Kkaennip Kimchi 깻잎김치

kkaen-nip gim-chi

SARAH
세라

Picture this: You're at a Korean restaurant with friends and your partner. On the table is a serving of nicely seasoned perilla leaves. These leaves are notorious for being challenging to pick up individually (you usually pick them up by the stem and hope that that a single leaf peels off the pile). You notice your friend struggling, as multiple leaves continue to stick together. Is it okay for your partner to use their chopsticks to help the friend peel off a leaf, or should they refrain, as this might cross social boundaries? This is the great Perilla Leaf Debate that captured Korea's and social media's attention. Though this debate is entirely silly, it highlights the intricate expectations and dynamics of relationships. Some argue that helping a friend is just an act of kindness, while others argue that this action is inappropriate. It's a lighthearted yet thought-provoking question that often sparks surprising responses! The debate aside, perilla leaves are one of my favorite herbs. (They're sometimes labeled as sesame leaves, but this is a mistranslation.) They're part of the mint family but don't have the cooling sensation of mint. Instead, they boast a unique taste that I'd describe as acerbic. Perilla leaves can be enjoyed raw as wraps (they pair well with Korean barbecue), cooked in a dish, or as pickles or kimchi. In this kimchi, their bold aromatic quality meets the umami flavor of soy sauce and fish sauce. And yes, these leaves will stick together and put you in a predicament! (They're a bit of a challenge to wrangle when preparing them, too, so stacking them in bundles as instructed and having a 3-quart storage container on hand will help keep things under control.)

Umma's Kitchen Wisdom

Look for perilla leaves that are 3 to 4 inches in diameter. Larger perilla leaves tend to be chewier and stiff and are less pleasant to eat.

Soaking the leaves in salt water is necessary to draw out excess moisture from the leaves before preparing the kimchi.

MAKES about 2 cups   TOTAL TIME 1 hour

2 teaspoons fine salt
4 ounces (113 grams) perilla leaves, washed
¼ cup soy sauce
3 tablespoons maesil cheong (plum extract syrup)
2 tablespoons gochugaru
1½ tablespoons fish sauce
1½ tablespoons sesame seeds, toasted and finely ground
2 teaspoons minced garlic
1½ teaspoons sugar
½ yellow onion (142 grams), halved across equator, sliced thin crosswise
¾ cup (85 grams) coarsely grated carrot
4 green onions (60 grams), sliced thin
½ Fresno chile, stemmed, seeded, and chopped fine
½ jalapeño chile, stemmed, seeded, and chopped fine

1 Dissolve the salt in 1 quart cold water in a large bowl. Stack the perilla leaves in 8 bundles, keeping the stems aligned in each bundle. Submerge the bundles in the brine, alternating the stem sides of the bundles, to create an even layer. Place a small plate or pickling weight on top to ensure the leaves remain submerged and let sit for 10 minutes, rotating the bundles halfway through soaking so that the bottom bundles are on top.

2 Meanwhile, whisk the soy sauce, maesil cheong, gochugaru, fish sauce, sesame seeds, garlic, and sugar together in a separate large bowl. Stir in the yellow onion, carrot, green onions, Fresno chile, and jalapeño until well combined. Let sit for 10 minutes.

3 Working with 1 bundle of perilla leaves at a time, fold them in half lengthwise and gently squeeze to remove excess water. Unravel the bundle. Stir to recombine the kimchi filling. Arrange 1 bundle of perilla leaves on a cutting board, dark green side up; using your gloved hands, spread 1 teaspoon kimchi filling evenly over the top of each leaf. Restack the leaves as you go, keeping the stems aligned, and place the bundle in a 3-quart storage container.

Stir the kimchi filling to recombine. Repeat with the remaining perilla leaf bundles, alternating the stem ends of the bundles in the container to create even layers. Spread any remaining kimchi filling over the top. Serve immediately, or cover and refrigerate for 12 hours. If you do refrigerate the kimchi, rotate the perilla leaf bundles (bottom to top) to redistribute any liquid that forms in the container before serving. (Refrigerate for up to 3 weeks; the flavor will continue to develop over time.)

Yeolmu Putbaechu Kimchi 열무풋배추김치

yuhl-moo poot-bae-choo gim-chi

SARAH
세라

One scorching summer night, Umma served my family three types of kimchi on a banchan platter. On the left was a serving of this "summer kimchi" made with young summer radish and baby napa cabbage; in the middle was Oi Kimchi (Cucumber Kimchi; page 132), also considered a "summer kimchi;" and on the right was the classic Mat Kimchi (Cut Napa Cabbage Kimchi; page 115). Although mat kimchi is the type most commonly enjoyed at Korean dining tables and is stocked in our fridge almost year-round, on that hot summer night my family gravitated toward the cucumber kimchi and this particular kimchi, which incorporates produce that is at its freshest and most delicious in the summer months (see page 31 for more information about young summer radish and page 32 for more information about young napa cabbage). It offers a quenching burst of cold spice, perfect for beating the summer heat. In Umma's version, she omits the usual gochugaru and relies entirely on Fresno chiles to give the kimchi its spicy kick. Not only do they add heat, but they also introduce a refreshing, juicy element. You'll need a large bowl or basin (at least 6 quarts) to comfortably salt and toss the radishes and cabbage, as well as a 4-quart storage container with a tight-fitting lid.

MAKES about 12 cups   TOTAL TIME 1½ hours, plus 1 hour salting and sitting and 2 weeks fermenting

- 1 large yellow onion (453 grams), one-third onion coarsely chopped, two-thirds onion sliced ⅜ inch thick, divided
- ½ ounce (14 grams) dried large anchovies, gutted and heads removed (see page 43)
- ½ ounce (14 grams) dashima (dried kelp), rinsed and broken into 2-inch pieces
- ¼ ounce (7 grams) dried large-eyed herring
- 2 pounds (907 grams) yeolmu (young summer radish), skinny root ends trimmed, cleaned
- 1 pound (454 grams) putbaechu (young napa cabbage), cut into rough 3-inch pieces
- 6 tablespoons (108 grams) plus 1½ teaspoons fine salt, divided
- 3 tablespoons all-purpose flour
- 3 tablespoons saeujeot (salted shrimp)
- 7 Fresno chiles (198 grams), stemmed and coarsely chopped
- 6 tablespoons (84 grams) minced garlic
- ¼ cup maesil cheong (plum extract syrup)
- 3 tablespoons fish sauce
- 1½ teaspoons grated fresh ginger
- 1½ teaspoons sugar

RECIPE CONTINUES

1 Bring 2 cups water, the chopped onion, anchovies, dashima, and herring to a boil in a small saucepan. Reduce the heat to a vigorous simmer and cook for 10 minutes. Immediately strain the broth through a fine-mesh strainer into a 2-cup liquid measuring cup; discard the solids. Add extra water to the broth as needed to equal 2 cups and let the broth cool completely.

2 Cut the radishes and their greens into 3-inch lengths. Halve smaller root sections lengthwise and quarter larger root sections lengthwise (the roots should be about ¼ inch thick). Submerge the radishes, radish greens, and cabbage in a large bowl of water and agitate with your hands to loosen any dirt. Transfer to a large colander; discard the water. Repeat rinsing the radishes, radish greens, and cabbage once more with fresh water and let drain.

3 Place one-third of the radishes, radish greens, and cabbage in the now-empty bowl to create a layer and sprinkle with 2 tablespoons salt. Repeat with the remaining radishes, radish greens, and cabbage and ¼ cup salt in 2 more layers. Toss the radishes, radish greens, and cabbage to thoroughly distribute the salt, then spread everything into an even layer. Cover and let sit for 1 hour, tossing the vegetables halfway through salting (set a timer so you don't forget!).

4 Meanwhile, transfer the reserved 2 cups broth to the now-empty saucepan. Whisk the flour into the broth until well combined, then bring to a boil, whisking constantly. Reduce the heat to a simmer and cook, whisking contantly, until thickened, about 1 minute. Remove from the heat and let cool completely.

5 Process 1 quart water and the saeujeot in a blender until smooth, about 15 seconds. Add the Fresno chiles and pulse until finely chopped, about 5 pulses; transfer the mixture to a separate large bowl. Stir in the garlic, maesil cheong, fish sauce, ginger, sugar, cooled flour paste, and remaining 1½ teaspoons salt until the sugar has dissolved; set the seasoning mixture aside.

6 Transfer the radishes, radish greens, and cabbage to a large colander; discard the liquid left in the bowl and rinse away any remaining salt. Working in batches, submerge the vegetables in a large bowl or basin of water, agitate gently to remove excess salt, and transfer to the colander. Discard the water. Repeat rinsing the vegetables once more with fresh water and let drain.

7 Transfer one-quarter of the radishes, radish greens, and cabbage to a 4-quart storage container and sprinkle one-quarter of the sliced onion over the top. Repeat with the remaining radishes, radish greens, cabbage, and onion in 3 more layers. Stir the seasoning mixture to recombine, then pour evenly over the vegetables. Gently press on the vegetables to create an even layer. Cover the container and place in a 50- to 70-degree location away from direct sunlight for 3 to 5 hours. Transfer the kimchi to the refrigerator and let ferment for 2 weeks. Serve. (Refrigerate for up to 2 months; the flavor will continue to develop over time.)

Prepping Young Summer Radish

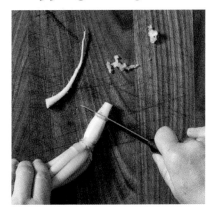

Trim off the skinny ends of the roots and clean the radish by using a knife to scrape off the thin skin.

Cut the radishes (roots and greens) into 3-inch lengths.

If the root sections are small, halve them lengthwise. If the root sections are large, quarter them lengthwise.

PICKLED RADISH SLICES

Ssammu 쌈무

ssahm-moo

SARAH 세라 It's very common for Koreans to wrap pieces of food using items such as red lettuce, gim, perilla leaves, or these pickled radish slices as the wrapper. Ssammu, which translates as "wrap radish," is prepared by slicing Korean radish into very thin disks. These pickles are commonly served at Korean barbecue restaurants, where they're used to wrap meat and other fillings for a perfectly balanced bite. Sweet and tangy, they are the perfect complement to barbecued meats, as well as a variety of deep-fried foods. In my family, we often use this pickle to make Jeongigui Tongdak Yachae Mussam Mari (Pickled Radish Chicken-Vegetable Wraps; page 311). You'll need a 1½-quart storage container with a tight-fitting lid.

MAKES 6 cups
TOTAL TIME 25 minutes, plus 2 weeks pickling

- 1 cup water
- 1 cup distilled white vinegar
- ¾ cup (149 grams) sugar
- 1 teaspoon fine salt
- 1½ pounds (680 grams) Korean radish, cut paper-thin (less than ⅟₁₆ inch thick)

Stir the water, vinegar, sugar, and salt in a medium bowl until the sugar has dissolved. Add the radish and brine to a 1½-quart storage container. Make sure the radish is fully submerged. Cover and refrigerate for 2 weeks to pickle before serving. (Refrigerate for up to 3 months.)

> ### Umma's Kitchen Wisdom
>
> *If your radishes are larger than 3 inches in diameter, cut them in half lengthwise before slicing them.*
>
> *These pickles need to be really thin in order to be used for wrapping food, so I strongly recommend using a mandoline to slice the radishes.*

CHICKEN RADISH

Chicken Mu 치킨무

chicken moo

SARAH 세라 Chicken mu is made using the same brine as ssammu, but this pickle is typically cubed rather than sliced. It is often served as an accompaniment at restaurants serving Korean fried chicken—hence its name! It doesn't have to be served only with fried chicken; like ssammu, this pickle pairs well with any deep-fried foods. Besides serving it with Korean Fried Chicken (page 198), try this pickle with Dwaeji Deunggalbi Twigim (Fried Pork Ribs with Cumin Seasoning Salt; page 176). Umma likes to add carrots to her version for some color and contrasting flavor. You'll need a 1½-quart storage container with a tight-fitting lid.

MAKES 6 cups
TOTAL TIME 25 minutes, plus 2 weeks pickling

- 1 cup water
- 1 cup distilled white vinegar
- ¾ cup (149 grams) sugar
- 1 teaspoon fine salt
- 1½ pounds (680 grams) Korean radish, cut into ½-inch cubes
- 1 large carrot (100 grams), peeled and cut into ½-inch cubes

Stir the water, vinegar, sugar, and salt in a medium bowl until the sugar has dissolved. Add the radish, carrot, and brine to a 1½-quart storage container. Make sure the radish and carrot are fully submerged. Cover and refrigerate for 2 weeks to pickle before serving. (Refrigerate for up to 3 months.)

Umma's Kitchen Wisdom

Two weeks is the optimum time for pickling these radishes, but you can enjoy them sooner, as soon as the next day. They won't be as pickled and will be crunchier in texture, so the Ssammu won't be suitable for using to wrap foods.

Modeum Jangajji 모듬장아찌

moh-deum jahng-ah-jji

SARAH
세라

When Umma owned her restaurant, every weekend on her way home she would drive along Route 91 West to pick up wang mandu (king dumplings) from a Korean-owned mom-and-pop shop. Unlike typical mandu, which are dumplings made from wheat flour and enjoyed pan fried or steamed, wang mandu are yeasted, steamed dumplings that are big, white, and fluffy on the outside, with a meat or kimchi filling. (Making this type of dumpling is a handful, requiring both baking and cooking skills.) This shop would serve the dumplings with assorted pickles, but they would only pack enough pickles for about half the amount of dumplings. I would eye the dwindling supply of pickles in their little containers as my family and I took bites of the dumplings, wondering with every passing minute when I would have to eat a dumpling by itself. Witnessing everyone's obsession with these pickles, Umma decided to re-create them at home so that we could always have a plentiful supply on hand. Lo and behold, she made a better, more flavorful version than what we got from the dumpling shop. The best part? These pickles can be enjoyed immediately, though we recommend refrigerating them for a day for maximum crunch. In addition to being delicious with any type of dumpling, these pickles are great with just about anything, especially fatty, oily foods and meat. You'll need a 3-quart storage container with a tight-fitting lid.

MAKES 8 cups
TOTAL TIME 40 minutes, plus 2 hours cooling

1¼ cups water
1¼ cups distilled white vinegar
1¼ cups soy sauce
1¼ cups (248 grams) sugar
1 pound (454 grams) Korean radish, sliced ⅛ inch thick, slices cut into rough 1-inch pieces
1 large yellow onion (453 grams), halved, cut into 1-inch pieces, layers separated
6 jalapeño chiles (210 grams), stemmed and sliced into ¼-inch-thick rounds

1 Combine the water, vinegar, soy sauce, and sugar in a large saucepan. Bring to a boil, stirring to dissolve the sugar. Remove the saucepan from the heat and let the brine cool for about 5 minutes. (It should still be hot when you pour it over the vegetables.)

2 Toss the radish, onion, and jalapeños together in a bowl, then transfer to a 3-quart storage container. Pour the brine over the vegetables and let cool to room temperature, about 2 hours. Enjoy immediately, or cover tightly and refrigerate. (Refrigerate for up to 3 months.)

Enjoy these pickles on their
own or as we love to do—
with dumplings!

SOY SAUCE RADISH PICKLES

Ganjang Mu Jangajji 간장무장아찌

gahn-jahng moo jahng-ah-jji

SARAH
세라

I remember the first time I saw Umma make these pickles. I was in awe of how the radishes transformed into beautiful shiny brown planks with irresistible crunch and flavor. It was love at first sight—in my mind, this picture-perfect dish had it all: a rich, sweetened soy sauce marinade that infused the radishes with deep flavor, while the radishes, in turn, enhanced the marinade with their sweetness. They also can be transformed into Ganjang Mu Jangajji Muchim (Seasoned Soy Sauce Radish Pickles; page 67). You'll need a 3-quart storage container with a tight-fitting lid.

Kitchen Conversation

SARAH I have always loved this pickle so much. There are so many flavors going on with the sweetness of the Korean radish and the salty-sweet soy sauce marinade. Did you like this as a kid too?

UMMA *No, I disliked it!*

SARAH What! Why?

UMMA *It didn't taste this good back then. Nowadays, we have the privilege of preparing foods that are both nutrtitious and tasty. Back then, we bought and prepared food to survive—not to be healthy or to enjoy, but just to satiate our hunger. Remember I told you about how kimchi was prepared and how we just ate that for months? We would also take advantage of Korean radish and pickle it by making it extremely salty so that it kept longer. Since it was so salty, we would have to rinse it in water and then season it. I remember asking Halmeoni as a young kid, "Please, Umma, can you salt this less so we can enjoy it?" You wouldn't believe how salty it was. Now that we have refrigeration and don't need to make the pickle so salty, I brine the radish in sugar water and use a sweetened soy sauce pickling liquid. Oddly enough, though, I've found myself craving Halmeoni's salty mu jangajji at times.*

MAKES 12 cups   TOTAL TIME 30 minutes, plus 8 days brining and marinating

    2 cups (397 grams) sugar
    3 pounds (1.4 kilograms) Korean radish
    1 cup soy sauce
    1 cup maesil cheong (plum extract syrup)
    5 dried small red chiles (optional)

1 Add the sugar to a large bowl. Cut the radish in half lengthwise, then slice each half lengthwise into ¾-inch-thick planks. Working with one radish plank at a time, thoroughly coat in sugar and arrange in even layers in a 3-quart storage container. Pour any remaining sugar on top of the radish and place small plates on top so that the radish will be fully submerged in the sugar water that will form. Cover tightly and place the container in a 50- to 70-degree location away from direct sunlight. Let sit for 24 hours.

2 Using tongs, transfer the radish planks to a rimmed baking sheet. (The radish planks should feel soft enough to be bendable at this stage.) Whisk the sugar water to fully dissolve any sugar that has settled to the bottom of the storage container. Return the radish to the container, starting with the pieces that were originally on top, and place the small plates back on top. Cover tightly and place the container in a 50- to 70-degree location away from direct sunlight. Let sit for 48 hours.

3 Combine the soy sauce and maesil cheong in a small bowl. Using tongs, transfer the radish planks to a bowl; discard the sugar water (do not rinse the container). Return the radish planks to the now-empty storage container and add the soy mixture and red chiles, if using. Place the small plates back on top to fully submerge the radish in the soy mixture. Cover tightly and let marinate in a 50- to 70-degree location away from direct sunlight for 3 days. Transfer to the refrigerator and continue to marinate for 2 days.

4 Drain the radishes, reserving the soy marinade for another use, and return the radishes to the storage container. Serve. (Refrigerate for up to 1 week.)

Umma's Kitchen Wisdom

*The small dried red chiles that I buy for
this pickle at the Korean grocery store
have a mild flavor. Use what you like,
keeping in mind the heat tolerance of the
people who will be eating this.*

*I keep the reserved soy sauce mixture
from step 4 and use it in other recipes,
including Avocado-Jang (Marinated
Avocado; page 75) and Ganjang Mu
Jangajji Muchim (Seasoned Soy Sauce
Radish Pickles; page 67). This mixture is
fully flavored from the Korean radish
and has a depth of flavor that makes it a
great cooking and marinating ingredient.*

Maneul Jangajji 마늘장아찌

mahn-neul jahng-ah-jji

SARAH
세라

I grew up eating maneul jangajji at least once a day. I remember my close friends would innocently ask, "Why does it smell like garlic around here?" as they sniffed around, only to discover that the garlic scent was coming from me! The culprit was this beloved pickle. I would eat five or six of these pickled garlic cloves a day because they are so flavorful and pair well with just about any main meal. They are crunchy, sweet, and of course garlicky, yet not too spicy and pungent despite being raw. While I still enjoy these pickles nearly every day, I try not to overindulge to avoid smelling like garlic. But feel free to indulge as you please! The pickling process here involves two steps. First, since the garlic is not cooked, we submerge it in a vinegar-and-water brine for 2 weeks to minimize the garlic's spiciness and pungency. The second step is to flavor it with soy sauce, sugar, and more vinegar, then let it pickle further. You'll need a 2-quart glass storage jar with a tight-fitting lid, or you can divide the garlic and brine between two smaller jars.

Umma's Kitchen Wisdom

I buy prepeeled garlic to avoid spending lots of time peeling garlic cloves.

Garlic—especially older garlic—often produces blue and green pigments in the presence of an acid (such as the vinegar in this recipe). Don't worry about it if this happens. The garlic is perfectly safe to eat and the unusual hue will be masked by the dark color of the soy marinade.

MAKES 7 cups   **TOTAL TIME** 20 minutes, plus 1 hour cooling and 15 weeks pickling

  2 pounds (907 grams) garlic cloves, peeled, root ends trimmed, and washed
  3 cups water, divided
  3 cups distilled white vinegar, divided
  1 cup soy sauce
  1 cup (198 grams) sugar

1 Pack the garlic into a 2-quart glass jar, then add 2 cups water and 2 cups vinegar. Place a small dish or pickling weight over the garlic to completely submerge it. Cover tightly and place the jar in a 50- to 70-degree location away from direct sunlight. Let pickle for 2 weeks.

2 Drain the garlic, then return it to the jar. Combine the soy sauce, sugar, remaining 1 cup water, and remaining 1 cup vinegar in a large saucepan. Bring to a boil, stirring to dissolve the sugar. Remove from the heat and let cool completely, about 1 hour.

3 Pour the cooled brine over the garlic until just covered and place a small dish or pickling weight over the garlic to completely submerge it. Cover tightly and place the jar in a 50- to 70-degree location away from direct sunlight. Let sit for 1 week.

4 Transfer the garlic to the refrigerator and let pickle for 3 months. Serve. (Refrigerate for 1 year or longer; the flavor will continue to develop over time.)

CUCUMBER PICKLES

Oiji 오이지

oh-e-ji

UMMA 엄마

One of my favorite foods prepared by Halmeoni was her oiji. She made it differently than I do, though. She would simply use coarse salt and make the cucumber pickle with just that one ingredient. It would be incredibly salty, so before preparing it as a banchan, she would submerge the pickled cucumber in water to reduce the saltiness. Although that saltiness bothered me when she made radish pickles, I didn't mind it with these cucumber pickles. For many years, I tried replicating her method but wasn't able to achieve her oiji taste using only salt. I later experimented with adding sugar and vinegar. I'm not sure why this worked, but that was when I was finally able to figure out how to approximate the flavors of one of my favorites from Halmeoni.

SARAH 세라

One thing I have always appreciated about Umma is her dedication to preparing Korean food without taking shortcuts that compromise flavor. This admirable trait is evident here. Though store-bought pickled cucumber is readily available at Korean grocery stores, Umma has never resorted to buying prepared oiji because homemade ones far surpass the store-bought options in both taste and quality, plus they come together easily. Once the cucumbers have completely pickled, make Umma's Oiji Muchim (Spicy Cucumber Pickles; page 68), and you will never consider buying a prepared version of that banchan again. You'll need a 6-quart rectangular storage container or a 6-quart glass jar with a tight-fitting lid; it should be long enough to store the whole cucumbers without needing to cut them.

MAKES about 2½ pounds
TOTAL TIME 20 minutes, plus 9 weeks pickling

  1 cup (198 grams) sugar
  ½ cup (144 grams) fine salt
  3 pounds (1.4 kilograms) pickling cucumbers or
      oi (Korean cucumbers)
  1 cup distilled white vinegar

1 Combine the sugar and salt in a bowl. Wipe the cucumbers clean and dry with paper towels. Create a single layer of cucumbers in a 6-quart rectangular storage container, then add a generous amount of the sugar mixture. Repeat the layering with the remaining cucumbers and sugar mixture. Pour the vinegar over the top. Cover tightly and place the container in a 50- to 70-degree location away from direct sunlight. Let sit for 24 hours.

2 Using tongs, transfer the cucumbers to a plate. Whisk the liquid to fully dissolve any sugar and salt that has settled to the bottom of the container. Return the cucumbers to the container, starting with the pieces that were originally on top, and place a plate or pickling weight on top of the cucumbers. Cover tightly and place the container in a 50- to 70-degree location away from direct sunlight. Let sit until the cucumbers turn olive green and have pruned, about 1 week.

3 Transfer the cucumbers to the refrigerator and let pickle for 2 months. Serve. (Refrigerate for 1 year or longer; the flavor will continue to develop over time.)

Umma's Kitchen Wisdom

Do not wash these cucumbers. It's not good to add moisture to the cucumbers before we pickle them. I rinse the pickled cucumbers when it's time to serve them or prepare them for other recipes such as Oiji Muchim.

Initially, you may question whether there are enough ingredients to create a brine that will submerge the cucumbers. It will be more than enough, as the cucumbers will excrete water as they pickle.

Korean cucumbers are great, but these thin-skinned, crisp cucumbers are typically available only in the summer. Kirby or other small pickling cucumbers are a good year-round alternative. Persian cucumbers are not.

GREEN CHILE PICKLES

Gochu Jangajji 고추장아찌

goh-choo jahng-ah-jji

UMMA
엄마

I grow Korean chiles in abundance in my backyard garden, picking them when they're green and serving them to my family in many ways: dipped into Yangnyeom Gochujang (Seasoned Gochujang; page 34), in stews, or as this pickle. When pickled, these chiles transform into a sweet, salty, crunchy bite that's delicious and so convenient to have in the refrigerator. Enjoy them as is or turn them into a banchan with additional seasonings (see page 70) and serve them with rice!

SARAH
세라

When April rolls around, Umma's annual desire to garden takes hold of her. Without fail, she will ask me sometime during the first two weeks of April if I want to visit our favorite Korean nursery with her. I will jokingly respond, "Ah, your annual gardening craving has kicked in," and we'll make plans to drive to this nursery. There, she will select her essential seeds and baby plants of perilla leaves, Korean lettuce, aehobak, eggplants, kale, pickling cucumbers, and Korean green chiles, which we will carefully pack into the trunk of my car. Then, Appa will build plant beds from scratch while Umma and I drive around town to find the best bargain deal for soil mix, as the cost can easily add up. For the rest of the spring and summer seasons, Umma will attend to her plants like they are her children, reminding me of how beautifully they have grown and how singsinghada (fresh and lively) her fruits and vegetables have become. You'll need a 2-quart glass jar with a tight-fitting lid.

MAKES 9 cups   TOTAL TIME 30 minutes, plus 2 hours cooling and 13 weeks pickling

- 1½ pounds (680 grams) putgochu (young green Korean chiles), washed, stems trimmed
- 1¼ cups water
- 1¼ cups distilled white vinegar
- 1¼ cups soy sauce
- 1¼ cups (248 grams) sugar

1 Pat the chiles dry with paper towels and pierce on one side with a fork. Tightly pack the chiles in a 2-quart glass jar.

2 Combine the water, vinegar, soy sauce, and sugar in a large saucepan. Bring to a boil, stirring to dissolve the sugar. Remove the saucepan from the heat and let the brine cool for about 5 minutes. (It should still be hot when you pour it over the vegetables.)

3 Pour the brine over the chiles until just covered (you may have extra brine) and place a small dish or pickling weight over the top of the chiles to completely submerge them. Let cool to room temperature, about 2 hours. Cover tightly and place the jar in a 50- to 70-degree location away from direct sunlight. Let sit until the chiles turn olive green and have pruned, about 1 week.

4 Transfer the chiles to the refrigerator and let pickle for 3 months. Serve. (Refrigerate for 1 year or longer; the flavor will continue to develop over time.)

Umma's Kitchen Wisdom

Putgochu (young green Korean chiles) have a mild heat and retain their crunch nicely when pickled. Although you can substitute Anaheim chiles in cooked preparations, I don't recommend any substitute for putgochu in these pickles.

When trimming the stems of the chiles, don't cut too close to the stem ends, otherwise the seeds will be exposed and a hole will form at the top of the chile.

You'll know the pickles are ready to eat when they have turned brownish green all over.

MEAT, POULTRY, AND SEAFOOD

A Korean Journey of Guilt and Gratitude

SARAH
세라

Thanks to my work on Ahnest Kitchen, Umma and I had a special opportunity to travel to Korea to work on a marketing campaign with TikTok. I remember receiving an email from TikTok late one weekday evening, inviting us to be featured in a commercial that would take place in the hot spot of Korea—Seoul. Additionally, they invited us on an all-expense paid trip to Busan alongside other content creators. Without hesitation, I bolted out of bed and woke up Umma to share this exciting news.

Accepting this offer filled us with excitement and anticipation for the once-in-a-lifetime opportunities it afforded. In addition to the work and the media exposure, this trip also meant that we could reunite with our family in Korea. The few months of waiting for the time to come were filled with glee and hope. It was an excitement that I hadn't felt in a very long time.

Upon landing in Korea, we were treated to luxuries we had never experienced before. This included a stay at a 5-star hotel overlooking the waters of Busan and gourmet meals prepared by chefs. But the most important experience of all was a heartwarming reunion between Umma and her older sister, whom she hadn't seen in 30 years.

We immediately got to work and filmed for the TikTok commercial. This involved getting professional hair and makeup done for the first time and trying our hand at acting. Umma was surprisingly great at this, completing her parts in one take. I, on the other hand, quickly learned that I am a terrible actor—it took more than 2 hours to film a 10-second clip of me acting surprised. We filmed for 12 hours straight and returned to our hotel exhausted but exhilarated.

As Umma washed up and prepared to head out for dinner, the excitement and chaos subsided, and I finally found myself alone with my thoughts. I broke down in tears as waves of emotion coursed through my body. I couldn't believe that a comfortable life like this could exist. Experiencing the extravagant, luxurious aspects of life was great, but having the opportunity to travel so freely and reunite with family across the world was another thing altogether.

A larger part of me also felt a sense of guilt. As I sat on the pristine white-sheeted queen bed, freshly made earlier by housekeeping, I felt guilty for enjoying my time away far from home as Appa worked back at home. Going on vacation has never felt right to me since becoming an adult, and it's something I've continued to struggle with.

Left: Umma and her oldest sister at Umma's high-school graduation in 1978.

Right: Umma and her oldest sister in 2023, reunited in Korea after 30 years apart.

Umma walked out of the bathroom, looking refreshed after a long day of filming. Confused by my facial expression, she asked me what was wrong. I asked her if we could talk about it over dinner. I told her I was craving godeungeo jorim, a familiar and comforting braised mackerel dish that always eased my mind (see page 207 for the recipe). After we were seated comfortably at the restaurant and had this dish, along with bowls of rice, in front of us, we had this conversation:

UMMA *So do you want to tell me what's wrong?*

ME Nothing really. I just have a lot on my mind. I feel really grateful, if anything.

UMMA *What makes you say that?*

ME I feel so happy to be here and share this experience with you. I hope I can live a life like this in the future where we can all travel together and enjoy the small things together as we have been doing here. I feel so bad that Appa isn't here. It just doesn't feel right.

Umma sat in silence as she picked out the bones of the mackerel for me. I was tempted to tell her she didn't need to do this, but I resisted my urge to stop Umma's kind gesture. I know it brings Umma joy to feel like a mother to me, regardless of my age. She removed all the bones from the mackerel and set the plate of boneless fish in front of me to enjoy.

UMMA *Don't worry, Soojin. You will live a life like that.*

Mandu 만두

mahn-doo

SARAH
세라

As I work, Umma tells me, "Mix the meat filling in one direction, adding water in batches, for 10 minutes. This method binds the meat together uniformly, resulting in a sticky, tender filling. It's a traditional technique used in Chinese cooking." Curious, I researched this technique and learned that it often sparks a heated debate, especially between Asian cooks and Western cooks. On the Asian side, renowned chefs, cooks, and aunties explain this technique as Umma did—that mixing in one direction only, beyond just combining the ingredients, stretches the long chain-like proteins into a tender, cohesive filling that cooks up juicy. On the Western side, chefs and cooks argue that the "one-direction method" isn't entirely necessary—mixing in any direction for a sufficient period will bind the proteins and yield an equally tender, juicy filling. I don't pretend to know who is correct. It's similar to how Asian, Caribbean, and African cuisines, among others, wash bone-in chicken (Umma does so in milk), but Western cooks do not. I don't question such long-standing traditions too deeply. While I understand that Western cooks have tested their methods, I believe there is another perspective we should delve into more and respect as well. A part of me wants to preserve these traditions. Perhaps these methods are indeed old wives' tales, or perhaps they require further understanding and testing. For now, I'll follow Umma's lead and mix in one direction; it's easier on my hand and wrist! Over the years, I've watched Umma prepare hundreds of mandu in our living room. She sets up her mandu station on our low wooden table, meticulously filling wrappers and sealing them perfectly into half-moons while watching her favorite K-dramas. When I was younger I would sometimes assemble some mandu myself, feeling proud of the ones I had filled and folded on my own. Afterward, I would eagerly ask Umma to steam the ones I had wrapped. Nowadays, I make sure to be home whenever Umma is preparing mandu to give her a helping hand. After finishing all that assembly, we immediately savor a batch ourselves, reaping the fruits of our hard work. These freeze well: Simply freeze the mandu as they are on the baking sheet or platter (flat, not touching, in a single layer), covered with plastic wrap, then transfer them to a zipper-lock bag for storage once frozen.

MAKES 30 to 60 mandu   **TOTAL TIME** 2 hours

- 3 ounces (85 grams) dangmyeon (Korean glass noodles)
- 2½ tablespoons neutral cooking oil, divided, plus more for pan-frying (optional)
- 8 ounces (227 grams) mung bean sprouts
- 5 ounces (142 grams) firm tofu
- 8 ounces (227 grams) 80 percent lean ground pork
- 4 ounces (113 grams) 80 percent lean ground beef
- 10 tablespoons hot water (150 degrees), divided
- 2½ tablespoons oyster sauce, divided
- 2 tablespoons toasted sesame oil, divided
- 2 tablespoons plus ½ teaspoon soy sauce, divided
- 2 tablespoons minced garlic, divided
- 1 tablespoon plus ½ teaspoon sugar, divided
- 1 tablespoon mirin
- 2½ teaspoons Dasida beef stock powder, divided
- 1½ teaspoons grated fresh ginger
- 1 teaspoon black pepper, divided
- 1 teaspoon fish sauce
- ⅓ cup finely chopped daepa (jumbo green onion; 85 grams), white and light green parts only
- 4 ounces (113 grams) garlic chives, chopped fine
- 30–60 store-bought mandu pi (dumpling wrappers)
  Cho Ganjang (Vinegar Soy Sauce; page 35)

1 Bring 6 cups water to a boil in a large, wide pot. Add the dangmyeon, using tongs as needed to fully submerge the noodles. Stir in 1 tablespoon neutral oil. Turn off the heat, cover, and let the noodles soak until softened but still very chewy, 6 to 9 minutes. Drain the noodles in a colander and shake to remove excess water. Let the noodles sit until cool enough to touch, then arrange them in a single straight mound on a cutting board. Cut the noodles crosswise into 1-inch sections and transfer to a large bowl; set aside.

RECIPE CONTINUES

2 Meanwhile, add the mung bean sprouts and 1 cup water to the now-empty pot. Cover and cook over medium-high heat until steam begins to rise out of the pot, about 5 minutes. Turn the sprouts once, remove the pot from the heat, and let sit, covered, for 1 minute. Drain the sprouts and let sit until cool enough to touch. Chop the sprouts, then, working in batches, squeeze the sprouts by hand to remove excess water. Transfer to a separate bowl; set aside.

3 Arrange a clean dish towel or triple layer of cheesecloth in a separate bowl. Crumble the tofu into the prepared bowl, then gather the ends of the towel and squeeze firmly to remove excess liquid from the tofu. Discard the liquid and set aside the tofu, still in the towel (you will squeeze it once more before adding it to the filling).

4 Using a wooden spoon or your gloved hands, combine the pork and beef in a small pot or bowl with tall sides. Add ¼ cup hot water, stirring vigorously in a circular motion until the water is thoroughly incorporated and the mixture becomes stringy, about 3 minutes. Stir in 1 tablespoon oyster sauce, 1 tablespoon sesame oil, 1 tablespoon soy sauce, 1 tablespoon garlic, 2 teaspoons sugar, the mirin, 1 teaspoon Dasida powder, the ginger, and ½ teaspoon pepper until thoroughly incorporated, about 3 minutes. Add 3 tablespoons hot water and continue to stir vigorously in a circular motion until the meat mixture starts to become whipped, about 3 minutes. Add the remaining 3 tablespoons hot water and continue to stir vigorously in a circular motion until the meat mixture is stringy and whipped, about 3 minutes. Stir in the remaining 1½ tablespoons neutral oil until thoroughly incorporated.

5 Squeeze the tofu once more to remove any remaining liquid. Separate the tofu crumbles and add them to the noodles along with the meat mixture. Stir in the remaining 1½ tablespoons oyster sauce, remaining 1 tablespoon sesame oil, remaining 3½ teaspoons soy sauce, remaining 1 tablespoon garlic, remaining 1½ teaspoons sugar, remaining 1½ teaspoons Dasida powder, remaining ½ teaspoon pepper, and the fish sauce in a circular motion until well incorporated.

6 Squeeze the mung bean sprouts once more to remove any remaining liquid. Separate the sprouts and add to the meat mixture along with the daepa and chives. Gently stir in a circular motion until thoroughly combined, then smooth the surface. Using a silicone spatula, mark the filling with a cross to divide it into 4 equal portions. Transfer 1 portion to a separate bowl and refrigerate the remaining filling.

7 Line a rimmed baking sheet or platter with parchment paper. Working with 1 wrapper at a time (keep the remaining wrappers covered), place a rounded 2½ tablespoons filling in the center of the wrapper. Brush away any flour clinging to the surface of the wrapper, then lightly moisten the edge with water. Fold the wrapper in half to make a half-moon shape. Using your index finger and thumb, pinch the mandu closed, using the end of the spoon to push down any filling that bulges out. (If desired, lay the mandu on the counter and press down on the sealed edge with a fork to create a decorative edge.)

8 Transfer the mandu to the prepared sheet. Repeat with additional wrappers and the first portion of filling. When the first layer of assembled mandu is on the tray, add another layer of parchment paper on top and continue to add assembled mandu on top. Continue the mandu-making process with additional wrappers and the remaining 3 portions filling on separate parchment-lined sheets or platters. (The mandu can be frozen on the sheet until solid, then transferred to a zipper-lock bag and frozen for up to 1 month. Do not thaw frozen mandu before cooking.)

9 TO STEAM Add about 1 inch water to a large, wide pot, then place a collapsible steamer basket with a silicone steamer basket liner in the pot (the water should reach just below the base of the steamer basket). Cover and bring the water to a boil over high heat. Arrange 8 mandu evenly in the prepared basket, leaving at least a ½-inch space between each mandu. Steam until the mandu wrappers have a translucent, glossy sheen, about 7 minutes if fresh or about 11 minutes if frozen. Serve immediately with the cho ganjang. (Before cooking the next batch of dumplings, replenish the water in the pot.)

10 TO PAN-FRY Steam the mandu as instructed. Heat 2 tablespoons neutral oil in a 12-inch nonstick skillet over medium heat until shimmering. Add the mandu and cook until crisp and light golden brown on both sides, about 2 minutes, flipping occasionally. Serve immediately with the cho ganjang. (Before pan-frying the next batch of mandu, wipe the skillet clean with paper towels.)

TURN TO SEE HOW TO SHAPE MANDU →

Umma's Kitchen Wisdom

I save time by using store-bought mandu pi (dumpling skins/wrappers; labeled as 만두피 on packages). The brand I prefer is Surasang, because these wrappers are 4 to 4½ inches in diameter. If you're only able to find 3½-inch wrappers (which are more common), you'll need to reduce the amount of filling for each dumpling to a rounded 2 teaspoons.

I fill each wrapper with about 2½ tablespoons of the filling, but this does take practice! For beginners, it's better to start with 1 rounded tablespoon and gradually increase the amount as you get more comfortable. If you start with 1 tablespoon filling, you'll make closer to 60 mandu.

Assembling the mandu is a time-consuming process. For this reason, I'll work with one portion of the meat filling and keep the remaining filling in the refrigerator, replenishing it as needed. Similarly, I place stacks of mandu pi in a sandwich bag to keep them from drying out, and remove them as needed.

If you don't have a perforated silicone steamer basket liner, you can poke about 20 holes in a 9-inch parchment round. Place the round in the basket just before adding the mandu; replace it with a fresh round between each batch.

Shaping Mandu

Top Working with 1 wrapper at a time, place a rounded 2½ tablespoons filling in the center of the wrapper.

Bottom left Brush away any flour clinging to the wrapper's surface, then lightly moisten the edge with water.

Bottom right Fold the wrapper in half to make a half-moon shape.

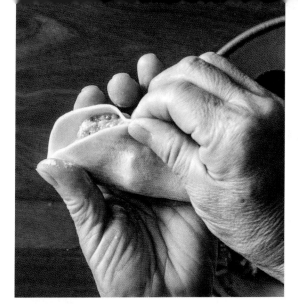
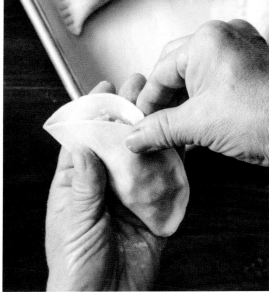

Top Pinch the mandu closed with your index finger and thumb, using the end of a spoon to push down any filling that bulges out.

Bottom If you like, press down on the sealed edge of the mandu with a fork to make a decorative edge. Transfer the mandu to the prepared baking sheet.

KOREAN BBQ SHORT RIBS

LA Galbi 갈비

LA gahl-bee

SARAH
세라

If you ever visit South Korea, you must visit one of their Costco locations. They are the Disneyland of grocery stores and have almost everything you can imagine—not just groceries but many other necessities too—only better and cuter at wholesale prices. When Umma and I visited our first Costco in South Korea, we easily spent four hours there, in awe of what was available in the store. We picked up several items such as perfectly sized stainless steel pots, red ginseng extract, and great skincare products that were extremely affordable. But amid all this retail fun and excitement, there was one item that had me scratching my head: LA galbi was being sold at this South Korean Costco. I found it interesting that it was labeled LA galbi, and I immediately wondered why. Is LA galbi different from just galbi? And did LA galbi originate in Los Angeles? I asked Umma if she knew anything about this, and all she could tell me was that she didn't try any type of galbi until she moved to the United States. Upon further research, I learned that galbi and LA galbi do differ from each other (they use different cuts of meat) and that there are a lot of theories about the origins of LA galbi. Some suggest it has nothing to do with the city, but instead with how the ribs are cut—across the lateral axis. Another plausible theory, based on my research, suggests that LA galbi was developed by Korean immigrants who relocated to Los Angeles. There, they adapted to working with the flanken cut, a preferred cut among American butchers. Pretty interesting, huh? What makes this recipe special is that Umma doesn't use any water in her marinade, a common ingredient you will find elsewhere. Her galbi marinade is made purely from fruits and other seasonings so it's not diluted. You'll taste it in the flavor! Washing and thoroughly scrubbing the ribs is especially important here since flanken-style ribs tend to have a fair amount of bone fragments stuck to them because they are cut with a band saw (also pretty interesting).

SERVES 4 to 6   TOTAL TIME 1¼ hours, plus 25 hours soaking, draining, and marinating

1 tablespoon sugar
3 pounds (1.4 kilograms) flanken-style short ribs, ¼ inch thick, trimmed

MARINADE

1¼ cups fresh Asian pear juice (see page 41)
5 tablespoons soy sauce
¼ cup fresh Fuji apple juice (see page 41)
¼ cup fresh onion juice (see page 41)
¼ cup pineapple juice
¼ cup mirin
2 green onions, chopped fine
3 tablespoons sugar
2 tablespoons toasted sesame oil
2 tablespoons minced garlic
1½ teaspoons fish sauce
1 teaspoon grated fresh ginger
1 teaspoon black pepper

2 green onions, sliced thin

1 Dissolve the sugar in 2 quarts cold water in a large bowl. Add the ribs and refrigerate for 30 minutes.

2 Transfer the ribs to a colander and discard the water. Under cold running water, rinse each rib thoroughly, removing any bone fragments (we like to use a designated toothbrush to scrub the bones). After all the ribs have been rinsed, give each rib another quick rinse. Let the ribs drain for 30 minutes in the colander. (Tip: Tilt the strainer to make sure the meat doesn't sit in any liquid that doesn't drip out of the colander.)

3 FOR THE MARINADE Whisk all the ingredients together in a large bowl until the sugar has dissolved. Working with one rib section at a time, coat in the marinade, then transfer to a storage container, alternating the bone and meat sides of ribs facing up as you layer them. Pour the remaining marinade over the ribs, cover, and refrigerate for at least 24 hours or up to 3 days, flipping the ribs halfway through marinating.

4 Arrange 3 or 4 ribs in a 12-inch nonstick skillet and add 1 tablespoon marinade per section; heat over medium-high heat. Cook until the marinade is slightly reduced and the edges of the ribs begins to brown, about 5 minutes. Flip the ribs and continue to cook until the marinade has reduced by half, occasionally redistributing the marinade under the ribs, about 5 minutes. Using kitchen shears, cut between each bone to create smaller rib pieces.

5 Reduce the heat to medium and continue to cook, turning the ribs occasionally, until the marinade is completely evaporated and the ribs are slightly caramelized and charred, 3 to 5 minutes. Transfer the ribs to a platter and tent with aluminum foil. Wipe the skillet clean with paper towels, return to medium-high heat, and repeat with the remaining ribs in batches; transfer to the platter. After cooking the last batch, return all the ribs to the skillet briefly to warm through. Sprinkle with the sliced green onions and serve.

Umma's Kitchen Wisdom

The best ribs for this are about 8 inches long and have a large amount of marbling.

If you don't want to eat all the galbi in one sitting, you can snip the marinated rib sections into pieces and freeze them in zipper-lock bags along with spoonfuls of the marinade. Thaw the ribs overnight in the refrigerator before cooking.

If you like, serve this over griddled sliced yellow onion. Preheat a 12-inch cast-iron griddle or skillet over medium heat for 5 minutes while getting ready to cook the last batch of ribs. Add 1 yellow onion (283 grams), halved and sliced thin, along with 2 to 3 tablespoons marinade and cook, stirring occasionally, until crisp-tender, about 3 minutes. Arrange the galbi and its juices over the onion and serve.

Sausage Yachae Bokkeum 소시지야채볶음

sausage ya-chae boh-kkeum

UMMA
엄마

I don't refer to Sarah as Sarah; I call her by her Korean name, Soojin. Soojin's appa, though, calls her by her English name, Sarah. Conversely, we refer to Soojin's older brother only by his English name, Kevin. When we realized this together as a family, we all laughed and wondered how this came to be. It was never intentional; life just somehow led us to call our kids by these names. In any case, Kevin has loved sausages and bacon since he was little. One day, while preparing lunch with a fridge that needed restocking, I threw together this dish on a whim using beef franks, leftover produce, and pantry condiments I had on hand. I served it with some warm white rice, and Kevin devoured the whole thing. I still make this dish whenever Kevin comes home, and it is always met with the same enthusiastic reaction.

SARAH
세라

I can understand why my brother, Kevin, loves this dish, and why Umma makes it whenever he comes home. For one, the sweet and savory sauce complements the sausage beautifully, while the contrast of the tender sausage and slightly crunchy vegetables make each bite enjoyable. Plus, it's incredibly easy to prepare and comes together in no time. And to add to the mystery of what my brother and I are called in our household: I don't address Kevin as "Oppa" (a term used by females to refer to a close, older male). Interestingly, though, I do refer to him as "Oppa" when talking about him with others in Korean. Funny how that works!

Umma's Kitchen Wisdom

I blanch the franks here to remove some of the salt and fat. This also preheats it before stir-frying, which helps to expedite the cooking process.

Feel free to use whatever vegetables you have available. I personally enjoy using bell peppers because they add vibrant color to the dish. Cabbage, mung bean sprouts, and mushrooms are also great options.

SERVES 4   TOTAL TIME 40 minutes

- 3 tablespoons ketchup
- 1 tablespoon soy sauce
- 1 tablespoon Worcestershire sauce
- 1½ teaspoons minced garlic
- 1 teaspoon grated fresh ginger
- 1 tablespoon sugar
- 12 ounces (340 grams) beef franks, cut ⅜ inch thick on bias
- 1 tablespoon neutral cooking oil, divided
- ¼ red bell pepper (57 grams), cut into rough 1-inch pieces
- ¼ green bell pepper (57 grams), cut into rough 1-inch pieces
- ½ yellow onion (142 grams), cut into rough 1-inch pieces
- ⅓ cup coarsely chopped fresh cilantro
- ¼ teaspoon black pepper

1 Whisk the ketchup, soy sauce, Worcestershire, garlic, ginger, and sugar together in a small bowl; set the sauce aside.

2 Bring 1 quart water to a boil in a 14-inch flat-bottomed wok or 12-inch nonstick skillet. Add the beef franks and blanch for 1 minute. Drain well.

3 Heat 1½ teaspoons oil in the now-empty wok over medium-high heat until shimmering. Add the bell peppers and onion and cook, tossing constantly, until the onion becomes translucent, about 2 minutes. Add the remaining 1½ teaspoons oil and the beef franks, toss to coat with the oil, and cook for 1 minute. Add the sauce and cook, stirring frequently, until the sauce clings to the vegetables and franks and reduces to 2 tablespoons, about 1 minute. Remove the wok from the heat and stir in the cilantro and pepper. Serve.

Maeun Dwaejibulgogi 매운 돼지불고기

mae-oon dwae-ji bool-goh-ghee

SARAH
세라

When it comes to consuming meat, the preferred option for Koreans is pork, according to a 2023 research survey on South Korea's meat consumption per capita. It's enjoyed in many forms—dumplings, braises, Korean barbecue, and more. Though Korea produces pork, including from the renowned Jeju Black pig, the high demand for the meat has made the country one of the top five pork importers in the world. Meat consumption is so high in Korea that it has surpassed rice consumption per capita in recent years, with pork leading this trend. It's quite a change from the 1970s, when rice and meat were rare luxuries reserved for special occasions. So why do Koreans love pork so much? It's likely because pork is relatively affordable and highly versatile. It's the meat we naturally gravitate toward for affordable feasts with friends, coworkers, and family for any occasion. (Plus, the fattier cuts pair wonderfully with drinks!) This rich pork version of bulgogi blends the balance of bold and sweet flavors that beef bulgogi is known for with additional heat from gochujang and gochugaru. Tenderized by an overnight marinade, the pork is cooked with complementary vegetables, notably perilla leaves, to balance the heat with herbaceous, aromatic notes.

Umma's Kitchen Wisdom

For tender bulgogi, make sure to select pork cushion or pork belly that has a decent amount of fat. Look for pork that's sliced ⅛ inch thick. For the ultimate tenderized bulgogi, marinate for the full 24 hours. (I do the 3-hour marination when I'm in a rush.)

Look for perilla leaves that are 3 to 4 inches in diameter. Larger ones tend to be unpleasantly chewy.

If you like, serve this with lettuce leaves and rice to make wraps.

SERVES 4   TOTAL TIME 40 minutes, plus 3 hours marinating

MARINADE
- 2 tablespoons gochujang
- 2 tablespoons minced garlic
- 1½ tablespoons fish sauce
- 1½ tablespoons toasted sesame oil
- 1½ tablespoons maesil cheong (plum extract syrup)
- 1½ tablespoons gochugaru
- 1½ tablespoons sugar
- 1 tablespoon distilled white vinegar
- 1 tablespoon lemon juice
- 2 teaspoons grated fresh ginger
- 1½ teaspoons soy sauce
- ½ teaspoon black pepper

- 1 pound (454 grams) thinly sliced pork cushion or skinless pork belly
- 1 tablespoon neutral cooking oil
- 1 carrot (75 grams), peeled and cut into 3-inch matchsticks
- ½ yellow onion (142 grams), sliced ¼ inch thick
- 3 green onions (45 grams), cut into 1½-inch lengths, white and light green parts halved lengthwise
- 1 ounce (28 grams) perilla leaves, sliced into ½-inch strips
- 1 teaspoon sesame seeds, toasted

1 FOR THE MARINADE Whisk all the ingredients together in a large bowl.

2 Separate the slices of pork and pat dry with paper towels. Cut the pork into rough 3 by 1½-inch pieces. Add the pork to the marinade and toss until evenly coated. Cover and refrigerate the pork for at least 3 hours or up to 24 hours.

3 Heat the oil in a 14-inch flat-bottomed wok or 12-inch nonstick skillet over high heat until shimmering. Add the pork and marinade and cook, tossing constantly, until the juices have thickened and cling to the meat, 3 to 5 minutes.

4 Reduce the heat to medium-high, add the carrot, and toss to combine. Add the yellow onion and cook, tossing constantly, until the vegetables begin to soften, about 30 seconds. Add the green onions and toss to combine. Turn off the heat, add the perilla leaves, and toss to combine. Transfer to a serving platter and sprinkle with the sesame seeds. Serve.

Daepae Samgyeopsal Yachae Jjim
대패삼겹살야채찜

dae-pae sahm-gyuhp-sahl yah-chae jjim

UMMA
엄마

This recipe is one of my favorites to serve to guests. It's incredibly simple and it makes a beautiful presentation. You can use a round or square pan here; it just needs to be deep enough to accommodate all the layered ingredients. After cooking, the pork and vegetables should be tender and fresh tasting. They are meant to be enjoyed together, dipped into the flavorful soy-based sauce punched up with Korean mustard and cilantro.

SARAH
세라

The pork and vegetables here offer a simple yet elegant flavor profile, with a clean and pure taste. Much of the seasoning flavors come from Umma's dipping sauce, which is uniquely nuanced thanks to minced cilantro and Korean mustard. You can find this hot yellow mustard sold in tubes at Korean grocery stores; it's much spicier than American yellow mustard. If you see pre-rolled pork belly, buy that; if only flat strips are available, cut them into 3-inch lengths and layer them like shingles. This dish is meant to be shared, so place the pan at the center of the table for everyone to serve themselves. Appa enjoys this with a bowl of rice, while Umma, my brother, and I prefer it without rice.

Umma's Kitchen Wisdom

Look for pork belly sliced 1/16 inch thick; it's sometimes labeled "Pork for Hot Pot" or "Shabu-Shabu."

Any shallow 6-quart round or square pan or similar sized large, wide pot will work here. Just make sure you have a tight-fitting lid so that the pork and vegetables steam properly.

I like enoki mushrooms, but other varieties also work. White button, shiitake, or oyster mushrooms are all great; remove any long stems and thinly slice the caps into long strips.

SERVES 4 to 6   TOTAL TIME 45 minutes

12 ounces (340 grams) mung bean sprouts
 8 ounces (227 grams) enoki mushrooms, ends trimmed, separated at the base
 ¼ cup (71 grams) thinly sliced yellow onion
 1 large carrot (100 grams), peeled and cut into 3-inch matchsticks
 4 ounces (113 grams) garlic chives, cut into 2-inch lengths
 4 ounces (113 grams) napa cabbage, innermost yellow leaves only, cut into 2-inch pieces
14 ounces (397 grams) thinly sliced skinless rolled pork belly
 ½ cup water
 1 green onion, sliced thin
 ½ teaspoon fine salt
 ¼ teaspoon black pepper
 ½ cup soy sauce
 6 tablespoons distilled white vinegar
 2 tablespoons maesil cheong (plum extract syrup)
 2 tablespoons minced garlic
 2 tablespoons minced fresh cilantro
   Prepared Korean mustard

1 Arrange the bean sprouts in an even layer in a shallow 6-quart pan, followed by a layer of mushrooms. Scatter the yellow onion over the mushrooms, then arrange the carrot, chives, and cabbage on top in 3 even rows. Arrange the pork on top in rows over the vegetables. Drizzle the water through the gaps in the pork belly. Sprinkle with the green onion, salt, and pepper. Cover and cook over medium-high heat until the pork is cooked through, 12 to 15 minutes.

2 Combine the soy sauce, vinegar, maesil cheong, garlic, and cilantro in a bowl, then divide the sauce among individual small bowls; place a small portion of mustard in each bowl for each person to mix into the sauce to their liking. Place the pan at the center of the table and serve with the dipping sauce.

This dish is as beautiful
to look at before cooking
as it is delicious to eat
after cooking.

BRAISED MARINATED PORK NECK

Dwaeji Moksal Yangnyeom Gui
돼지목살양념구이

dwae-ji mohk-sahl yahng-nyuhm goo-e

SARAH
세라

Although the Korean name of this dish ("gui") translates directly as "grilled," the pork here is actually braised. Meat prepared this way in Korean cuisine is often served alongside a variety of raw, unseasoned vegetables including green chiles, onions, and garlic. Beyond these vegetables, two greens pair exceptionally well with this style of meat: chives and perilla leaves. Although the other vegetables can do the job of creating a satisfying bite, both chives and perilla leaves complement grilled or braised meats so well that sometimes I think that the meat tastes incomplete without one of them! It's a longstanding tradition to enjoy grilled or braised meats wrapped in leafy greens to create bites that are balanced with flavor, texture, and aromatics. Here, the chives are turned into a well-seasoned salad and served as a bed for the braised pork. Instead of being wrapped, a piece of meat is picked up with chopsticks along with a few pieces of the seasoned chive salad. To create this irresistible pairing of pork and chives, Umma marinates pork neck overnight in a savory and sweet tenderizing marinade to produce juicy meat that glistens when cooked. She then tosses together the vibrant chive salad right before serving. Umma finishes this dish with a squeeze of fresh lemon juice for a bright, zesty boost that unifies the elements into a perfect bite.

Umma's Kitchen Wisdom

You can substitute pork collar or pork butt for the pork neck; you'll want to trim any excess fat from the edges of the slices.

If using an electric stovetop, increase the heat to medium-high before proceeding with step 5.

SERVES 4 to 6   **TOTAL TIME** 1¼ hours, plus 24 hours marinating

PORK

1½ pounds (680 grams) boneless pork neck, sliced ½ inch thick
½ cup fresh Asian pear juice (see page 41)
2 tablespoons pineapple juice
2 tablespoons toasted sesame oil
2 tablespoons soy sauce
2 tablespoons mirin
2 tablespoons corn syrup
2 tablespoons sugar
2 tablespoons minced garlic
1 tablespoon fish sauce
2 teaspoons grated fresh ginger
½ teaspoon black pepper

CHIVE SALAD

2 teaspoons maesil cheong (plum extract syrup)
2 teaspoons toasted sesame oil
1½ teaspoons gochugaru
1½ teaspoons sesame seeds, toasted
1½ teaspoons fish sauce
1 teaspoon distilled white vinegar
1 teaspoon minced garlic
1 teaspoon sugar
4 ounces (113 grams) garlic chives, cut into 2-inch lengths
¼ cup thinly sliced yellow onion (36 grams)
   Lemon wedges

1 FOR THE PORK Pat the pork dry with paper towels. Using a sharp knife, cut a ½-inch crosshatch pattern, about ⅛ inch deep, on each side of the pork slices, being careful not to cut all the way through. Cut the pork slices crosswise into 1-inch-wide strips.

2 Whisk the pear juice, pineapple juice, oil, soy sauce, mirin, corn syrup, sugar, garlic, fish sauce, ginger, and pepper together in a bowl until the sugar has dissolved. Combine the pork and marinade in a storage container, making sure that the pork is evenly coated. Cover and refrigerate for at least 24 hours or up to 2 days, flipping the pork halfway through marinating.

3 FOR THE CHIVE SALAD Whisk the maesil cheong, oil, gochugaru, sesame seeds, fish sauce, vinegar, garlic, and sugar together in a medium bowl until the sugar has dissolved; set the dressing aside.

4 Using tongs, coat the pork fully in the marinade once more, then add the pieces to a 12-inch nonstick skillet in a single layer; discard the remaining marinade. Cook over high heat until the juices in the skillet begin to boil. Cover, reduce the heat to medium, and cook until the pork is mostly brown but some pink color still remains, about 13 minutes.

5 Uncover the pork and continue to cook until it begins to caramelize on the bottom and the sauce has nearly evaporated, 6 to 8 minutes. Flip the pork and continue to cook until the sauce has evaporated and the pork is caramelized (but not charred) on the second side, 1 to 2 minutes. Remove the skillet from the heat.

6 Add the chives and onion to the reserved dressing and toss to combine. Spread the salad evenly over a serving platter and arrange the pork on top. Serve with lemon wedges.

The Intuitive Art of Sonmat

SARAH
세라

Whenever Umma and I prepare a dish together that requires mixing ingredients, she always steps aside to let me do it. I attempt to mirror her movements that I grew up observing, striving to mix the ingredients thoroughly yet gracefully, the way Umma has always done. She stands close by each time, observing my every move with a blend of patience for my learning curve and concern for the recipe process. Eventually, she reclaims her position and instructs me through her motions. Umma's hands and wrists always move with precision and elegance.

Umma explains that timing and the handling of ingredients are of the utmost importance when cooking—seasonings must be added at precise moments, heat levels are adjusted constantly, and mixing and adding pressure when working with ingredients must begin and end at just the right times. This careful orchestration of events allows any given dish's flavors to meld perfectly, creating a harmonious balance that is hard to capture with instructions alone. This is the art of sonmat (손맛).

Kitchen Conversation

UMMA *Do you know what sonmat means?*

SARAH No, not really. What is it?

UMMA *Sonmat translates as "taste of the hands," but it signifies a special cooking talent or intuition. If you have it, practice can make you better, but practice alone won't give you sonmat. When someone has sonmat, the food they prepare reveals a unique, intangible quality and flavor. This taste comes not only from years of experience but also from the heart and from sincere love for both the food being prepared and the people it feeds. Science cannot explain sonmat, but in Korean cuisine, sonmat is one of the important elements in the art of cooking. It's a talent, a sense, and a phenomenon that one possesses. Give two people the same recipe, and the person with sonmat will make a tastier dish.*

SARAH From how you have described Halmeoni to me, it sounds like Halmeoni had sonmat. I remember extended relatives and friends speaking highly of her food. They said it remains memorable to their taste buds even today.

UMMA *Yes, everyone said Halmeoni had sonmat. And they still compliment her cooking all these years later.*

SARAH I think you have sonmat too, Umma.

Umma smiles softly. At that moment, I realized that Umma's sonmat is unparalleled to me, as her love for her family finds its deepest expression through her cooking.

BRAISED PORK BACK RIBS AND KIMCHI

Dwaeji Deunggalbi Kimchi Jjim
돼지등갈비김치찜

dwae-ji deung-gahl-bee gim-chi jjim

SARAH
세라

Late one afternoon, Imobu (Uncle; husband to an aunt on the maternal side) came over and walked to our stove to see what was cooking as the pot gurgled and emanated enticing aromas. He marveled, as it was a dish he had yet to try in his lifetime. He watched the braise bubbling away and said excitedly, "Wow, today is the day I get to finally try kimchi jjim!" Once the braise was ready, Umma served Imobu this dish with a warm bowl of rice, some banchan, and a red-capped soju (the red cap indicates a stronger soju). He took a big bite, then let out a long, satisfied sigh, repeating, "Masisseo... masisseo" ("Delicious... delicious"). At this point, I couldn't help but ask why this was Imobu's first time trying this dish. Umma explained that this is a very modern recipe and reminded me that in times past, they just ate kimchi and rice. I think this recipe serves as a bridge from the past to the present: The first bites are all about the flavor of that long-fermented pogi kimchi, evoking gimjang days when Halmeoni and the neighborhood ajummas would make huge batches of pogi kimchi (see page 123). After several bites, the focus falls on the luscious, tender pork that falls off the bone, bringing the more bountiful present into focus. The flavors of this braise carry the essence of history paired with its progression, the sonmat (taste of the hands), and a myriad of complexities. Balanced between tradition and modernity, this dish is a testament to the enduring legacy and ongoing adaptability of pogi kimchi.

SERVES 4 to 6   TOTAL TIME 2¾ hours, plus 30 minutes soaking

¼ cup (25 grams) sugar, divided

2 pounds (907 grams) pork loin back ribs, membrane removed, ribs separated (see page 43)

3½ pounds (1.6 kilograms) well-fermented Pogi Kimchi (Whole Napa Cabbage Kimchi; page 127), plus ½ cup kimchi juice

1 yellow onion (283 grams), halved and sliced ½ inch thick

1 Fresno chile, stemmed and sliced ¼ inch thick on bias

1 jalapeño chile, stemmed and sliced ¼ inch thick on bias

1 daepa (jumbo green onion; 130 grams), trimmed and cut into 1½-inch lengths, white and light green parts halved lengthwise

2 tablespoons minced garlic

1½ tablespoons doenjang (fermented soybean paste)

1½ tablespoons fish sauce

1 Dissolve 1 tablespoon sugar in 2 quarts cold water in a large, wide pot. Add the ribs and refrigerate for 30 minutes.

2 Transfer the ribs to a bowl and discard the water; rinse the pot well. Bring 2 quarts water to a boil in the pot. Add the ribs, return to a boil, and cook for 5 minutes.

3 Transfer the ribs to a colander and discard the water; rinse the pot. Under cold running water, rinse each rib thoroughly, removing coagulated particles at the end of each rib (we like to use a designated toothbrush to scrub the ribs). After all the ribs have been rinsed, give each rib another quick rinse.

4 Remove the excess filling from the surface of the kimchi pieces and put it back into the container. Cut the kimchi pieces in half lengthwise through the core. Arrange half the kimchi cut side up in the pot. Arrange the ribs evenly over the top, followed by the remaining kimchi, cut side down, and any kimchi juice from the kimchi pieces.

5 Set aside a small portion of the yellow onion, Fresno chile, jalapeño, and daepa (about 1 cup total; choose the thinner slices). Whisk 6 cups water, the garlic, doenjang, fish sauce, kimchi juice, and remaining 3 tablespoons sugar together in a bowl until the sugar has dissolved. Pour the mixture into the pot and arrange the remaining vegetables evenly over the top. Gently press on the vegetables with the back of a spoon to submerge them in the broth.

6 Bring to a boil. Reduce the heat to a vigorous simmer, cover, and cook for 5 minutes. Reduce the heat to a simmer and continue to cook until the ribs are nearly falling off the bones, the kimchi has softened significantly, and the liquid has thickened slightly, about 1½ hours. Add the reserved vegetables, gently press on them with the back of a spoon to submerge in the broth, and continue to cook for 2 minutes. Serve.

Umma's Kitchen Wisdom

For the deepest. richest flavor, I let my pogi kimchi ferment for at least 2 months before using it in this dish. You can use well-fermented store-bought kimchi (see page 20 for purchasing tips). You'll need about 8 cups for this recipe. If you use store-bought, taste the broth and adjust the seasonings as needed.

When measuring out the kimchi, simply pick it up with tongs with the juices intact.

Pork front leg is commonly used, but this cut is hard to find. Pork loin back ribs (also often labeled as baby back ribs) are also regularly used, so that's my pick (spareribs also work). The best ribs for this dish are 4 to 6 inches long and have ½ to 1 inch of meat on them.

Don't trim the fat from the ribs—it's needed for this flavorful braise.

If you'd like extra spice, add 1½ teaspoons gochugaru to the broth mixture in step 5. The cooking time will be slightly less, as the gochugaru will thicken (and darken) the braise more.

FRIED PORK RIBS WITH CUMIN SEASONING SALT

Dwaeji Deunggalbi Twigim
돼지등갈비튀김

dwae-ji deung-gahl-bee twee-gim

SARAH
세라

"Oh my goodness, I could cry eating this" was the first reaction from my friend Marian after trying these ribs. This type of compliment is usually followed by "What are these ribs seasoned with?" The answer, and what makes these ribs so irresistible, involves a two-step seasoning process. First, the ribs are coated with a warm spice blend that includes garlic powder, onion powder, and ground ginger. Then, after bathing them in a starch slurry to give them a crispy crunch when fried, the final step after cooking is to toss them with a blend of sesame seeds, cumin, gochugaru, and MSG salt, among other pantry staples. This cumin-forward seasoning is the final flourish that gives these ribs a big flavor boost.

SERVES 4 to 6   TOTAL TIME 1½ hours, plus 1½ hours soaking and seasoning

    4 teaspoons sugar, divided
    3 pounds (1.4 kilograms) pork loin back ribs, membrane removed, ribs separated (see page 43)
    1 tablespoon miwon matsogeum (MSG seasoning salt), divided
    2 teaspoons garlic powder, divided
    1 teaspoon onion powder
    1 teaspoon black pepper, divided
  ½ teaspoon ground ginger
    1 cup plus 2 tablespoons (170 grams) potato starch
1½ tablespoons sesame seeds, toasted and coarsely ground (see page 38)
    1 tablespoon gochugaru
    2 teaspoons ground cumin
2–3 quarts vegetable oil for frying

1 Dissolve 1 tablespoon sugar in 2 quarts cold water in a large bowl. Submerge the ribs and refrigerate for 30 minutes.

2 Combine 1 teaspoon seasoning salt, 1 teaspoon garlic powder, the onion powder, ½ teaspoon pepper, and the ginger in a small bowl. Drain and rinse the ribs, then pat dry with paper towels. Arrange the ribs meat side up in a large dry bowl. Sprinkle the ribs with the seasoning mixture, then massage the seasoning into the ribs to coat them evenly. Cover and refrigerate the ribs for at least 1 hour or overnight.

3 Meanwhile, whisk the potato starch and 2 cups water in a small bowl. Let sit until the mixture separates and the starch settles to the bottom, about 30 minutes. Combine the sesame seeds, gochugaru, cumin, remaining 1 teaspoon sugar, remaining 2 teaspoons seasoning salt, remaining 1 teaspoon garlic powder, and remaining ½ teaspoon pepper in a separate small bowl; set aside.

4 Set a wire rack in a rimmed baking sheet. Following the manufacturer's instructions, heat the oil in an electric fryer to 330 degrees. Measure out and reserve 3 tablespoons liquid from the surface of the water-starch mixture. Carefully pour off the remaining water from the bowl, making sure not to discard any starch. Mix the reserved water back into the starch until it becomes smooth and pourable. Pour the starch mixture over the ribs and toss until thoroughly coated.

5 Working with 1 rib at a time, use tongs to coat the rib in the starch mixture once more, then carefully lower the rib, meat side up, into the hot oil; hold for 5 seconds, then release the piece into the oil. Repeat with 3 more ribs. Cook, undisturbed, for about 2 minutes, then use the tongs to release the ribs from the fryer basket base. Continue to cook, turning occasionally, until the coating has puffed and crisped and the pork is light golden brown and registers at least 200 degrees, 12 to 14 minutes.

6 Using tongs, transfer the ribs to the prepared rack. Return the oil to 330 degrees and repeat with the remaining ribs in batches. Add the ribs and 2 tablespoons cumin seasoning salt to a large bowl and toss gently to coat. Serve, passing the remaining cumin seasoning salt separately.

Umma's Kitchen Wisdom

Use a pure potato starch, with no additional ingredients, to ensure it forms a slurry that adheres well to the ribs. This is crucial to create a crispy exterior.

Look for ribs that are 4 to 6 inches long and have ½ to 1 inch of meat on them. Pork loin back ribs are sometimes labeled as baby back ribs. Pork spareribs will also work.

Since you're frying for 15 minutes per batch and there are 4 batches, I keep the coated ribs in the refrigerator until the moment before frying. This also enhances their crispiness. The starch slurry will settle at the bottom of the bowl, so use a spoon to scoop it up and coat the ribs again.

I like the convenience of using an electric deep fryer. A large, wide pot or Dutch oven that holds 6 quarts or more also works. Add the oil to the pot until it measures about 2 inches deep and heat it over medium-high heat to 330 degrees. Adjust the heat as needed to maintain the temperature.

Sogogijeon 소고기전

soh-goh-ghee-juhn

UMMA
엄마

This simple dish is so delicious that I enjoy it on its own as a snack. It also makes excellent sandwiches and a great noodle topping. Leftovers freeze great— I pop them into my air fryer at 375 degrees for 5 minutes and they're ready for more snacking.

SARAH
세라

To make any jeon (pancake), you start by coating seasoned vegetables, kimchi, seafood, or, in this case, thinly sliced beef, with a seasoned flour mixture and/or an egg batter mixture, and then you pan-fry it to golden-brown crispy perfection. We love the convenience and flavor that Korean frying mix (see page 21) brings to jeon. This is one of my favorite ways to enjoy beef, as it offers so much more than meets the eye. The beef turns out tender and savory, with a hint of sweetness and a delicate exterior. I like this dish as a meal with rice and various banchan, but like Umma, you can also enjoy it as a snack. After cooling leftovers to room temperature, Umma freezes them. If you don't have an air fryer for reheating the pancakes (as we do), reheat them on the stovetop in a skillet with a little oil or pop them into a 375-degree oven.

SERVES 4 to 6   TOTAL TIME 1 hour, plus 1 hour marinating

- 2 teaspoons Dasida beef stock powder, divided
- 1 tablespoon onion powder
- 1 teaspoon ground ginger
- 1 teaspoon miwon matsogeum (MSG seasoning salt), divided
- ½ teaspoon black pepper
- 2 tablespoon maesil cheong (plum extract syrup)
- 2 tablespoons toasted sesame oil
- 1 pound (454 grams) thinly sliced beef sirloin or rib-eye
- 2 tablespoons plus 1 teaspoon sugar, divided
- 3 tablespoons minced garlic
- 1⅔ cups (220 grams) Korean frying mix
- 8 large eggs
- ½ cup neutral cooking oil, plus extra as needed

1 Mix 1 teaspoon Dasida powder, the onion powder, ginger, ½ teaspoon seasoning salt, and the pepper in a small bowl. Combine the maesil cheong and sesame oil in a separate small bowl.

2 Separate the slices of beef, pat dry with paper towels, and arrange in a single layer on a large tray or cutting board. Lightly sprinkle the tops with 1 tablespoon sugar and 2 teaspoons seasoning mixture, rub lightly with all of the garlic, and brush lightly with half of the maesil cheong mixture. Flip the slices and repeat seasoning with 1 tablespoon sugar, the remaining seasoning mixture, and the remaining maesil cheong mixture. Transfer the seasoned beef to a large plate, stacking the slices as needed. Cover tightly with plastic wrap and refrigerate for at least 1 hour or up to 24 hours.

3 Spread the frying mix in a shallow dish. Beat the eggs, remaining 1 teaspoon Dasida powder, remaining ½ teaspoon seasoning salt, and remaining 1 teaspoon sugar in a second shallow dish.

4 Set a wire rack in a rimmed baking sheet. Heat 1 tablespoon oil in a 12-inch nonstick skillet over medium-high heat until shimmering, then reduce the heat to medium. Press 1 beef slice into the frying mix, shaking off excess; dip in the egg mixture, allowing excess to drip off; and then gently place in the skillet. Repeat with additional slices, spacing them about ½ inch apart in the skillet. Drizzle 1 tablespoon oil around the edges of the slices and cook until light golden brown on the first side, 1 to 2 minutes. Using tongs, gently separate the slices, flip, and continue to cook until light golden brown on the second side, 1 to 2 minutes. Transfer the slices to the prepared rack. Repeat with the remaining oil and slices, wiping the skillet clean between batches if needed. Serve.

Umma's Kitchen Wisdom

Look for sirloin sliced ⅟₁₆ inch thick; it's sometimes labeled "Beef for Hot Pot" or "Shabu-Shabu." If you can't find it, you can use rib-eye, but sirloin is preferable.

I find that keeping the sugar separate from the beef seasoning results in better seasoning overall.

For optimal flavor, don't skimp on the amount of oil in the skillet.

Beef Gaseu 비프가스

beef gah-seu

UMMA
엄마

While chicken or pork is a more common choice for this dish, I wanted to show Sarah how delicious gaseu can be when made with beef. Instead of the sweet and savory sauce that's typically served with gaseu, I serve these cutlets with my special curry sauce. I also serve these cutlets to my family uncut—that's how I learned to make it and that's just how some Koreans serve it! I clapped my hands and laughed when Sarah explained to me the historical context for serving gaseu uncut rather than sliced, as it is served in Japan. I recommend serving this dish with either Kkakdugi (Radish Kimchi; page 118) or store-bought danmuji (yellow pickled radish). These fermented foods pair exceptionally well with this fried cutlet.

SARAH
세라

While there is no definitive English spelling for this dish, when I see gaseu (or ggasu / kkasu / ggaseu), I immediately recognize it as Korea's version of Japan's katsu, a breaded and fried cutlet that's similar to a German schnitzel. This is a dish that arrived in Korea during the 1930s under Japanese colonial rule. Korea's version is much thinner, served uncut, and doused with sauce. The tradition of serving it uncut in Korea stems from the 1980s, when slicing food at the table with a knife was associated with Western cuisine and considered a symbol of wealth, as Korean table utensils primarily consisted of just spoons and chopsticks. To this day, it is not uncommon to be served uncut gaseu, though it is sometimes served cut for convenience. In Umma's version, you will find all the characteristics of Korea's classic dish: She pounds the beef into thin pieces, serves it uncut, and smothers it in her own special curry sauce. Then, she serves it with rice and a creamy cabbage salad.

SERVES 4   TOTAL TIME 1¾ hours, plus 1 hour refrigerating

CUTLETS

- 4 (4- to 6-ounce / 113- to 170-gram) boneless beef short ribs, 1½ to 2 inches thick and 6 to 7 inches long, trimmed
- 1 teaspoon onion powder
- 1 teaspoon garlic powder
- ½ teaspoon miwon matsogeum (MSG seasoning salt), divided
- ¼ teaspoon ground ginger
- ¼ teaspoon black pepper
- 1 tablespoon maesil cheong (plum extract syrup)
- 2 cups (160 grams) panko bread crumbs
- 7 tablespoons (53 grams) Korean frying mix
- 2 large eggs
- 1 tablespoon milk
- ¼ teaspoon sugar

CURRY

- 2 tablespoons salted butter
- ½ yellow onion (142 grams), sliced ¼ inch thick
- 2 ounces (57 grams) white mushrooms, trimmed and sliced thin
- 3 cups water
- 3 cubes (57 grams) mild curry sauce mix

3–4 quarts vegetable oil for frying

DRESSING

- ½ cup (104 grams) mayonnaise
- ¼ cup (68 grams) ketchup
- ¼ cup Worcestershire sauce

- ½ head green cabbage (454 grams), cored and sliced ⅛ inch thick
- 4 cups (740 grams) cooked short- or medium-grain white rice

RECIPE CONTINUES

1 FOR THE CUTLETS Cut each short rib in half crosswise, then butterfly each piece lengthwise, starting on the narrowest side and stopping ½ inch away from the bottom so the halves remain attached. Open up the short ribs and lightly score on both sides. Cover the short ribs with plastic wrap and pound to a ¼-inch thickness.

2 Mix the onion powder, garlic powder, ¼ teaspoon seasoning salt, ginger, and pepper in a small bowl. Pat the cutlets dry with paper towels and sprinkle both sides with the seasoning mixture. Brush both sides of the cutlets with the maesil cheong, using the brush to also distribute the seasoning evenly.

3 Spread the panko and frying mix in separate shallow dishes. Beat the eggs, milk, sugar, and remaining ¼ teaspoon seasoning salt together in a third shallow dish. Working with 1 cutlet at a time, press it first into the frying mix; shake off any excess; dip it in the egg mixture, allowing excess to drip off; then coat in the panko, pressing with your fingers to form an even, cohesive coating. Stack the breaded cutlets in an airtight container and refrigerate for at least 1 hour or overnight.

4 FOR THE CURRY Meanwhile, melt the butter in a 14-inch flat-bottomed wok or 12-inch nonstick skillet over medium-high heat. Add the onion and mushrooms and cook, tossing constantly, until the onion has softened (but still has a bit of crunch to it), about 5 minutes. Stir in the water. Cover, increase the heat to high, and bring to a boil. Uncover, reduce the heat to a vigorous simmer, and cook until the flavors meld, about 5 minutes.

5 Stir in the curry cubes until completely dissolved, about 1 minute. Continue to cook until the sauce thickens slightly, about 6 minutes. Remove the wok from the heat; set aside.

6 Set a wire rack in a rimmed baking sheet. Following the manufacturer's instructions, heat the oil in an electric fryer to 330 degrees. Lower 1 cutlet into the oil and cook until golden brown, about 2 minutes per side. Transfer the cutlet to the prepared rack. Return the oil to 330 degrees and repeat with the remaining 3 cutlets.

7 FOR THE DRESSING Whisk the mayonnaise, ketchup, and Worcestershire sauce together in a bowl.

8 Return the curry to a brief simmer over medium-high heat. Arrange the cutlets and cabbage on plates and put the rice in individual bowls. Spoon the curry over the top of the cutlets and the dressing over the cabbage. Serve.

Preparing Beef Cutlets

After cutting the ribs crosswise, butterfly each rib in half lengthwise, starting on the narrowest side and stopping ½ inch away from the bottom so that the halves remain attached.

Open up the short ribs and score them lightly on both sides.

Cover the short ribs with plastic wrap and pound them to a ¼-inch thickness.

Umma's Kitchen Wisdom

Refrigerating the breaded beef for an hour before frying allows the panko to moisten, ensuring that the outer part fries evenly with the inner meat.

I like House Foods Vermont Curry with Apple and Honey sauce mix, but other brands, such as Ottogi, work too.

A mandoline will make it easier to slice the cabbage paper-thin.

An electric deep fryer is so convenient, but you can also use a 6-quart or larger wide pot or Dutch oven. Add the oil to the pot until it measures 2 inches deep and heat over medium-high heat to 330 degrees; adjust the heat as needed to maintain the temperature.

You can replace the beef with thin fish fillets such as flounder or with boneless chicken thighs or pork loin steaks pounded to a ¼-inch thickness.

Seoul-Sik Bulgogi
서울식 불고기

seoul-shik bool-goh-ghee

SARAH
세라

I finally had the opportunity to visit Korea as an adult in 2017. Samchon was generous enough to buy me a round-trip ticket and let me stay with him and his family in Suwon for two weeks. He gave me an in-depth tour of Korea, during which I got to visit Appa's family in Incheon, visit the border of South and North Korea, and participate in festivals and activities throughout Seoul. One particular day, he took me to watch a folktale musical at Korea House called *The Tale of Sim Chong*. Not knowing what to expect, I left the theater in a flood of tears (and was perhaps the only person who reacted this way). Embarrassed, I told Samchon that I was having an allergy attack from the dust outside.

Through this musical, I suddenly felt deeply connected to my Korean roots in a way I had never experienced before. The sound of the drumbeats hitting the janggu, the strings of the gayageum vibrating across the room, and the story of Sim Chong's desire of wanting to sacrifice herself for her blind father all felt like home to me. I was experiencing a true sense of Korean identity and connection, and as everyone else enjoyed the show, I silently released what felt like a river of tears. That day, I felt more at home in Korea than I had ever felt at home in America, and looking back, I understand that shedding those tears was a cathartic release for all the years that I had hidden my Korean pride as a Korean American.

Soon after this awakening, Samchon took me to a local restaurant near his home to enjoy some bulgogi. This wasn't the bulgogi that I was used to, though—this bulgogi featured a broth that was kept at a simmer tableside. Samchon showed me how to enjoy it step by step: Add the meat and vegetables on top of your rice, add a spoonful of the bubbling broth over it, scoop it all up, and enjoy. I followed his lead, then scarfed down the entire dish. I remember Samchon saying, "Wow, you ate that well!" He took me back to this same restaurant every day for the remaining week I had with him.

CONTINUES

When I returned home, I shared my excitement and love with Umma for the musical and the bulgogi I had with Samchon. Umma did not hesitate to learn how to re-create this dish for me. It's a dish that is not only savory and comforting but also homey because it reminds me of a place I never knew could feel like home—Korea.

This type of bulgogi is best enjoyed family-style, setting the pot or skillet on a hot plate in the center of the table to keep the bulgogi at a simmer. Each person helps themselves, usually one bite at a time. I highly recommend enjoying this as Samchon taught me: Give everyone a serving of rice; add some meat, noodles, and vegetables on top of the rice, pour over a spoonful of the broth; then scoop up a mouthful and enjoy. Don't forget to set out some kimchi!

SERVES 4 to 6   TOTAL TIME 45 minutes, plus 3 hours soaking and marinating

   2 ounces (57 grams) dangmyeon (Korean glass noodles)

MARINADE
1⅔ cups fresh Asian pear juice (see page 41)
 ½ cup fresh Fuji apple juice (see page 41)
 ⅓ cup soy sauce
 ¼ cup fresh onion juice (see page 41)
  2 green onions, finely chopped
  3 tablespoons mirin
  3 tablespoons sugar
  2 tablespoons pineapple juice
  2 tablespoons toasted sesame oil
  2 tablespoons minced garlic
  2 tablespoons oyster sauce
  1 tablespoon fish sauce
  1 teaspoon grated fresh ginger
  1 teaspoon black pepper

  2 pounds (907 grams) thinly sliced sirloin,
    cut into rough 4-inch pieces
  1 small carrot (35 grams), peeled and cut into
    3-inch matchsticks
  1 ounce (28 grams) enoki mushrooms,
    ends trimmed, separated at the base
  1 ounce (28 grams) thinly sliced yellow onion
  2 green onions, white and light green parts halved
    lengthwise, cut into 3-inch lengths

1 Cover the dangmyeon with 1 inch water in a large bowl and let soak at room temperature for at least 3 hours or overnight. Drain the noodles and rinse thoroughly; set aside.

2 FOR THE MARINADE Whisk all the ingredients together in a large bowl until the sugar has dissolved. Separate the slices of beef and pat dry with paper towels. Add the beef to the marinade and toss gently until thoroughly coated. Cover and let marinate for 2 hours.

3 Add the beef and marinade to a 12-inch wide pot or skillet, cover, and bring to a boil over high heat, stirring occasionally to break up the slices of beef. Stir in the carrot, mushrooms, yellow onion, green onions, and dangmyeon and return to a boil. Cook until the vegetables and noodles are softened and the beef is cooked through, about 1 minute. Serve.

Umma's Kitchen Wisdom

Look for sirloin sliced 1/16 inch thick; it's sometimes labeled "Beef for Hot Pot" or "Shabu-Shabu." Since this cut is so thin, don't marinate it for longer than 2 hours.

The easiest way to prepare Korean glass noodles is to submerge them in water for a minimum of 3 hours. There's no need to cook them separately, since they will achieve the proper texture once mixed into the hot cooking liquid. If your noodles are very long, cut them into 10-inch lengths just before serving.

I like using enoki mushrooms, but you can use any mushroom (trim long stems and slice the caps).

If you have a portable burner, cook this tableside, as I do. Reduce the heat to low before serving.

BRAISED BEEF RIBS

Galbi Jjim 갈비찜

gahl-bee jjim

UMMA
엄마

I love using an Instant Pot to cook recipes with braised meat. It speeds up the cooking process by up to 70 percent, I don't have to constantly check on the meat, and I can step away from cooking to do other things. It's very beginner-friendly, and I encourage my kids to use it to make our galbi jjim recipe. When developing this recipe, I created a flavorful marinade using three different fruit juices plus plenty of other bold ingredients. All that fruit juice tenderizes the meat instantly when pressure-cooked. Additionally, I add jujubes for their natural subtle sweetness. If you're curious and wondering whether to eat the jujubes, the answer is of course! I usually just add them whole, but you can pit them first, if you prefer (see page 38). Jujubes are delicious and are rich in antioxidants. Take a bite and you will appreciate their deep, distinctive sweetness, which stands out from the marinade. I have two jujube trees in my yard that I planted many years ago. Every fall, we harvest these dates and carefully sun-dry and then freeze them to use in dishes such as this and to make tea infusions.

SARAH
세라

Fear not the Instant Pot. When I learned this recipe, it was my first time using an Instant Pot—an appliance that felt daunting to me. But after mastering Umma's galbi jjim, I am convinced that every home cook should have one, much like the air fryer. The pressure-cook setting truly makes anyone look like a professional cook. It tenderizes meat with a click of a button and is not at all difficult to learn and use. You'll need a 6- or 8-quart pressure cooker here.

SERVES 4 to 6   **TOTAL TIME** 2½ hours, plus 2½ hours soaking and marinating

1 tablespoon sugar
4 pounds (1.8 kilograms) beef back ribs, membrane removed, ribs separated (see page 43)
1 ounce (28 grams) fresh ginger, peeled and chopped, divided
1 tablespoon black peppercorns

MARINADE
1⅔ cups fresh Asian pear juice (see page 41)
½ cup fresh Fuji apple juice (see page 41)
½ cup fresh onion juice (see page 41)
½ cup pineapple juice
5 tablespoons soy sauce
¼ cup corn syrup
3 tablespoons oyster sauce
2 tablespoons sugar
2 tablespoons mirin
2 tablespoons toasted sesame oil
2 tablespoons minced garlic
1 tablespoon fish sauce
2 teaspoon grated fresh ginger
2 teaspoons black pepper
3 green onions (45 grams), chopped fine

3 carrots (227 grams), peeled and sliced 1 inch thick, edges trimmed if desired (see page 40)
8 ounces (227 grams) Korean radish, sliced 1 inch thick, slices cut into 2-inch pieces, edges trimmed if desired (see page 40)
1 ounce (28 grams) dried jujubes
2 bay leaves
2 green onions (30 grams), white and light green parts halved lengthwise, cut into 3-inch lengths

RECIPE CONTINUES

1 Dissolve the sugar in 3 quarts cold water in a large stockpot. Add the ribs and refrigerate for 30 minutes.

2 Transfer the ribs to a bowl and discard the water; clean the pot. Bring 4 quarts water to a boil in the pot. Add the ribs, half the ginger, and the peppercorns; return to a boil; and blanch for 10 minutes.

3 Transfer the ribs to a colander and discard the water; clean the pot thoroughly. Under cold running water, rinse each rib thoroughly, removing any coagulated particles at the end of each rib (we like to use a designated toothbrush to scrub them off). After all the ribs have been rinsed, give each rib another quick rinse.

4 FOR THE MARINADE Whisk all the ingredients together in a large bowl. Measure out and reserve 1½ cups marinade. Add the ribs to the remaining marinade and toss to coat, then arrange the ribs meat side down. Cover and refrigerate the ribs (and the reserved marinade) for at least 2 hours or up to 24 hours.

5 Add the reserved marinade, carrots, and radish to an electric pressure cooker. Lock the lid in place and close the pressure-release valve. Select the high pressure-cook function and cook for 7 minutes. Turn off the pressure cooker and quick-release the pressure. Carefully remove the lid, allowing the steam to escape away from you. Using a slotted spoon, transfer the carrots and radish to a bowl and set aside.

6 Add the ribs, meat side down, and their marinade to the pressure cooker. Add the jujubes, bay leaves, and remaining ginger. Make sure the bay leaves are submerged in the marinade. Lock the lid in place and close the pressure release valve. Select the high pressure-cook function and cook for 20 minutes. Turn off the pressure cooker and quick-release the pressure. Carefully remove the lid.

7 Turn on the highest sauté or browning function, cover the pot without locking the lid, and cook for 15 minutes, flipping the ribs halfway through cooking using tongs. Stir in the carrots and radish and any accumulated juices (try to submerge them in the sauce) and cook until the vegetables are heated through, about 5 minutes. Turn off the pressure cooker and add the green onions. Transfer the ribs, vegetables, and sauce to a serving dish. Serve.

Umma's Kitchen Wisdom

The best ribs to buy for this recipe are 5 to 7 inches long and have ½ to 1 inch of meat on them. I strongly prefer back ribs because they're tasty and more affordable than short ribs (which are often used).

You must submerge the meat in water for 30 minutes to get rid of the myoglobin, and the meat must be scrubbed and rinsed after boiling it in step 2 to avoid an off-aroma in the finished dish.

To get the right size carrot pieces for this dish, look for jumbo carrots that are at least 1½ inches in diameter at the stem end.

I like to trim around the edges of the carrots and Korean radish for this particular dish, a common practice in Korean cooking. This creates a smooth surface and nicer appearance when the vegetables are cooked tender.

Jeongigui Tongdak Yangbaechu Mari
전기구이 통닭 양배추말이

juhn-ghee-goo-e tohng-dahk yahng-bae-choo ma-ri

SARAH
세라

I went through a challenging period in my life post-college. Though I was thankful to land a job in my field of study immediately upon graduation, I soon realized that this job and career path weren't right for me. I struggled to adjust, feeling trapped by my student loans, clinging to the hope that things would eventually get better. But something just felt off, and instead of dissipating, my unhappiness deepened into misery. Saturday-morning grocery trips to the Korean grocery store and Costco with Umma became more meaningful to me during this time. We would catch up about the long week we'd just had, discussing the highs and lows as I drove us down the winding roads. Umma has always been open to listening and evolving. She was never dismissive of my unhappiness, but there was a clear cultural difference between what I needed in my life and what she had experienced in Korea's office-work culture of 6-day workweeks with long hours, work-related social demands, and grinding commutes. When I told her during one of these drives that I was going to give my notice at work and confided my fear about it, she looked straight ahead and said, "You know, you're much wiser than I was when I was your age. Back then, I didn't think so deeply about my future. I just followed orders and didn't think twice about it. But look at you. You're questioning your desires, what makes you happy, and what you need to do to have a better future. I'm not worried about you, Soojin. I fully understand and support your decision." That night, Umma made this new dish for the first time, just for me. She said, "Let's celebrate this new chapter in your life." It's a delicious, easy meal that I continue to enjoy. Umma combines store-bought rotisserie chicken with shredded imitation crab and savory, earthy Korean seasonings, then wraps the mixture in a tender cooked cabbage leaf. I always make these rolls with all three dipping sauces that she originally served to me, so feel free to add the Honey-Mustard Sauce (page 36) and/or the Perilla Seed Sauce (page 37).

MAKES 8 rolls   TOTAL TIME 1 hour

    1 head green cabbage (907 grams)
   12 ounces (340 grams) finely shredded rotisserie chicken
    3 green onions (45 grams), chopped fine
    3 tablespoons toasted sesame oil
    4 teaspoons maesil cheong (plum extract syrup)
    4 teaspoons fish sauce
    4 teaspoons perilla seed powder
    4 teaspoons minced garlic
    1 teaspoon sugar
   5½ ounces (156 grams) imitation crab, lightly squeezed and pulled apart into fine strands
    1 recipe Gochujang-Mustard Sauce (page 37)

1 Using a small knife, carefully cut out and discard the conical core from the cabbage. Continue to carve out the remaining portions of the thick core as needed. Bring 6 cups water to a boil in a large, wide pot. Place the cabbage cored side down in the boiling water, and cook until the outer leaves are pliable, about 1 minute. (If the cabbage is too big to submerge fully, rotate the cabbage in the water until the leaves are pliable.) Using tongs, carefully remove the wilted outer leaves; set aside. Cover and repeat until all the leaves are wilted and separated from the head. Keep the water boiling.

2 Select 10 leaves that are roughly 8 inches in diameter, without any tears; set aside the remaining leaves to enjoy separately. (Only 8 leaves are needed for the filling, but working with 10 gives you a cushion in case of tearing.) Working in 2 batches, blanch the leaves by submerging them in the boiling water until softened but still maintaining some crunch, about 2 minutes. (If you prefer softer leaves, you can boil for longer, until it reaches your preference.) Using tongs, transfer the leaves to a colander to drain and cool.

RECIPE CONTINUES

3 Working with one leaf at a time, place it flat on a cutting board with the thicker side of the rib (the outer side of the leaf) facing up. Holding a knife parallel to the leaf, trim the thick rib to be level with the remaining leaf, being careful not to create any holes.

4 Toss the chicken, onions, oil, maesil cheong, fish sauce, perilla seed powder, garlic, and sugar in a bowl until well combined. Add the crab and toss gently to combine.

5 Place 1 cabbage leaf on a cutting board with the rib parallel to the board edge. Arrange ½ cup loosely packed filling in the leaf, leaving about 1 inch of the bottom and side edges free of filling. Fold the bottom of the leaf over the filling, then fold in the sides. Roll the leaf tightly around the filling. Repeat with the remaining leaves and remaining filling. Arrange the rolls seam side down on a serving platter. (The rolls can be wrapped tightly in plastic wrap and refrigerated for up to 24 hours.) Slice in half and serve with dipping sauce.

> ### Umma's Kitchen Wisdom
>
> *You can freeze the skin and leftover meat from the rotisserie chicken to use in our Jeongigui Tongdak Kalguksu (Rotisserie Chicken Knife-Cut Noodle Soup; page 304) or Jeongigui Tongdak Yachae Mussam Mari (Pickled Radish Chicken-Vegetable Wraps; page 311).*
>
> *For a quick banchan, I sometimes prepare just the rotisserie chicken mixture on its own, without the cabbage wraps.*
>
> *The leftover steamed cabbage can be refrigerated. Enjoy the leftover leaves as a simple wrap: Cut them in half if large, fill them with rice, and top them with a dab of Yangnyeom Gochujang (Seasoned Gochujang; page 34), then serve with banchan.*

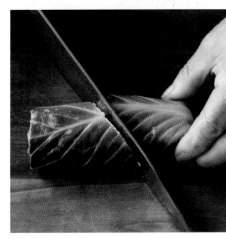

Top Place a blanched leaf flat on a cutting board with the thicker side of the rib facing up. Holding a knife parallel to the leaf, trim the thick rib to be level with the remaining leaf, being careful not to create any holes.

Middle Place a trimmed leaf on a cutting board with the rib parallel to the board edge. Arrange the filling in the leaf, leaving 1 inch of the bottom and side edges free of filling. Fold the edge of the leaf closest to you over the filling, then fold in the right and left sides.

Bottom Roll the leaf tightly around the filling. Slice in half before serving.

Honey-Garlic Chicken 허니갈릭치킨

SARAH 세라

In August 2014, two major snack food brands, Haitai from South Korea and Calbee from Japan, joined forces to create a new snack that quickly went viral and became a top-selling snack, dominating the Korean market that year. What these two companies created is a snack known as Honey Butter Chips. These chips became so popular that they sparked a trend known as the "honey-butter craze," making the chips nearly impossible to purchase, with resale prices online reaching triple the original price. As Korean Americans, we watched this phenomenon unfold from home on our TV screens, eagerly awaiting the arrival of these chips at our local Korean grocery stores. Ultimately, we just couldn't wait and asked our Korean relatives to pack some of these snacks in their luggage when they visited us. Since trying these chips, which did not disappoint one bit, my family has been obsessed with any food that combines honey and butter. These drumsticks, sweetened with honey, spiced with plenty of garlic, and finished with a dollop of butter, remind me so much of those chips. They're sweet and savory with a satisfying richness in every bite—just like the irresistible flavor of those honey butter chips (which are now available in the United States and have even been imitated by American snack brands).

SERVES 4 to 6   **TOTAL TIME** 1¼ hours, plus 2 hours refrigerating and marinating

   3 pounds (1.4 kilograms) chicken drumsticks, trimmed
2½ cups milk
 ¼ cup extra-virgin olive oil
   1 teaspoon fine salt, divided
   1 teaspoon black pepper, divided
 ¼ cup honey
   2 tablespoons soy sauce
   2 tablespoons distilled white vinegar
   2 tablespoons sugar
   6 tablespoons (87 grams) finely chopped garlic
2½ tablespoons salted butter

1 Rinse and drain the chicken, then transfer to a large bowl or container. Add the milk and toss to coat. Arrange the chicken in an even layer, making sure all the chicken is submerged in the milk. Cover and refrigerate for 1 hour.

2 Drain and thoroughly rinse the chicken until the water runs clear. Clean and dry the bowl. Using a sharp knife, make 4 to 6 slashes in each drumstick (each slash should reach the bone). Pat the chicken dry with paper towels and transfer to the bowl.

3 Add the oil, ½ teaspoon salt, and ½ teaspoon pepper and toss the chicken to coat. Cover and refrigerate for at least 1 hour or up to overnight.

4 Whisk the honey, soy sauce, vinegar, sugar, remaining ½ teaspoon salt, and remaining ½ teaspoon pepper together in a small bowl; set the sauce aside.

5 Toss the chicken again to coat in the oil that has settled in the bowl. Working with 1 drumstick at a time, stretch the skin to evenly cover the meat, then arrange skin side down in a 12-inch nonstick skillet. Drizzle any remaining oil left in the bowl over the chicken. Cook over medium-high heat, turning the chicken occasionally, until spotty golden brown, about 10 minutes.

6 Reduce the heat to medium, cover, and continue to cook, turning the chicken occasionally, until it registers at least 185 degrees, about 20 minutes.

7 Spoon the garlic into the spaces between the drumsticks where the oil has pooled. Cook, spreading the garlic into the skillet with the back of a spoon, until fragrant, about 30 seconds. Gently toss the chicken until evenly coated with the garlic. Add the sauce, stirring in any browned bits in the skillet. Increase the heat to medium-high and cook, continuously coating and basting the chicken in the sauce, until the sauce has thickened, about 2 minutes. Stir in the butter until the sauce has thickened into a glaze, about 30 seconds. Serve.

Umma's Kitchen Wisdom

I call for extra-virgin olive oil here, rather than neutral cooking oil, because its fruity, peppery flavor and richness complement the honey and butter perfectly.

Dakgogi Ganjang Jorim 닭고기간장조림

dahk-go-ghee gahn-jahng joh-rim

SARAH
세라

To make this sublime dish, simply toss tenderized chicken wings in a stir-together sauce and cook until they transform into a sweet and spicy delight. What takes the longest in this recipe—though it's completely hands-off—is the part where Umma soaks the chicken in milk and then rinses it. According to Umma, there are two reasons for this. First, the lactic acid and the calcium in the milk work in different ways to tenderize the chicken. Second, this method helps remove any gamy flavor or aroma. I asked Umma more about this method, speculating that it was outdated, and she explained that she uses this method for all bone-in meats (she submerges bone-in beef and pork in water). She reiterated that washed meat tastes different than unwashed meat, the latter being described in Korean cooking as unpleasant. I was still unconvinced and asked her one last time if it was necessary to add this step. In response, Umma made two batches of this braise—one where the chicken was soaked in milk and one where it was not soaked. I blind-tasted both versions and noticed that one version had a distinctive gamy flavor and aroma and the other version had no gaminess and was more tender. She reminded me that if she didn't have to add this step, she wouldn't. But after many years of cooking and learning from early rookie mistakes, she has learned what's necessary to make good food that satisfies. We enjoy this braise with rice and Chicken Mu (Chicken Radish; page 140).

Umma's Kitchen Wisdom

I love the convenience of buying pre-split chicken wings for this recipe (sometimes called party wings) and opt for smaller wings whenever possible.

SERVES 4 to 6
TOTAL TIME 1¼ hours, plus 1 hour soaking

    3 pounds (1.4 kilograms) chicken wings,
      cut at joints, wingtips discarded
 2½ cups milk

SAUCE
 4½ tablespoons (19 grams) sugar
 4½ tablespoons corn syrup
   ¼ cup soy sauce
    3 tablespoons water
    2 tablespoons mirin
    2 tablespoons minced garlic
    1 tablespoon distilled white vinegar
    1 tablespoon ketchup
    1 tablespoon toasted sesame oil
    1 teaspoon black pepper
    1 teaspoon grated fresh ginger

   ¼ cup neutral cooking oil
    3 ounces (85 grams) garlic cloves, peeled
    1 Fresno chile, stemmed, halved lengthwise,
      and sliced ¼ inch thick on bias
    1 large jalapeño chile (43 grams), stemmed, halved
      lengthwise, and sliced ¼ inch thick on bias
    3 green onions (45 grams), cut into 2-inch lengths
    1 tablespoon sesame seeds, toasted, plus extra
      for sprinkling

1 Rinse and drain the chicken, then transfer to a large bowl or container. Add the milk and toss to coat the chicken; make sure all the chicken is submerged in the milk. Cover and refrigerate for 1 hour.

2 FOR THE SAUCE Meanwhile, whisk all the sauce ingredients together in a small bowl; set aside.

3 Drain and thoroughly rinse the chicken until the water runs clear. Using a sharp knife, make 2 slashes on each side of each wing, making sure to penetrate beyond the skin and into the meat. Pat the chicken dry with paper towels.

4 Heat the oil in a 12-inch nonstick skillet over medium-high heat until shimmering. Add the chicken skin side down in a single layer and cook until golden brown, about 5 minutes per side. Add the garlic and continue to cook, stirring occasionally, until the chicken is nearly cooked through, about 10 minutes.

5 Add the sauce and cook, continuously tossing the chicken, until the sauce has thickened slightly, 5 to 7 minutes. Stir in the Fresno chile and jalapeño and cook until the sauce has thickened into a glaze that clings to the chicken, about 2 minutes. Remove the skillet from the heat and stir in the green onions and sesame seeds. Sprinkle with extra sesame seeds and serve.

Korean Fried Chicken
프라이드치킨

SARAH
세라

I never used to be a big fan of fried chicken. There wasn't anything in particular that I disliked about it, but I just never craved it or cared much for it. That all changed when I tried Korean fried chicken for the first time at Jin Mi Chicken, a bustling restaurant in Suwon, South Korea. There, they serve only two flavors: plain fried chicken and spicy glazed fried chicken. My uncle had ordered two large plates of each flavor for us. "Is this for the entire family?" I asked him. "No, this is just for you. Trust me, you'll finish the entire thing." I recall feeling a bit anxious as I faced Samchon's expectation that I would be able to finish two plates full of fried chicken; however, as I took my first bite, my concern gave way to amazement. This was the most delicious fried chicken I had tasted to date, and my memories will not let me forget it. The outside was perfectly crisp and seasoned with a blend of savory spices, complementing the soft and juicy chicken meat underneath. Before I knew it, I had two buckets in front of me filled with nothing but bones. Upon returning home to the United States, I struggled to find Korean fried chicken that matched the quality and taste I had experienced at Jin Mi Chicken. While many restaurants offer decent versions, nothing was as memorable as what I had eaten in Korea. That is, until Umma developed her own fried chicken recipe, inspired by my described memory. To me, Umma's fried chicken is not just "good enough"—it's exceptional. It brings me back to the amazement that I felt in Korea. Her fried chicken is a work of art—perfectly crispy, yet light and flavored with a harmonious blend of spices. Described by Umma as a "wave-patterned" crust (meant to resemble the waves of the ocean) and accomplished by "shocking" the battered chicken by tapping it against the bowl before frying it, the distinctive pattern is key to achieving the signature crisp and crunch. Having now shared this with friends, family, and fried chicken lovers in my life, I can say that Umma's fried chicken has been repeatedly hailed as some of the best.

CONTINUES

SERVES 4 to 6   TOTAL TIME 1¼ hours,
plus 3 hours soaking and seasoning

    3 pounds (1.4 kilograms) chicken wings, cut at joints,
        wingtips discarded
2½ cups milk
    2 teaspoons black pepper, divided
    1 teaspoon miwon matsogeum (MSG seasoning salt)
3½ cups (420 grams) Korean frying mix, divided
    5 tablespoons (50 grams) curry powder, divided
    1 tablespoon Dasida beef stock powder
    1 tablespoon garlic powder
    1 tablespoon onion powder
1½ cups cold water
2–3 quarts vegetable oil for frying

1 Rinse drain the chicken, then transfer it to a large bowl
or container. Add the milk and toss to coat. Arrange the
chicken in an even layer, making sure all the chicken is
submerged in the milk. Cover and refrigerate for 1 hour.

2 Drain and thoroughly rinse the chicken until the water
runs clear. Clean and dry the bowl. Using the tip of a sharp
paring knife, pierce each wing 3 to 5 times on each side
around the bone (the tip of the knife should puncture through
to the other side). Pat the chicken dry with paper towels and
transfer to the bowl.

3 Add 1 teaspoon pepper and the seasoning salt and toss
the chicken to coat. Cover and refrigerate for at least 2 hours
or overnight.

4 Set a wire rack in a rimmed baking sheet. Following
the manufacturer's instructions, heat the oil in an electric
fryer to 330 degrees. Whisk 1½ cups (180 grams) frying
mix, 3 tablespoons curry powder, the Dasida powder, garlic
powder, and onion powder together in a separate large bowl.
Gradually whisk in the cold water until the batter is just
combined (it's okay if small lumps remain; be careful not to
overmix). Add the chicken and toss to coat it in the batter.

5 Whisk the remaining 2 cups (240 grams) frying mix,
remaining 2 tablespoons curry powder, and remaining
1 teaspoon pepper together in a medium bowl. Working
with 1 piece at a time, use tongs to fully coat the chicken in
the batter once more. Lift the wing, allowing excess batter to
drip back into the bowl, and transfer it to the seasoned frying
mixture. Using your hands, toss the wing to coat it (do not
press the piece into the flour), then gently tap the wing against
the side of the bowl twice to "shock" it (this is what gives the
fried chicken its wave pattern). Carefully lower half of the
wing piece into the hot oil, hold for 3 seconds, then release
the piece completely into the oil. Repeat with 5 more wing
pieces. Cook, undisturbed, for about 2 minutes, then use the
tongs to release the wings from the base of the fryer basket.
Continue to cook, turning the wings occasionally, until
golden brown and crisp and the chicken registers at least
165 degrees, 5 to 7 minutes for wingettes and 7 to 10 minutes
for drumettes.

6 Using a slotted spoon, transfer the wings to the prepared
rack as they finish cooking. Return the oil to 330 degrees and
repeat with the remaining wings in batches. Serve.

Umma's Kitchen Wisdom

*I prefer to use Ottogi brand mild curry powder for this
recipe, but other mild curry powders work too.*

*I love the convenience of pre-split chicken wings and
opt for smaller wings whenever possible. I also cook the
wingettes and drumettes separately, since they have
different cooking times.*

*I use an electric deep fryer for my fried chicken, though
you can also use a large, wide pot or Dutch oven that
holds 6 quarts or more. Add the oil to the pot until it
measures about 2 inches deep and heat over medium-
high heat to 330 degrees. Adjust the heat as needed to
maintain the temperature.*

Yangnyeom Chicken
양념치킨

yahng-nyuhm chicken

MAKES enough sauce for 1 recipe
Korean Fried Chicken

- 7 tablespoons (119 grams) ketchup
- 7 tablespoons (105 grams) sriracha
- ⅓ cup water
- 5 tablespoons honey
- 3 tablespoons minced garlic
- 2 tablespoons sugar
- 2 tablespoons mirin
- 1 tablespoon soy sauce
- 1 tablespoon gochujang
- 1 tablespoon gochugaru
- 1 teaspoon Dasida beef stock powder

Whisk all of the ingredients together in a small saucepan. Bring to a simmer and cook, stirring occasionally, until thickened, about 4 minutes. Remove the pan from the heat and set aside while frying the chicken. Once all of the chicken wings have been fried, brush the sauce onto the wings. (You can also dip the wings individually into the sauce to coat them, but avoid tossing all the wings with the sauce at once, as this will break apart the delicate crunchy "wave" coating on the chicken.)

Yangnyeom Gejang 양념게장

yahng-nyuhm gae-jahng

SARAH
세라

Both of my parents grew up enjoying gejang (marinated raw crab). Surprisingly, crabs were abundant and widely accessible when they were young. Umma recalls how Halmeoni and her sister-in-law would buy them in bulk and each prepare a different variation of gejang: this spicy version, along with ganjang gejang (raw crabs marinated in soy sauce). They would then exchange these variations with each other, allowing each family to enjoy both styles of crab. According to Umma, making ganjang gejang is much trickier than making yangnyeom gejang and requires much more preparation. She fondly recalls how delicious Halmeoni's ganjang gejang was. It was so flavorful and memorable that extended family members have contacted both us and relatives in Korea asking for Halmeoni's recipe. Unfortunately, there is no record of it, but Umma has made it her ongoing project to replicate Halmeoni's ganjang gejang, chasing the flavors she remembers from her childhood. For me, it serves as a powerful reminder of the deep significance of family recipes. The true value of preserving them often becomes apparent only when it's too late. I encourage everyone to spend time with loved ones, especially elder cooks. Be patient as you learn how to create some of their dishes—and be sure to get exact measurements, even if they don't use measuring cups and spoons! Show gratitude for their guidance in passing down these recipes, and give them a big hug for helping to preserve a tradition that will live on with future generations. You'll thank yourself later when you taste the memories they've left behind. In the meantime, enjoy the bold flavors of this spicy, buttery, umami-rich yangnyeom gejang. When Appa tried this recipe, his first words from his very first bite were, "Wow, this reminds me of the old days."

SERVES 4   TOTAL TIME 45 minutes, plus 24 hours marinating

7 tablespoons (87 grams) sugar
6 tablespoons (42 grams) gochugaru
¼ cup (58 grams) minced garlic
¼ cup fish sauce
2 tablespoons soy sauce
2 tablespoons toasted sesame oil
2 tablespoons mirin
1 tablespoon maesil cheong (plum extract syrup)
1 tablespoon grated fresh ginger
1 tablespoon sesame seeds, toasted
18 ounces (510 grams) frozen half-cut swimming crabs, thawed
¼ yellow onion (71 grams), sliced ¼ inch thick, divided
1 large jalapeño chile (43 grams), stemmed and sliced ¼ inch thick on bias, divided
2 green onions, sliced thin, divided
1 Fresno chile, stemmed and sliced ¼ inch thick on bias, divided

1 Stir the sugar, gochugaru, garlic, fish sauce, soy sauce, oil, mirin, maesil cheong, ginger, and sesame seeds in a large bowl until combined; set aside.

2 Place the crabs in a colander. Rinse each crab thoroughly under running water, removing any dirt and loose shells. After all the crabs have been rinsed, give each one another quick rinse. Using kitchen shears, trim off the claw pincers and the flat pieces of each leg that do not contain meat. Remove any spikes on the claws and legs to make them safer and easier to eat. Add the crabs to the bowl with the sauce.

3 Set aside a small portion of the yellow onion, jalapeño, green onions, and Fresno chile (about ½ cup total) for garnishing. Add the remaining yellow onion, jalapeño, green onions, and Fresno chile to the bowl with the crabs. Using 2 wooden spoons, gently toss the crabs until fully coated, making sure that the sauce reaches the inside of the cut bodies, claws, and legs. Transfer the crabs and any additional sauce to a storage container and spread them into an even layer. Sprinkle with the reserved vegetables. Cover and refrigerate for 24 hours. Serve.

Umma's Kitchen Wisdom

This recipe contains raw seafood, which comes with inherent risks.

I prefer to purchase frozen half-cut crabs, as they come pre-shelled and pre-cut, making them convenient and easy to eat.

Thaw the crabs in the refrigerator for 24 hours. They don't need to be completely thawed before beginning.

This is messy to eat, so I wear food-handling gloves to gently squeeze the meat out with my hands, then delicately squeeze the shells between my teeth to extract every delicious morsel.

TURN TO SEE HOW TO TRIM SWIMMING CRABS →

Top Use kitchen shears to trim off the claw pincers of each crab half.

Middle Cut off the flat pieces of each leg that do not contain meat, including the swimmerets.

Bottom Cut off any remaining spikes on the claws or the legs.

Godeungeo Jorim 고등어조림

goh-deung-uh joh-rim

UMMA
엄마

When Sarah was a child, she made an interesting observation about this dish and asked me about it. She often watched adults enjoying this braised fish and wondered if it was particularly favored by older individuals for some reason. I replied that it's a comforting dish that ordinary people enjoy regardless of age or background.

SARAH
세라

Braised fish is a traditional dish enjoyed by Koreans from all walks of life. While we use mackerel in our version, other types of firm-fleshed fish such as trout, hairtail, cutlassfish, and Pacific saury can also be used. Regardless of the type of fish, the subtly spicy flavors and tender textures of this braise make it a staple dish in Korean households. I have always found this particular braise comforting but have come to appreciate it even more as I grow older. While I agree with Umma that it's universally popular among all age groups, I do think that with age and wisdom comes a greater appreciation for its satisfying flavor. I understand now why so many older adults enjoy it, since I savor it myself more and more with every year that goes by.

Umma's Kitchen Wisdom

This is a forgiving braise, so don't worry if your mackerel is a little over 1 pound. (Likewise, if you find 8- to 10-ounce mackerel, you can buy two.) You can ask the fishmonger at Korean grocery stores to prepare the mackerel for jorim (braises). They will remove the scales, clip the fins, gut the fish, and chop the fish into cylindrical pieces.

This dish is enjoyed with the bones in the final cooked fish. Simply remove the bones as you eat.

SERVES 4 to 6   TOTAL TIME 1¼ hours

- 1 (1-pound / 454-gram) whole mackerel, scaled, gutted, head removed, and tail and fins snipped off with scissors
- 3 tablespoons mirin, divided
- ¼ teaspoon fine salt
- ¼ teaspoon ground ginger
- ¼ cup (26 grams) gochugaru
- ¼ cup soy sauce
- 1 tablespoon doenjang (fermented soybean paste)
- 1½ tablespoons sugar
- 1 tablespoon fish sauce
- 1 teaspoon grated fresh ginger
- 1 tablespoon minced garlic
- 1 tablespoon maesil cheong (plum extract syrup)
- ½ teaspoon black pepper
- ½ yellow onion (142 grams), sliced ½ inch thick
- 1 Fresno chile, stemmed and sliced ¼ inch thick on bias, larger rounds halved lengthwise
- 1 jalapeño chile, stemmed and sliced ¼ inch thick on bias, larger rounds halved lengthwise
- 4 green onions (60 grams), white and light green parts halved lengthwise, cut into 1½-inch lengths
- 2½ cups water
- 12 ounces (340 grams) Korean radish, halved lengthwise, halves sliced into ½-inch-thick planks
- 1 russet potato (226 grams), peeled and sliced into ½-inch-thick rounds

RECIPE CONTINUES

1 Using a sharp knife, cut the mackerel crosswise into 4 pieces, leaving the piece closest to the tail slightly larger because it's thinner. Using the tip of a knife, butterfly each piece through the belly and spine. Open each piece, except for the piece that was closest to the head (we leave the 2 halves of that piece connected, since there is less meat on them), and use kitchen shears to cut the halves apart. Rinse the mackerel thoroughly under running water, then drain. Drizzle with 1 tablespoon mirin and sprinkle with the salt and ground ginger; set aside.

2 Whisk the gochugaru, soy sauce, doenjang, sugar, fish sauce, fresh ginger, garlic, maesil cheong, pepper, and remaining 2 tablespoons mirin together in a bowl. Set aside a small portion of the yellow onion, Fresno chile, jalapeño, and green onions (about ½ cup total).

3 Combine the water and 1 rounded tablespoon sauce in a large, wide pot. Arrange the radish evenly in the pot, cover, and bring to a boil. Reduce to a vigorous simmer, cover, and cook until the radish is nearly tender, about 7 minutes.

4 Arrange the potato in an even layer over the radish, followed by the mackerel, skin side up. Dollop the remaining sauce over the top (use some of the broth in the pot to help rinse the bowl and get all the sauce!) and gently press on the mackerel with the back of a spoon to dissolve the sauce into the broth. Add the remaining yellow onion, Fresno chile, jalapeño, and green onions and gently press on the vegetables to submerge them in the broth. Cover and bring to a boil, then reduce the heat to a vigorous simmer and cook until the potatoes are tender, about 11 minutes. Gently stir in the reserved vegetables, cover, and cook for 1 minute. Serve.

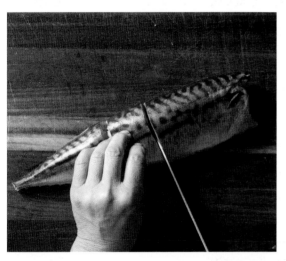

Top Use kitchen shears to cut off the tail and fins from the mackerel.

Middle Use a sharp knife to cut the fish crosswise into 4 pieces.

Bottom Butterfly each piece lengthwise through the belly and spine, then cut into 2 pieces using kitchen shears (don't cut apart the piece closest to the head).

PAN-FRIED SALTED AND DRIED CROAKER

Gulbi Gui 굴비구이

gool-bee goo-e

UMMA
엄마
When I was growing up, our family would enjoy eating grilled fish from time to time. I noticed that Halmeoni would only eat the heads of the fish, a pattern that struck me as odd when I was a child. One day, I asked her, "Umma, why do you only eat the heads of the fish and not the body?" She replied, "Because the heads are tastier." Years later, as an adult and an umma myself, I decided to follow Halmeoni's tradition and pan-fry fish with the heads still attached. Remembering her words from my childhood about the heads being tastier, I tried some myself, only to discover that there was barely any meat in the head! That's when I realized that Halmeoni didn't eat the heads because they were tastier; she did it because she wanted to give her family the meatiest parts—the bodies of the fish.

SARAH
세라
White fish simply pan-fried in a skillet until crispy and golden brown, gulbi gui is a staple protein often found on the tables of Korean households. "Gulbi" refers to yellow croaker or yellow corvina that has been salted and partially dried, a method of preservation that has been used for hundreds of years in Korea. They are typically tied with a rope (a plastic one in modern times) to keep them separated and then partially dried using the cold ocean breeze during the winter months. Then they're sprinkled with mounds of sea salt for seasoning and preservation. This process results in perfectly firm, seasoned fish that cooks up with tender meat and crispy skin that stays intact. This is one of the first dishes that I can remember enjoying as a child, and I still love it to this day.

SERVES 4   TOTAL TIME 30 minutes, plus 30 minutes salting

    4 (4- to 6-ounce / 113- to 170-gram) frozen gulbi, thawed, scaled, tail and fins snipped off with scissors
    ½ teaspoon miwon matsogeum (MSG seasoning salt)
    ⅓ cup (40 grams) Korean frying mix
    ¼ cup neutral cooking oil, divided

1 Working with 1 gulbi at a time, rinse the fish under cold running water. Grasp the head with 1 hand and grab the body, just behind the gills, with your other hand and twist to separate. Discard the head. (If the gulbi has not been previously gutted, you will need to use kitchen shears to cut along the base of the belly and remove the innards.) Rinse the gulbi once more and set aside on a large plate. Sprinkle the fish evenly with the seasoning salt, inside and out, and let sit for at least 30 minutes.

2 Spread the frying mix in a shallow dish. Turn the gulbi to moisten the skin with accumulated liquid on the plate. Working with 1 gulbi at a time, coat the fish in the frying mix, pressing to adhere. Gently shake off any excess and transfer to a separate plate.

3 Heat 2 tablespoons oil in a 12-inch nonstick skillet over medium-high heat until shimmering. Cook the gulbi until light golden brown on the first side, about 2 minutes. Flip the gulbi, drizzle the remaining 2 tablespoons oil around the edge of the skillet, and cook until light golden brown on the second side, about 2 minutes.

4 Reduce the heat to medium-low. Using tongs, hold the gulbi together so that they stand on their bellies. Cook until light golden brown, about 2 minutes. Continue to cook, turning the fish occasionally, until golden brown and the thickest part of the fish registers at least 160 degrees, 3 to 5 minutes. Serve.

Umma's Kitchen Wisdom

Gulbi (salted and semi-dried croaker or corvina) can be found in the freezer section of the Korean grocery store. They typically come gutted and are usually sold tied with ropes separating the fish. Thaw them in the refrigerator for 24 hours and remove the scales with a sharp knife before starting. Don't confuse gulbi for jogi (fresh croaker or corvina), which are available at the seafood counter.

While gulbi is salted, I've found that it's often not enough for my family's taste, so I always add more salt. I prefer using MSG seasoning salt, but regular salt works fine too.

I remove and discard the heads from the bodies of the fish because they don't contain much meat and can end up absorbing cooking oil if left intact.

SOUPS
AND
STEWS

Sundubu Gyerantang 순두부계란탕

soon-doo-boo gye-rahn-tahng

UMMA
엄마

I don't rely on many shortcuts in my cooking, but one modern convenience that I really make the most of is instant seafood broth tablets. For this flavorful, quick soup, instead of the traditional from-scratch anchovy broth, I use these broth tablets to make an easy seafood broth. These wondrous little coin-shaped pellets (see page 21 for more information) are packed with umami flavor. For this soup, I suggest using 4 tablets with 5 cups water to make the broth. This soup is great for busy families or individuals, since boiling the broth is the most time-consuming step.

SARAH
세라

This comforting dish is truly perfect for those days when you're feeling either rushed or lazy. It's incredibly flavorful and loaded with protein, and comes together in minutes. Initially, I was skeptical about using broth tablets, thinking nothing could beat the traditional anchovy broth. However, after my first sip of broth made with them, I asked Umma, "What is this amazing broth?" to which she replied, "It's from those broth tablets!" They are packed with umami-rich ingredients, including various fish and shellfish and vegetables such as radish, cabbage, celery, and carrots. They are truly one of the most convenient innovations in Korean cooking, in my opinion.

SERVES 4   TOTAL TIME 30 minutes

- 4 large eggs
- ¼ teaspoon fine salt
- ¼ teaspoon sugar
- 5 cups seafood broth
- 11 ounces (312 grams) extra-soft or silken tofu
- 1 tablespoon fish sauce
- 3 green onions (45 grams), sliced thin
- Black pepper
- Shredded roasted seaweed

1 Lightly beat the eggs, salt, and sugar in a bowl until combined. Set aside.

2 Bring the broth to a boil in a large, wide pot, then reduce the heat to a vigorous simmer. Break the tofu into 2-inch pieces with your fingers and add it the broth along with the fish sauce.

3 Return the broth to a vigorous simmer, then slowly pour the egg mixture into the pot in a spiral pattern. Let the eggs set, without stirring, for about 1 minute, as the broth comes back to a simmer. Mix gently to combine evenly and break up any large clumps of egg. Turn off the heat and gently stir in the onions. Serve immediately, topping individual servings with pepper and shredded seaweed.

Kimchi Jjigae 김치찌개

gim-chi jji-gae

SARAH
세라

To me, kimchi jjigae is the ultimate comfort meal that reminds me of home. For Umma, this is the dish she can always rely on, as kimchi is always stocked in our household. It is the dish she prepared to welcome my brother and me home after many months away during our college days, the dish she meticulously packed in zipper-lock plastic bags for my brother to freeze as he studied out of state for medical school, and the dish she served to our Korean relatives after their 13-hour flight to California. It's the epitome of comfort food, featuring a tangy flavor from the aged kimchi, richness stemming from the pork belly fat and butter, and savory depth from the addition of beef franks and Spam. This recipe will always hold a special place in my heart. For now, while I have Umma in my life, this stew carries the transformative and comforting flavors of kimchi that I grew up with—the flavors that I experienced when I was just 4 years old, mimicking Umma's squat and washing the discarded cabbage scraps, emulating her every move as she made kimchi in our small condominium backyard. However, I'm certain that its significance will deepen as I continue to age and eventually live a life without Umma by my side. While I dread that inevitable day, when the time comes, I know that this dish will have the power to transport me back to the cherished moments spent making kimchi with her, much like how Gosu Musaengchae (Seasoned Cilantro Radish Shreds; page 79) transports Umma back to the days with her own mother.

SERVES 4 to 6   TOTAL TIME 1 hour

- 12 ounces (340 grams) beef franks, cut ⅜ inch thick on bias
- 6 ounces (170 grams) Spam, sliced into ½-inch-thick planks
- 1½ tablespoons salted butter
- 8 ounces (227 grams) sliced skinless pork belly or pork cushion, ½ inch thick
- 1½ pounds (680 grams) well-fermented cabbage kimchi, plus 6 tablespoons kimchi juice
- 2½ teaspoons fish sauce
- 2½ teaspoons sugar, plus extra for seasoning
- 2 teaspoons Dasida beef stock powder

1 Bring 6 cups water to a boil in a large, wide pot. Add the beef franks and Spam and blanch for 1 minute. Drain well and rinse the pot. Set the beef franks aside.

2 Cook the Spam in the now-empty pot over medium heat until golden brown and crisp, 5 to 7 minutes per side. Transfer the Spam to a cutting board; once cool enough to handle, cut it into bite-size pieces.

3 Melt the butter in the now-empty pot over medium-high heat. Add the pork belly and cook until beginning to brown but some pink color still remains (don't cook it all the way through, or else it will overcook later), 1 to 2 minutes. Add the kimchi and cook, stirring occasionally, for 5 minutes. Stir in 3 cups water, the fish sauce, sugar, Dasida powder, and kimchi juice and bring to a boil. Reduce the heat to a simmer, cover, and cook until the kimchi has wilted and become translucent, 7 to 10 minutes. Stir in the Spam and beef franks and bring back to a boil. Reduce the heat to a simmer, cover, and cook for 5 minutes. Adjust the sweetness of the stew with extra sugar to taste. Serve.

Umma's Kitchen Wisdom

I prefer the flavor of well-fermented Mat Kimchi (Cut Napa Cabbage Kimchi; page 115). If you wish to use store-bought kimchi instead, see page 20 for tips on how to purchase it.

When measuring out the kimchi, simply pick it up with tongs with the juices clinging to it.

Blanching the Spam and beef franks is entirely optional, but I like to do this to remove some of their salt and fat.

Spam Gochujang Jjigae 스팸고추장찌개

spam goh-choo-jahng jji-gae

UMMA 엄마

While this stew looks similar to Kimchi Jjigae (Kimchi Stew; page 216), it offers a completely different flavor profile. By uniting the much-loved ingredients of Spam, gochujang, and doenjang with hearty potatoes and squash, it creates a nostalgic and comforting dish. Like so many ingredients used in Korean cooking, Spam has a rich history rooted in humble origins. Koreans were introduced to Spam during the Korean War in the 1950s, when these shelf-stable cans served as a portable protein source for American soldiers. Since nutritious food, especially meat, was very scarce during that time, Spam (and other processed meats) slowly made their way into the mouths of Koreans through connections, smuggling, and salvaging from the trash cans used by soldiers. Even after Korea recovered from the war and entered a time of economic growth and development, Spam remained a treat with symbolic significance.

SARAH 세라

Fun fact: According to the BBC, Korea is the largest consumer of Spam outside the United States. While I understand that Spam isn't perceived as the most appealing food in the United States, the perception is quite the opposite in Korea, where Spam is used in a variety of dishes, such as Kimchi Jjigae (Kimchi Stew; page 216) and Gyeran Mari (Rolled Omelet; page 104). During Chuseok (Autumn Harvest Festival) and Seollal (Lunar New Year), many Koreans purchase elegantly packed gift sets of Spam to give to colleagues, friends, and family. My brother and I used to jump in excitement whenever Umma bought Spam, which was a special treat that appeared only when it was on sale. (It's not that cheap!) So why do Koreans love Spam so much? Simply put, it's delicious and pairs wonderfully with a bowl of rice even when it's just pan-fried. As kids, my brother and I would often enjoy that pairing with a side of ketchup.

SERVES 4   TOTAL TIME 1¼ hours

6 ounces (170 grams) Spam

14 ounces (397 grams) russet potatoes, peeled, halved lengthwise, and sliced crosswise ½ inch thick

½ yellow onion (142 grams), sliced ½ inch thick

7 teaspoons gochujang

2 tablespoons gochugaru

1 tablespoon doenjang (fermented soybean paste)

1 tablespoon sugar

7 ounces aehobak (Korean summer squash; 198 grams), trimmed and cut into rough 1-inch pieces

5 green onions (75 grams), sliced ¾ inch thick

1 large jalapeño chile (43 grams), stemmed, halved lengthwise, and sliced ¼ inch thick

1½ teaspoons minced garlic

1½ teaspoons fish sauce

1 Bring 6 cups water to a boil in a large, wide pot. Add the Spam and blanch for 1 minute. Transfer the Spam to a cutting board. Discard the blanching liquid and rinse the pot.

2 Once cool enough to handle, cut the Spam into rough ½-inch-thick slices, then use the flat side of the knife to gently mash each slice into bite-size pieces. (The goal is to make very irregular small pieces, but don't go so far as to turn the Spam into a paste.) Add 3 cups water, the Spam, potatoes, yellow onion, gochujang, gochugaru, doenjang, and sugar to the pot and stir until well combined and the pastes have dissolved. Bring to a boil. Reduce to a simmer, cover, and cook until the potatoes are tender and easily pierced with a chopstick, about 20 minutes.

3 Stir in the aehobak, green onions, jalapeño, garlic, and fish sauce and bring to a boil. Reduce the heat to a simmer, cover, and cook until the aehobak is tender, about 12 minutes. Serve.

Umma's Kitchen Wisdom

This is a very flexible recipe that is easily adjustable to what you have on hand. For example, if you don't have squash, simply increase the amount of potatoes to make up for it. And vice versa if you don't have potatoes on hand. If you can't find aehobak (see page 31), substitute zucchini or gray squash.

Blanching the Spam is optional, but I like to take this step to remove some of its salt and fat.

GROUND SOYBEAN STEW

Kongbiji Jjigae 콩비지찌개

kohng-bi-ji jji-gae

UMMA
엄마

This is a nostalgic stew for me. I can distinctly remember Halmeoni reaching her hand down through the blended soybean mixture to feel its texture between her fingertips and decipher whether or not she needed to blend more. When I tried re-creating her kongbiji jjigae recipe later in my life, I wasn't able to get it right. The first time, I blended the soybeans just about completely, and the second time, I blended the soybeans too coarsely. Neither method made a good stew in the end. Then I recalled the memories I had of Halmeoni reaching her hand down to feel the soybeans, and everything clicked for me. There's a certain texture that you need to achieve with the soybeans to perfect this stew—and it requires you to feel the texture with your fingertips.

SARAH
세라

According to Umma, Halmeoni used to make two versions of this stew: one with well-fermented kimchi and one with plain cabbage instead. Umma finds herself drawn to this plain cabbage version because it's a bit more convenient in that it doesn't require the use of well-fermented kimchi. Plus, we love the creamy off-white color this stew offers from the blended soybeans and plain cabbage. In texture, this is sort of like a porridge, but thinner in consistency, with a pleasing grainy texture from the ground soybeans. (If you feel them with your fingertips, as Umma does, they should feel slightly grainy yet tender, similar to how cooked lentils break down but don't become completely smooth.) You can enjoy this stew by itself, topped with the complementary sauce full of green onions and ground sesame seeds, or you can add some rice and kimchi for a full meal. Any pork is fine to use, but we prefer less fatty cuts such as shoulder here. You can use an equal amount of napa cabbage leaves in place of the young napa cabbage; cut the leaves into rough 3-inch pieces before blanching them.

SERVES 4 to 6
TOTAL TIME 1¼ hours, plus 6 hours soaking

SAUCE

2 tablespoons soy sauce
1 tablespoon maesil cheong (plum extract syrup)
1 tablespoon toasted sesame oil
2 tablespoons sesame seeds, toasted and coarsely ground (see page 38)
3 green onions (45 grams), sliced thin

STEW

6 ounces (170 grams) dried soybeans, picked over and rinsed
1 tablespoon saeujeot (salted shrimp)
7 ounces (198 grams) young napa cabbage, leaves separated, trimmed, and thoroughly washed
1 tablespoon toasted sesame oil
1 tablespoon neutral cooking oil
1 tablespoon minced garlic
6 ounces (170 grams) boneless pork shoulder (cushion or butt), trimmed of excess fat and coarsely chopped
6 ounces (170 grams) Korean radish, sliced ¼ inch thick, slices cut into ¾-inch pieces
1 tablespoon fish sauce
2 teaspoons Dasida beef stock powder
½ teaspoon miwon matsogeum (MSG seasoning salt; optional)

1 FOR THE SAUCE Combine all the ingredients in a bowl; set aside for serving.

2 FOR THE STEW Submerge the soybeans in water and let soak at room temperature for at least 6 hours or overnight. Drain and rinse the soybeans, discarding any loose soybean skins.

RECIPE CONTINUES

3 Process 3 cups water and the saeujeot in a blender until smooth, about 15 seconds. Add the soybeans and process until finely ground, about 30 seconds; set aside. (The mixture will have the texture of thin porridge; do not process until completely smooth.)

4 Bring 1 quart water to a boil in a large pot. Add the cabbage and submerge completely. Blanch until the cabbage is bright green but still has some bite, about 30 seconds. Using tongs, quickly transfer the cabbage to a large bowl of cold water and gently run your hands through the cabbage to cool it down. Drain the cabbage and repeat covering with cold water until the cabbage has completely cooled. Working in batches, squeeze the cabbage to remove excess water, then chop into rough ½-inch pieces; set aside.

5 Cook the sesame oil, neutral oil, and garlic in the now-empty pot over medium heat until fragrant, about 2 minutes. Add the pork and cook until beginning to brown but some pink color still remains, about 2 minutes. Stir in the cabbage and radish and cook for 2 minutes. Increase the heat to medium-high, add the fish sauce, and cook, stirring frequently, until the radish turns opaque, about 1 minute.

6 Stir in 1 quart water and bring to a boil. Reduce the heat to medium, cover, and cook for 5 minutes. Stir in the soybean mixture, bring to a vigorous simmer, and cook, stirring continuously, until the foam subsides and the stew thickens slightly, about 15 minutes. (During the first few minutes of simmering, the stew may quickly boil over if the heat is too high or you pause from stirring it. If this begins to happen, immediately remove the pot from the heat and allow the foam to settle before continuing to simmer and stir.) Stir in the Dasida powder and seasoning salt, if using, and cook for 2 minutes. Serve with the sauce for spooning on top.

Umma's Kitchen Wisdom

The trickiest part of this recipe is blending the soybeans. You don't want them too coarse, but they should not be completely smooth. The soybeans should still maintain 10 to 15 percent of their texture.

You must constantly stir the stew as it cooks, otherwise the soybeans will fall to the bottom and scorch.

The MSG seasoning salt is optional but will give this stew a restaurant-quality taste!

Sogogi Muguk 소고기뭇국

soh-goh-gi moo-ggook

UMMA
엄마

When planning my weekly meals, the first thing I think about is what ingredients are in season. Then I'll create a mental list of the dishes I want to make and head to the Korean grocery store with that in mind. Once I'm there, I prioritize the dishes where most of their ingredients are on sale, as well as the seasonal ingredients that I want my family to enjoy before they're gone. For example, in the winter season, Korean radish is an ingredient I'll prioritize whether it's on sale or not. It's nutrient-rich, adds a sweet flavor to dishes, and cooks up pleasantly tender. Then, I'll let the grocery store guide my decision on which dishes to make with this radish, depending on what items are on sale or recently stocked. One week, I had already prepared my Sogogi Yuksu (Beef Broth and Shredded Beef; page 250), so all I needed was some Korean radish to make this soup. Our Korean grocery store had recently restocked Korean radishes from Jeju Island, so I bought a few since they aren't always available and are very high quality. A lot of other home cooks were stocking up on those too. Then I came home and made this traditional soup that Appa really loves.

SARAH
세라

This classic Korean-household staple is beloved by people of all ages, from young children to the elderly. And with good reason—it can be made fairly quickly and offers a comforting, soothing meal with tender radishes and beef in a flavorful broth. Umma elevates her sogogi muguk with a homemade aromatic broth. This broth does all the heavy lifting, bringing the umami flavors to the forefront and infusing the onion and radish with rich depth, thus enhancing the overall umami profile of the soup. Since first using this beef broth as the base in this recipe, she hasn't reverted to the more common method of preparing it, which actually uses a quicker beef broth. Once you try her approach, you'll understand why!

SERVES 4 to 6   TOTAL TIME 1 hour

- 9 cups beef broth plus 2 cups (170 grams) shredded beef from Sogogi Yuksu (Beef Broth and Shredded Beef; page 250)
- 2 pounds (907 grams) Korean radish, sliced into 1-inch-thick rounds, rounds cut into 1-inch strips and sliced crosswise ¼ inch thick
- ½ yellow onion (142 grams), sliced ½ inch thick
- 3 tablespoons fish sauce
- 1 teaspoon fine salt
- 2 tablespoons minced garlic
- 4 green onions (60 grams), sliced thin
  Black pepper

1 Bring the broth to a boil in a covered large, wide pot. Stir in the radish, yellow onion, fish sauce, and salt and return to a boil. Reduce the heat to a simmer and cook until the radish is tender, about 15 minutes.

2 Stir in the shredded beef and garlic and return to a boil. Turn off the heat and stir in the green onions. Sprinkle individual portions with black pepper before serving.

Baechu Mu Doenjangguk 배추무된장국

bae-choo moo doen-jahng-gook

UMMA
엄마

When I was in elementary school, there was a bustling street that led to the gimjang farmers' market, with stacks of napa cabbage and radish that seemed as high as our home's roof to me. Farmers would stand atop the vegetables, loudly asking how many cabbages and radishes customers wanted and tossing down quantities to the farmers below, who then handed them off to customers. It was a busy and lively street during this season as we all prepared to make gimjang kimchi (see page 123) and other dishes with these winter vegetables. As the farmers handled the cabbages, the outer leaves would naturally fall off and pile up on the street, to the point where you couldn't see the street. Everyone in my family—my own halmeoni and harabeoji, your halmeoni and harabeoji, and my sisters and I—would go to these markets and pick up those outer leaves to bring home. It wasn't something we felt embarrassed about. It was very normal to do this. Aigoo (goodness), we really lived through that.

SARAH
세라

This soup originated as a simple dish made with minimal ingredients, primarily cabbage and radish, during times of scarcity. Through multiple generations and increasing wealth, it evolved to include protein such as beef or tofu. Despite these additions, the essence of this humble soup remains unchanged, featuring savory umami flavors from the anchovy broth and doenjang, the earthy-funky fermented soybean paste. The vegetables and beef are ultra-tender, creating an inviting dish that feels like a warm, welcoming hug.

Umma's Kitchen Wisdom

Soft or firm tofu is a great alternative to the shredded beef in this soup. Simply use half a block and slice it into rectangles that are 2 inches long, 1¼ inches wide, and ¼ inch thick.

SERVES 6 to 8   TOTAL TIME 1¾ hours

- 12 cups water
- 1 ounce (28 grams) dried large anchovies, gutted and heads removed (see page 43)
- ½ ounce (14 grams) dashima (dried kelp), rinsed and broken into 2-inch pieces
- ½ ounce (14 grams) dried large-eyed herring
- 2½ tablespoons red miso paste
- 2½ tablespoons doenjang (fermented soybean paste)
- 1½ pounds (680 grams) napa cabbage, cut into rough 3-inch pieces
- 12 ounces (340 grams) Korean radish, sliced into ½-inch-thick rounds, rounds halved and cut crosswise into ½-inch-wide pieces
- ½ yellow onion (142 grams), sliced ½ inch thick
- 2 tablespoons fish sauce
- 1⅔ cups (142 grams) beef from Sogogi Yuksu (Beef Broth and Shredded Beef; page 250)
- 1 tablespoon minced garlic
- 4 green onions (60 grams), sliced thin

1 Bring the water, anchovies, dashima, and herring to a boil in a large, wide pot. Reduce the heat to a vigorous simmer and cook for 15 minutes. Using a slotted spoon, discard the solids.

2 Add the miso paste, doenjang, cabbage, radish, yellow onion, and fish sauce and stir until well combined and the pastes have dissolved. Bring to a boil. Reduce the heat to a vigorous simmer, cover, and cook, stirring occasionally, until the vegetables are softened and turn opaque, about 50 minutes.

3 Add the shredded beef and garlic, and return to a vigorous simmer. Turn off the heat and stir in the green onions. Serve.

Kitchen Conversation

SARAH So the farmers didn't mind you all taking the outer leaves? And what did you do with them? Make kimchi?

UMMA *No, they didn't mind. I mean, people would eventually step all over them anyway. At that point, they were considered trash. And, no, we didn't make kimchi—it's not possible to make pogi kimchi with detached outer leaves. Halmeoni would make a simple version of this soup with those outer leaves. And she would serve it to the family and neighbors when she hosted gimjang at our home.*

SARAH How does that change make you feel—from having to scour for cabbage to now being able to buy it so easily at the grocery store? And having the luxury to enrich this soup with additional ingredients like beef?

UMMA *It's truly a privilege to be able to easily buy food at the grocery store and have the option to not finish your food if you're too full. I remember Harabeoji would drink this soup until there was no trace of it, along with every grain of rice. It was considered too wasteful for even a single grain of rice to go uneaten.*

Taking Rice to the Mill for Tteok

UMMA *Tteok manduguk [rice cake soup with dumplings] is something we Koreans traditionally eat every New Year.*

SARAH But we have it every Sunday too.

UMMA *These days, yes. Nowadays, we can easily buy tteok off the shelves at Korean grocery stores to have anytime, in addition to making the rice cake soup to enjoy on the first of January. But in the past in Korea, obtaining the tteok for tteokguk (rice cake soup) was primarily reserved for Seollal (Lunar New Year) celebrations. We looked forward to Seollal because it was the one day we got to enjoy tteokguk. I remember walking with Halmeoni to the tteok mill with a lot of excitement and anticipation. The day before our trip to the mill, Halmeoni would wash our white rice and submerge it in water. The next morning, she would wake up early to drain the bloated rice and transfer it into a large aluminum bowl. Then she would carry it to the mill atop her head.*

SARAH Why did she rest it on her head?

UMMA *It was a large, heavy bowl filled with soaked rice, and that was the easiest way to transport the rice on foot. I think the amount of rice was greater than the 15-pound bags of rice we buy for ourselves today. It was a lot—but I could be mistaken since I was just a little kid at that time! She would put a cotton cloth directly on her head to create a soft barrier between her head and the bowl.*

SARAH Was the bowl as big as the one we use to make kimchi?

UMMA *No, it was much larger than that—a size you can't imagine. She used it to transport all kinds of things across the city, not just food. Once we arrived at the mill, there would be a very long line of customers, all eager to make tteokguk. When we reached the front of the line, we would give the mill workers our prepared rice. They would immediately grind it and mix it with water, then steam it. Once steamed, a rice dough would form and be placed into a machine that would extrude cylindrical tteok known as garaetteok. They would make the garaetteok extra long, about 3 feet in length, as length symbolized longevity.*

SARAH I can imagine how exciting that must have felt to watch, all the while knowing that a special dish was going to be prepared very soon with that tteok. It must have been akin to the excitement I felt watching Krispy Kreme doughnuts being made fresh as a child, though in your case, this was a special outing and treat that only happened once a year.

UMMA *Exactly, it was a limited-time treat for us. From there, Halmeoni would let the garaetteok sit out, uncovered, for a day or two to firm up so that it could be easily sliced to make tteokguk. Sometimes, if the garatteok sat out for too long and got too firm, Korean parents would use that to spank their kids. [We both laugh at the thought of being spanked with a long, cylindrical rice cake stick.] Think about it. We lived during a time when white rice was scarce, but every year, all of us Koreans were committed to making tteokguk, no matter the circumstances, to celebrate Seollal. It's quite an experience to recall and share.*

Left: Umma, age 8, with her two older sisters, likely on a rare trip to Seoul in 1967. Above: Halmeoni on the right (year unknown).

Right: Umma, age 7 months, being carried on her oldest sister's back in 1959.

TURN FOR UMMA'S TTEOK MANDUGUK RECIPE →

RICE CAKE SOUP WITH DUMPLINGS

Tteok Manduguk 떡만둣국

ttuhk mahn-doo-ggook

SARAH
세라

Tteok (rice cakes) come in many shapes and sizes and are a common ingredient in Korean cooking. These pleasingly chewy cakes are probably best known in the United States as the main ingredient in tteokbokki, a very popular Korean street food consisting of cylinder-shaped rice cakes simmered in gochujang sauce. Mainstream grocery stores such as Trader Joe's have caused them to take off in popularity. Today they seem like a humble ingredient, but when Umma was growing up in Korea, they were not. In this soup, we use tteokguk tteok, thinly sliced rice cake ovals. The soup comes together quickly and delivers a comforting, hearty array of flavors originating from the aromatic beef broth Umma has prepared beforehand and frozen for convenience. There are also so many appealing textures in this soup. In addition to the tteok, there's shredded beef and tender dumplings, plus toppings of delicate egg ribbons and shredded roasted seaweed. When paired with some freshly made kimchi, a bowl of this soup will evoke memories of home for everyone present.

Umma's Kitchen Wisdom

Look for tteokguk tteok (sliced rice cake ovals, often labeled as 떡국떡) at Korean grocery stores. See page 22 for buying tips.

If you buy frozen rice cakes, thaw them in the refrigerator for 24 hours or on the counter for about 1 hour before soaking.

You can also make Tteokbokki (Spicy Rice Cakes; page 319) using these sliced cakes, rather than the cylindrical rice cakes that are more commonly used.

I use frozen vegetable and pork mandu in this soup, but feel free to use any flavor of prepared frozen mandu that you like, including beef, shrimp, or kimchi. Our Mandu (Dumplings; page 157) are a little too big to use here.

SERVES 4
TOTAL TIME 30 minutes, plus 1 hour soaking

- 2 pounds (907 grams) tteokguk tteok (sliced rice cakes)
- 8 cups beef broth plus 2 cups (170 grams) shredded beef from Sogogi Yuksu (Beef Broth and Shredded Beef; page 250), divided
- 8 frozen mandu (dumplings)
- 2 tablespoons minced garlic
- 2½ tablespoons fish sauce
- 1 teaspoon fine salt
- 4 green onions (60 grams), sliced thin
- 1 recipe Egg Ribbons (page 42)
  Shredded seasoned roasted seaweed
  Black pepper

1 Submerge the tteok in 6 cups water in a large bowl for 1 hour.

2 Bring the beef broth to a boil in a large, wide pot. Drain the tteok and stir the slices into the broth, separating any pieces that stick together. Stir in the beef, mandu, garlic, fish sauce, and salt; cover; and return to a boil.

3 Uncover, reduce the heat to a vigorous simmer, and cook for 2 minutes. Turn off the heat and stir in the green onions. Top individual portions with egg ribbons, shredded seaweed, and black pepper before serving.

BEEF RIB SOUP

Galbitang 갈비탕

gahl-bi-tahng

SARAH
세라

Umma is pretty open-minded, but sometimes we misconstrue what we're saying to each other. Assumptions get made that lead to conflict and hurt feelings. Communication is of course key to clearing the air, but sometimes communication can be difficult in our bilingual world. Both my parents speak only Korean, and unfortunately I am not fluent. There have been many times when I wished for deep, complex conversations with my parents, times when I wanted to read them my college essays that I felt so proud of, and times when I wanted to clear up any misunderstandings and conflicts we had. There was an instance when Umma and I got into a big argument, and frustrated by the fact that we couldn't fully articulate what we wanted to say due to the language barrier, we decided to step away from the situation and cool off. She had cooked some galbitang that night, and when we sat down to eat, we took a sip of the broth. A cathartic sigh of relief and laughter escaped us, breaking the silent, awkward tension between us. Immediately, we talked again and resolved our conflict with a clearer mind. Lesson learned: This soup heals conflicts. Though the preparation time is long, this is actually an easy dish—it is essentially just making a very flavorful broth.

Umma's Kitchen Wisdom

The best ribs to buy for this soup are 5 to 7 inches long with ½ inch to 1 inch meat on them. I prefer back ribs because they have a richer flavor than short ribs (which are commonly used).

You must submerge the meat in water for 30 minutes to get rid of the myoglobin, and the meat must be thoroughly rinsed after blanching, or else the broth won't taste right.

The Dasida powder is optional, but I highly recommend it for restaurant-quality flavor.

Don't be shy—get in there and eat the ribs with your hands!

SERVES 4 to 6   TOTAL TIME 3½ hours, plus 3 hours soaking and brining

2 ounces (57 grams) dangmyeon (Korean glass noodles)
1 tablespoon sugar
4 pounds (1.8 kilograms) beef back ribs, trimmed and membranes removed (see page 43)
1½ pounds (680 grams) Korean radish, cut into rough 1-inch pieces
½ yellow onion (142 grams), chopped coarse
1 daepa (jumbo green onion; 130 grams), roots left intact, chopped coarse
4 ounces (115 grams) garlic cloves, peeled
⅓ cup (40 grams) coarsely chopped peeled ginger
¼ cup fish sauce
1 tablespoon black peppercorns
3 bay leaves
¼ cup soy sauce
4 teaspoons distilled white vinegar
Wasabi paste
1½ teaspoons fine salt
1½ teaspoons Dasida beef stock powder (optional)
12 green onions (180 grams), sliced thin
1 recipe Egg Ribbons (page 42)
Black pepper

1 Cover the dangmyeon with 1 inch water in a large bowl and let soak at room temperature for at least 3 hours or overnight. Drain the noodles and rinse thoroughly; set aside.

2 Meanwhile, dissolve the sugar in 3 quarts water in a large stockpot. Add the ribs and refrigerate for 30 minutes. Transfer the ribs to a bowl and discard the water; clean the pot thoroughly.

3 Bring 4 quarts water to a boil in the pot. Add the ribs, return to a boil, and blanch for 10 minutes. Transfer the ribs to a colander and discard the water; rinse the pot thoroughly.

Under cold running water, rinse each rib thoroughly, removing coagulated particles at the end of each rib (we like to use a designated toothbrush to scrub them). After all the ribs have been rinsed, give each rib another quick rinse; set aside.

4 Bring 6½ quarts water to a boil in the pot. Add the ribs, radish, yellow onion, daepa, garlic, ginger, fish sauce, peppercorns, and bay leaves. Return to a boil and cook until the ribs are tender and the meat is nearly falling off the bone, 1 to 1½ hours.

5 Using tongs, transfer the ribs to a bowl. Strain the broth through a fine-mesh strainer into a separate large bowl; discard the solids. Transfer 12 cups broth to the now-empty pot; save the remaining broth for another use. Let the broth settle for 5 minutes, then skim off excess fat from the surface

using a wide, shallow spoon or ladle. (The ribs and broth can be refrigerated separately for up to 4 days or frozen for up to 1 month; if frozen, thaw completely before proceeding.)

6 Combine the soy sauce and vinegar in a medium bowl, then divide among individual small serving bowls; place a small portion of wasabi paste in each bowl. Bring the broth to a boil over medium-high heat. Stir in the salt and Dasida powder, if using, and season with extra salt to taste.

7 Add the ribs to the broth and bring to a brief boil to warm through. Divide the ribs among serving bowls and top with the dangmyeon and green onions. Ladle the broth over the ribs, then top with the egg ribbons and sprinkle with pepper to taste. Serve with the soy-vinegar sauce for dipping.

A Green Composition Notebook and a Trip to Busan

SARAH
세라

Every morning, after Umma completes her long list of chores and morning routine, you can find her resting on our living room floor in front of the TV. As she sips on her trademark 900-calorie drink that she fills with essential nutrients, Umma takes her first break of the day to catch up on her Korean dramas and documentaries. She has some quirky habits when it comes to watching her shows. Vexingly for me, Umma will insist upon watching the ending of her favorite Korean dramas first, instead of watching the episodes in chronological order. We often tease Umma about this, because we'll catch her clicking away with the remote control, fast-forwarding through every episode just to know what happens at the end of the story. When that happens, we know that the drama must be exceptionally good and binge-worthy!

Aside from Korean dramas, Umma also enjoys watching documentaries about everyday life in Korea. She says it's a way for her to stay connected with her roots and her homeland. She particularly enjoys shows that visit and promote humble, yet popular, restaurants throughout Korea, many of which showcase novel cooking techniques demonstrated by each restaurant's owner or chef. I'll often see Umma writing down the names of these restaurants and locations in her green composition notebook.

Watching Umma whimsically yet methodically jot down these restaurants into a list that grew over time was both endearing and disheartening as the years passed. For my family, traveling was never a simple privilege or activity that we could enjoy recreationally, as my parents worked tirelessly as small business owners and first-generation immigrants to America. Umma never missed a day at the restaurant she was running, and Appa, a general contractor painting homes, takes advantage of nearly every day to get his job done. So as Umma continued to build her list, I wistfully dreamed of visiting each restaurant with her, though I couldn't help but wonder whether this was all just a pipe dream.

One place Umma always wanted to visit was Jagalchi Market, which, along with Gukje Market, is the largest fish market in South Korea and a lively traditional marketplace, located in the heart of Busan. Whenever the documentaries we watched with Umma took us on tours through these bustling markets, Umma would gasp and express her craving for all the seafood from Busan. One thing Umma craved in particular was the eomuk (fish cakes) sold by the street vendors. Eomuk (also known as odeng) is made by processing and frying fish, flour, and seasonings together. As a street food, it is simmered in a savory broth and sold on skewers, to be dipped in a seasoned soy sauce. It's a widely popular snack on cold days and nights, especially in Busan.

Fast-forward to 2023, when Umma and I had a serendip-itous opportunity to visit Busan (see page 154 for more on that). We woke up to a crisp fall morning—perfect weather for eomuk! Within our first 12 hours in this seafood haven, we spotted an eomuk street cart. Without hesitation, Umma, who is in her mid-60s mind you, took off running toward the cart with a childlike excitement. I didn't know she still had that kind of vigor in her!

"Jeogi, jeogi!" (Over there!), Umma exclaimed, pointing eagerly at the very thing she had dreamed of eating for many years. When I caught up to her at the cart, Umma showed me how to enjoy the eomuk, pierced through with a wooden skewer and dipped in soy sauce, while we happily sipped on the savory broth that the vendor handed to us in plastic cups. As Umma and I looked at one another and savored each bite in front of that street cart, we fell into laughter in appreciation of this simple and blissful moment we had dreamed of enjoying together.

FISH CAKE SOUP

Eomukguk 어묵국

uh-mook-ggook

SARAH
세라

Eomuk (fish cakes) are a classic Korean street food; vendors simmer these fried cakes made of ground white fish and seasonings in a savory broth and serve them up on skewers with a soy dipping sauce. Eomukguk encapsulates the same flavors and essence of this street food favorite of Umma's, with the tender, seasoned fish cakes simmering in a savory, umami-rich broth. Look for fish cake circles for this soup (or fun shapes such as stars or hearts!). Umma enhances the signature umami quality of this soup by adding bonito flakes to the broth. These flakes are rich in amino acids, which help create deep flavor. As an homage to the street food version of eomuk, Umma serves this soup with a dipping sauce on the side, inviting us to pick out the fish cakes, dip them, and reconnect with the flavors of home.

SERVES 4 to 6   TOTAL TIME 1¼ hours

¼ ounce (7 grams) bonito flakes
1 ounce (28 grams) dried large anchovies, gutted and heads removed (see page 43)
½ ounce (14 grams) dashima (dried kelp), rinsed and broken into 2-inch pieces
½ ounce (14 grams) dried large-eyed herring
1 pound (454 grams) Korean radish, quartered lengthwise and sliced crosswise ¼ inch thick
½ yellow onion (142 grams), sliced ½ inch thick
2½ tablespoons fish sauce
½ teaspoon fine salt
10 ounces (283 grams) frozen fish cake pieces, thawed
2 tablespoons minced garlic
4 green onions (60 grams), sliced thin
3 tablespoons soy sauce
1 tablespoon distilled white vinegar
Wasabi paste
Black pepper

1 Place the bonito flakes in a seasoning strainer or cheesecloth bundle. Add 10 cups water, the anchovies, dashima, and herring to a large, wide pot. Submerge the strainer in the pot, cover, and bring to a boil. Reduce the heat to a vigorous simmer and cook for 15 minutes. Remove the strainer and press on the bonito flakes to extract as much liquid as possible; discard the bonito flakes. Using a slotted spoon, discard the remaining solids.

2 Stir the radish, yellow onion, fish sauce, and salt into the broth. Cover and bring to a boil. Reduce the heat to a vigorous simmer and cook until the radish is tender, about 15 minutes.

3 Meanwhile, submerge the fish cake pieces in hot tap water, let soak for 1 minute, then drain. Repeat soaking and draining the cakes. Stir the fish cakes and garlic into the soup, return to a vigorous simmer, and cook until heated through, about 2 minutes. Turn off the heat and stir in the green onions.

4 Combine the soy sauce and vinegar in a bowl, then divide the sauce among individual small bowls; place a small portion of wasabi in each bowl for each person to mix into the sauce to their liking. Sprinkle individual portions of the soup with pepper before serving with the dipping sauce.

Umma's Kitchen Wisdom

If you have leftovers, separate the fish cakes from the broth before storing them in order to prevent the fish cakes from soaking up the broth and becoming bloated. To reheat, simply return the fish cakes to the broth and reheat together.

SEAWEED SOUP

Miyeokguk 미역국

mi-yuhk-ggook

SARAH
세라
When I was growing up, there was one dish my family could count on to be served on our birthdays. It wasn't cake or any kind of dessert unless requested; it was miyeokguk, a traditional seaweed soup that symbolizes the celebration of life and honors the mothers who brought us into it. Though this soup is consumed regularly in Korean households, we greet it with open arms every birthday. We enjoyed it upon waking up, alongside a bowl of warm rice and kimchi, before indulging in one of Imobu's luscious cakes (see page 329) in the evening. We grew to love this tradition and this soup more with every birthday celebration. This soup is also commonly served to women after childbirth to aid in postpartum recovery due to its plentiful health benefits. Umma always told me that if I ever became a mother myself, she would make this soup for me after I gave birth. And she advised me that if she were unable to do so or was no longer around, I should be sure I had found a partner who would make this soup for me without hesitation, as she would. Umma takes a distinctly different approach to the common method for this soup (sautéing the miyeok—dried seaweed—and beef and then adding water to create a broth). She uses a separately made beef broth as the base and continuously sautés the miyeok in this broth, adding the broth in batches to tenderize the seaweed and extract as much umami flavor as possible. The result is an incredibly rich, deeply flavored soup where the seaweed's complex flavors are brought to the forefront.

SERVES 4 to 6   TOTAL TIME 1¼ hours,
plus 30 minutes soaking

   1 ounce (28 grams) miyeok (dried seaweed) strips
   1 tablespoon toasted sesame oil
   2 tablespoons fish sauce, divided
 2¼ teaspoons Dasida beef stock powder, divided
   1 tablespoon minced garlic
 10 cups broth, divided, plus 3 cups (255 grams) shredded beef from Sogogi Yuksu (Beef Broth and Shredded Beef; page 250)
   ½ teaspoon fine salt

1 Submerge the miyeok in 2 quarts water in a large, wide pot and let soak for about 30 minutes to rehydrate. Drain and rinse the miyeok in a colander, gently pressing to extract the excess water.

2 Untangle the miyeok and arrange in a single straight mound on the cutting board. Cut the miyeok crosswise into 2-inch lengths, then rotate each section and cut crosswise 2 or 3 times to achieve rough 2-inch pieces.

3 Toss the miyeok with the sesame oil in the now-empty pot. Stir in 1 tablespoon fish sauce, 1 teaspoon Dasida powder, and the garlic until well combined. Add ½ cup beef broth and cook over medium-high heat, stirring constantly, until most of the liquid has been absorbed, 5 to 7 minutes. Stir in an additional ½ cup beef broth and cook, stirring constantly, until most of the liquid has been absorbed, 5 to 7 minutes.

4 Stir in the remaining 1 tablespoon fish sauce, 1 teaspoon Dasida powder, and 6 cups broth and bring to a boil. Reduce the heat to a simmer, cover, and cook for 25 minutes.

5 Stir in the remaining 3 cups broth, remaining ¼ teaspoon Dasida powder, salt, and shredded beef and bring to a boil, using a wide, shallow spoon to skim off any fat that accumulates on the surface of the soup. Reduce the heat to a simmer, cover, and cook for 10 minutes, occasionally skimming additional fat that rises to the surface. Serve.

Umma's Kitchen Wisdom

Miyeok (a type of dried kelp, also called sea mustard or wakame) is sold as either large sheets or cut strips. Make sure to buy the cut strips for this soup, since the sheets require a different preparation.

Don't take any shortcuts when preparing and cooking the miyeok. These steps are all essential to tenderize it and extract its umami flavors.

Kongnamulguk 콩나물국

kohng-nah-mool-gook

SARAH
세라

South Korea definitely has a culture of social drinking, whether with friends, family, coworkers, or clients. So it's to be expected that there would also be some popular "hangover foods." This is considered one of the best hangover soups in Korean cuisine, and after having learned how to make it alongside Umma, I can understand why. Aside from the medicinal aspects of the untrimmed soybean sprouts, this traditional Korean soup is light yet comforting, and savory with a sweet crunchiness from the soybean sprouts—making it an ideal homey dish to enjoy anytime, not just after a long night on the town. The Fresno chile is optional, but we like the color and the fruity warmth it adds to this soup.

Umma's Kitchen Wisdom

Be sure to thoroughly wash the soybean sprouts to remove excess skins before cooking.

The soybean sprouts should retain their crunch, so be careful not to overcook them. This can be prevented by not putting the lid back on the pot once the soup is done cooking.

If you have any leftovers, refrigerate the rest and enjoy it cold, especially in warmer seasons.

SERVES 6 to 8   TOTAL TIME 1 hour

 10 cups water
  1 ounce (28 grams) dried large anchovies, gutted and heads removed (see page 43)
 ½ ounce (14 grams) dashima (dried kelp), rinsed and broken into 2-inch pieces
 ½ ounce (14 grams) dried large-eyed herring
 12 ounce (340 grams) soybean sprouts
 10 ounces (283 grams) soft or firm tofu, cut into ¾-inch cubes
 ½ yellow onion (142 grams), sliced ½ inch thick
 2½ tablespoons fish sauce
  1 teaspoon fine salt
  1 tablespoon minced garlic
  3 green onions (45 grams), sliced thin
 ½ Fresno chile, sliced thin crosswise (optional)
    Gochugaru

1 Bring the water, anchovies, dashima, and herring to a boil in a large, wide pot. Reduce the heat to a vigorous simmer and cook for 15 minutes. Using a slotted spoon, discard the solids.

2 Stir in the soybean sprouts, tofu, yellow onion, fish sauce, and salt; cover; and bring a boil. Reduce the heat to a simmer and cook for 10 minutes. Stir in the garlic and cook for about 30 seconds (just to take the raw edge off the garlic).

3 Remove from the heat and stir in the green onions and Fresno chile, if using (don't put the cover back on the pot). Serve, passing gochugaru separately at the table for seasoning.

Kitchen Conversation

UMMA *Don't remove the stringy root ends of the soybean sprouts.*

SARAH Why not? Some people take them off when making this soup.

UMMA *This soup is known to cure hangovers. Soybean sprouts have a lot of asparagine, and most of it is said to come from these root ends. Asparagine helps support liver function, assisting with recovery after alcohol consumption.*

SARAH So why do some Koreans remove them?

UMMA *The benefits haven't always been widely known. Also, there are aesthetic reasons, since keeping the stringy ends on can make certain dishes look a little "messy." I don't get rid of them because the health benefits outweigh any minor aesthetic concerns.*

SARAH But won't you feel their stringiness in your mouth when you eat this soup?

UMMA *Nope. Let me show you how to make this soup and you'll see.*

SPICY SOFT TOFU STEW

Sundubu Jjigae 순두부찌개

soon-doo-boo jji-gae

UMMA
엄마
Sundubu jjigae holds a nostalgic significance for Koreans from many walks of life—it's a nurturing meal to enjoy with family, friends, and colleagues after a long day of work or following a church service, or to feed students taking a break from studying for exams. The humble yet spicy piping-hot broth, combined with a variety of seafood (oysters, shrimp, and/or clams), meat (pork or beef), soft tofu, vegetables, and an egg stirred in at the end of cooking, makes it a truly comforting and satisfying dish. I use seafood broth tablets to make the broth here, using 2 tablets with 1½ cups water.

SARAH
세라
My brother and I always knew when Appa arrived home from work. Our ears would perk up like puppies when we heard his rumbling white cargo van, with ladders strapped on top, parking nearby. Once we confirmed that the noise was Appa's work van, we would run straight to the garage door and eagerly wait to greet him. When he opened the door with his empty cooler in hand, we would welcome him by saying, "Danyeoosyeosseoyo!" (dah-nyuh-oh-ssyuh-ssuh-yoh; a welcome back greeting to an older person) and Umma would kindly take his cooler away to wash. I always felt excited for Appa's return in the evening because it made our home feel complete. He occasionally brought used toys from clients' homes when their children no longer wanted them, so my eyes would instinctively look at his hand that didn't hold the cooler, checking for any toys he might have. Immediately after settling in, Appa would take a long, hot shower to rinse off his day's work. Afterward, we would sometimes go to Kaju Soft Tofu, and later BCD Tofu House, a neighborhood Korean restaurant renowned for its hot, bubbling sundubu jjigae. Umma and Appa always paired this stew with LA Galbi (Korean BBQ Short Ribs; page 162). These were the only two dishes we ordered, and I can remember the overwhelming sense of joy in simply being together and sharing these meals as a family. After filling our stomachs, my brother and I would doze off in our car seats, returning home with the soft-spoken voices of Umma and Appa in the front.

SERVES 4   TOTAL TIME 50 minutes

1½ teaspoons fine salt, divided
4 ounces (113 grams) frozen shucked oysters, thawed
4 ounces (113 grams) ground pork
¼ cup (71 grams) chopped yellow onion
4 green onions (60 grams), chopped, divided
2 tablespoons toasted sesame oil
2 tablespoons gochugaru
1 tablespoon oyster sauce
1½ cups seafood broth
2 teaspoons Dasida beef stock powder (optional)
22 ounces (624 grams) extra-soft or silken tofu
4 shell-on jumbo shrimp (head-on if possible; 1 to 1½ ounces each)
½ aehobak (Korean summer squash; 113 grams), trimmed, halved lengthwise, and sliced crosswise ¼ inch thick
1 tablespoon minced garlic
1 large egg
1 jalapeño chile, stemmed and chopped fine
¼ teaspoon black pepper

1 Dissolve 1 teaspoon salt in 1 quart water in a large bowl. Add the oysters and thoroughly mix to rinse. Drain the oysters and rinse them again in fresh unsalted water; drain thoroughly.

2 Add the pork, yellow onion, three-quarters of the green onions, and the sesame oil to a large, wide pot. Cook over medium-high heat, breaking up the meat with a wooden spoon, until the pork begins to brown but some pink color still remains, 4 to 5 minutes. Reduce the heat to medium and stir in the gochugaru until evenly distributed.

3 Stir in the oyster sauce until combined. Stir in the broth; Dasida powder, if using; and remaining ½ teaspoon salt; cover and bring to a boil. Break the tofu into 2-inch pieces with your fingers and add it to the broth. Stir in the shrimp, aehobak, and oysters, gently breaking up the tofu into

rough 1½-inch pieces (it's normal if some bits of tofu crumble into the broth). Cover, return to a boil, and cook until the shrimp are opaque throughout, about 5 minutes.

4 Stir in the garlic and cook for about 30 seconds. Working quickly, crack the egg into the center of the pot, then top with the jalapeño, pepper, and remaining green onions. Serve immediately, breaking up the egg upon serving.

Umma's Kitchen Wisdom

I love the convenience of frozen oysters, but you can also use fresh shucked oysters.

If you can't find aehobak (see page 31), use zucchini or grey squash.

For a milder stew, use 1 tablespoon gochugaru and ½ jalapeño.

Bring the whole pot to the table so that each person can ladle some out for themselves into a smaller bowl and enjoy it with their rice.

PUMPKIN PORRIDGE

Hobakjuk 호박죽

hoh-bahk-jook

SARAH
세라

Hobakjuk is a traditional porridge that's often characterized as a nourishing, healing dish that people of all ages enjoy. It's slightly sweetened to bring out the nutty flavors of kabocha squash, the flavor of which is often described as a blend of sweet potato and pumpkin (it's sometimes called Japanese pumpkin). Hobakjuk is commonly served during the colder months, as well as at weddings and memorial ceremonies. It's my favorite way to welcome the fall season. (I'll take pumpkin porridge over a pumpkin spice latte any day.) Whenever I have visited Korea, I've made sure to visit a particular street food vendor located in Seoul, in Gwangjang Market, one of Korea's largest and oldest traditional markets. It's home to some widely known vendors that have been featured on television and in documentaries. Among the many vendors and wide variety of foods, there is one particular stall I always return to when I have the chance. This stall specializes in just two items: hobakjuk and patjuk (savory red bean porridge). The welcoming woman who runs it serves some of the best-tasting porridges I've ever had. I'll sit down and savor both types of porridge and often purchase more to take with me and enjoy during the rest of my trip. When I most recently took Umma to this market and she saw me ordering more of these porridges to go, right after we had enjoyed some, she realized how much I love traditional Korean foods. Though I enjoy Korean fusion dishes as much as anyone, nothing ever beats the comforting, familial taste of dishes made by those closest to our grandmothers.

SERVES 4 to 6   TOTAL TIME 1 hour,
plus 30 minutes soaking

¼ cup (52 grams) short- or medium-grain white rice
1 kabocha squash (907 grams) halved lengthwise
    and seeded
5 tablespoons (64 grams) sugar, plus extra for seasoning
1 teaspoon fine salt, plus extra for seasoning
    Toasted pumpkin seeds
    Chopped dried jujube or jujube "flowers"
    Ground cinnamon

1 Add the rice to a medium bowl and cover by 1 inch with water. Using your hands, gently swish the rice to release excess starch. Carefully pour off the water, leaving the rice in the bowl. Repeat about 3 times, until the water runs almost clear. Cover the rice with water and let sit for at least 30 minutes or up to 12 hours. Drain and set aside.

2 Cut each squash half into 2- to 3-inch wedges. Add about 1 inch water to a large, wide pot, then place a collapsible steamer basket in the pot (the water should reach just below the base of the steamer basket). Cover and bring the water to a boil. Arrange the squash evenly in the steamer basket and cook, covered, until tender, about 15 minutes.

3 Transfer the squash to a large plate and let sit until it's cool enough to touch. Transfer any remaining steaming liquid to a 4-cup liquid measuring cup and add water as needed to equal 3 cups. Using a vegetable peeler or paring knife, remove the squash skin and green flesh just below the skin (the squash pieces should be completely orange). Transfer the squash to a blender with the steaming liquid and process until smooth, about 30 seconds, scraping down the sides of the blender jar as needed. Transfer the mixture to the now-empty pot.

4 Add the rice and 1½ cups water to the now-empty blender and pulse to clean the squash puree from the sides of the blender jar and coarsely grind the rice, 2 or 3 pulses; transfer to the pot. Bring the squash mixture to a boil, stirring and scraping the bottom of the pot frequently to prevent scorching. Reduce to a simmer and cook until the rice is tender and the porridge has thickened slightly, 18 to 20 minutes. At the last minute of cooking, stir in the sugar and salt.

5 Turn off the heat. Using the back of a spoon, press any clumps of rice against the side of the pot to separate them. Adjust the consistency with extra hot water as needed and season with extra sugar and salt to taste. Sprinkle individual portions with pumpkin seeds, jujube, and cinnamon and serve.

Making a Jujube "Flower"

After pitting the jujube (see page 38), unravel any folded edges and then use a rolling pin to flatten the fruit. Tightly roll up the flattened jujube lengthwise.

Slice the rolled jujube crosswise ⅛ inch thick to reveal the flower pattern. The end pieces won't be pretty, so discard (or eat) them.

Danpatjuk 단팥죽

dahn-paht-jook

<table>
<tr><td>SARAH
세라</td><td>Like Hobakjuk (Pumpkin Porridge; page 244), patjuk is a traditional dish that has been passed down through generations and has become increasingly popular again in recent years. It is</td></tr>
</table>

particularly enjoyed during the winter months for its comforting, hearty flavors. There are actually two versions of this porridge: a sweetened version and a savory version. Because the red beans impart a subtly sweet nuttiness of their own, we enjoy the sweetened version, called danpatjuk. The porridge often includes rice cakes, rice, or noodles for added texture. Umma likes to add freshly made rice cake balls to her danpatjuk because that's how Halmeoni often used to prepare this dish. These are easy and fun to make using glutinous rice flour (also called sweet rice flour) and add a really nice chew. This velvety porridge can be served as either a filling meal or, in smaller portions, an anytime sweet snack.

Umma's Kitchen Wisdom

Make sure you use adzuki beans (sometimes labeled as red mung beans). Other types of red beans won't work in this recipe.

It's important to parcook the beans and then rinse them before cooking them in the porridge; this reduces their natural bitterness.

This is a very versatile porridge that can be adjusted to one's taste. If you prefer a savory version, add half the amount of sugar called for in step 6 and adjust the flavor with salt to your liking.

SERVES 4 to 6
TOTAL TIME 1¾ hours, plus 8 hours soaking

- 2 cups (400 grams) dried adzuki beans
- ¾ cup plus 2 tablespoons (136 grams) glutinous rice flour
- 6 tablespoons (57 grams) potato starch
- ½ cup (99 grams) plus ½ teaspoon sugar, divided, plus extra for seasoning
- 2 tablespoons plus ¾ teaspoon fine salt, divided, plus extra for seasoning
- 8–10 tablespoons boiling water

1 Soak the beans in 1 quart water in a large bowl or container for at least 8 hours or overnight. Carefully pour off the water, leaving the beans in the bowl. Repeat covering the beans with water and pouring it off about 3 times, until the water runs almost clear. Drain the beans and set aside.

2 Whisk the rice flour, potato starch, ½ teaspoon sugar, and ¼ teaspoon salt together in a medium bowl. Using a wooden spoon or spatula, stir in 8 tablespoons boiling water, 1 tablespoon at a time. Continue to stir in up to an additional 2 tablespoons boiling water, 1 teaspoon at a time, until a rough dough begins to form and no dry flour remains. Using your hands, knead the dough in the bowl until a cohesive ball forms. (The dough will be tacky, with the texture of Play-Doh.) Cover the bowl with plastic wrap and let rest for 10 minutes.

3 Bring 6 cups water to a boil in a large, wide pot. Fill a large bowl with 1 quart cold water. Pinch off and roll the dough into 1-teaspoon balls (about 6 grams each) and transfer the balls to a lightly floured large platter or baking sheet. Add the balls to the boiling water and cook, stirring occasionally, until the balls begin to float, about 3 minutes. Using a slotted spoon, transfer the balls to the prepared bowl of cold water; set aside. Discard the cooking water.

RECIPE CONTINUES

4 Bring 2 quarts water, the beans, and 2 tablespoons salt to a boil in the now-empty pot. Reduce the heat to a vigorous simmer, cover, and cook for 10 minutes. Drain and rinse the beans thoroughly in a colander.

5 Set a colander over a large bowl. Bring 2 quarts water and the beans to a boil in the now-empty pot. Reduce the heat to a vigorous simmer, cover, and cook until the beans are extremely tender and easily breakable, about 12 minutes. Drain the beans in the prepared colander. Measure out and reserve 1½ cups cooked beans and 5 cups cooking liquid separately; discard the remaining cooking liquid.

6 Process the remaining beans and the reserved cooking liquid in a blender until smooth, about 30 seconds, scraping down the sides of the blender jar as needed. Add the bean mixture to the now-empty pot. Drain the rice balls and add them to the pot along with the reserved beans, remaining ½ cup sugar, and remaining ½ teaspoon salt. Bring to a boil, stirring frequently to prevent scorching. Reduce to a simmer and cook until the porridge thickens slightly, 5 to 8 minutes. Adjust the consistency with hot water as needed and season with extra sugar and salt to taste. Serve.

Kitchen Conversation

UMMA *Halmeoni would prepare this red bean porridge for the family every Dongji [the winter solstice day] growing up. Consuming this porridge on this day was believed to ward off evil spirits and bring good fortune to the household.*

SARAH I've heard that some Koreans would splatter this porridge onto the walls of their home or their gate to drive away those evil spirits. Did your family do that too?

UMMA *[laughing] We barely got by with the food we had! There was never enough to have extra for splattering. Halmeoni's porridge wasn't the sweet version, known as danpatjuk; it was the savory version simply called patjuk. Her porridge was a little thinner than mine, and she would add either rice cake balls or, on some occasions, kalguksu [knife-cut noodles].*

SARAH Noodles seem like a strange addition to this porridge. Did you like that?

UMMA *Yes, Halmeoni added noodles to her porridge, but she would also include rice cakes or rice on different occasions. Personally, I wasn't too keen on patjuk and didn't eat it often. If it had been danpatjuk, I might have enjoyed it more as a child.*

SARAH Which one do you prefer now, as an adult? We had the savory version in Korea at Gwangjang Market, and I enjoy that one a lot!

UMMA *I would enjoy Halmeoni's patjuk now, but mainly for its nostalgic taste. I think I prefer danpatjuk, if I have to be completely honest [giggling]. I remember that patjuk from Gwangjang Market. You've got the taste buds of an old person and appreciate the true flavor of red beans.*

SARAH This sweet version is really good too, though. I like both equally. I wish I could have tried Halmeoni's. I think I would have loved it.

Top left Stir the boiling water into the rice flour mixture, 1 tablespoon at a time, until a rough dough begins to form.

Top right Knead the dough with your hands until a smooth, cohesive dough ball forms.

Bottom Pinch off 1 teaspoon at a time and roll the dough into little balls. Place the rice cake balls on a lightly floured baking sheet.

BEEF BROTH AND SHREDDED BEEF

Sogogi Yuksu 소고기육수

soh-goh-gi yook-ssoo

SARAH
세라

Homemade beef broth plays an essential role in taking soups from good to outstanding. Although Umma is known to sometimes take shortcuts when making seafood broth, she has found shortcut methods for beef broth to be unsatisfying. This recipe uses a method Umma learned from Halmeoni, where boneless beef and aromatic vegetables are boiled together for an hour. When Umma first used this broth, she was amazed by the way it transformed the flavors of her soups. She uses this broth as the base for many of her staple soup recipes, along with the cooked beef. Given the minimal additional seasoning required in soup recipes that use this broth, it proves to be well worth the time and effort invested. Umma essentially likes to "meal-prep" this broth—once she finishes making it, she uses some of it for that evening's meal, then cools down the remainder and ladles it into zipper-lock freezer bags. Then she seals each bag, covers each with a paper towel (this prevents them from sticking to each other as they freeze), and freezes them for future use. As for the beef, she shreds it with her hands while it's still warm and freezes it in a zipper-lock freezer bag. This way, Umma has broth and meat readily available for a variety of soup dishes.

Umma's Kitchen Wisdom

You might wonder why you need to pat the beef dry before adding it to the broth. This is a common Korean technique to reduce the myoglobin flavor.

I prefer not to skim the fat from the broth, but rather skim it away as needed in the particular recipe that the broth is used in.

I like to store the shredded meat in a zipper-lock bag in the freezer, spread into a thin, flat layer. This makes it easy to break off the desired amount I need when adding it to soups.

MAKES 12 cups broth and 3 cups shredded beef
TOTAL TIME 2 hours

    4 quarts water
    1 pound (454 grams) beef flank steak or brisket, quartered and patted dry
   12 ounces (340 grams) Korean radish, cut into rough 1½-inch pieces
    1 daepa (jumbo green onion; 130 grams), untrimmed, chopped coarse
  ½ yellow onion (142 grams), halved
 1½ tablespoons coarsely chopped fresh ginger
 1½ teaspoons black peppercorns
    2 bay leaves

1 Bring the water to a boil in a large stockpot. Add the beef, radish, daepa, onion, ginger, peppercorns, and bay leaves to the pot and return to a boil. Reduce the heat to a vigorous simmer, cover, and cook for 10 minutes. Reduce the heat to a simmer and continue to cook, covered, until the meat is tender, about 50 minutes.

2 Transfer the beef to a cutting board, let it cool enough to touch, then shred the beef with your hands into strands about 2 inches long and a little less than ½ inch thick.

3 Set a fine-mesh strainer in a large bowl or container. Using tongs or a slotted spoon, discard any large solids from the broth. Pour the broth through the prepared strainer; discard any remaining solids. (The cooled broth and shredded beef can be refrigerated separately for up 3 days or frozen for up to 1 month.)

Clockwise from top left: Sogogi Muguk
(Beef and Radish Soup; page 225),
Miyeokguk (Seaweed Soup; page 238), and
Baechu Mu Doenjangguk (Soybean Paste
Soup with Cabbage and Radish; page 226)

RICE AND
NOODLES

Gimbap and a Purple Lunch Pail

SARAH
세라

I've always taken pride in the food Umma makes because the amount of work and love that goes into her dishes is unparalleled. For example, dishes such as Japchae (Stir-Fried Glass Noodles; page 295) and Gimbap (Seaweed Rice Rolls; page 257) demand attention to detail for each and every ingredient—from seasoning and cooking eggs to sautéing each vegetable separately to rolling the gim or cooking the noodles.

This labor of love was always evident to me growing up. When I was in third grade, I wanted to bring Umma's gimbap to school for lunch and share it with my classmates. After all, for us Koreans, sharing and enjoying food with our friends and family is a significant part of our culture. It's a way for us to connect with others and build relationships. Plus, Umma's gimbap is unmatched, and I don't say that lightly!

Without question, Umma woke up bright and early to prepare this labor-intensive food, and she packed enough for me and my select classmates. I went to school proudly clutching the handle of my purple lunch pail, determined not to lose it. I recall constantly glancing at the classroom's clock, eagerly awaiting the 11:45 bell, which was when we ate lunch.

When it was finally time, I ran to grab my purple lunch pail and hurried to the lunch tables, eager to show off the gimbap to my classmates. I remember holding the container of gimbap as if offering these rolls was a once-in-a-lifetime opportunity for my classmates to witness and be a part of.

I opened the container and proudly looked at the pieces, marveling at the vibrant colors of the meticulously seasoned and layered vegetables that Umma had prepared. I even brought chopsticks for others to make sure everyone could enjoy the full experience of eating Korean food. As I picked up a piece, smiling from ear to ear, a classmate exclaimed, "Ew, why are you eating that? That looks so disgusting." The entire lunch table fell silent. I looked at the gimbap, feeling the heat of embarrassment flush my face red. Then, knowing I couldn't look at the gimbap any longer, I summoned the courage to meet my classmates' eyes. I noticed everyone was looking at the gimbap and then at me, silently agreeing with the classmate's remark.

I ate the gimbap in stubborn silence, but with a growing sense of shame. I went home gripping my purple lunch pail, not in excitement, but rather feeling bewilderment, pain, and anger. The Sarah who had taken such pride in her Korean culture now felt defeated and isolated.

Clockwise from top: A special day at the San Diego Zoo. Sarah, age 9, third grade. Sarah's brother, Kevin, giving her a kiss with Umma by her side.

When I arrived home, Umma asked me how the gimbap was. I told her it was good, and that all my classmates liked it. I lied because I didn't want to hurt her feelings and because I felt ashamed, embarrassed, and confused. Ashamed that I had brought this food to school. Embarrassed by how disgusting Korean food was to others. Confused about my own identity.

Later that night, I told Umma: "Umma, please don't pack me gimbap again. Can you please pack me a sandwich instead?"

From then on, for nearly 10 years, my interest in sharing Korean culture went dormant. I was certainly not ashamed of the culture I grew up with, but I had subconsciously come to terms with the idea that maybe Korean culture wasn't mainstream enough to be accepted in America. I thought, perhaps Americans just like American things. So, I kept my love for Korean food, music, and entertainment within the confines of my home.

I was reunited with my roots a decade later when I visited Korea for the first time as an adult. After devouring bulgogi nearly every day, I returned home with a renewed sense of identity. It was a memorable experience that caused me to reflect on this period of my life during which I had sequestered myself away from Korean culture.

Fast-forward to the present day: My Korean friends who have kids tell me that their kids happily pack gimbap to take to school for lunch and come home asking, "What Korean food can we pack next?"

TURN FOR UMMA'S GIMBAP RECIPE →

Gimbap 김밥

gim-bahp

UMMA 엄마

Growing up, I enjoyed gimbap during my school's annual field trip, a tradition for which Halmeoni would wake up early to pack rolls of freshly made gimbap, Chilsung cider, Samlip cream bread, and hard-boiled eggs. This was a typical picnic combo meal that students packed for these field trips. We would also pack extra food to give to our teachers. It was the one and only day when I got to indulge to my heart's content, and I would usually come home with a very full but happy stomach.

SARAH 세라

"So it's Korean sushi, right?" is a question we often get asked. And Umma's response is always the same, with a hint of confusion: No, it's gimbap. And sushi is sushi. Why would gimbap be called Korean sushi? I can understand why this question is asked, though. Gimbap and sushi share the commonality of being a seaweed wrap filled with rice, but from there they diverge. It's sort of like saying ravioli are Italy's dumplings—both consist of a dough with a variety of fillings, but then the comparison stops. As pastry writer Joy Cho wrote on the Institute of Culinary Education's Diced blog, "Growing up in a Korean household, there were good meals and really good meals. And then there were the meals that sparked a specific kind of joy because it felt special even though it was just another Tuesday evening." Gimbap sparks joy. Just as it was for Umma, gimbap remains a special treat that we enjoy on casual occasions, such as when everyone is in town or when we go camping together as a family. Umma's gimbap is extra special to me for two reasons. First, I have yet to perfect my gimbap to Umma's level. My rolls so far don't achieve the tightly packed, colorfully coherent aesthetic presentation of Umma's. But I think I'll eventually reach her skill level, and I eagerly await that day. Second, I have yet to find any gimbap better than Umma's. With its ideal rice-to-vegetables ratio and Umma's additions of seasoned vinegar to the rice and avocado to the roll, it's simply unbeatable: satisfying, buttery, and harmonious. Her gimbap embodies the essence of "made with Umma's love."

Umma's Kitchen Wisdom

Make sure to buy dried seaweed sheets designated for gimbap (gimbapgim, usually labeled as 김밥김) or nori sheets designated for sushi. This type of seaweed will not rip as you roll.

Danmuji is also sold pre-cut in strips for gimbap and can be used here as well.

So that everything is as fresh as possible, I suggest preparing the fillings while the rice cooks and setting up your "gimbap station" with all the ingredients lined up so you'll be ready to roll when the rice is cooked.

It's best to add the sushi seasoning and sesame oil to the rice when it is still warm from cooking, just before assembling the gimbap. I prefer Mizkan Sushi Seasoning, but other brands of seasoned rice vinegar also work.

I prefer to wrap my bamboo mat with plastic wrap before rolling gimbap. Otherwise, rice becomes lodged in the crevices of the mat, making it harder to clean and shortening its lifespan.

When cutting the roll, use a sharp, wet knife and cut at a 90-degree angle to the cutting board using a seesaw motion. Don't cut the roll from a slanted angle, as this may cause the filling to loosen.

I especially like to serve this with Eomukguk (Fish Cake Soup; page 237), Tteokbokki (Spicy Rice Cakes; page 319), or instant ramen.

RECIPE CONTINUES

SERVES 4 to 6
TOTAL TIME 2¼ hours, plus 1 hour soaking

- ¾ cup (160 grams) short- or medium-grain white rice
- ½ ounce (14 grams) dashima (dried kelp), rinsed and broken into 2-inch pieces
- 2¼ teaspoons plus ⅛ teaspoon sugar, divided
- ¾ teaspoon miwon matsogeum (MSG seasoning salt), divided
- ½ teaspoon plus ⅛ teaspoon Dasida beef stock powder, divided
- 1 teaspoon fine salt
- 8 ounces (227 grams) flat-leaf spinach
- 2 large eggs
- 8 teaspoons neutral cooking oil, divided
- 1 cup (100 grams) shredded carrot
- 3½ ounces (100 grams) frozen fish cake sheets, thawed and sliced crosswise ¼ inch thick
- 2½ teaspoons soy sauce
- 1½ tablespoons Mizkan Sushi Seasoning
- 7 teaspoons toasted sesame oil, divided
- 1½ teaspoons sesame seeds, toasted, plus extra for sprinkling
- 4 (8-inch square) sheets gimbapgim
- 2½ ounces (71 grams) danmuji (yellow pickled radish), cut into 8-inch-long by ⅜-inch-thick strips
- ½ avocado, sliced ¼ inch thick
- 2½ ounces (71 grams) imitation crab sticks, lightly squeezed and halved lengthwise

1 Add the rice to a medium bowl, cover by 2 inches water, and let sit for 1 hour. Soak the dashima in 1½ cups hot water in a separate bowl for 15 minutes. Measure out 1 cup dashima broth; discard the remaining broth and solids.

2 Using your hands, gently swish the rice to release excess starch. Carefully pour off the water, leaving the rice in the bowl. Cover the rice with water again, swish it, and pour off the water; repeat 2 or 3 more times, until the water runs almost clear. Drain the rice using a fine-mesh strainer.

3A FOR AN ELECTRIC RICE COOKER Transfer the rice to the cooking chamber of a 5- to 6-cup electric rice cooker. Stir in the reserved dashima broth, ¼ teaspoon sugar, ¼ teaspoon seasoning salt, and ¼ teaspoon Dasida powder; cover; and cook on the standard rice setting according to the manufacturer's directions. The machine will automatically shut off when cooking is completed (typically indicated by the "Keep Warm" light turning on).

Using a moistened rice paddle or silicone spatula, gently fluff the rice (this ensures even texture and moisture distribution). Cover and set aside.

3B FOR THE STOVETOP Transfer the rice to a large saucepan. Stir in the reserved dashima broth, ¼ teaspoon sugar, ¼ teaspoon seasoning salt, and ¼ teaspoon Dasida powder. Bring to a boil. Reduce the heat to low (medium if using an electric stove), cover, and cook until the rice is tender and the water is fully absorbed, about 20 minutes. Turn off the heat and let sit for 15 minutes to finish cooking. Using a moistened rice paddle or silicone spatula, gently fluff the rice. Cover and set aside.

4 Meanwhile, bring 1 quart water and the salt to a boil in a large saucepan. Add the spinach and submerge completely. Blanch until the spinach is bright green but still has some bite, about 10 seconds. Using tongs, quickly transfer the spinach to a large bowl of cold water and run your hands gently through the spinach to cool it down. Drain the spinach and repeat covering with cold water until the spinach has completely cooled. Working in batches, squeeze the spinach by hand to remove excess water. Untangle the spinach and transfer it to a medium bowl; set aside.

5 Beat the eggs, ⅛ teaspoon sugar, ⅛ teaspoon seasoning salt, and ⅛ teaspoon Dasida powder in a separate bowl until the eggs are thoroughly combined and the mixture is pure yellow. Heat 1 teaspoon neutral oil in an 8½ by 7½-inch rectangular nonstick skillet over medium heat until shimmering. Add the egg mixture, tilting and shaking the skillet gently until the egg evenly covers the bottom of the pan. Cook, undisturbed, until the bottom of the omelet is just set but the top is still slightly wet, 1 to 3 minutes.

6 Using two thin spatulas, gently lift one-third of the omelet (one of the long sides) over, then fold the omelet in half. Continue to cook, gently flipping and turning the omelet, until lightly set, about 30 seconds. Remove the skillet from the heat and let the eggs continue to cook using residual heat until fully set, 1 to 3 minutes. Transfer the omelet to a cutting board and let it rest while continuing to prepare the filling.

7 Heat 4 teaspoons neutral oil in a 14-inch flat-bottomed wok or 12-inch nonstick skillet over medium-high heat until shimmering. Add the carrot and cook, tossing constantly, until softened, about 2 minutes. Stir in ¼ teaspoon sugar and ¼ teaspoon seasoning salt until fully incorporated, about 30 seconds. Transfer the carrot to a plate and set aside.

8 Place the fish cake strips in a strainer and thoroughly rinse under hot water. Drain the strips well and pat dry with paper towels. Heat the remaining 1 tablespoon neutral oil in the now-empty wok over medium-high heat until shimmering. Add the fish cakes and cook, tossing constantly, until evenly coated in oil, about 15 seconds. Add the soy sauce and 1½ teaspoons sugar and mix until just combined, about 20 seconds (don't overcook or else the fish cakes will become hard and chewy). Transfer the fish cakes to a separate plate.

9 Just before you are ready to assemble the gimbap, transfer the rice to a large bowl, add the sushi seasoning and 1 tablespoon sesame oil, and gently fluff with a rice paddle or silicone spatula until well combined. Squeeze the spinach by hand to remove excess water that has accumulated. Add the remaining ¼ teaspoon sugar, remaining ⅛ teaspoon seasoning salt, remaining ¼ teaspoon Dasida powder, 1 tablespoon sesame oil, and sesame seeds to the spinach. Lift and loosen individual pieces of spinach and mix gently until evenly coated with the seasonings. Cut the omelet lengthwise into quarters.

10 Place 1 gim sheet shiny side down on a bamboo mat, with the longer side parallel to the bottom edge of the mat. Using your lightly moistened hands, scoop one-quarter of the seasoned rice, place the rice on the gim, and spread it out evenly all the way to the edges. (Parts of the gim should still be visible through the rice; the rice should not form a solid layer.) Starting 1 inch from the bottom edge of the gim, use one-quarter of the danmuji, one-quarter of the carrot, and one-quarter of the spinach to create three thin, adjacent rows. Use one-quarter of the avocado slices and one-quarter of the fish cakes to create two rows on top, followed by a row of crab and a row of omelet on top of the avocado and fish cakes, overlapping the ends if needed.

11 Using the bamboo mat as a guide, lift and roll the bottom edge of the gim sheet up and over the filling. Gently squeeze to tighten the roll. Lift up the top edge of the mat and continue to roll the remaining gim and rice into a log, using the mat to gently squeeze the roll to seal and tighten it as you go. When fully rolled, flip the bamboo mat over and roll the mat away from you to release the gimbap. Set the gimbap aside, seam side down, and repeat shaping 3 more gimbap using the remaining gim sheets, rice, and filling.

12 Brush the gimbap with the remaining 1 teaspoon sesame oil. Using a sharp knife, cut each roll into ½-inch-thick slices, dipping the knife in water between cuts if the slices begin to stick. Sprinkle with extra sesame seeds and serve.

TURN TO SEE HOW TO ROLL GIMBAP →

Rolling Gimbap

Top Place 1 gim sheet shiny side down on the mat, with the longer side parallel to the bottom edge of the mat. Scoop one-quarter of the seasoned rice, place it on the gim, and spread it out evenly all the way to the edges.

Bottom left Starting 1 inch from the bottom edge of the gim, use one quarter of the danmuji, carrot, and spinach to create three rows.

Bottom right Use one-quarter of the avocado slices and fish cakes to create two adjacent rows on top, followed by two rows of crab and omelet.

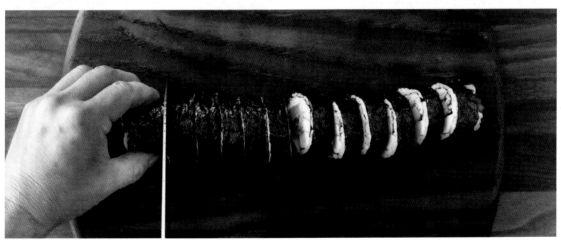

Top Using the mat as a guide, lift and roll the bottom edge of the gim up and over the filling. Squeeze to tighten the roll. Lift the edge of the mat and continue to roll the remaining gim and rice, squeezing as you go to seal and tighten the log.

Middle When fully rolled, flip the mat over and roll it away from you to release the gimbap.

Bottom Brush the gimbap with sesame oil. Cut each roll crosswise into ½-inch-thick slices, dipping the knife in water between cuts if the slices begin to stick.

Bibimbap 비빔밥

bee-beem-bahp

SARAH
세라

Here's a fun fact: In 2023, the most Googled recipe in the world was . . . bibimbap! Although it may be trending these days, this dish has a centuries-long history with many origin theories, and it has evolved into countless variations. Bibimbap, which translates to "mixed rice," is a hearty dish consisting of warm rice meticulously topped with an array of seasoned vegetables, a protein of choice, and seasoned gochujang. It's a savory, sweet, and all-around nutritious meal that's supremely satisfying. In our household, we tend to "unintentionally" make bibimbap as a way of using up our leftovers. We mix leftover rice with whatever banchan we have in our fridge, then add a dollop of prepared Yangnyeom Gochujang (Seasoned Gochujang; page 34) with a drizzle of sesame oil, mix it all up, and voilà, we have bibimbap. This is a great way to assemble a meal when possible, but you can also easily make bibimbap from scratch. Here's how Umma prepares bibimbap in a streamlined process that you can complete while the rice cooks. If you can't find the aehobak (see page 31), you can substitute grey squash or zucchini. I highly recommend Umma's method for making ultra-crispy fried eggs—the texture of these eggs pairs so well with the rest of the dish that I find myself deliberately picking out a bit of crispy fried egg to enjoy with every bite!

SERVES 4   TOTAL TIME 1¼ hours

- 5 ounces (142 grams) Korean radish, cut into 3-inch matchsticks
- 4 teaspoons sugar, divided
- 1 teaspoon distilled white vinegar
- ½ teaspoon gochugaru
- 1½ teaspoons fine salt, divided
- 6 ounces (170 grams) oyster mushrooms, trimmed
- 6 ounces (170 grams) soybean sprouts
- 7½ tablespoons neutral cooking oil, divided
- 2 large carrots (200 grams), peeled and cut into 3-inch matchsticks
- 1 aehobak (Korean summer squash; 227 grams), trimmed and cut into 3-inch matchsticks, ¼ inch thick
- 4 large eggs
- 4 cups (740 grams) cooked short- or medium-grain white rice
- 1½ cups (57 grams) shredded romaine lettuce
- 1 recipe Yangnyeom Gochujang (Seasoned Gochujang; page 34)
- 2 tablespoons toasted sesame oil, plus extra for serving (optional)

1 Combine the radish, 1 teaspoon sugar, vinegar, gochugaru, and ¼ teaspoon salt in a small bowl; set aside.

2 Using your hands, pull the mushrooms lengthwise into rough ½-inch-thick strands. Add the mushrooms to a 14-inch flat-bottomed wok or 12-inch nonstick skillet, cover, and cook over medium heat until the mushrooms release their liquid, about 10 minutes. Stir the mushrooms and continue to cook, covered, until they are fully softened, about 2 minutes. Drain the mushrooms, transfer to a separate bowl, and set aside to cool.

RECIPE CONTINUES

3 Add the soybean sprouts and ⅓ cup water to the now-empty wok. Cover and cook over medium-high heat until the sprouts begin to wilt and turn translucent, about 3 minutes. Stir the sprouts and continue to cook, covered, until fully softened, about 2 minutes. Drain the sprouts, then return them to the wok along with 1½ teaspoons neutral oil, ½ teaspoon sugar, and ¼ teaspoon salt. Cook over medium-high heat, tossing constantly, until the sprouts are evenly coated. Mound the sprouts on a large platter; set aside.

4 Heat 1 tablespoon neutral oil in the now-empty wok over medium-high heat until shimmering. Add the carrots and cook, tossing constantly, until softened and evenly coated, about 1 minute. Stir in 1 teaspoon sugar and ½ teaspoon salt and continue to cook until the carrots are crisp-tender but not browned, about 2 minutes. Arrange the carrots in a separate mound on the platter with the sprouts; set aside.

5 Heat 1 tablespoon neutral oil in the now-empty wok over medium-high heat until shimmering. Add the aehobak and cook, tossing constantly, until softened and evenly coated, about 1 minute. Stir in 1 teaspoon sugar and ¼ teaspoon salt and continue to cook until the aehobak is crisp-tender but not browned, 1 to 2 minutes. Arrange the aehobak in a separate mound on the platter with the vegetables; set aside.

6 Working in batches, squeeze the mushrooms by hand to remove excess water. (Do not over-squeeze, as the mushrooms should still be slightly moist.) Heat 1 tablespoon neutral oil in the now-empty wok over medium-high heat until shimmering. Add the mushrooms and toss to coat in the oil. Add the remaining ½ teaspoon sugar and remaining ¼ teaspoon salt and cook, tossing constantly, until heated through but not browned, about 15 seconds. Arrange the mushrooms in a separate mound on the platter with the vegetables; set aside.

7 Heat the remaining ¼ cup neutral oil in the now-empty wok over medium-high heat until just smoking. Working quickly, carefully crack 1 egg into the wok and use a silicone spatula to pull the egg whites toward the yolk to create an even circle. Repeat with a second egg, making sure the two eggs do not touch. Cook until the eggs are crisp around the edges and bottom and the whites just around the perimeter of the yolks are beginning to set, about 1 minute. Using a spoon, baste each egg twice with hot oil. (This will produce a runny yolk; continue to baste as desired to create a more set yolk.) Using a slotted spatula, transfer the eggs to a plate. Repeat with the remaining 2 eggs and the oil left in the wok.

8 Using a moistened rice paddle or silicone spatula, gently fluff the rice. Divide the rice among individual serving bowls and arrange the seasoned radish, stir-fried vegetables, and shredded lettuce attractively on top. Dollop a rounded tablespoon of yangnyeom gochujang in the center of each bowl, top each bowl with a fried egg, and drizzle each with 1½ teaspoons sesame oil. Serve, passing the remaining yangnyeom gochujang and extra sesame oil, if using, separately.

> ### *Umma's Kitchen Wisdom*
>
> *This is a very versatile dish, so don't feel limited by what's listed in this recipe. Feel free to use other cooked vegetables such as matchstick bell peppers, thinly sliced onions, and blanched spinach. You can also substitute other mushrooms for the oyster mushrooms.*
>
> *Leftovers of these banchan would also taste great as bibimbap toppings: Chwinamul Muchim (Seasoned Aster Scaber; page 58), Kongnamul Muchim (Seasoned Soybean Sprouts; page 51), Gaji Aehobak Muchim (Seasoned Eggplant and Squash; page 57), and Broccoli Dubu Muchim (Seasoned Broccoli Tofu; page 52).*
>
> *The fried egg makes a great addition because its contrasting crispy texture complements the tender vegetables well. Ground beef is also another common protein added to bibimbap.*
>
> *The ingredients in bibimbap should be enjoyed in harmony, with no particular ingredient standing out. The size and thickness of the ingredients are crucial for achieving this, so pay attention to your knife work.*

Pull the oyster mushrooms
by hand lengthwise into
½-inch-thick strands.

Avocado-Jang Myeongran Deopbap
아보카도장명란덮밥

avocado-jahng myuhng-nahn duhp-bbahp

SARAH
세라

Here's a fun, modern rice bowl that reminds me of something you would get at a brunch restaurant. We learned about this recipe when avocados became a craze in Korea and reached their peak import and supply leading up to 2020. As long-time consumers of avocados, Umma and I were intrigued by all the trending avocado dishes that Koreans were creating. We would hover over our family computer desk together and watch videos featuring Korean-fusion avocado dishes being shared online. Among them, one stood out: marinated avocado served alongside rice and a sunny-side-up egg. The buttery texture and umami richness of the avocados sounded like the perfect complement to warm rice and a runny egg yolk—it had my mouth instantly watering! Umma wasted no time in creating her own version, finding ways to elevate it with her radish-infused soy sauce and by adding seasoned pollack roe for a flavor and texture punch. This dish features our Avocado-Jang (Marinated Avocado; page 75), which includes avocado, tomatoes, and yellow onion that have been marinated in our special soy sauce blend infused with Korean radishes and maesil cheong (plum extract syrup). When we finally assembled this dish, we couldn't help but notice how pretty the colors of each ingredient looked next to each other. It brought us back to the few days Umma and I had spent in Seoul, enjoying a beautifully presented rice dish at a local café over cups of tea and coffee. Myeongranjeot (seasoned/salted pollack roe) is typically available in the freezer section of Korean markets; don't buy unseasoned pollack roe. To thaw the frozen roe, let it sit in the refrigerator for 24 hours. Although this dish comes together quickly, you do need to plan ahead to make its components. The Avocado-Jang requires at least 1 hour of marinating time, and to get the seasoned soy sauce for the Avocado-Jang, you must either make the Ganjang Mu Jangajji (Soy Sauce Radish Pickles; page 144) or the Instant Seasoned Soy Sauce (page 75).

SERVES 4   TOTAL TIME 30 minutes

- 5 ounces (142 grams) myeongranjeot (seasoned pollack roe)
- 2 tablespoons plus 1 teaspoon toasted sesame oil, divided
- 1½ teaspoons sesame seeds, toasted and coarsely ground (see page 38), plus extra for garnish
- 1½ teaspoons minced jalapeño chile
- 1½ teaspoons minced green onion
- 1 tablespoon finely chopped yellow onion
- ¼ teaspoon sugar
  Pinch black pepper
- 1 tablespoon neutral cooking oil
- 4 large eggs
- 4 cups (740 grams) cooked short- or medium-grain white rice
- 1 recipe Avocado-Jang (Marinated Avocado; page 75)
- 2 ounces (57 grams) vegetable sprouts or microgreens
  Shredded roasted seaweed

1 Remove the pollack roe from its sac by cutting lengthwise along 1 side with a sharp paring knife. Using a spoon, scrape the roe from the sac and transfer to a medium bowl; discard the membrane. Add 1 teaspoon sesame oil, the sesame seeds, jalapeño, green onion, yellow onion, sugar, and pepper and mix gently until well combined; set aside.

2 Heat the neutral oil in a 12-inch nonstick skillet over medium-high heat until shimmering. Working quickly, crack 2 eggs into 1 side of the pan and the remaining 2 eggs into the other side of the pan. Cover and cook for 1 minute. Remove the skillet from the heat and let sit, covered, for 15 to 45 seconds for runny yolks or 45 to 60 seconds for soft but set yolks.

3 Divide the cooked rice among individual shallow serving bowls and arrange the fried eggs, seasoned roe, and marinated avocado, tomatoes, and yellow onion from the avocado-jang attractively on top. Sprinkle with the sprouts, shredded seaweed, and extra sesame seeds and drizzle with the remaining 2 tablespoons sesame oil. Serve.

SOYBEAN SPROUT RICE

Kongnamulbap 콩나물밥

kohng-nah-mool-bahp

SARAH
세라

Kongnamulbap is a staple in our family's dinner rotation. It's one of our go-to recipes when we're low on banchan but want a hearty meal. Because it's so substantial on its own, we usually serve it with just kimchi, without any additional banchan. It's a very simple dish to make, as the rice cooker does most of the work. The rice cooks in a savory broth conveniently made from seafood broth tablets (see page 21; we use 2 broth tablets with 2 cups water for this broth). While the rice cooks, you can prepare the other components. First, there's Buchu Yangnyeomjang—a savory and sweet stir-together sauce featuring plentiful chopped chives, ground sesame seeds, sesame oil, and maesil cheong—which will be spooned over the individual servings. You'll also grind some beef and cook it with a little sugar and soy sauce. Then, simply top the cooked rice and soybean sprouts with the beef and the chive seasoning sauce, and enjoy. You will need an electric rice cooker with a 5½-cup or greater capacity for this recipe.

SERVES 4 to 6
TOTAL TIME 1 hour, plus 35 minutes freezing

    12 ounces (340 grams) beef flap meat, trimmed and
        cut into ½-inch pieces
    1½ cups (312 grams) short- or medium-grain white rice
     2 cups seafood broth
     1 pound (454 grams) soybean sprouts
    5½ teaspoons sugar
    1½ tablespoons soy sauce
     ½ teaspoon black pepper
     1 recipe Buchu Yangnyeomjang (Chive Seasoning
        Sauce; page 35)

1 Arrange the beef in a single layer on a rimmed baking sheet and freeze until very firm and starting to harden around the edges but still pliable, 35 to 45 minutes.

2 Working in 2 batches, pulse the beef in a food processor until finely ground into ⅛-inch pieces, about 12 pulses, stopping to redistribute the meat as needed. Transfer the meat to a bowl, cover, and refrigerate until needed.

3 Add the rice to a medium bowl and cover by 2 inches water. Using your hands, gently swish the rice to release excess starch. Carefully pour off the water, leaving the rice in the bowl. Repeat 2 or 3 more times, until the water runs almost clear. Using a fine-mesh strainer, drain the rice, then transfer to the cooking chamber of an electric rice cooker. Stir in the broth, then arrange the soybean sprouts evenly over the top. Cover and cook on the standard rice setting according to the manufacturer's directions.

4 Ten minutes before the rice is finished cooking (indicated by the rice cooker), cook the beef in a 14-inch flat-bottomed wok or 12-inch nonstick skillet over high heat, breaking up the meat with a wooden spoon, until the beef begins to brown but some pink color still remains, 2 to 3 minutes. Tilt the wok and, holding a wad of paper towels with tongs, blot away any accumulated liquid. Add the sugar and toss to combine. Stir in the soy sauce until the beef is evenly coated. Stir in the pepper and cook, stirring frequently, until the sauce clings to the beef, about 45 seconds. Remove the wok from the heat to prevent the beef from overcooking.

5 Using a moistened rice paddle or silicone spatula, gently fluff the rice and soybean sprouts to combine. Divide the rice among individual serving bowls and top with the beef. Serve with the buchu yangnyeomjang.

Umma's Kitchen Wisdom

I grind my own beef for this recipe because I find freshly ground beef to be much more tender than store-bought ground beef. I use flap meat (also called steak tips). Flank steak also works well. If you don't wish to grind your own beef, you can substitute 12 ounces store-bought ground beef.

Make sure to wash the soybean sprouts well to remove excess skins. However, I don't remove the stringy roots from the soybean sprouts, as they provide nutritional benefits.

ASTER SCABER RICE

Chwinamulbap 취나물밥

chwee-nah-mool-bahp

SARAH
세라
Another fixture in our family's dinner rotation, much like Kongnamulbap (Soybean Sprout Rice; page 268), is chwinamulbap, which shares a similar concept but presents a uniquely different flavor profile provided by the earthy herbal notes of chwinamul (aster scaber). Although this recipe is enjoyed regularly in Korea, I find it particularly special because it's relatively unknown outside Korea. Perhaps that's because this dish involves more steps than its counterpart, or it could be because chwinamul is less readily accessible than soybean sprouts. Rest assured, the extra steps are approachable and straightforward and make great practice for making Chwinamul Muchim (Seasoned Aster Scaber; page 58), where the aster scaber plays the starring role. Laced with earthy, rooty notes of chwinamul throughout, then topped with Umma's highly requested chive seasoning sauce, this hearty dish deserves wider recognition and consideration. The Dasida powder is optional but adds an umami flavor boost. You will need an electric rice cooker with a 5½-cup or greater capacity for this recipe.

Umma's Kitchen Wisdom

Dried chwinamul can be found in Korean grocery stores in the dried food section or purchased online.

Don't be tempted to skip the rinsing step after you rehydrate the aster scaber; rinsing will get rid of any lingering acridness.

Flap meat is sometimes labeled as steak tips. You can substitute flank steak for the flap meat, if you like. I find freshly ground beef to be much more tender than store-bought; however, you can substitute store-bought ground beef if you prefer.

SERVES 4 to 6
TOTAL TIME 2¼ hours, plus 12 hours soaking

- 3½ ounces (99 grams) dried chwinamul (aster scaber)
- 12 ounces (340 grams) beef flap meat, trimmed and cut into ½-inch pieces
- ¼ cup plus 1½ teaspoons soy sauce, divided
- 7 teaspoons sugar, divided
- 2 tablespoons toasted sesame oil
- 1 teaspoon Dasida beef stock powder (optional)
- 1½ cups (312 grams) short- or medium-grain white rice
- ½ teaspoon black pepper
- 1 recipe Buchu Yangnyeomjang (Chive Seasoning Sauce; page 35)

1 Submerge the chwinamul in 5 quarts water in a large bowl or container and let soak for about 12 hours to rehydrate.

2 Drain the chwinamul and rinse thoroughly in a bowl of water, using your hands to rub the chwinamul leaves against each other. Drain and rinse again. Repeat the process until the water runs clear.

3 Add the chwinamul and 3 quarts water to a large, wide pot and bring to boil. Reduce the heat to a simmer and cook, stirring occasionally to push the chwinamul that has risen to the surface back under the water, until the stems are tender, about 45 minutes.

4 Meanwhile, arrange the beef in a single layer on a rimmed baking sheet and freeze until very firm and starting to harden around the edges but still pliable, 35 to 45 minutes.

5 Drain the chwinamul, transfer to a large bowl, and submerge in cold running water. Using your hands, gently agitate the leaves to untangle any knotted sections. Drain, cover, and gently agitate again. Continue to repeat the process until the chwinamul is completely cooled.

RECIPE CONTINUES

6 Working in batches, squeeze the chwinamul by hand to remove excess water, then transfer to a cutting board. (Do not over-squeeze, as the chwinamul should still be slightly moist.) Lift and loosen individual leaves of chwinamul to untangle any knotted sections. Arrange half the strands in a single straight mound on a cutting board. Cut the mound crosswise into 1-inch sections and transfer to the bowl. Repeat with the remaining chwinamul.

7 Separate any clumps of chwinamul. Add 3 tablespoons soy sauce, 1½ teaspoons sugar, the sesame oil, and the Dasida powder, if using. Using your gloved hands, lift and loosen individual pieces of chwinamul and gently mix until evenly coated with the seasonings; set aside.

8 Working in 2 batches, pulse the beef in a food processor until finely ground into ⅛-inch pieces, about 12 pulses, stopping to redistribute the meat as needed. Transfer the meat to a bowl, cover, and refrigerate until needed.

9 Add the rice to a medium bowl and cover by 2 inches water. Using your hands, gently swish the rice to release excess starch. Carefully pour off the water, leaving the rice in the bowl. Repeat 2 or 3 more times, until the water runs almost clear.

Using a fine-mesh strainer, drain the rice, then transfer to the cooking chamber of an electric rice cooker. Stir in 2 cups water, then arrange the chwinamul evenly over the top. Cover and cook on the standard rice setting according to the manufacturer's directions.

10 Ten minutes before the rice is finished cooking (indicated by the rice cooker), cook the beef in a 14-inch flat-bottomed wok or 12-inch nonstick skillet over high heat, breaking up the meat with a wooden spoon, until the beef begins to brown but some pink color still remains, 2 to 3 minutes. Tilt the wok and, holding a wad of paper towels with tongs, blot away any accumulated liquid. Add the remaining 5½ teaspoons sugar and toss to combine. Stir in the remaining 1½ tablespoons soy sauce until the beef is evenly coated. Stir in the pepper and cook, stirring frequently, until the sauce clings to the beef, about 45 seconds. Remove the wok from the heat to prevent the beef from overcooking.

11 Using a moistened rice paddle or silicone spatula, gently fluff the rice and chwinamul to combine. Divide the rice among individual serving bowls and top with the beef. Serve with buchu yangnyeomjang.

EGG RICE WITH AVOCADO

Gyeranbap 계란밥

gye-rahn-bahp

SARAH
세라

Gyeranbap is the quintessential pantry meal for Koreans. It's the dish ummas prepare for their little ones when they want to make a quick and convenient meal; the dish that follows those not-so-little ones to college when they want a taste of home without breaking the bank; and the dish we find ourselves coming back to well into adulthood, when we understand our parents more than ever before and seek the nostalgic, comforting flavors of childhood. For many, it's the first dish we learn to make after watching our ummas effortlessly prepare it for years, back when kitchen counters felt like towers to us. The foundation of this dish is the same across Korean households: rice, eggs, soy sauce, and sesame oil are all you need. However, every household can prepare it differently according to their preferences and upbringing. Umma likes to scramble the eggs and mix them into the rice with the liquid seasonings. Her special touch is that she includes avocado slices for creamy richness and seasoned roasted seaweed for crispy texture and extra nutrients. I highly recommend topping this dish with the avocado and seaweed, because they pair together wonderfully, but it's no biggie if you don't have those items on hand. However, a side of kimchi is a must—the dish will feel naked without it. At least, that's how it is for me! One bite of this and you'll understand why people continue to come back to it. And if you want to share it with a friend, it's easily doubled.

SERVES 1   TOTAL TIME 15 minutes

2 teaspoons neutral cooking oil
2 large eggs
1 cup (185 grams) cooked short- or medium-grain white rice
1 tablespoon soy sauce
2½ teaspoons toasted sesame oil
½ avocado (136 grams), sliced crosswise ¼ inch thick
Shredded seasoned roasted seaweed

1 Heat the neutral oil in a 10-inch nonstick skillet over medium-high heat until shimmering. Add the eggs, scramble quickly using a silicone spatula, and cook until very little liquid egg remains, about 1 minute. Transfer the scrambled eggs to a medium bowl and break apart any large curds.

2 Add the cooked rice, soy sauce, and sesame oil to the bowl with the eggs and toss, breaking up any clumps of rice, until thoroughly combined. Transfer the rice mixture to a serving bowl and top with the avocado and shredded seaweed. Serve.

Umma's Kitchen Wisdom

You can use freshly cooked rice here if you like, but I usually use leftover rice to make this, warming it up in the microwave just before mixing it with the eggs. It tastes just as good this way and lives up more to the pantry meal idea of this dish!

Sigeumchi Bokkeumbap 시금치볶음밥

shi-geum-chi boh-kkeum-bap

UMMA
엄마

Whenever I serve this to my family, I always hear the spoons clanking against the plates as they try to get every last bite. This packed dish is a surprising twist on fried rice that features a pound of spinach, along with scrambled eggs, topped with flavorful stir-fried beef and drizzled with toasted sesame oil. It maintains the delicious characteristics of fried rice while offering a nutrition-packed boost from all that spinach.

SARAH
세라

This fried rice recipe is one of my favorites. It offers a satisfying mix of flavors and textures, and the colors of this dish are inviting, with vibrant green spinach, browned beef, and fluffy yellow eggs suffusing every bowlful. What makes this recipe unique is the extra steps that Umma takes to remove the excess water from all the ingredients, especially the spinach. She uses a salad spinner to remove the water after washing the fresh spinach. In her initial test of this recipe, she wiped away the water only as she stir-fried the spinach, which resulted in fried rice that was too mushy and wet. Upon further development, she refined the process by first wiping away the excess water, then gently patting the spinach with a paper towel, and then allowing the remaining water to evaporate. This method produced the perfect texture, so be sure to follow these steps to achieve the optimal results. And plan ahead: You'll need cold, day-old rice for this recipe—another step Umma takes to remove extra moisture from the ingredients to create just the right texture.

SERVES 4   TOTAL TIME 1¾ hours, plus 24½ hours cooling and chilling

- 1½ cups (312 grams) short- or medium-grain white rice
- 2 cups water
- 3 large eggs
- 2¾ teaspoons sugar, divided
- ½ teaspoon fine salt, divided
- 1 teaspoon neutral cooking oil
- 2 tablespoons salted butter, cut into 3 pieces, divided
- 1 pound (454 grams) flat-leaf spinach, chopped fine
- 5 tablespoons Kikkoman Hon Tsuyu soup and sauce base
- 8 ounces (227 grams) thinly sliced beef brisket, cut into rough 2-inch pieces
- 1½ teaspoons soy sauce
- 4 teaspoons toasted sesame oil

1 Add the rice to a medium bowl and cover by 2 inches water. Using your hands, gently swish the rice to release excess starch. Carefully pour off the water, leaving the rice in the bowl. Repeat 2 or 3 more times, until the water runs almost clear. Drain the rice using a fine-mesh strainer.

2A FOR AN ELECTRIC RICE COOKER Transfer the rice to the cooking chamber of a 5- to 6-cup electric rice cooker. Stir in the water, cover, and cook on the standard rice setting according to the manufacturer's directions. The machine will automatically shut off when cooking is completed (typically indicated by the "Keep Warm" light turning on).

2B FOR THE STOVETOP Transfer the rice to a large saucepan. Stir in the water and bring to a boil. Reduce the heat to low (medium if using an electric stove), cover, and cook until the rice is tender and the water is fully absorbed, about 20 minutes. Turn off the heat and let sit for 15 minutes to finish cooking.

RECIPE CONTINUES

3 As soon as the rice is finished cooking, using a moistened rice paddle or silicone spatula, gently fluff the rice (this ensures an even texture and even moisture distribution). Transfer the rice to a storage container and allow it to cool to room temperature, about 30 minutes. Cover and refrigerate the rice for at least 24 hours or up to 3 days.

4 Lightly beat the eggs, ¼ teaspoon sugar, and ¼ teaspoon salt in a bowl until well combined. Heat the neutral oil in a 14-inch flat-bottomed wok or 12-inch nonstick skillet over medium-high heat until shimmering. Add the egg mixture, and cook, stirring constantly, until very little liquid egg remains, about 1 minute. Transfer the scrambled eggs to a plate, break apart into large curds, and set aside.

5 Melt one piece of the butter in the now-empty wok over medium heat. Add the rice and break up any large clumps by pressing down on them with the back of a ladle or large spoon. Add the remaining two pieces of butter and cook, stirring to break up any remaining clumps with a wooden spoon, until the rice is evenly coated in butter, about 2 minutes. Increase the heat to medium-high. Add 1 teaspoon sugar and the remaining ¼ teaspoon salt and cook, tossing constantly, until the rice is heated through and any excess moisture is removed, about 3 minutes. Transfer the rice to a bowl, spread into an even layer, and set aside.

6 Add the spinach to the now-empty wok and cook over high heat, tossing constantly, until the spinach is wilted and has released most of its moisture, about 3 minutes. Tilt the wok and, holding a wad of paper towels with tongs, blot away any accumulated liquid. Continue to toss the spinach, using the tongs and paper towels to blot more liquid from the spinach, until no liquid remains.

7 Reduce the heat to medium. Return the rice to the wok and cook, tossing constantly, until the spinach and rice are evenly combined, about 1 minute. Increase the heat to medium-high, add the tsuyu, and cook, tossing constantly, until the rice is evenly coated, about 1 minute. Add the eggs and cook, tossing constantly, until some parts of the rice begin to crisp, about 1 minute. Remove the wok from the heat.

8 Separate the slices of beef and pat dry with paper towels. Cook the beef in a 10- or 12-inch nonstick skillet over medium-high heat, tossing constantly, until beginning to brown but some pink color still remains, about 2 minutes.

Tilt the skillet and, holding a wad of paper towels with tongs, blot away any accumulated liquid. Continue to toss the beef, using the tongs and paper towels to blot more liquid from the beef, until no excess liquid remains. Add the remaining 1½ teaspoons sugar and toss to coat. Stir in the soy sauce and toss to combine. Remove the skillet from the heat and, using kitchen shears, cut the beef into rough ½-inch pieces. Divide the spinach fried rice among individual serving bowls and top with the beef. Drizzle with the sesame oil and serve.

Umma's Kitchen Wisdom

Look for brisket sliced 1/16 inch thick. I prefer point-cut brisket here, but flat-cut brisket is acceptable too.

When separating the cold, day-old rice, I prefer using a large stainless steel ladle; its broad surface area swiftly and efficiently breaks up the clumped rice.

It's essential to remove as much moisture as possible from the rice, spinach, and beef. This is why the rice is refrigerated for 24 hours and why I use paper towels to blot away the excess liquid from the spinach and beef while they cook.

KIMCHI FRIED RICE

Kimchi Bokkeumbap 김치볶음밥

gim-chi boh-kkeum-bap

SARAH
세라

Umma isn't afraid to use flavorful ingredients to craft dishes that leave everyone craving seconds. Her philosophy when it comes to cooking and eating is simple: Make it incredibly tasty and allow yourself to genuinely enjoy it. She's never been one to consistently try to make foods "healthier" or diet-based—she believes in a balanced lifestyle that embraces everything in moderation. Umma's kimchi bokkeumbap is a great example of this philosophy. She uses pork belly and incorporates a generous amount of fat from stir-frying the pork to both moisten the dish and infuse it with richness. She also adds oyster sauce and Dasida beef stock powder to further enhance the tangy, umami-rich kimchi, creating a boldly flavored dish that's truly irresistible. Is it the healthiest dish? Absolutely not. Does it nourish the soul? Absolutely yes. And who doesn't love fried rice and kimchi? When these favorites come together, you get the ultimate comfort food for sharing over drinks with friends after a Friday night out or for cozying up while binge-watching Netflix on a Saturday night in.

SERVES 4 to 6
TOTAL TIME 1½ hours, plus 30 minutes cooling

1½ cups (312 grams) short- or medium-grain white rice
2 cups water
3 large eggs
1 tablespoon plus ¼ teaspoon sugar, divided
¼ teaspoon fine salt
1 teaspoon neutral cooking oil
12 ounces (340 grams) thinly sliced skinless pork belly
4 green onions (60 grams), chopped
1 tablespoon minced garlic
2½ cups (510 grams) well-fermented cabbage kimchi, sliced thin
1 tablespoon gochugaru
1½ teaspoons Dasida beef stock powder
2 tablespoons oyster sauce
½ cup (14 grams) shredded seasoned roasted seaweed, plus extra for garnish
Toasted sesame oil (optional)

1 Add the rice to a medium bowl and cover by 2 inches water. Using your hands, gently swish the rice to release excess starch. Carefully pour off the water, leaving the rice in the bowl. Repeat 2 or 3 more times, until the water runs almost clear. Drain the rice in a fine-mesh-strainer.

2A FOR AN ELECTRIC RICE COOKER Transfer the rice to the cooking chamber of a 5- to 6-cup electric rice cooker. Stir in the water, cover, and cook on the standard rice setting according to the manufacturer's directions. The machine will automatically shut off when cooking is completed (typically indicated by the "Keep Warm" light turning on).

2B FOR THE STOVETOP Transfer the rice to a large saucepan. Stir in the water and bring to a boil. Reduce the heat to low (medium if using an electric stove), cover, and cook until the rice is tender and the water is fully absorbed, about 20 minutes. Turn off the heat and let sit for 15 minutes to finish cooking.

3 As soon as the rice is finished cooking, using a moistened rice paddle or silicone spatula, gently fluff the rice (this ensures even texture and moisture distribution). Transfer the rice to a storage container and allow it to cool down to room temperature, about 30 minutes.

4 Lightly beat the eggs, ¼ teaspoon sugar, and salt in a bowl until well combined. Heat the neutral oil in a 14-inch flat-bottomed wok or 12-inch nonstick skillet over medium-high heat until shimmering. Add the egg mixture and cook, stirring constantly, until very little liquid egg remains, about 1 minute. Transfer the scrambled eggs to a plate and set aside.

5 Cook one-third of the pork belly in the now-empty wok over medium-high heat, flipping occasionally, until rendered and beginning to brown in spots, 2 to 3 minutes.

RECIPE CONTINUES

Using tongs, transfer the pork to a paper towel–lined plate; pour off and reserve the fat. Repeat with the remaining pork in 2 batches. Wipe the wok clean with paper towels. Using kitchen shears, cut the pork into rough ½-inch pieces.

6 Heat 3 tablespoons reserved pork fat in the wok over medium-high heat until shimmering; discard the remaining fat. Add the onions and garlic and cook until fragrant, about 1 minute. Add the kimchi and cook until heated through, 2 to 3 minutes. Stir in the gochugaru, Dasida powder, and remaining 1 tablespoon sugar and cook for about 30 seconds. Add the pork belly and stir to combine.

7 Reduce the heat to medium. Add the rice, breaking up any large clumps by pressing down on them with the back of a ladle or large spoon. Cook, tossing frequently until thoroughly combined and heated through, about 2 minutes. Add the oyster sauce and toss to combine. Add the scrambled eggs and shredded seaweed and gently toss to combine, being careful not to break up the egg curds. Serve, sprinkling individual portions with extra shredded seaweed and drizzling with sesame oil, if using.

Umma's Kitchen Wisdom

Look for pork belly sliced ⅛ inch thick.

I don't use day-old rice for this fried rice, as I do in the Sigeumchi Bokkeumbap (Spinach Fried Rice; page 277). The rice in this recipe should be a little more moist than that, while not being as moist as Baekmibap (Steamed White Rice; page 284). The amount of water used to cook the rice here achieves the proper texture.

I use well-fermented Mat Kimchi (Cut Napa Cabbage Kimchi; page 115). For convenience, you can use well-fermented store-bought kimchi instead (see page 20 for purchasing tips). Because the taste of kimchi can vary greatly, adjust the seasoning to taste.

When measuring out the kimchi, simply pick it up with tongs with the juices intact.

There are seasoned gim toppers sold specifically for rice and noodle dishes, but seasoned gim snacks, snipped into smaller pieces, also work. My kids like to add more seasoned gim to their rice as they eat it.

Chadolbagi Mu Sotbap 차돌박이무솥밥

chah-dohl-bah-gi moo soht-bbap

UMMA
엄마

As my family gathered for dinner one evening, I set down our bright-red Dutch oven at the center of the table and lifted the cover. Immediately, the room was filled with a smoky, sweet, and savory scent. We were enjoying this dish together when suddenly, as if transported through a time machine, I recalled a dish from my childhood. "I grew up with a dish like this," I said, "but it was a much more simplified version. It was mubap (steamed radish rice), a dish that Halmeoni made often. I had forgotten about that after all these years." As I continued to eat, I noted the flavors and textures that reminded me of Halmeoni's dish. Sarah asked how I could have forgotten about a dish I had eaten so often as a kid. Truthfully, I was never a big fan of mubap. It always seemed to me like a food that adults enjoyed more than kids. But I told Sarah, "Now that I've reached Halmeoni's age, I finally understand why she and the other adults loved it. The radish has a sweet element to it that flavors this dish just right. I remember Halmeoni enjoying plain mubap so much."

SARAH
세라

Watching Umma revisit this dish from her childhood as an adult sparked a reflective moment for me. I tried hard to recall the foods that I never liked too much growing up but saw Umma and Appa enjoying deeply. I wondered if these dishes, many of which I barely remember, will become ones I learn to appreciate as I grow older and wiser. I'm unsure what memories these dishes may unlock, but I know that they'll at least bring me back to those moments when I saw Umma and Appa enjoying them, just as Umma's chadolbagi mu sotbap reminded her of Halmeoni. Umma's modern take combines rice cooked in an umami-rich broth with seasoned beef brisket and green onion charred with a kitchen torch, infusing the dish with a savory, smoky, and subtly sweet flavor. The kitchen torch is important to achieve the charred flavor. A Dutch oven is also important, since this heavy pot helps the rice to form a scorched-rice layer, known as nurungji, at the bottom of the pot. This nutty, crunchy rice, a traditional treat, is mixed into the moist parts of the rice for added flavor and texture.

SERVES 4 to 6   TOTAL TIME 1¼ hours

- 2½ cups water
- ¼ ounce (7 grams) bonito flakes
- ½ ounce (14 grams) dashima (dried kelp), rinsed and broken into 2-inch pieces
- 1½ cups (312 grams) short- or medium-grain white rice
- 8 ounces (227 grams) Korean radish, cut into 3-inch matchsticks, ¼ inch thick
- 2 tablespoons Kikkoman Hon Tsuyu soup and sauce base
- 12 ounces (340 grams) thinly sliced beef brisket, cut into rough 1½-inch pieces
- 4 teaspoons sugar
- 2 teaspoons minced garlic
- 2 tablespoons soy sauce
- ½ teaspoon black pepper
- 8 green onions (120 grams), sliced thin

1 Bring the water to a boil in a small saucepan. Remove the saucepan from the heat, submerge the bonito flakes and dashima in the water, cover, and let sit for 15 minutes. Drain the mixture through a fine-mesh strainer into a bowl, pressing on the solids to extract as much liquid as possible; discard the solids. Measure out and reserve 2 cups broth; discard the remaining broth.

2 Add the rice to a medium bowl and cover by 2 inches water. Using your hands, gently swish the rice to release excess starch. Carefully pour off the water, leaving the rice in the bowl. Repeat 2 or 3 more times, until the water runs almost clear. Using a fine-mesh strainer, drain the rice, then transfer to a 3½- to 7-quart Dutch oven and spread into an even layer. Arrange the radish evenly over the top. Add the reserved broth and tsuyu and bring to a boil. Reduce the heat to low (medium if using an electric stove), cover, and cook until the rice is tender and the water is fully absorbed, about 15 minutes. Turn off the heat and let sit for 10 minutes to finish cooking.

3 Meanwhile, separate the slices of beef and pat dry with paper towels. Cook the beef in a 14-inch flat-bottomed wok or 12-inch nonstick skillet over medium-high heat, tossing constantly, until beginning to brown but some pink color still remains, 3 to 5 minutes. Tilt the skillet and, holding a wad of paper towels with tongs, blot away any accumulated liquid. Continue to toss the beef, using the tongs and paper towels to blot away more liquid, until no liquid pools in the pot but the beef is still moist. Add the sugar and garlic and toss to coat. Stir in the soy sauce and cook until slightly reduced and the beef is glazed, about 30 seconds. Stir in the pepper and toss to coat.

4 Remove the wok from the heat. Ignite a kitchen torch and, holding the flame 4 to 5 inches from the beef, sweep the flame over the surface to lightly char the edges.

Toss the beef and repeat charring the edges with the torch; set aside.

5 Remove the Dutch oven from the stovetop. Using a moistened rice paddle or wooden spoon, gently fluff the rice and radish to combine, being sure to scrape up any nurungji (scorched rice) from the bottom of the pot. Arrange the beef over half of the rice and add any accumulated juices. Arrange the onions over the other half of the rice. Ignite the kitchen torch and, holding the flame 4 to 5 inches from the beef and onions, sweep the flame over the surface to lightly char the edges. Cover and let sit for 2 minutes. Gently mix the rice, beef, and onions just before serving.

STEAMED WHITE RICE

Baekmibap 백미밥

baeng-mi-bap

SARAH
세라

My family enjoys rice daily, and we have two favorite preparations. First, there's this classic white rice. Sometimes Umma serves it plain, while other times she adds color and protein, mainly frozen green peas or cooked black soybeans. Umma always says, "Isn't the color against the white rice so pretty?" We like to enjoy this rice for convenience's sake or when a meal specifically calls for it over our second type of rice. This second type of rice, which we eat more often, is Umma's Japgokbap (Multigrain Rice; page 288). This rice is a bit heartier, offering a texture that is not as uniform as plain white rice. We love both of these types of rice, choosing between the two depending on the occasion. To store leftovers, put them in an airtight container and let the rice cool to room temperature, then refrigerate. When reheating leftover rice, add 1 tablespoon of water per serving of rice and reheat in the microwave.

Umma's Kitchen Wisdom

If you use green peas, use the larger amount of water listed in the ingredients.

If you use cooked black soybeans, increase the water to 2⅔ cups. I usually add ½ cup (81 grams) soybeans; you can use canned, or see page 289 to learn how to cook them in a pressure cooker.

SERVES 4 to 6   TOTAL TIME 50 minutes

1¾ cups (380 grams) short- or medium-grain white rice
2¼–2½ cups water
⅓ cup (50 grams) frozen green peas (optional)

1 Add the rice to a medium bowl and cover by 2 inches water. Using your hands, gently swish the rice to release excess starch. Carefully pour off the water, leaving the rice in the bowl. Repeat 2 or 3 more times, until the water runs almost clear. Drain the rice using a fine-mesh strainer.

2A FOR AN ELECTRIC RICE COOKER Transfer the rice to the cooking chamber of a 5- to 6-cup electric rice cooker. Stir in the water and peas, if using. Cover and cook on the standard rice setting according to the manufacturer's directions. The machine will automatically shut off when cooking is completed (typically indicated by the "Keep Warm" light turning on). Once the cooking is complete, immediately fluff the rice with a moistened rice paddle or a silicone spatula (this ensures an even texture and even moisture distribution). Serve.

2B FOR THE STOVETOP Transfer the rice to a large saucepan. Stir in the water and peas, if using, and bring to a boil. Reduce the heat to a very gentle simmer (typically low heat but this may vary depending on your stovetop), cover, and cook until the rice is tender and the water is fully absorbed, about 20 minutes. Turn off the heat and let sit for 15 minutes to finish cooking. Immediately fluff the rice with a moistened rice paddle or silicone spatula (this ensures an even texture and even moisture distribution). Serve.

The Days of No Rice

UMMA
엄마

Every autumn when I was growing up, Halmeoni would buy one gamani filled with white rice freshly harvested from the paddy fields. These sacks were handwoven from straw by street vendors and were said to preserve the new rice crop well. Each gamani held 60 kilograms of rice, and one of these sacks would last us the entire following year.

Like having a new, fancy car parked in the driveway, having a rice gamani in the home felt like a luxury, and it was quite a sight for us. It meant that we could enjoy white rice without worrying about running out for some time. It also meant that we didn't have to eat barley every day, a grain we often dreaded—Halmeoni included.

I remember going to the movie theater in the 1960s and 1970s and seeing a government news campaign called the "Mixed-Grain and Flour-Based Foods Campaign." It urged Korean citizens to consume more flour-based foods and to mix grains such as barley or millet into white rice. The demand for rice was high and the supply was low after the Japanese occupation (1910–1945), as Korea's once abundant agricultural land was used to address Japan's rice shortage. We went from having about 1,500 indigenous varieties of rice to nearly none. Following the occupation, the Korean War (1950–1953) devastated the nation, resulting in a destroyed infrastructure, widespread poverty, food shortages, and inflation. Under the leadership of former President Park Chung-Hee in the '60s and '70s, policies and initiatives to modernize and increase rice production domestically played a substantial role in making rice an accessible staple at the table.

From 1969 to 1977, we had "no-rice days" on Wednesdays and Saturdays from 11AM to 5PM, during which time rice dishes were prohibited from being sold. Police would enforce this order by going undercover and "dining in" at restaurants. If restaurants were caught selling rice dishes during these hours, they would be prohibited from operating for up to six months. There were even monetary rewards for those who reported restaurants that served rice during the no-rice hours. Radios would broadcast orders for parents to mix grains into rice for their children's school lunches, in order to include only a certain percentage of white rice. (Some parents, desiring the best for their children, would covertly include white rice beneath this multigrain rice.) This is also why you'll see noodles in dishes such as seolleongtang (beef bone soup)—it originates from this relatively recent historical campaign to limit rice consumption.

Such initiatives stabilized rice consumption and inflation, and by the end of the 1970s Korea was able to achieve self-sufficiency in domestic rice production. Shortly after, Korea progressed from an impoverished country to a fully developed industrial nation.

This campaign also diversified Korean cuisine. The enforcement of these policies resulted in Koreans finding creative ways to prepare meals without rice, leading to the emergence of noodle dishes such as Janchi Guksu (Banquet Noodles; page 302), as well as Uyusikppang (Milk Bread; page 333) and fried foods like Yachae Twigim (Fried Vegetables; page 322).

To many, rice is just a simple filling food, something that's not given much thought, but for Koreans who grew up during these transformative years, a single grain of white rice was once considered a luxury. Today, white rice stands as a powerful symbol of resilience, adaptability, and the collective efforts that have shaped modern South Korea.

From top: Gamani, traditional sacks made from straw. South Korean President Park Chung-Hee planting rice saplings in observance of National Farmers' Day. Rice harvest in the Slow City Samjicheon Village, Changpyeong, Jeollanam-do. Rice and grains, along with the wooden box used for measuring them.

Kitchen Conversation

SARAH What did Halmeoni think of mixed rice, japgokbap, especially when it was enforced during the "no-rice days" campaign?

UMMA *She wasn't a huge fan of the classic japgokbap, which included portions of barley. Its earthy flavor and texture reminded her a lot of barley rice, which was the main grain we ate growing up before rice became accessible to us. White rice was scarce, and it's what we all preferred whenever we could get our hands on it.*

SARAH We enjoy japgokbap so much today, though!

UMMA *Right, but our japgokbap is more aligned with Halmeoni's tastes. She loved adding millet, beans, and green peas to white rice, leaving out barley entirely. That's also considered a version of japgokbap. Since millet is expensive for everyday consumption here, I use quinoa instead and add chickpeas too.*

SARAH Do you think Halmeoni would like your version?

UMMA *Yes, definitely. It continues her tradition, just with a little update.*

Japgokbap 잡곡밥

jahp-ggok-bbahp

SARAH
세라

It's somewhat ironic that this style of multigrain rice, born out of necessity during the Korean government's campaign to limit rice consumption (see page 286), is once again popular, for both its flavor and its nutrition. Umma's japgokbap is a hearty rice blend featuring a variety of textures and tastes to keep you coming back for another bite, and it's the most frequently eaten rice in our home. It combines the fluffy texture and mild flavor of white rice with the crunchy texture and nuttiness of quinoa, studded with tender beans throughout. This rice offers diverse yet harmonious flavors—just as Halmeoni preferred. And, inspired by Halmeoni, Umma includes no trace of barley. Whenever Halmeoni managed to obtain a sack of white rice during the "no-rice days" campaign, she would forgo barley and stretch her limited supply by mixing in beans and various other grains. To make this rice convenient to prepare anytime, Umma cooks large quantities of beans in her pressure cooker and freezes them to keep on hand. The cooked beans can be frozen for up to 1 month (or refrigerated for up to 3 days). To store leftovers of the rice, seal the warm rice with a lid and let the rice cool to room temperature, then refrigerate. Reheat leftovers in the microwave, adding 1 tablespoon water per serving of rice.

Umma's Kitchen Wisdom

Since I make this rice so often, I always keep cooked soybeans and chickpeas on hand in the freezer (an electric pressure cooker is a super convenient way to cook them), but you can also use canned soybeans and chickpeas.

I sometimes rotate dried pinto beans into the mix, applying the same cooking method and duration. Feel free to substitute any other type of beans that you prefer.

SERVES 4 to 6   TOTAL TIME 1 hour

 1 cup (208 grams) short- or medium-grain white rice
⅓ cup (66 grams) prewashed quinoa
2¼ cups water
⅓ cup (54 grams) cooked black soybeans (recipe follows)
⅓ cup (52 grams) cooked chickpeas (recipe follows)
⅓ cup (50 grams) frozen green peas

1 Add the rice and quinoa to a medium bowl and cover by 2 inches water. Using your hands, gently swish the rice and quinoa to release excess starch. Carefully pour off the water, leaving the rice and quinoa in the bowl. Repeat 2 or 3 more times, until the water runs almost clear. Using a fine-mesh strainer, drain the rice and quinoa.

2A FOR AN ELECTRIC RICE COOKER Transfer the rice and quinoa to the cooking chamber of a 5- to 6-cup electric rice cooker. Stir in the water, soybeans, chickpeas, and peas. Cover and cook on the standard rice setting according to the manufacturer's directions. The machine will automatically shut off when cooking is completed (typically indicated by the "Keep Warm" light turning on). Once the cooking is complete, immediately fluff the rice with a moistened rice paddle or silicone spatula (this ensures even texture and moisture distribution). Serve.

2B FOR THE STOVETOP Transfer the rice and quinoa to a large saucepan. Stir in the water, soybeans, chickpeas, and peas and bring to a boil. Reduce the heat to low (medium if using an electric stove), cover, and cook until the rice is tender and the water is fully absorbed, about 20 minutes. Turn off the heat and let sit for 15 minutes to finish cooking. Immediately fluff the rice with a moistened rice paddle or silicone spatula (this ensures even texture and moisture distribution). Serve.

Pressure-Cooker Beans

You'll need a 6- or 8-quart electric pressure cooker.
This recipe can be easily doubled (the cooking time is
the same). Feel free to combine chickpeas and soybeans
together, but be aware that the black soybeans will
bleed color onto the chickpeas.

MAKES 4 cups
TOTAL TIME 15 minutes, plus 8 hours soaking

  1½ cups (292 grams) dried chickpeas or
       black soybeans, picked over and rinsed

1 Soak the beans in 1 quart cold water in a large
container for at least 8 hours or overnight. Drain
and rinse well.

2 Add about 1 inch water and a collapsible steamer
basket to an electric pressure cooker (the water
should not hit the steamer basket). Add the beans
to the basket in an even layer. Lock the lid in place
and close the pressure-release valve. Select the high
pressure-cook function and cook for 7 minutes.

3 Turn off the pressure cooker and quick-release
the pressure. Carefully remove the lid, allowing the
steam to escape away from you. Remove the steamer
basket from the pot and let the beans cool to room
temperature.

Angel Hair Bibimguksu
엔젤 헤어 비빔국수

angel hair bee-beem-gook-ssoo

SARAH
세라

I started Ahnest Kitchen in 2018 during my "quarter-life crisis." I was very unhappy and unfulfilled in my first full-time job, and I hoped this wasn't something that I just needed to get used to and accept as an adult. During those years, one thing made me feel fulfilled: Umma's food. It wasn't just the taste and flavor that comforted me; the process of making these dishes also fascinated me. Learning and replicating the recipes felt like therapy, and sharing and cooking these recipes for others brought me joy, just as it does for Umma. This new-found practice was exactly what I needed during this phase of my life, and it eventually motivated me to collect all of Umma's recipes to keep forever. Initially, I documented them in my notebook until I decided to upload them online to share with enthusiastic cooks around the world. Soon enough, people took notice of our work, and traction followed. We eventually received our first opportunity to collaborate with a Korean food brand we both grew up with. Umma and I felt beyond excited and determined to develop a unique recipe that would not disappoint. When we took our first bites of the final dish—after multiple rounds of testing and critiques—we both nodded in agreement and said, "This is it!" That very dish was this unique noodle masterpiece, which relies on gochujang to create a sauce that delivers the perfect balance of spice, tang, and sweetness. Here we opt for angel hair pasta instead of somyeon (thin wheat noodles) for a different flavor and texture, as well as added convenience.

Umma's Kitchen Wisdom

I use a mandoline to slice the cabbage about ⅛ inch thick.

You can substitute fish sauce for the tuna extract sauce: Use 2 tablespoons fish sauce and reduce the sugar to 2 tablespoons.

SERVES 4 to 6   TOTAL TIME 50 minutes

- ½ cup (176 grams) gochujang
- ½ cup maesil cheong (plum extract syrup)
- ¼ cup tuna extract sauce
- ¼ cup distilled white vinegar
- ¼ cup toasted sesame oil
- 3 tablespoons minced garlic
- 3 tablespoons sugar
- 2 tablespoons gochugaru
- 12 ounces (340 grams) angel hair pasta
- 3 Persian cucumbers (240 grams), cut into 3-inch matchsticks, divided
- 4 cups (226 grams) very thinly sliced green cabbage, divided
- 4 teaspoons sesame seeds, toasted
- 2 or 3 hard-boiled large eggs, halved
  Lemon wedges

1 Whisk the gochujang, maesil cheong, tuna extract sauce, vinegar, oil, garlic, sugar, and gochugaru together in a large bowl; set aside.

2 Bring 2½ quarts water to a boil in a large, wide pot. Add the pasta and cook, stirring occasionally, until softened, about 4 minutes. Drain the noodles and rinse under cold running water until chilled. Drain and gently squeeze the noodles to remove excess liquid.

3 Add the pasta, two-thirds of the cucumbers, and two-thirds of the cabbage to the bowl with the sauce. Using your gloved hands, gently toss the mixture until the noodles and vegetables are evenly coated with the sauce. Divide the pasta among individual serving bowls. Spoon any sauce left in the mixing bowl around the pasta, then sprinkle with the sesame seeds. Top with the remaining cucumber, remaining cabbage, and egg halves. Serve with lemon wedges.

Kimchi Bibimguksu 김치비빔국수

gim-chhi bee-beem-gook-ssoo

SARAH
세라

When I was growing up, we rarely turned on our window air conditioners. Financially, being able to afford that electricity bill was a major challenge. Emotionally, Umma and I felt a sense of guilt relaxing in a cool, air-conditioned home while Appa worked tirelessly under the scorching desert sun, painting houses in temperatures that climbed into the triple digits. In a way, enduring the heat of our home made us feel a sense of solidarity with Appa. As irrational as it may sound, these emotions felt validated when Appa would return home in the late evening with visibly leathered, sunburned skin, seemingly always a shade darker than the day before. During heat waves, we would find creative ways to cool down, such as lying down in the hallway of our home, which was the coolest part surrounded by the walls of our bedrooms; visiting the public library often; taking cold showers; repeatedly soaking cooling towels in ice-cold water; and eating cold noodles such as kimchi bibimguksu. A bite of these cold noodles felt like a burst of coolness that reinvigorated the entire body, providing temporary relief from the summer heat. We would enjoy bowls of these noodles along with naengmyeon (cold noodles in chilled beef broth), which Umma frequently bought from the Korean grocery store, while wearing our thinnest tank tops and shorts. After college, I saved money from my first full-time job and helped my parents purchase a new central air conditioner. We still turn on this air conditioner somewhat sparingly, but much more frequently than before. It's one of my proudest purchases.

SERVES 6   TOTAL TIME 50 minutes

3½ cups (680 grams) well-fermented cabbage kimchi
3 tablespoons toasted sesame oil
7 teaspoons sugar
2 tablespoons sesame seeds, toasted
1 tablespoon maesil cheong (plum extract syrup)
2 teaspoons Dasida beef stock powder
2 teaspoons fish sauce
12 ounces (340 grams) somyeon (dried thin white wheat noodles)
Shredded seasoned roasted seaweed (optional)
2 hard-boiled large eggs, halved

1 Using your gloved hands, squeeze the kimchi in batches over a bowl to collect the juice. (Don't over-squeeze the kimchi; it should still be juicy.) Transfer the kimchi to a cutting board and thinly slice. Reserve 1 cup kimchi juice from the bowl, adding extra kimchi juice from the storage container if needed.

2 Whisk the kimchi juice, oil, sugar, sesame seeds, maesil cheong, Dasida powder, and fish sauce in a large bowl.

3 Bring 2½ quarts water to a boil in a large, wide pot, then add the noodles and stir. Once the water returns to a boil, add ½ cup cold water and continue to cook, stirring occasionally, until the noodles are tender, about 2 minutes. Drain the noodles and rinse under cold running water. Transfer the noodles to a large bowl and cover with cold water. Using your hands, rub the noodles against each other to remove excess starch, then drain and rinse again until the noodles are completely chilled. Gently squeeze the noodles to remove excess liquid.

4 Add the noodles and kimchi to the bowl with the sauce. Using your gloved hands, gently toss until the noodles are evenly coated. Divide the noodles among individual serving bowls. Spoon any sauce left in the bowl around the noodles. Top with shredded seaweed, if using, and egg halves. Serve.

Umma's Kitchen Wisdom

I prefer the flavor of well-fermented Mat Kimchi (Cut Napa Cabbage Kimchi; page 115). For convenience, you can use well-fermented store-bought kimchi instead (see page 20 for purchasing tips). Because the taste of kimchi can vary greatly, adjust the seasoning to taste.

When measuring out the kimchi, simply pick it up with tongs with the juices intact.

There are seasoned gim toppers sold specifically for noodle and rice dishes, but seasoned gim snacks, snipped into smaller pieces, work just as great. My kids like to add more seasoned gim to their noodles as they eat it. Avoid mixing it in with the sauce, as the gim will absorb the liquid and lose its texture.

Japchae 잡채

jahp-chae

SARAH
세라

Japchae is undoubtedly one of the most popular dishes that's enjoyed during a variety of celebrations, including Seollal (Lunar New Year) and Chuseok (Autumn Harvest Festival), as well as weddings, birthdays, potlucks, and even on regular dinner nights. I frequently find Umma making this dish on a whim, seasoning the springy glass noodles in her classic, ergonomic squat position on the kitchen floor, where she feels most comfortable. In a short time, containers of japchae are neatly arranged on our dinner table, with tongs nearby for serving. It's a dish I grew up enjoying regularly, whether it was for a special occasion or a casual meal at home. While the recipe may seem intimidating at first glance, making japchae is surprisingly straightforward. It does require some patience and effort, but this labor of love is characteristic of what Korean cuisine entails. Plus, the payoff—bouncy, salty-sweet glass noodles studded with an array of colorful, crisp vegetables and savory, smoky beef—is entirely worth the effort. Japchae is enjoyed both as a standalone meal and as a banchan, and it can be served either warm or at room temperature. It's the perfect dish to bring to a party or potluck in a disposable foil tray, to serve guests on a beautiful platter, or to enjoy straight from the container as a quick snack. It's best enjoyed the day it's made, but after your first taste, we don't think that will be a problem!

Umma's Kitchen Wisdom

The ingredients in japchae should be harmoniously enjoyed together, with no particular ingredient standing out. The size and thickness of the ingredients are crucial for achieving this balance, so pay attention to your knife work. It's also important to maintain the crispness of each vegetable, so don't overcook them.

I like to wait about 10 minutes before eating the japchae. This allows the noodles to fully absorb all of the flavors of the seasonings.

SERVES 4 to 6   TOTAL TIME 1½ hours

- 10 ounces (284 grams) flat-leaf spinach
- ¼ cup plus ½ teaspoon neutral cooking oil, divided
- 2 carrots (150 grams), peeled and cut into 3-inch matchsticks
- ¼ cup (50 grams) plus 5¼ teaspoons sugar, divided
- 1 tablespoon plus 1¼ teaspoons Dasida beef stock powder, divided
- ¾ teaspoon miwon matsogeum (MSG seasoning salt), divided
- ½ red bell pepper (113 grams), cut into 3-inch matchsticks, ¼ inch thick
- ½ yellow bell pepper (113 grams), cut into 3-inch matchsticks, ¼ inch thick
- ½ yellow onion (142 grams), sliced ¼ inch thick
- 8 ounces (227 grams) beef flap meat or flank steak, trimmed
- 6 tablespoons plus 2½ teaspoons soy sauce, divided
- 1 teaspoon minced garlic
- 12 ounces (340 grams) dangmyeon (Korean glass noodles)
- 3 tablespoons plus 1½ teaspoons toasted sesame oil, divided
- 3 tablespoons sesame seeds, toasted
- 1 teaspoon black pepper

1 Bring 1 quart water to a boil in a large, wide pot. Add the spinach and submerge completely. Blanch until the spinach is bright green but still has some bite, about 10 seconds. Using tongs, quickly transfer the spinach to a large bowl of cold running water and gently run your hands through the spinach to cool it down. Drain the spinach and repeat covering it with cold water until the spinach has completely cooled.

RECIPE CONTINUES

2 Working in batches, squeeze the spinach by hand to remove excess water and transfer it to a cutting board. Lift and loosen individual leaves of spinach to untangle any knotted sections. Arrange the strands in a single straight mound and cut crosswise into 1½-inch sections. Transfer the spinach to a bowl and set aside.

3 Heat 3½ teaspoons neutral oil in a 14-inch flat-bottomed wok or 12-inch nonstick skillet over medium-high heat until shimmering. Add the carrots and cook, tossing constantly, until softened and evenly coated in oil, about 2 minutes. Stir in ½ teaspoon sugar, ¼ teaspoon Dasida powder, and ¼ teaspoon seasoning salt and continue to cook until the carrots are crisp-tender (don't let them brown), about 2 minutes. Transfer the carrots to a separate large bowl and spread into an even layer; set aside.

4 Heat 2½ teaspoons neutral oil in the now-empty-wok over medium-high heat until shimmering. Add the bell peppers and cook, tossing constantly, until softened and evenly coated in oil, about 1 minute. Stir in ¼ teaspoon sugar, ⅛ teaspoon Dasida powder, and ⅛ teaspoon seasoning salt and continue to cook until the peppers are crisp-tender (don't let them brown), about 2 minutes. Transfer the peppers to the bowl with the carrots and spread into an even layer.

5 Heat 3½ teaspoons neutral oil in the now empty-wok over medium-high heat until shimmering. Add the onion and cook, tossing constantly, until softened and evenly coated in oil, 1 to 2 minutes. Stir in ½ teaspoon sugar, ⅛ teaspoon Dasida powder, and ⅛ teaspoon seasoning salt and continue to cook until the onion is crisp-tender (don't let it brown), about 1 minute. Transfer the onion to the bowl with the vegetables and spread into an even layer.

6 Cut the beef with the grain into 1½-inch-wide strips, slice each strip crosswise into ¼-inch-thick planks, then cut the planks lengthwise into ½-inch-thick strips. Cook the beef in the now-empty wok, breaking it up with a wooden spoon, until the beef begins to brown but some pink color still remains, 1 to 2 minutes. Tilt the wok and, holding a wad of paper towels with tongs, blot away any accumulated liquid. Add 1½ teaspoons soy sauce, the garlic, 2½ teaspoons sugar, and ½ teaspoon Dasida powder and cook, tossing constantly, until the beef is evenly coated, about 1 minute. Transfer the beef to the bowl with the vegetables and spread into an even layer. Set the wok aside.

7 Bring 2 quarts water to a boil in the now-empty pot. Add the dangmyeon, using tongs as needed to fully submerge the noodles. Stir in the remaining 1 tablespoon neutral oil. Turn off the heat, cover, and let the noodles soak until softened but still very chewy, 6 to 9 minutes. Drain the noodles in a colander and shake to remove excess water. Spread the noodles into an even mound and use kitchen shears to cut the mound into quarters. Transfer the noodles to the now-empty wok; add 2 tablespoons sugar, 1½ teaspoons Dasida powder, 2 tablespoons soy sauce, and 1 tablespoon sesame oil; and gently toss until evenly coated.

8 Squeeze the spinach by hand to remove excess water that has accumulated and separate clumps. Add ½ teaspoon sugar, ¼ teaspoon Dasida powder, 1½ teaspoons sesame oil, and the remaining ¼ teaspoon seasoning salt to the spinach and toss to coat. Add the seasoned noodles and spinach to the bowl with the vegetables and beef and toss gently to combine. Add the remaining 7 teaspoons sugar, remaining 1½ teaspoons Dasida powder, remaining ¼ cup plus 1 teaspoon soy sauce, remaining 2 tablespoons sesame oil, the sesame seeds, and pepper. Gently toss until the mixture is evenly combined and coated with the seasonings, unraveling any remaining clumps of spinach. Serve.

Dongchimi Guksu 동치미국수

dohng-chi-mi gook-ssoo

UMMA
엄마

This dish feels full of history, bringing me back to my childhood in my hometown of Incheon, Korea. I used to eat it often as a young child, especially during the winter months. The flavor of the dongchimi juice is unique and pairs so well with the somyeon.

SARAH
세라

Appa likes to have dongchimi plain, while Umma likes to have dongchimi either plain or as part of a noodle dish, which is specifically called dongchimi guksu. I recall the first time I tried this dish. Gasping at how amazing it was, I yelled out, "Michelin! Michelin!," praising Umma for this masterpiece because it genuinely tasted like something I could order at a Michelin-starred restaurant! This dish truly is a work of art. Not only is it simply beautiful, but it also made me feel a strong connection to my Korean roots when I first took a bite. I could taste the rich, unique flavors of the fermented juice that were both refreshing and complex, a taste that has taken Umma years to achieve. When paired with freshly cut Asian pear, there is an added note of subtle crunch that enhances the overall textural experience of this dish. If you like, you can also garnish the noodles with the chiles from the dongchimi.

Umma's Kitchen Wisdom

Adding a splash of cold water to the somyeon while they are cooking contributes a pleasant chewy texture to the noodles that Koreans describe as jjolgit-jjolgit. It's a common technique used when preparing this type of noodle. You could skip it, but I highly recommend doing it for the best texture.

SERVES 4   TOTAL TIME 35 minutes

- 12 ounces (340 grams) somyeon (dried thin white wheat noodles)
- 8 pieces (113 grams) fermented radish, thinly sliced lengthwise, from Dongchimi (Radish Water Kimchi; page 120)
- ¼ Asian pear (100 grams), peeled, cored, and thinly sliced
- 8 pieces (28 grams) fermented green onion from Dongchimi (Radish Water Kimchi; page 120)
- 2 hard-boiled large eggs, halved
- 4 cups juice from Dongchimi (Radish Water Kimchi; page 120)
  Thinly sliced cucumbers (optional)

1 Bring 2½ quarts water to a boil in a large, wide pot, then add the noodles and stir. Once the water returns to a boil, add ½ cup cold water and continue to cook, stirring occasionally, until the noodles are tender, about 2 minutes. Drain the noodles and rinse under cold running water.

2 Transfer the noodles to a large bowl and cover with cold water. Using your hands, vigorously rub the noodles against each other to remove excess starch, then drain and rinse again until the noodles are completely chilled. Gently squeeze the noodles to remove excess liquid.

3 Divide the noodles among individual serving bowls and top with the radish and pear. Garnish with the onion and eggs, then pour the pickling juice around the noodles so as not to disrupt the toppings. Top with cucumbers, if using, and serve.

STIR-FRIED UDON WITH BEEF BELLY

Usamgyeop Bokkeum Udon
우삼겹볶음우동

oo-sahm-gyuhp bo-kkeum oo-dohng

SARAH
세라

When Halmeoni and Harabeoji visited us from Korea, Halmeoni observed Umma making dinner for the family and later said to Imo (maternal aunt; Umma's sister), "Wow, did you know your sister has a knack for cooking?" As Umma recalled this story to me, it was clear that this was a compliment she cherished deeply. Umma opened a restaurant when I was in middle school, and that became our primary source of income for a little over a decade. At her restaurant, she specialized in serving Mongolian BBQ noodles. ("Mongolian BBQ" is a misleading name, by the way. This type of noodle dish originated in Taiwan in the 1950s, not in Mongolia.) Umma perfected her recipes, especially the sauces, down to the last detail—so much so that other restaurateurs would inquire about her recipes, often offering substantial sums for them, but she always refused. At her restaurant, customers would assemble the ingredients for their bowls from a salad-like bar and then hand them off to the cooks. Using wooden sticks as tall as me, the cooks would stir-fry the ingredients together over a large, circular industrial grill, about 4 feet wide, in front of the customers. This concept fascinated and entertained diners—an experience that concluded with a freshly stir-fried, slightly smoky-tasting, steaming noodle dish that couldn't be reproduced elsewhere. Since the closing of her restaurant, we deeply miss Umma's Mongolian BBQ noodles for both the flavor and the stability they provided us. Umma would enjoy a bowl of these noodles every day, never growing tired of the food that sustained us for so long. While we can't replicate the dishes at home, many of the preparations that Umma once used at her restaurant can be. In the case of this udon dish, the sauce incorporates two key ingredients that Umma used to make her Mongolian BBQ sauces: oyster sauce instead of fish sauce and lemon juice instead of vinegar. The chewy, thick udon and richly flavored, subtly smoky sauce, alongside the spicy chiles, chives, and thinly sliced beef, evoke delicious memories of Umma's past noodles.

SERVES 4 to 6   TOTAL TIME   45 minutes

- 2 tablespoons soy sauce
- 2 tablespoons oyster sauce
- 1½ tablespoons sugar
- 1 tablespoon Kikkoman Hon Tsuyu soup and sauce base
- 1 tablespoon lemon juice
- 1½ teaspoons maesil cheong (plum extract syrup)
- 1 teaspoon black pepper
- 2¼ pounds (1 kilogram) frozen udon noodles
- 12 ounces (340 grams) thinly sliced beef plate
- 1 tablespoon salted butter
- 2 Fresno chiles (50 grams), stemmed, seeded, and sliced thin lengthwise
- 2 green onions, chopped
- 1 tablespoon minced garlic
- 4 ounces (113 grams) garlic chives, cut into 3-inch lengths
- 1 teaspoon gochugaru (optional)

1 Whisk the soy sauce, oyster sauce, sugar, tsuyu, lemon juice, maesil cheong, and pepper in a bowl; set aside.

2 Bring 2 quarts water to a boil in a large, wide pot. Add the noodles and cook, stirring occasionally, until tender, 2 to 3 minutes. Drain and rinse under cold running water, using your hands to toss the noodles to remove excess starch. Gently squeeze the noodles to remove excess liquid; set aside.

3 Separate the beef slices, pat dry with paper towels, and cut into pieces 4 to 6 inches long and about 1 inch wide. Working in 2 batches, cook the beef in a 14-inch flat-bottomed wok or a 12-inch nonstick skillet over medium-high heat, tossing constantly, until beginning to brown but some pink color remains, 1 to 2 minutes. Using tongs, transfer the beef to a plate. Discard the fat left in the wok and wipe the wok clean with paper towels.

Umma's Kitchen Wisdom

Look for beef plate sliced ⅟₁₆ inch thick, which is sometimes labeled "Beef for Hot Pot" or "Shabu-Shabu."

I like to use frozen Japanese udon noodles in my stir-fries; I think they have a better texture than refrigerated fresh udon or dried udon. Since the frozen noodles are already parboiled, you only need to heat them in boiling water until they're pliable. Be careful not to overcook them.

A wok makes easy work of tossing the noodles with the sauce in step 4. If you're using a nonstick skillet, use wooden spoons to gently toss the noodles, as the skillet will be quite full.

I add a small amount of sauce to the beef before adding the noodles and the rest of the sauce. Doing this ensures that a bit of sauce penetrates each piece of beef, rather than being all absorbed by the noodles.

4 Melt the butter in the wok over medium-high heat. Add the Fresno chiles, onions, and garlic and cook until fragrant, about 30 seconds. Add the beef and toss to combine. Add 2 tablespoons sauce and toss to coat. Increase the heat to high, add the noodles and remaining sauce, and cook, tossing constantly, until heated through and well combined, about 1 minute. Add the garlic chives and gochugaru, if using, and toss to combine. Serve.

BANQUET NOODLES

Janchi Guksu 잔치국수

jahn-chi gook-ssoo

UMMA
엄마

I remember my older colleagues asking me, "When will you feed me noodles?" when I was approaching my late 30s. This was a typical question from people of an older generation as a way of asking others when they would marry. The noodles that they were referring to were janchi guksu, which were frequently served at Korean weddings, as the noodles symbolized good health and longevity for newlywed couples. It is incredibly simple and affordable to make these noodles, which is another reason why the dish was often featured at celebrations such as weddings. I remember a point in my life when the majority of Koreans were unable to afford rice, so the government created mass campaigns encouraging people to use flour in their everyday cooking. This gave rise to the creation and popularity of many flour-based dishes, including this one. It is still common to see this dish served at Korean weddings nowadays, though it is more likely to be served as part of a buffet. These noodles are a testament to the adversities Koreans faced—and they are also simply delicious.

SARAH
세라

Umma's take on janchi guksu is somehow both easier and elevated. These noodles are typically made using a from-scratch anchovy broth, but Umma takes a shortcut and combines Kikkoman Hon Tsuyu soup and sauce base, a Japanese convenience product made from soy sauce, bonito flakes, and mirin, with bonito flakes to create a broth full of bold umami flavors, as opposed to the mellow and comforting flavors of anchovy broth. Instead of using egg ribbons—which are typically used to top this dish—for added protein, Umma uses shrimp that she has seasoned with the same soup base plus additional Korean pantry ingredients. (If you buy prepeeled shrimp, as Umma does, you'll need 6 ounces.) If you can't find aehobak (see page 31), use grey squash or zucchini. Enjoy these noodles simply on their own, and don't forget to release a sigh of happiness on your first bite!

SERVES 4   TOTAL TIME 1¼ hours

8 ounces (227 grams) medium-large shrimp (31 to 40 per pound), peeled, deveined, and tails removed
1 cup plus 4 teaspoons Kikkoman Hon Tsuyu soup and sauce base, divided
2 teaspoons toasted sesame oil
1 teaspoon sugar
1 teaspoon mirin
Pinch fine salt
Pinch black pepper
¼ ounce (7 grams) bonito flakes
4 ounces aehobak (Korean summer squash; 113 grams), trimmed and cut into 3-inch matchsticks
1 carrot (76 grams), peeled and cut into 3-inch matchsticks
12 ounces (340 grams) somyeon (dried thin white wheat noodles)
Shredded roasted seaweed
3 green onions (45 grams), sliced thin

1 Halve the shrimp lengthwise, then toss with 2 teaspoons tsuyu, the oil, sugar, mirin, salt, and pepper in a medium bowl; set aside.

2 Place the bonito flakes in a seasoning strainer or cheesecloth bundle. Bring 7 cups water, the aehobak, carrot, and remaining 1 cup plus 2 teaspoons tsuyu to a boil in a large saucepan. Remove the saucepan from the heat, submerge the seasoning strainer in the liquid, and let sit for 10 minutes. Remove the seasoning strainer and press on the bonito flakes to extract as much liquid as possible back into the saucepan; discard the bonito flakes and set the broth aside.

3 Meanwhile, cook the shrimp in a 10- or 12-inch nonstick skillet over medium-high heat, stirring occasionally, until opaque throughout, 4 to 5 minutes. Set the shrimp aside.

4 Bring 2½ quarts water to a boil in a large, wide pot, then add the noodles and stir. Once the water returns to a boil, add ½ cup cold water and continue to cook, stirring occasionally, until the noodles are tender, about 2 minutes. Drain the noodles and rinse under cold running water. Transfer the noodles to a large bowl and cover with cold water. Using your hands, vigorously rub the noodles against each other to remove excess starch, then drain and rinse again until the noodles are completely chilled. Gently squeeze the noodles to remove excess liquid; set aside.

5 Divide the noodles among individual serving bowls. Using a slotted spoon, transfer the aehobak and carrot to the bowls. Top with the shrimp and shredded seaweed. Return the broth to a brief boil, then ladle into the bowls along the sides so as to not disrupt the toppings. Sprinkle with the onions and serve.

Jeongigui Tongdak Kalguksu
전기구이 통닭 칼국수

juhn-ghee-goo-e tohng-dahk kal-gook-ssoo

UMMA
엄마

I first learned to make chicken broth using store-bought rotisserie chicken from Sarah's gomo (paternal aunt; Appa's sister). When I saw it being done, I thought it was such an ingenious idea that it should have been obvious to me all along. The bones and carcass of a perfectly seasoned rotisserie chicken can be used to create a rich, flavorful broth that can enhance dishes in any cuisine, not just Korean. Gomo used it to make classic American chicken soup, for example. As someone who loves noodles, I felt inspired to create a rotisserie chicken version of dak kalguksu (chicken knife-cut noodle soup) that merges American-style convenience with Korean flavors into one hearty meal.

SARAH
세라

For my family, no grocery trip to Costco would be complete without purchasing a rotisserie chicken. We always buy one so we can make the most of its supreme convenience and endless versatility. While it obviously can be enjoyed on its own, we love using it as an ingredient to elevate flavors and create satisfying dishes such as this one. The aromatic broth paired with the seasoned chicken, fresh knife-cut noodles (traditionally, wheat noodles hand-cut from a block of dough), and Umma's spicy seasoning sauce creates a comforting, wholesome meal where each bite makes you feel as though nothing else matters in that moment. If you can't find aehobak (see page 31), use grey squash or zucchini.

Umma's Kitchen Wisdom

Be sure to toss the shredded chicken meat well, both to distribute the seasoning and to make sure that the white and dark meat are evenly distributed.

You'll have about 2 cups leftover broth to refrigerate or freeze. Use it in any other dish that calls for chicken broth.

SERVES 6 to 8   **TOTAL TIME** 2 hours

- 5 quarts water
- 1 (2½-pound / 1.1 kilogram) rotisserie chicken, skin and bones reserved, meat shredded into bite-size pieces (3½ cups [397 grams], divided)
- 12 ounces (340 grams) Korean radish, cut into rough 1½-inch pieces
- 1 daepa (jumbo green onion; 130 grams), untrimmed, chopped coarse
- 2 celery ribs (123 grams), chopped coarse
- 15 garlic cloves (45 grams), peeled, plus 1 tablespoon minced garlic
- 1½ tablespoons coarsely chopped peeled fresh ginger
- 1½ teaspoons black peppercorns, plus ground black pepper for serving
- 1 tablespoon perilla seed powder
- 1 tablespoon toasted sesame oil
- 3½ tablespoons fish sauce
- 1 teaspoon fine salt
- 1 russet potato (227 grams), peeled, halved lengthwise, and sliced crosswise ⅛ inch thick
- ½ yellow onion (142 grams), sliced ¼ inch thick
- 1 large carrot (100 grams), peeled and cut into 3-inch matchsticks
- 20 ounces (567 grams) kalguksu (fresh knife-cut wheat noodles)
- 4 ounces aehobak (Korean summer squash; 113 grams), trimmed and cut into 3-inch matchsticks
- 4 green onions (60 grams), chopped fine
- 1 recipe Kalguksu Yangnyeomjang (Seasoning Sauce for Kalguksu; page 36)

1 Bring the water to a boil in a large, wide pot. Add the reserved chicken skin and bones, radish, daepa, celery, garlic cloves, ginger, and peppercorns and bring back to a boil. Reduce the heat to a vigorous simmer and cook, stirring occasionally, for 45 minutes.

2 Toss 1½ cups shredded chicken with the perilla seed powder and oil; cover and set aside for serving.

3 Set a fine-mesh strainer in a large bowl or container. Using tongs or a slotted spoon, discard any large solids from the broth. Pour the broth through the prepared strainer; discard any remaining solids. Measure out and reserve 13 cups broth; save the remaining broth for another use.

4 Return the broth to the now-empty pot. Bring to a boil and stir in the fish sauce and salt. Add the potato, yellow onion, carrot, and remaining 2 cups shredded chicken and return to a boil.

5 Rinse and untangle the kalguksu in a large bowl of water to remove excess starch (which otherwise would make the broth too thick). Stir the kalguksu into the broth and boil until just fully cooked, about 3 minutes. Stir in the aehobak and minced garlic. Turn off the heat and stir in the green onions. Top individual portions with ground pepper, seasoned chicken, and a spoonful of kalguksu yangnyeomjang and serve, passing the remaining sauce separately.

YASIK AND DESSERTS

Yasik, Now and Then

SARAH
세라

Yasik, which refers to "midnight snacks," has evolved into a late-night culture deeply ingrained in modern Korean life. With South Korea's economic prosperity in recent decades, the tradition of indulging in these comforting snacks has steadily grown in popularity. Enjoyed alone or with others, yasik has become a way for those up late— from socializing, working, or studying—to unwind with something crave-worthy. Whether it's a plate full of fiery Tteokbokki (Spicy Rice Cakes; page 319), brown sugary Sikppang Hotteok (Sweet Pancake Sandwiches; page 320), or even something more substantial such as a steaming pot of ramen served with a side of vibrant kimchi or Korean Fried Chicken (page 198) paired with an ice-cold beer (known as chimaek, a mash-up of chicken and maekju, the Korean word for beer), these snacks hold a special charm, tasting even better in the quiet of the night for reasons unknown.

SARAH What were some of your favorite snacks growing up?

UMMA *Back then, we didn't really have many snacks. We simply ate to fill our stomachs.*

SARAH So, Korea in general didn't have snacks when you were growing up?

UMMA *I'm not sure what was fully available when I was in elementary school, as my view of the world was limited then. However, I distinctly remember always keeping an eye out for scraps of burnt and unusable aluminum from cookware in our home. When I found a piece, I would excitedly run down the street with my collected aluminum to buy some beondegi, a popular street food snack made from silkworm pupae. I knew when the vendors were around because they would announce their arrival by tapping loudly on their aluminum bowl filled with cooked silkworms, singing, "Degi degi, beondegi, degi degi beondegi!" in a fun rhythm. Neighboring kids and I would exchange aluminum or money for a newspaper cone filled with seasoned silkworms. Then, the vendor would profit from the aluminum that kids had exchanged for the beondegi.*

SARAH How did it taste? I remember beondegi being sold right next to Han River on our most recent trip to Korea. Do you remember that?

UMMA *Yes, I remember. It's still around because it's a nostalgic snack. I enjoyed the beondegi a lot. It's nutty, savory, sweet, and meaty—everything we wanted in a snack. All the kids loved it. We didn't get to eat much protein, so you can only imagine how much of an indulgent treat this was. In middle school, I recall the moment I realized one of my childhood friends was living comfortably. She took piano classes, and her parents would bribe her to practice using chocolate as a reward. I remember feeling surprised when I saw that.*

Umma and I sat in silence as I finally understood what snacks meant to Umma and what had been available to her.

Umma, age 5, with her oldest sister, Halmeoni, and Harabeoji at her sister's high-school graduation in 1964.

UMMA *But now that I think more about it, there were some snacks that we enjoyed, although on rare occasions. Dalgona (sugar candy), for example, is one. Back then, we called it ttoppopgi. Halmeoni would buy us these candies for a few cents each on rare occasions. Dalgona was featured in the show* Squid Game *as a challenge. Remember when the contestants were aggressively licking the dalgona and using needles to carve out the engraved shape without breaking it?*

SARAH Yeah, I remember that. You licked the candy like that too?

Umma and I burst into hysterical laughter, recalling the intense licking scene from *Squid Game.*

UMMA *Yeah, I did, but there was a reason. I would bring a needle from home because, you know, Halmeoni had plenty as a hanbok seamstress. All the neighboring kids and I would line up and squat with our needles in one hand, licking away and working diligently with sweat running down our foreheads to carve out the shape in perfect condition. If successful, that meant we could get another piece of dalgona for free from the street vendor.*

SARAH The dalgona must've been really good for you to put in so much effort. This sounds really cute.

UMMA *In some sense, it's kind of sad too, don't you think? We didn't work hard to get the shapes out just because it was candy, but because we could get another one for free. We rarely came by free things, let alone a sweet treat. And similarly, we collected aluminum to get a taste of protein.*

SARAH What other snacks were you able to enjoy?

UMMA *On rare occasions, another snack we were able to buy was boiled squid dipped in gochujang sold by street vendors. It was surprisingly cheap back then. We also ate freshly puffed rice that street sellers would spin in these cannons. Right before the rice puffed, the sellers would yell, "Ppeongiyo!" to warn everyone of the incoming big bang. When I was in middle school, fried foods sold on the street became more common, and once in a great while, I got to indulge in yachae twigim (fried vegetables; see page 322), eomukguk (fish cake soup; see page 237), or tteokbokki (spicy rice cakes; see page 319).*

SARAH Oh right, you told me that you used the money Harabeoji gave you to buy schoolbooks to buy these!

UMMA *When I became a mother in America, seeing a pantry full of snacks made me incredibly happy. Being able to give a snack to my children so easily each day meant a lot to me.*

Jeongigui Tongdak Yachae Mussam Mari
전기구이 통닭 야채무쌈말이

juhn-ghee-goo-ee yah-chae moo-ssahm mah-ri

SARAH
세라

For a quick and beautiful finger food that's perfect for a potluck or party and looks like you spent more time on it than you actually did, try mussam mari. This dish requires no cooking, thanks to the convenience of store-bought rotisserie chicken. There's just ingredient preparation and then the assembly of wrapping the sliced vegetables and chicken in a pickled radish wrap. These are zesty, crunchy, and light, and they pair wonderfully with the honey-mustard sauce we suggest here. Or try them with Gochujang-Mustard Sauce (page 37) and/or Perilla Seed Sauce (page 37).

Umma's Kitchen Wisdom

Homemade ssammu (pickled radish slices) are ideal here. You can buy ssammu at Korean markets, but keep in mind that their flavor may vary depending on the brand. Either way, you want the slices to be at least 3½ inches in diameter to ensure that you'll have plenty of space for the fillings.

For the prettiest presentation, I use a combination of three bell pepper colors; however, you can use a single large bell pepper instead (340 grams). Try to cut the bell peppers as straight and evenly as possible.

SERVES 4   TOTAL TIME 30 minutes

20 slices Ssammu (Pickled Radish Slices; page 140), drained
½ red bell pepper (113 grams), cut into 3-inch-long matchsticks, ¼ inch wide
½ orange bell pepper (113 grams), cut into 3-inch-long matchsticks, ¼ inch wide
½ yellow bell pepper (113 grams), cut into 3-inch-long matchsticks, ¼ inch wide
¾ ounce (21 grams) radish, broccoli, or arugula sprouts, trimmed
5 ounces (142 grams) cooked rotisserie chicken breast, skin discarded, torn into 3-inch-long strands, ½ inch wide
1 recipe Honey-Mustard Sauce (page 36)

1 Place several pickled radish slices on a cutting board. Arrange 1 piece of each bell pepper, roughly 6 radish sprouts, leafy ends pointing outward, and a piece of chicken in the center of each radish slice, allowing a portion of the filling to overhang slightly on one side of the radish slice.

2 Fold the radish slices in half to create half-moon-shaped wraps and arrange on a serving platter. Repeat with the remaining radish slices, bell peppers, sprouts, and chicken. Serve with the dipping sauce.

Kimchi Grilled Cheese 김치그릴치즈

SARAH 세라

Thanksgiving has always meant a trip to Costco with Umma to purchase their premade holiday foods. Of these, one staple we never skip is their macaroni and cheese. It's creamy, cheesy, and comforting—a perfect complement to our annual Thanksgiving meal. Despite our love for this dish, my family never quite manages to finish it all on Thanksgiving Day. Of course, as with many other leftovers, Umma has found a way to bring the macaroni and cheese back to life after the holiday by pairing it with kimchi. The spicy kick of the kimchi elevates the creamy richness of the mac and cheese to a whole new level. It's now a ritual in our household to enjoy them together after every Thanksgiving—a fusion of comfort food and Korean flavors that we cannot get enough of. Inspired by this family tradition and its delicious blend of traditional American and Korean foods, Umma and I endeavored to create a kimchi grilled cheese sandwich that celebrates this pairing. Our recipe brings together the rich and gooey goodness of melted Muenster cheese with the spicy, tangy flavors of kimchi, sandwiching them between buttery griddled sourdough bread slices. For even more depth, we include a layer of chopped green onion, along with a blend of seasonings.

Umma's Kitchen Wisdom

A sturdy bread, such as sourdough, is ideal here to prevent the sandwich from becoming soggy.

I use well-fermented Mat Kimchi (Cut Napa Cabbage Kimchi; page 115) to make this dish. If you wish to use store-bought kimchi instead, see page 20 for purchasing tips.

When measuring out the kimchi, simply pick it up with tongs with the juices intact.

SERVES 1   TOTAL TIME 30 minutes

- 2 tablespoons salted butter, divided
- ½ cup (100 grams) well-fermented cabbage kimchi, chopped fine
- 2 teaspoons sugar, plus extra for sprinkling
- ½ teaspoon fish sauce
- ½ teaspoon gochugaru
- ¼ teaspoon Dasida beef stock powder
- 2 (½-inch-thick) slices sourdough bread
- 3 slices (61 grams) Muenster cheese, halved
- ½ teaspoon garlic powder
- ½ teaspoon onion powder
- ¼ teaspoon black pepper
- 2 green onions, chopped fine

1 Melt ½ tablespoon butter in a 12-inch nonstick skillet over medium-high heat. Add the kimchi and cook, stirring occasionally, until heated through and it begins to sizzle. Stir in the sugar, fish sauce, gochugaru, and Dasida powder and cook until the liquid has just evaporated, about 1 minute. (Don't let the kimchi dry out.) Transfer the seasoned kimchi to a small plate and set aside. Wipe the skillet clean with paper towels.

2 Melt half of the remaining butter in the skillet over medium-high heat. Add the bread slices and swirl them around the skillet to coat them in butter on the first side; transfer the bread to a separate plate. Repeat melting the remaining butter and coating the second sides of the bread slices. Continue to toast the bread on the second sides until just golden brown and crisp, about 1 minute.

3 Reduce the heat to low and flip the bread slices. Arrange the cheese evenly on top of the bread slices, then sprinkle with the garlic powder, onion powder, and pepper. Sprinkle 1 slice of the bread with the onions, then neatly arrange the seasoned kimchi on top. Place the second slice of bread over the kimchi, cheese side down. Using a spatula, gently press down on the sandwich to help seal it. Cover and cook until the cheese is fully melted, about 2 minutes, flipping the sandwich halfway through cooking. Transfer the sandwich to a wire rack and sprinkle with sugar on both sides to taste. Garnish the sandwich with any green onions that fell out into the skillet. Slice and serve.

VEGETABLE PANCAKES

Yachaejeon 야채전

yah-chae-juhn

SARAH
세라

Along with Kimchijeon (Kimchi Pancakes; page 316), we all regularly enjoy yachaejeon as a snack when passing through our kitchen. These pancakes contain no kimchi—this is purely a vegetable pancake made up of an array of punchy vegetables such as garlic chives, yellow and green onions, and herbaceous perilla leaves. What I like about Umma's pancakes is that she loads them up with vegetables and uses a minimal amount of flour. To me, this is the preferred ratio, allowing the flavors of the vegetables to shine without being over-shadowed by the batter. This approach—minimizing the use of flour or rice so that the flavors of the other ingredients, usually vegetables, can be fully enjoyed—is common through-out her cooking; see Gimbap (Seaweed Rice Rolls; page 257) for another example of this technique. Here, Umma's perfected ratio of vegetables to flour batter yields a harmonious blend of savory, umami taste from the seasoning, chewy and crispy textures (the outer perilla leaves are so crispy they just shatter with each bite!), and an array of fresh, savory flavors from all the vegetables.

SERVES 6 to 8 (makes 18 pancakes)
TOTAL TIME 1½ hours

   2 cups (240 grams) Korean frying mix
1½ teaspoons Dasida beef stock powder
   1 teaspoon sugar
1½ cups cold water
   1 tablespoon Kikkoman Hon Tsuyu soup and sauce base
   ½ yellow onion (142 grams), sliced thin
   4 ounces (113 grams) imitation crab sticks, lightly squeezed and pulled apart into fine strands
   3 ounces (85 grams) perilla leaves, sliced into ½-inch strips
   3 ounces (85 grams) garlic chives, cut into 2-inch lengths
   4 green onions (60 grams), white and light green parts halved lengthwise, cut into 2-inch lengths
   1 Fresno chile, stemmed, seeded, and finely chopped
   1 cup plus 2 tablespoons neutral cooking oil, divided

1 Using a wooden spoon, stir the frying mix, Dasida powder, and sugar in a large bowl. Gradually stir in the water and tsuyu until the batter is just combined (be careful not to overmix).

2 Toss the yellow onion, crab, perilla leaves, chives, green onions, and Fresno chile together in a separate bowl. Add the vegetable mixture to the bowl with the batter and toss gently until well combined.

3 Set a wire rack in a rimmed baking sheet. Heat 2 table-spoons oil in a 12-inch nonstick skillet over medium heat until shimmering. Using a ⅓-cup dry measuring cup, place 3 portions of the vegetable mixture in the skillet. Using a shallow spoon or ladle, press each portion into a 3-inch round that is ¼ inch thick and evenly distribute the vegetables. (If there are any large gaps between vegetable pieces, you can fill them with a portion of the batter.) Cook, occasionally tilting and shaking the skillet in a circular motion to distribute oil under the pancakes, until the pancakes are just set around the edges and the oil has been absorbed, 2 to 3 minutes.

4 Using a thin spatula, carefully flip the pancakes; press down gently on the pancakes with the spatula. Drizzle 1 tablespoon oil around the edges of the pancakes and cook, tilting and gently shaking the skillet to distribute oil under the pancakes, until the second side begins to crisp and turn light golden brown and the oil has been absorbed, 2 to 3 minutes. Flip the pancakes and continue to cook on the first side until golden brown and the edges begin to crisp, about 2 minutes. Transfer the pancakes to the prepared rack.

5 Stir the vegetable mixture to recombine. Repeat frying the pancakes in 5 more batches, stirring the vegetable mixture before starting each successive batch. Serve immediately.

Umma's Kitchen Wisdom

Avoid overmixing the batter, as this will cause the pancakes to be dense and chewy.

Look for perilla leaves that are 3 to 4 inches in diameter, and halve the larger leaves lengthwise before slicing.

These are so well seasoned and savory that we often eat them plain. If you'd like to serve a dipping sauce, I suggest Cho Ganjang (Vinegar Soy Sauce; page 35) made with plenty of gochugaru.

Kimchijeon 김치전

gim-chi-juhn

<table>
<tr><td>SARAH
세라</td><td>I often see Umma enjoying these pancakes in the kitchen. She spontaneously and quickly whips up the batter using the same frying mix she always buys from the Korean grocery store, adding</td></tr>
</table>

minimal seasonings and her homemade aged kimchi to create crispy pancakes that are mouthwatering at first sight and smell. Pan-fried in oil to produce a spicy, tangy crunch, these pancakes are guaranteed to satisfy any time the munchies hit. This is a popular snack commonly served at restaurants as well as in Korean households because it's so easy to make.

Kitchen Conversation

SARAH Did you have kimchijeon as a snack growing up? You eat that all the time and enjoy it a lot.

UMMA *Kimchijeon back then wasn't considered a snack for us like it is now. Its history is a part of kimchi's history; we found creative ways to use and serve kimchi because kimchi and rice were all we had. So, at that time, it wasn't considered a snack that we indulged in. It was just another common kimchi dish, and there was a lot of flour in the pancake mixture to fill our stomachs.*

SARAH So why do you think you enjoy it so much even now?

UMMA *Nowadays, we don't eat kimchi every day for every meal. We have the privilege to eat and indulge in lots of different foods, transforming kimchijeon into a snack we can now enjoy on our own terms. But also, kimchijeon will always be timelessly delicious. It easily ranks among the top 10 yasik for me, and arguably for all Koreans. I mean, it's kimchi that's been fried in oil, so how can it not be good?*

SERVES 4 to 6 (makes 11 pancakes)
TOTAL TIME 1 hour

1¾ cups (400 grams) well-fermented cabbage kimchi, coarsely chopped, plus 3 tablespoons kimchi juice
1¾ cups (210 grams) Korean frying mix
½ yellow onion (142 grams), halved across equator, sliced crosswise ¼ inch thick
1 cup cold water
1½ tablespoons sugar
2½ teaspoons Dasida beef stock powder
¾ cup plus 2 tablespoons neutral cooking oil, divided

1 Using a wooden spoon, stir the kimchi and kimchi juice, frying mix, onion, water, sugar, and Dasida powder in a large bowl until just combined and no streaks of flour remain (be careful not to overmix).

2 Set a wire rack in a rimmed baking sheet. Heat 2 tablespoons of the oil in a 12-inch nonstick skillet over medium heat until shimmering. Using a ⅓-cup dry measuring cup, place 3 portions of the kimchi mixture in the skillet. Using a shallow spoon or ladle, press each portion into a 4-inch round, evenly distributing the kimchi and onion. Cook, tilting and shaking the skillet occasionally in a circular motion to distribute the oil under the pancakes, until the pancakes are just set around the edges and the oil has been absorbed, 2 to 3 minutes.

3 Using a thin spatula, carefully flip the pancakes. Drizzle 2 tablespoons oil around the edges of the pancakes and cook, tilting and gently shaking the skillet to distribute the oil under the pancakes, until the second side begins to crisp and turn light golden brown and the oil has been absorbed, 3 to 5 minutes. Flip the pancakes and continue to cook on the first side until golden brown and the edges begin to crisp, 1 to 2 minutes. Transfer the pancakes to the prepared rack.

4 Stir the remaining batter to recombine, then repeat with 2 cups batter and ½ cup oil in 2 more batches; transfer the pancakes to the rack. Heat the remaining 2 tablespoons oil in the now-empty skillet and repeat with the final 2 pancakes; you will not need to add any additional oil after flipping. Serve immediately.

Umma's Kitchen Wisdom

I prefer the flavor of well-fermented Mat Kimchi (Cut Napa Cabbage Kimchi; page 115). If you'd rather use store-bought kimchi, see page 20 for purchasing tips.

When measuring out the kimchi, simply pick it up with tongs with the juices intact.

Avoid overmixing the batter, as this will cause the pancakes to be dense and chewy.

Sometimes you'll see large kimchi pancakes. I use less flour than typical in my pancakes, since I think it lets the kimchi flavor shine through more strongly. With less flour, they're a little harder to flip, which is why I make smaller pancakes.

SPICY RICE CAKES

Tteokbokki 떡볶이

ttuhk-bboh-kki

SARAH
세라

Tteokbokki is a widely enjoyed street food in Korea—it's especially favored by students seeking a quick and affordable post-school or late-night bite. As a student, Umma enjoyed tteokbokki after school too. She recalls savoring these chewy, plush rice cakes smothered in a sweet and savory sauce made with gochujang, soy sauce, sugar, and other seasonings, along with a side of twigim (deep-fried foods similar to tempura) and sundae (steamed blood sausage) that were dipped into the tteokbokki's thick, bolstering red sauce. Today, as you walk down the streets of South Korea, you'll find carts selling tteokbokki with an assortment of twigim displayed at the front, meant to be enjoyed together. This includes yakki mandu (dumplings filled with seasoned dangmyeon), Gim Mari (Fried Seaweed Rolls; page 325), squid, shrimp, sweet potato, perilla leaves, and more. Though it isn't necessary to enjoy tteokbokki with these accompaniments—this dish is plenty good on its own!—there's no denying that the added flavors and textures elevate it. At home, Umma usually serves tteokbokki alone or with assorted twigim (both store-bought and homemade), which she crisps up in her air fryer. Other nonfried foods such as Gimbap (Seaweed Rice Rolls; page 257) pair wonderfully as well, thanks to tteokbokki's versatile sauce.

Umma's Kitchen Wisdom

Look for cylindrical rice cakes, often labeled as 떡볶이떡 *(tteokbokki tteok), at Korean grocery stores. See page 22 for purchasing tips.*

If you purchase frozen rice cakes, thaw them either in the refrigerator for 24 hours or on the counter for about 1 hour before soaking.

I like the sweetness of daepa (jumbo green onion) in this dish, but you can use an equal weight of green onions.

SERVES 4   TOTAL TIME 45 minutes

- 2 ounces (57 grams) frozen fish cake sheets, thawed
- 2 tablespoons neutral cooking oil
- ½ yellow onion (142 grams), sliced ½ inch thick
- ½ daepa (jumbo green onion; 65 grams), trimmed, halved lengthwise, and cut into 2½-inch lengths
- 10 ounces (284 grams) tteokbokki tteok (rice cakes)
- 2 cups water
- 7 teaspoons sugar
- 2 tablespoons gochujang
- 2½ teaspoons gochugaru
- 2 teaspoons Dasida beef stock powder
- 1½ teaspoons soy sauce
- 1 tablespoon minced garlic
- 1 tablespoon toasted sesame oil
- 1½ teaspoons sesame seeds, toasted, plus extra for sprinkling

1 Submerge the fish cake sheets in hot water, let soak for 1 minute, then drain. Repeat soaking and draining the cakes. Halve the fish cake sheets lengthwise, then slice crosswise ¾ inch thick.

2 Heat the neutral oil in a 14-inch flat-bottomed wok or 12-inch nonstick skillet over medium-high heat until shimmering. Add the yellow onion and daepa and cook, tossing constantly, until fragrant and evenly coated in the oil, about 1 minute. Add the fish cakes and tteok and toss to combine. Stir in the water, sugar, gochujang, gochugaru, Dasida powder, and soy sauce until thoroughly combined. Bring to a boil and cook, stirring occasionally, until the sauce thickens and coats the tteok, 10 to 12 minutes.

3 Stir in the garlic. Turn off the heat and stir in the sesame oil and sesame seeds. Transfer the tteokbokki to a serving platter, sprinkle with extra sesame seeds, and serve.

Sikppang Hotteok 식빵호떡

shik-bbahng hoh-ttuhk

<table>
<tr><td>SARAH
세라</td><td>In our kitchen, the oven is always filled . . . with stored pots and pans, that is. Umma very rarely bakes or uses our oven. (We have a countertop convection oven that we use for roasting nuts</td></tr>
</table>

and sweet potatoes, but that's about it.) Making baked desserts at home was not a part of our routine. As a child, I never noticed this, as my sweet tooth cravings were always satisfied with Imobu's pastries and prepared desserts purchased from rice cake and ice cream shops. As an adult, I understand why Umma didn't have a strong inclination to make desserts from scratch—it simply wasn't a part of her childhood and upbringing, during which desserts were considered an even greater luxury than snacks. For her, there's no nostalgia or family tradition for making desserts beyond Sikhye (Rice Punch; page 358). However, there was one dessert that Umma would prepare for us on special occasions, something that she had enjoyed as a young adult: hotteok. Hotteok is a very popular street food "dessert" in South Korea. While there are many variations, the classic version features carefully crafted yeasted dough filled with a sweet brown sugar–based filling that is pan fried to golden, gooey perfection. While the original version is a favorite, Umma prefers to prepare hotteok with greater ease and convenience. Sometimes she buys a hotteok pancake mix from the Korean grocery store (these make great hotteok, by the way), but often she prepares an even simpler, modified version using sandwich bread. This sandwich bread version is much less intimidating and faster to prepare, and the results are reminiscent of the original hotteok—chewy, crispy, and filled with a satisfyingly sweet filling.

SERVES 8 (makes 8 sandwiches)
TOTAL TIME 45 minutes

- 3 tablespoons roasted peanuts, pecans, and/or almonds
- 1 tablespoon roasted pumpkin seeds
- 1 tablespoon sesame seeds, toasted
- 3 tablespoons packed brown sugar
- 1 teaspoon ground cinnamon
- 6 tablespoons honey
- 16 slices Uyusikppang (Milk Bread; page 333), ½ inch thick, divided
- 6 tablespoons (85 grams) salted butter, melted

1 Combine the nuts and pumpkin seeds in a zipper-lock bag. Using a rolling pin, gently smash the nuts and seeds to break them into smaller pieces. Transfer the contents of the bag to a small bowl. Add the sesame seeds, sugar, and cinnamon. Stir together, then stir in the honey until well combined.

2 Arrange 8 bread slices on a cutting board and spoon 1 tablespoon filling in the center of each slice. Top the slices with the remaining bread to create 8 sandwiches. Using an inverted 4-inch round cutter, stamp out the center of each sandwich, using a twisting motion to fully cut through the bread. Discard the crusts or save for another use.

3 Working with 1 hotteok at a time, pinch the edges together to seal in the filling and brush both sides with melted butter.

4A TO AIR-FRY Arrange 4 hotteok in the basket of an air fryer. Place the basket in the air fryer and set the temperature to 360 degrees. Cook until light golden brown, 8 to 10 minutes, flipping the hotteok halfway through cooking. Transfer to a large plate and repeat cooking the remaining hotteok. Serve.

4B TO PAN-FRY Arrange 4 hotteok in a 12-inch nonstick skillet. Cook over medium heat until light golden brown, about 10 minutes, flipping the hotteok halfway through cooking and adjusting the temperature as needed if the hotteok begin to brown too quickly. Transfer to a large plate and repeat cooking the remaining hotteok. Serve.

Umma's Kitchen Wisdom

If you don't want to make the Uyusikppang (Milk Bread; page 333) and you can't find an Asian milk bread at a bakery, you can substitute a soft white sandwich bread.

We use a 4-inch round cutter for these sandwiches. If your bread is smaller, opt for a smaller cutter and adjust the filling accordingly. Using the rounded side of the cutter instead of the sharp side helps seal the slices together. You can also use a large mug or a bowl as a substitute for the cutter.

My family prefers to cook these sandwiches in the air fryer instead of on the stove. The air fryer produces hotteok that are evenly toasted all around.

FRIED VEGETABLES

Yachae Twigim 야채튀김

yah-chae twee-gim

SARAH
세라

My best friend, Paige, always asked me for just one thing for her birthday when we were growing up: Umma's yachae twigim. Every year, Umma would lovingly pack Paige a four-tiered dosirak (Korean lunchbox) with layers of yachae twigim, gimbap, rice, an assortment of banchan, and a large jar of freshly made kimchi on the side. Umma would always go above and beyond when preparing home-cooked food as a gift to a loved one. Then, as we carefully wrapped the dosirak in Halmeoni's bojagi (a Korean traditional wrapping cloth), Umma would say, "Okay, go deliver it to her now, while it's hot." We have continued this tradition every year for over 20 years. Each year, Paige and I grow more grateful for Umma's cooking and the love she shows through it. Fortunately, Paige's mom also happens to be an amazing cook! Every Thanksgiving, I look forward to Paige stopping by my home with a plate of her family's feast. Yachae twigim is simply matchstick vegetables coated in batter and deep-fried until crispy. It's a timeless classic enjoyed by all ages. While any vegetables can be used, this trio of carrots, onions (two kinds), and potatoes creates what I think is a perfect blend of flavor, color, and texture in every bite. Carrots contribute mild sweetness, the onions add a gentle astringency, and potatoes provide a starchy, soft texture. Be sure to dip these bad guys into Umma's cho ganjang to complete the experience!

Umma's Kitchen Wisdom

I like the convenience of using an electric deep fryer, but you could also use a wide pot or Dutch oven that holds 6 quarts or more. Add the oil to the pot until it measures about 2 inches deep and heat over medium-high heat to 350 degrees. Adjust the heat as needed to maintain the temperature.

SERVES 4 to 6   TOTAL TIME 45 minutes

1½ cups (180 grams) Korean frying mix
1 cup cold water
1 yellow onion (283 grams), halved and sliced ¼ inch thick
1 russet potato (227 grams), peeled and cut into 3-inch matchsticks, ¼ inch thick
2 large carrots (200 grams), peeled and cut into 3-inch matchsticks, ¼ inch thick
8 green onions (120 grams), white and light green parts quartered lengthwise, cut into 3-inch lengths
2–3 quarts vegetable oil for frying
1 recipe Cho Ganjang (Vinegar Soy Sauce; page 35)

1 Using a wooden spoon or spatula, stir the frying mix and water in a large bowl until just combined and no streaks of flour remain (be careful not to overmix). Add the yellow onion, potato, carrots, and green onions to the batter and toss until all the pieces are coated with the batter. Transfer the vegetable mixture to the refrigerator and chill while heating the oil.

2 Set a wire rack in a rimmed baking sheet. Following the manufacturer's instructions, heat the oil in an electric fryer to 350 degrees. Stir the vegetable mixture to recombine. Using tongs, grab a small portion of the vegetables (about ¼ cup; try to get a balanced selection of vegetables), slowly lower the bundle into the oil, hold for 2 seconds, then release the bundle. If any of the vegetables separate from the bundle, use two chopsticks or a separate, clean pair of tongs to gently press the vegetables together until they stick. Repeat adding 3 more portions of the vegetable mixture. Fry until light golden brown and crisp, about 2 minutes, flipping halfway through frying. Using a slotted spoon, transfer the vegetable bundles to the prepared rack.

3 Discard any loose vegetable pieces left in the oil. Return the oil to 350 degrees and repeat with the remaining vegetable mixture in batches. Serve immediately with the cho ganjang.

Gim Mari 김말이

gim mah-ri

SARAH
세라
If japchae and gimbap had a baby, gim mari would be the result. This popular street food, commonly paired with Tteokbokki (Spicy Rice Cakes; page 319), combines signature elements from both japchae and gimbap. You have seasoned dangmyeon and vegetables prepared similarly to japchae (but with much less effort!), and you roll the gim tightly around this dangmyeon filling, mimicking the process of making gimbap (but with much less effort here too). What makes this my all-time favorite snack, though, is the additional step of coating it in batter and deep-frying it, resulting in next-level rolls with a multitude of textures, tastes, and colors. If you can't get to the streets of South Korea to sample freshly fried gim mari, rest assured that Umma's ultra-flavorful recipe will transport you to those street-food carts laden with tteokbokki, gim mari, and other twigim options.

Umma's Kitchen Wisdom

The saffron is optional but adds a vibrant, natural yellow color to the batter.

Any mild green chile, such as Anaheim, can be substituted for the putgochu. (Or for an extra kick, use jalapeño instead.)

Make sure to buy dried seaweed designated specifically for gimbap (gimbapgim, usually labeled as 김밥김). This type of seaweed will not rip as you roll it.

I like the convenience of using an electric deep fryer, but you could use a wide pot or Dutch oven that holds 6 quarts or more instead. Add the oil to the pot until it measures about 2 inches deep and heat over medium-high heat to 350 degrees. Adjust the heat as needed to maintain the temperature.

You can freeze leftovers for up to 1 month. To reheat, pop them into an air fryer at 400 degrees for 15 minutes. Or reheat at 400 degrees for 20 minutes in an oven.

SERVES 12 to 15 (makes 60 rolls)
TOTAL TIME 2 hours, plus 1 hour soaking

Pinch saffron (optional)
3½ cups (420 grams) Korean frying mix, divided

FILLING

10 ounces (284 grams) dangmyeon (Korean glass noodles)
2 tablespoons neutral cooking oil, divided
1½ cups (142 grams) coarsely grated carrot
1 putgochu (young green Korean chile; 85 grams), stemmed, seeded, quartered lengthwise, and sliced thin crosswise
6 green onions (90 grams), sliced thin
1 tablespoon plus 1½ teaspoons sugar, divided
1 tablespoon plus ½ teaspoon Dasida beef stock powder, divided
¾ teaspoon miwon matsogeum (MSG seasoning salt), divided
2 tablespoons toasted sesame oil
1½ tablespoons oyster sauce
1½ tablespoons soy sauce
1 teaspoon black pepper

15 (8-inch square) sheets gimbapgim, halved
2–3 quarts vegetable oil for frying
1 recipe Cho Ganjang (Vinegar Soy Sauce; page 35)

1 Steep the saffron, if using, in 2 cups water in a small bowl for at least 1 hour or overnight. Strain the saffron water through a fine-mesh strainer into a separate bowl or container; discard the solids.

2 Add 3 cups frying mix to a large bowl. Using a wooden spoon or spatula, gradually stir in the water until the batter is just combined (be careful not to overmix). Cover and refrigerate the batter until ready to use.

RECIPE CONTINUES

3 FOR THE FILLING Bring 2 quarts water to a boil in a large, wide pot. Add the dangmyeon, using tongs as needed to fully submerge the noodles. Stir in 1 tablespoon neutral oil. Turn off the heat, cover, and let the noodles soak until softened but still very chewy, 6 to 9 minutes. Drain the noodles in a colander and shake to remove excess water. Using kitchen shears, cut the noodles into 6- to 7-inch-long pieces. Set aside to cool slightly.

4 Meanwhile, heat the remaining 1 tablespoon neutral oil in a 14-inch flat-bottomed wok or 12-inch nonstick skillet over medium-high heat until shimmering. Add the carrot and putgochu and toss to coat. Add the onions, 1 teaspoon sugar, ½ teaspoon Dasida powder, and ¼ teaspoon seasoning salt and cook, tossing constantly, until the vegetables are just beginning to soften, about 2 minutes. Transfer to a large bowl; do not wipe the wok clean.

5 Add the noodles, sesame oil, oyster sauce, soy sauce, pepper, remaining 3½ teaspoons sugar, remaining 1 table-spoon Dasida powder, and remaining ½ teaspoon seasoning salt to the now-empty wok and toss until evenly coated. Add the vegetables and toss until thoroughly combined. Transfer the filling to the bowl.

6 Place 1 gim sheet half shiny side down on a counter, with the longer side parallel to the bottom edge of the counter.

Starting ½ inch from the bottom edge of the gim, arrange ¼ cup filling in a 1-inch row across the length of the gim. Using your fingers, lightly moisten the top edge of the gim with water. Lift and roll the bottom edge of the gim sheet up and over the filling, then continue to roll into a tight log. Using kitchen shears, trim any filling that protrudes from the ends of the gim mari (so that they will fry cleanly), then cut the gim mari in half. Transfer the gim mari seam side down to a large platter and repeat rolling with the remaining gim sheets and filling; stack the rolls as needed.

7 Set a wire rack in a rimmed baking sheet. Following the manufacturer's instructions, heat the oil in an electric fryer to 350 degrees. Spread the remaining ½ cup frying mix in a shallow dish. Whisk the batter to recombine. Working with 7 gim mari at a time, roll in the frying mix, shaking off the excess, then submerge in the batter. Using tongs, remove the gim mari from the batter 1 at a time, allowing excess batter to drip off, and submerge in the hot oil. Hold for 5 seconds, then release the gim mari into the oil. Fry, stirring with a wooden chopstick or skewer to prevent sticking, until light brown and crisp, about 3 minutes. Using tongs, transfer the gim mari to the prepared rack. Use a spider skimmer to remove any loose pieces left in the oil. Return the oil to 350 degrees and repeat with the remaining gim mari in 8 more batches. Serve immediately with cho ganjang.

Place 1 gim sheet half shiny side down, with the longer side parallel to the bottom edge of the counter. Starting ½ inch from the bottom edge of the gim, arrange ¼ cup filling in a 1-inch row across its length. Using your fingers, moisten the top edge of the gim with water.

Lift and roll the bottom edge of the gim sheet up and over the filling, then continue to roll into a tight log. Trim any filling that protrudes from the ends of the roll, then cut the roll in half. Transfer the pieces seam side down to a platter and repeat with the remaining gim sheets and filling.

Working with 7 gim mari at a time, roll in the frying mix, shaking off the excess, then submerge in the batter. Using tongs, remove the gim mari from the batter 1 at a time, allowing excess batter to drip off, and slowly submerge in the hot oil.

Fry, stirring with a chopstick or wooden skewer to prevent sticking, until light brown and crisp, about 3 minutes. Remove with tongs.

The Hands That Shape Tradition

SARAH
세라

A person's hands tell a story. A cook's hands carry the scars from accidental cuts and burns, a house painter's hands become leathered and calloused from working under the hot summer sun, and a baker's hands become permanently slanted and swollen from shaping dough into balls and piping cream onto cakes and into buns. At her restaurant, Umma always had finger covers available so that her bandaged cuts would look presentable to her hungry customers. Appa always has a tub of industrial-grade paint removal cleanser sitting on our bathroom counter to rinse away the crackled paint embedded in the creases of his worn-out hands. And Imobu (Uncle; husband to an aunt on the maternal side, whom I refer to as Uncle Baker Chun on social media) is often seen massaging his fingers with Salonpas and Tiger Balm, trying to ease the curling from decades of work.

Imobu is a seasoned professional baker who has been serving Korean pastries to Southern California for nearly four decades. He honed his craft through formal training in Korea under the guidance of both Korean and European pastry chefs. He then worked for multiple bakeries in America as the head pastry chef, baking a multitude of classic Korean pastries and cakes for primarily Korean Americans who wished to enjoy the not-too-sweet desserts reminiscent of home.

Eventually, his skills led him to open his own bakery in Tustin, California. The bakery enjoyed considerable success, particularly within the Korean American community in Orange County. Today, he is a semi-retired pastry chef and currently bakes for a local bakery specializing in both Korean and French pastries.

One of my favorite memories of Imobu dates back to fifth grade. For my 11th birthday, I wanted to bring cupcakes to class to celebrate with my classmates, but I didn't want them to have just any cupcakes—I wanted them to taste Imobu's cupcakes. Having grown up with Imobu's cakes for most of my life's celebrations, I took a lot of pride in his craft and knew just how delicious his pastries and cakes were. They were simple and elegantly light, yet sweet enough for all to enjoy, embodying the essence of Korean desserts. I wanted to share that with those closest to me outside of my family—my classmates. However, at this time Imobu was incredibly busy due to the success of his bakery. Umma warned me that Imobu might lack the bandwidth to bake me cupcakes.

I nervously dialed Imobu on our landline phone, with my fingers crossed behind my back, hoping that this wasn't the case. I asked for this favor, and without hesitation, he said, "Of course, what flavors would you like?"

CONTINUES

That next week, Imobu prepared about 50 vanilla cupcakes for my classmates, teachers, and staff to enjoy. I felt a surge of pride as I watched everyone, including several teachers and staff members, enjoy his perfectly baked cupcakes topped with sweetened whipped cream. I recall the adults in particular saying, "I've never tasted a dessert this light and delicious. I could easily eat 10 of these!" To which I proudly responded, "They're Korean cupcakes! That's why!"

Fast-forward to the present day. Inspired by the milk cream doughnuts that Umma and I found at our Korean grocery store and that were selling out nationally (see page 345), I wondered what I could do to get my hands on them again and share them with others. I reached out to Imobu to see if he would be interested in collaborating with me to develop some recipes. Unsurprisingly, he responded with, "Of course, what pastries were you thinking?"

He came over the following week with a box of his pastry tools and decorating tips, along with his notebooks from the 1980s that contained all his original recipes—the same recipes that helped support his own family. Ready to pass down his knowledge, he smiled and said, "All right, let's start with these cream doughnuts!" The resulting doughnuts are far superior to the store-bought ones—so much so that others have remarked that they're even better than the ones they've tasted in Korea and Japan.

Later in our collaboration, when Imobu showed me how to shape the Sobboroppang (Peanut Butter Streusel Bread; page 341), he dipped the perfectly smooth dough balls into a light, crumbled peanut butter streusel we had prepared the day before. Ever so subtly he curved his fingers to sculpt each one into a uniform dome, ready for baking. As he repeated this process with each dough ball, I noticed his weathered hands, a sight that reminded me of my own parents' hands over the years. I said, "Your hands have gone through a lot too, Imobu."

Imobu replied "Oh, you noticed? Yeah, they've changed shape throughout the decades. My left hand is permanently slanted and my right hand is swollen. My left hand is used to shape dough into balls and domes like this, while my right hand is used to hold piping bags filled with cream. Korean pastries tend to be round and curved, so my hands just adapted to that over time."

As I watched him work, I realized that the hands that shaped these pastries were not just tools of the trade but storytellers in their own right—holding the tradition of Korean pastries passed down through generations, brought to America with hopes and dreams.

In baking, precision is everything. Like many pastry chefs, Imobu never relies on guesswork or volume measurements—he uses a scale to weigh every ingredient down to the gram. So get your scales ready and your oven preheated, and let's dive into the world of Korean baking.

MILK BREAD

Uyusikppang 우유식빵

oo-yoo-shik-bbahng

SARAH
세라

Imobu sold three types of sliced loaf bread at his bakery: multigrain, chestnut, and milk bread. Whenever I tagged along on Umma's visits to the bakery to offer a helping hand, I would be tasked with closing these bagged loaves with a metallic twist tie. The first time I did this, I painstakingly braided each twist tie by hand, carefully looping one strip around another with both hands. However, I quickly learned to twist the entire tie with just my thumb and index finger and a few turns after watching Umma and Imo (aunt from maternal side; Umma's sister) close the bags with a pinch of their fingers, in a factory assembly-line fashion. At the end of the day, Imobu would sometimes swing by our home to drop off some of the leftover bread. But one type of bread was never included in these drop-offs, because it was always guaranteed to be sold out by midday: his tender, fluffy, beloved milk bread, lightly sweetened with milk and sugar. Imobu's bakery closed when the Korean grocery store it was located in shut down, and I struggled to find this bread elsewhere. Other Korean bakeries sold milk bread, but like Imobu's bakery, they would sell out fast due to high demand. (To this day, I always have to make sure to go to the bakery extra early to grab myself this loaf before they're gone!) I tried baking this bread myself using online tutorials but found the kneading and proofing process far too time-consuming. Thankfully, I was reunited with Imobu's milk bread when he passed down his bakery recipe and adjusted it so that it could be baked in a home kitchen. He showed me how to cut down on proofing time without a proofer by placing a pan of boiling water in the oven with the prepared dough. This makes bread baking a bit less daunting. Oh, and if you're curious about how milk bread differs from white bread found at the grocery store, just imagine white bread elevated to a luxurious, elegant, and cloudlike version of itself. Milk bread is softer, fluffier, and much more delicate, making it far better for sandwiches, toast with butter and sugar, and sweet snacks.

MAKES 1 loaf   TOTAL TIME 1¾ hours, plus 2 hours rising, resting, and cooling

302 grams bread flour
 15 grams sugar
  5 grams instant or rapid-rise yeast
  5 grams fine salt
220 grams warm milk (110 degrees), plus 55 grams milk, divided
 30 grams unsalted butter, softened
  1 large egg yolk

1 Stir the flour, sugar, yeast, and salt together in the bowl of a stand mixer, then add the warm milk. Fit the stand mixer with the dough hook and mix on low speed until all the ingredients are moistened, about 30 seconds. Increase the speed to medium and continue to mix until a sticky dough just forms, about 2 minutes, scraping down the sides of the bowl as needed.

2 With the mixer running, add the butter and continue to mix until fully incorporated and the dough is smooth and elastic and clears the sides of the bowl, 15 to 17 minutes, scraping down the bowl halfway through mixing. Transfer the dough to a lightly greased large bowl. Cover with plastic wrap and let sit at room temperature until doubled in volume, about 30 minutes.

3 Divide the dough into 3 equal portions (about 189 grams each). Working with 1 piece of dough at a time, form into a rough ball by stretching the dough around your thumb and pinching the edges together so that the top is smooth. Place the ball seam side down on a clean counter and, using your cupped hand, drag in small circles until the dough feels taut and round. Pinch the bottom seam to ensure it's sealed securely and cover with plastic. Let the dough balls rest for 20 minutes.

RECIPE CONTINUES

4 Lightly grease a clean counter. Place 1 dough ball seam side up on the counter and, using a rolling pin, press and roll into a 10-inch oval with a short side facing toward you. (It's best to use light pressure and avoid rolling rapidly back and forth. Instead, roll completely from one end to the other, then repeat in the other direction.) Fold the dough crosswise into thirds, like a business letter, to form a rough 5 by 2½-inch loaf and cover with plastic. Repeat with the remaining dough balls.

5 Grease an 8½ by 4½-inch loaf pan. Arrange 1 loaf on the counter with a short side facing you. Using a small greased rolling pin, press and roll the dough into a 10-inch strip. Starting on the short side closest to you, fold the 2 corners in to meet, then continue to roll the dough away from you into a tight cylinder. Pinch the seam to seal and arrange the loaf seam side down in the prepared pan, with the short side of the loaf facing the long side of the pan. Repeat with the remaining 2 loaves. Bring 1 quart water to a boil.

6 Adjust an oven rack to the upper-middle position. Place a shallow baking pan on the bottom of the oven. Preheat the oven to 200 degrees for 1 minute, then turn off the oven. Pour the boiling water into the prepared pan. Place the loaf pan on the rack, close the oven, and allow the loaf to rise until the dough is ½ inch from the top edge of the pan, about 25 minutes.

7 Carefully remove the baking pan from the oven and discard the water. Remove the loaf pan from the oven and heat the oven to 375 degrees. While the oven preheats, lightly mist the loaf with water to prevent the top from drying out. Return the loaf pan to the oven and bake until the loaf is deep golden brown and registers about 206 degrees, 25 to 27 minutes.

8 Whisk the remaining 55 grams milk and the egg yolk together in a small bowl until well combined. Using pot holders, carefully remove the pan from the oven and invert the bread onto a wire rack. Reinvert the loaf and immediately brush the top with the milk mixture (not all of the mixture will be used). Let cool completely before slicing.

> ### Uncle's Baking Wisdom
>
> *I prefer whole milk, but you can use low-fat milk. Just don't use skim milk.*
>
> *For all of the baked goods in this chapter, I like to use a small-diameter, short, handle-free rolling pin.*

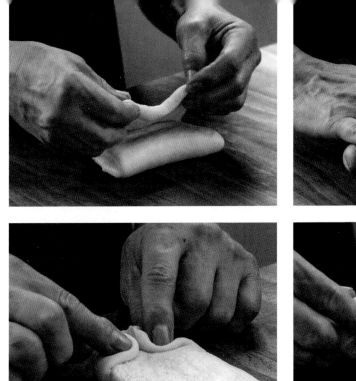
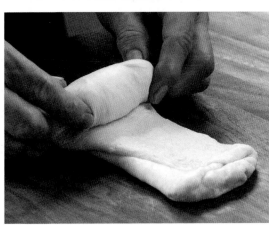
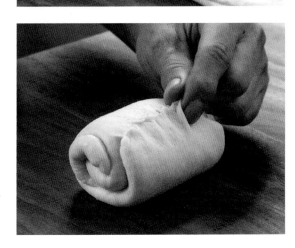

Top After rolling a dough ball into an oval, fold the dough oval crosswise into thirds, like a business letter, to form a rough 5 by 2½-inch loaf. Repeat with the remaining 2 dough balls. Arrange 1 dough piece on the counter with a short side facing you, and, using a rolling pin, press and roll the dough into a 10-inch strip.

Middle Starting on the short side closest to you, fold the 2 corners in to meet, then continue to roll the dough away from you into a tight cylinder.

Bottom Pinch the seam to seal and arrange the loaf seam side down in the prepared pan, with the short side of the loaf facing the long side of the pan. Repeat with the remaining 2 loaves.

SALT BREAD

Sogeumppang 소금빵

soh-guem-bbahng

SARAH
세라

What is salt bread, you might ask? This very trendy pastry bread has gained popularity and even become a craze among café-goers in South Korea. Said to have originated in Japan, this bread combines the best characteristics of a croissant, a baguette, and Uyusikppang (Milk Bread; page 333) into a single roll. Buttery and crispy yet also plush and cloud-like, this bread is rolled and baked with a block of butter at its core. (For maximum flavor, Imobu recommends using high-quality salted butter and whole milk.) As it bakes, the butter melts to create a crispy, golden crust on the bottom and a tender, fluffy interior. With a sprinkle of pretzel salt on top, these rolls are truly irresistible, combining all the elements of our favorite breads into one perfect bite. It's no wonder that salt bread has people lining up outside the doors of bakeries that sell it, rain or shine. Imobu learned this recipe during pastry school from Korean chefs who had originally learned it from Japanese chefs long before it became trendy. In fact, he pulled out his recipe notebooks from the 1980s to find his original recipe. Just as good music and certain fashion trends always make comebacks, it seems salt bread is doing the same.

MAKES 8 rolls   TOTAL TIME 2¼ hours, plus 1½ hours rising and resting

240 grams bread flour
 72 grams cake flour
 25 grams sugar
  5 grams instant or rapid-rise yeast
  3 grams fine salt
240 grams warm milk (110 degrees), plus 55 grams milk, divided
 24 grams salted butter, softened, plus 120 grams salted butter, chilled and cut into eight 15-gram pieces, divided
    Coarse pretzel salt
  1 large egg yolk

1 Whisk the bread flour, cake flour, sugar, yeast, and fine salt together in the bowl of a stand mixer, then add the warm milk. Fit the stand mixer with the dough hook and mix on low speed until all the ingredients are moistened, about 30 seconds. Increase the speed to medium and continue to mix until a sticky dough just forms, about 2 minutes, scraping down the sides of the bowl as needed.

2 With the mixer running, add the softened butter and continue to mix until fully incorporated and the dough is smooth and elastic and clears the sides of the bowl, about 16 minutes, scraping down the bowl halfway through mixing. Transfer the dough to a lightly greased large bowl. Cover with plastic wrap and let sit at room temperature until doubled in volume, about 30 minutes.

3 Transfer the dough to a lightly floured counter and press gently into a 10-inch square of even thickness. Fold the dough into thirds, like a business letter. Using a bench scraper or sharp knife, cut the rectangle in half lengthwise, then cut each strip crosswise into 4 equal pieces (about 75 grams each). Working with 1 piece of dough at a time, form into a rough ball by stretching the dough around your thumb and pinching the edges together so that the top is smooth. Place the ball seam side down on a clean counter and, using your cupped hand, drag in small circles until the dough feels taut and round. Pinch the bottom seam to ensure it's sealed securely and cover with plastic. Let the dough balls rest for 20 minutes.

4 Working with 1 piece of dough at a time and using your hands, shape into an 8-inch tapered log that is roughly 2 inches at the broadest end; cover with plastic. Let the dough logs rest for 20 minutes.

5 Line a rimmed baking sheet with parchment paper. Lightly grease the counter. Place 1 dough log on the counter with the tapered end facing you. (Allow space for rolling between the tapered tip and the counter edge.) Place a small greased rolling pin in the middle of the log with one hand and grip the tapered end with the other hand.

Working simultaneously, roll toward you while gently stretching the tapered end of dough toward the counter edge.

6 Return the rolling pin to the middle of the log and repeat rolling in the opposite direction, stretching the broad end of the log away from you while rolling. Continue rolling as needed to create a tapered dough strip that is about 18 inches in length and 3 inches wide at the broadest end.

7 Arrange 1 chilled butter piece across the broad top of the dough strip, 1½ inches from the top edge. Fold the top edge of the dough over the butter toward you and press gently to seal. Fold in the edges of the dough along the butter to enclose, then continue to roll the dough toward you into a tight roll. Arrange the roll seam side down on the rimmed baking sheet and cover with plastic. Repeat with the remaining dough logs and butter, spacing the rolls evenly on the sheet. Bring 2 quarts water to a boil.

8 Adjust an oven rack to the upper-middle position. Place a shallow baking pan on the bottom of the oven. Preheat the oven to 200 degrees for 1 minute, then turn off the oven. Pour the boiling water into the prepared pan. Remove the plastic, place the baking sheet on the rack, close the oven, and allow the rolls to rise until increased in size by half, about 20 minutes.

9 Carefully remove the baking pan from the oven and discard the water. Remove the rolls from the oven and heat the oven to 375 degrees. Lightly mist the rolls with water and sprinkle with pretzel salt. Return the rolls to the oven and bake until the rolls are deep golden brown, 15 to 17 minutes, rotating the sheet after 12 minutes of baking.

10 Whisk the remaining 55 grams milk and the egg yolk in a small bowl. Transfer the rolls to a wire rack and immediately brush the tops with the milk mixture (not all of the mixture will be used). Let cool for 10 minutes before serving.

TURN TO SEE HOW TO SHAPE SALT BREAD →

Shaping Salt Bread

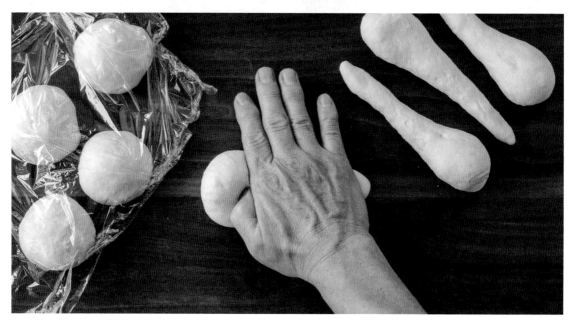

Top left After folding the dough into thirds like a business letter, cut the dough rectangle in half lengthwise, then cut each strip crosswise into 4 equal-size pieces.

Top right Working with 1 piece of dough at a time, form it into a rough ball by stretching the dough around your thumb and pinching the edges together so that the top is smooth. Place the ball seam side down on the counter and, using your cupped hand, drag in small circles until the dough feels taut and round.

Bottom Working with 1 piece of dough at a time and using your hands, shape it into an 8-inch tapered log that is roughly 2 inches at the broadest end.

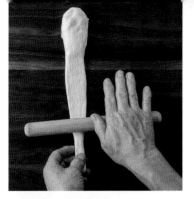
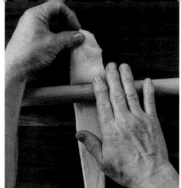
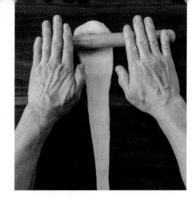
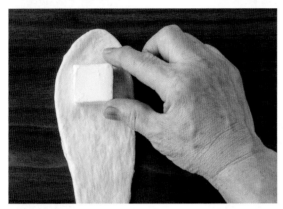

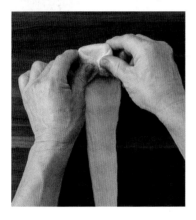

Top Arrange 1 dough log on the counter with the tapered end facing you. Place the rolling pin in the middle of the log and grip the tapered end with your other hand. Roll toward you while stretching the tapered end toward the counter edge. Return the rolling pin to the middle of the log and repeat rolling in the opposite direction while stretching the broad end of the log away from you to create an 18-inch-long strip.

Middle Arrange 1 butter piece across the broad top of the dough strip, 1½ inches from the top edge. Fold the top edge of the dough over the butter toward you and press the sides to seal.

Bottom Fold in the edges of the dough along the butter to enclose it, then roll the dough toward you into a tight roll.

Soboroppang 소보로빵

soh-boh-roh-bbahng

SARAH
세라

As Imobu and I shaped the dough balls covered in peanut butter streusel into domes, I noticed his experienced baker's hands and asked about them, nodding my head in respect as he showed them to me and explained why they looked the way they do (see page 330). Later that night, Umma brought up the conversation she had overheard between me and Imobu. She asked how I felt when I saw his hands. I told her that I had experienced a range of emotions and mentioned it wasn't the first time I felt these emotions about someone's hands. After all, hands can reveal much about a person and their dedication to providing for their family. I told Umma that seeing her and Appa's hands has always elicited in me a mix of pain, gratitude, and utmost respect. Their hands weather and wear so that their children's hands can remain unblemished and unburdened. Soboroppang, one of Imobu's best-selling pastries when he owned and operated his bakery, certainly shaped his hands over the years, leaving them with a permanent curve that tells a story of dedication. A beloved, traditional Korean bakery item, this pastry features a soft, delicate sweetened bun topped with a light, crunchy peanut butter streusel. The contrasting textures of the bun and streusel, with hints of peanut flavor, always left Imobu's customers wanting more. Whenever Imobu brought these rolls over for my family and me to enjoy, we would devour them immediately. They pair exceptionally well with coffee, tea, or milk.

Uncle's Baking Wisdom

I prefer whole milk, but you can use low-fat milk. Don't use skim milk, though.

Corn flour, also known as maize flour, is a finely ground flour made from whole corn kernels. It is not the same as cornmeal (or cornstarch).

MAKES 8 rolls   **TOTAL TIME** 2 hours, plus 13 hours 10 minutes refrigerating, rising, and resting

PEANUT BUTTER STREUSEL

230 grams all-purpose flour
 15 grams corn flour
  5 grams baking powder
185 grams sugar
 90 grams unsalted butter, softened
 60 grams creamy peanut butter
 20 grams corn syrup
    Pinch fine salt
  1 large egg

DOUGH

295 grams bread flour
 60 grams sugar
  5 grams instant or rapid-rise yeast
  3 grams fine salt
 85 grams warm milk (110 degrees)
 35 grams water
  1 large egg
 55 grams unsalted butter, softened

1 FOR THE STREUSEL Whisk the all-purpose flour, corn flour, and baking powder together in a bowl. Using a stand mixer fitted with a paddle, mix the sugar, butter, peanut butter, corn syrup, and salt on low speed until combined, about 30 seconds. Increase the speed to medium and beat the mixture until pale and smooth, about 3 minutes, scraping down the sides of the mixer bowl as needed.

2 Add the egg and beat until the mixture has lightened in color and looks whipped, 4 to 5 minutes. Reduce the speed to low and scrape down the sides of the mixer bowl. Add the flour mixture and mix until just combined, about 30 seconds. Transfer the streusel mixture to an airtight storage container and refrigerate for at least 12 hours or up to 24 hours.

RECIPE CONTINUES

3 FOR THE DOUGH Whisk the flour, sugar, yeast, and salt together in the stand mixer bowl. Lightly beat the milk, water, and egg together in a separate bowl, then add to the flour mixture. Fit the stand mixer with the dough hook and mix on low speed until all the ingredients are moistened, about 30 seconds. Increase the speed to medium and continue to mix until a sticky dough just forms, about 2 minutes, scraping down the sides of the bowl as needed.

4 With the mixer running, add the butter and continue to mix until fully incorporated and the dough is smooth and elastic and clears the sides of the bowl, 15 to 18 minutes, scraping down the bowl halfway through mixing. Transfer the dough to a lightly greased large bowl. Cover with plastic wrap and let sit at room temperature until doubled in volume, about 30 minutes.

5 Transfer the dough to a lightly floured counter and gently press into a 10-inch square of even thickness. Fold the dough into thirds, like a business letter. Using a bench scraper or sharp knife, cut the rectangle in half lengthwise, then cut each strip crosswise into 4 equal pieces (about 71 grams each). Working with 1 piece of dough at a time, form it into a rough ball by stretching the dough around your thumb and pinching the edges together so that the top is smooth. Place the ball seam side down on a clean counter and, using your cupped hand, drag it in small circles until the dough feels taut and round. Pinch the bottom seam to ensure it's sealed securely and cover with plastic. Let the dough balls rest for 20 minutes.

6 About 5 minutes before the end of the resting time, remove the streusel mixture from the refrigerator and cut into quarters. Set a checkered wire rack over a cutting board. Press the streusel mixture through the rack to create small clumps; break up any clumps larger than ½ inch with your fingers. (If you don't have a checkered wire rack, you can break up the streusel by hand.)

7 Line a rimmed baking sheet with parchment paper. Fill a small bowl with water. Spread a rounded ½ cup streusel into a 4-inch round on a clean counter. Pinch the seam side of 1 dough ball again to ensure the seam is securely sealed, then dip smooth side down into the bowl of water. Place the ball smooth side down on top of the streusel round. Grab a small handful of streusel, about 1 rounded tablespoon, in one hand and press it into the top of the dough. Press the dough ball firmly down into the streusel round, spreading your fingers across the dough to press the streusel into it on both sides.

8 Carefully lift the streusel-covered roll and place, streusel side down, in the palm of your hand. Cup your hand to create a slight depression in the center of the roll, then invert the roll and transfer to the prepared sheet, streusel side up. Return any streusel that did not adhere to dough back to the bowl with the remaining streusel. Repeat with the remaining dough balls and streusel, spacing the rolls evenly on the sheet. Discard any leftover streusel. Bring 2 quarts water to a boil.

9 Adjust an oven rack to the upper-middle position. Place a shallow baking pan on the bottom of the oven. Preheat the oven to 200 degrees for 1 minute, then turn off the oven. Pour the boiling water into the prepared pan. Place the baking sheet on the rack, close the oven, and allow the rolls to rise until nearly doubled in size, about 20 minutes.

10 Carefully remove the baking pan from the oven and discard the water. Remove the rolls from the oven and heat the oven to 375 degrees. Return the rolls to the oven and bake until deep golden brown, 15 to 16 minutes, rotating the sheet after 12 minutes of baking. Transfer the rolls to a wire rack and let cool for 10 minutes before serving.

Cut the chilled streusel into quarters and press each quarter through a checkered wire rack to break it up into small clumps. You can also do this by hand; just make sure the clumps are ½ inch or smaller.

Spread a rounded ½ cup streusel into a 4-inch round on a counter. Place the dough ball smooth side down on top of the streusel round. Grab a small handful of streusel, about 1 rounded tablespoon, in one hand and press it into the top of the dough.

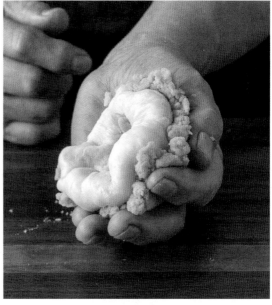

Press the dough ball firmly down into the streusel round, pressing the streusel into the dough on both sides.

Lift the streusel-covered roll and place, streusel side down, in the palm of your hand. Cup your hand to create a slight depression in the center of the roll, then invert the roll onto the prepared sheet (streusel side up).

Yasik and Desserts   343

Coating Peanut Butter Streusel Bread

Uyu Cream Doughnuts 우유크림도넛

oo-yoo cream doughnuts

SARAH
세라

One weekday evening, Umma and I went to the Korean grocery store to pick up some last-minute ingredients. Once inside, we instinctively went our separate ways. Umma headed to the produce section, while I went to the snack aisle. When I was a child, I would linger only in the snack aisle, but as I've grown older, I've found myself eventually making my way to the produce section too. No matter my age, one thing remains a constant—I always visit the snack aisle first. When I reached the end of this nostalgic aisle, my eyes fell upon a small box filled to the brim with individually wrapped cream doughnuts imported from Korea. It sat there untouched, seemingly unnoticed by the passing shoppers. Being a seasoned snacker, I could sense that this packaged dessert was something special—it was a treat that I had seen only in Korea's convenience stores and grocery stores, and now somehow it had arrived in the United States. Umma eventually met up with me as I stood in front of the box of doughnuts, brimming with excitement. I added my snacks to our cart, my eyes fixated on the cream doughnut. Once we were seated in the car, Umma and I immediately opened the package to try it. We gasped with our first bite—even though they had been frozen, the doughnuts retained their yeasty, buttery flavor, and the 2-inch-thick cream filling was just sweet enough and easy to finish, which was a rarity for Umma, as she often finds desserts too sweet. We devoured every last piece and then speed-walked right back into the grocery store and bought five more. I shared these moments on my social media, as I had recorded them on my phone. By the next week, the cream doughnuts were completely sold out and would be unavailable to buy for the next month! Everyone enjoyed these doughnuts just as much as we did, though many weren't able to get their hands on this hot item, including ourselves. But now, thanks to the expertise of Imobu, we—and you—can make a superior version at home. His cream doughnuts are everything you could ask for: perfectly sweetened and fluffy whipped cream sandwiched in a freshly fried split doughnut that's delicately buttery and lofty enough to support 2 inches of fluffy filling.

MAKES 10 doughnuts   **TOTAL TIME** 1¾ hours, plus 1 hour 50 minutes rising, resting, and cooling

DOUGHNUTS

350 grams bread flour
45 grams granulated sugar
7 grams instant or rapid-rise yeast
6 grams fine salt
183 grams warm whole milk (110 degrees)
1 large egg
50 grams unsalted butter, softened
2–3 quarts vegetable oil for frying

FILLING

700 grams heavy cream
100 grams granulated sugar
60 grams sweetened condensed milk, divided
170 grams strawberries, stemmed and sliced thin (optional)

Confectioners' sugar

1 FOR THE DOUGHNUTS Whisk the flour, sugar, yeast, and salt together in the bowl of a stand mixer. Lightly beat the milk and egg together in a separate bowl, then add to the flour mixture. Fit the stand mixer with the dough hook and mix on low speed until all the ingredients are moistened, about 30 seconds. Increase the speed to medium and continue to mix until a sticky dough just forms, 2 to 3 minutes, scraping down the sides of the bowl as needed.

2 With the mixer running, add the butter and continue to mix until fully incorporated and the dough is smooth and elastic and clears the sides of the bowl, about 15 minutes, scraping down the bowl halfway through mixing. Transfer the dough to a lightly greased large bowl. Cover with plastic wrap and let sit at room temperature until doubled in volume, about 30 minutes. Clean and dry the mixer bowl and place it in the freezer.

RECIPE CONTINUES

3 Transfer the dough to a lightly floured counter and gently press it into a 10-inch square of even thickness. Fold the dough into thirds, like a business letter. Using a bench scraper or sharp knife, cut the rectangle in half lengthwise, then cut each strip into 5 equal pieces (about 67 grams each). Working with 1 piece of dough at a time, form it into a rough ball by stretching the dough around your thumb and pinching the edges together so that the top is smooth. Place the ball seam side down on a clean counter and, using your cupped hand, drag it in small circles until the dough feels taut and round. Pinch the bottom seam to ensure it's sealed securely and cover with plastic. Let the dough balls rest for 20 minutes.

4 Cut ten 4-inch square pieces of parchment paper, arrange on two rimmed baking sheets, and lightly spray with vegetable oil spray. Working with 1 piece of dough at a time, gently flatten it with your hand to expel air, then reshape into a smooth, taut ball. Pinch the bottom seam to seal. Using a small greased rolling pin, press and roll the dough ball into a 3-inch round. Arrange the dough rounds seam side down on the prepared parchment squares. Bring 1 quart water to a boil.

5 Adjust the oven racks to the upper-middle and lower-middle positions. Place a shallow baking pan on the bottom of the oven. Preheat the oven to 200 degrees for 1 minute, then turn off the oven. Pour the boiling water into the prepared pan. Place the sheets on the racks, close the oven, and allow the doughnuts to rise until doubled in size, about 30 minutes. Remove the doughnuts from the oven and let sit for 5 minutes to allow their surface to dry.

6 About 20 minutes before the end of the rising time, following the manufacturer's instructions, heat the oil in an electric fryer to 350 degrees. Working with 1 doughnut at a time, lift it from the baking sheet along with the parchment square. Using the edge of the parchment to assist you, carefully flip and lower the doughnut into the hot oil, then peel away and discard the parchment. Repeat with 4 more doughnuts. Cook the doughnuts until golden brown on the undersides, about 90 seconds. Using a spider skimmer, flip the doughnuts and cook until the second sides are browned, about 90 seconds. Transfer the doughnuts to the prepared rack. Return the oil to 350 degrees and repeat with the remaining 5 doughnuts. Let the doughnuts cool completely, about 30 minutes.

7 FOR THE FILLING Using a stand mixer fitted with the chilled bowl and the whisk attachment, whip the cream and sugar on medium-low speed until foamy, about 1 minute. Increase the speed to medium and whip until stiff peaks form, 8 to 9 minutes.

8 Using a serrated knife, cut each doughnut in half horizontally, stopping about ½ inch before the edge. Working with 1 doughnut at a time, open the halves, being careful to leave the uncut section intact, and spread 6 grams (1 teaspoon) condensed milk over the bottom half. Spoon a rounded ½ cup whipped cream onto the bottom half, then fold over the top half. Gently press the halves together until the whipped cream extends just beyond the cut edges of the doughnut. (The doughnut should still be quite open.) Using an offset spatula, spread the whipped cream to fill in any gaps in the opening and create a smooth surface. Clean the edges of the doughnut, then press 4 or 5 strawberry slices, if using, into the whipped cream to create a decorative border. Dust the tops of the doughnuts with confectioners' sugar and serve.

> ### Uncle's Baking Wisdom
>
> *If you don't have a deep fryer, you can use a wide pot or Dutch oven that holds 6 quarts or more. Add the oil to the pot until it measures about 2 inches deep and heat it over medium-high heat to 350 degrees. Adjust the heat as needed to maintain the temperature.*
>
> *These doughnuts are best enjoyed the same day you make them, so plan to share them with friends and family.*

Top Using a serrated knife, cut each doughnut in half horizontally, stopping about ½ inch before the edge. Working with 1 doughnut at a time, open the halves, being careful to leave the uncut section intact, and spread 6 grams (1 teaspoon) condensed milk over the bottom half.

Middle Spoon a rounded ½ cup whipped cream onto the bottom half, then fold over the top half. Gently press the halves together until the cream extends just beyond the cut edges. Use an offset spatula to fill in any gaps and create a smooth surface.

Bottom Clean the edges of the doughnut, then press 4 or 5 strawberry slices, if using, into the whipped cream. Dust with confectioners' sugar.

TURN TO SEE HOW TO SHAPE AND FRY DOUGHNUTS →

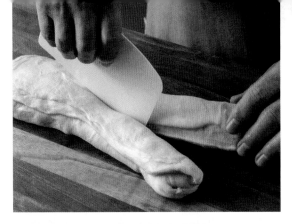

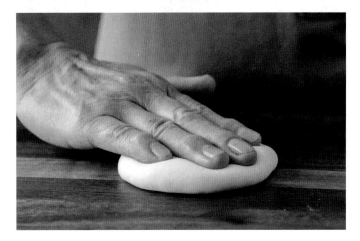

Top After pressing the dough into a 10-inch square and folding it into thirds, like a business letter, cut the dough rectangle in half lengthwise, then cut each strip into 5 equal pieces.

Middle Working with 1 piece of dough at a time, form it into a rough ball by stretching the dough around your thumb and pinching the edges together so that the top is smooth. Place the ball seam side down and, using your cupped hand, drag it in small circles until the dough feels taut and round.

Bottom Working with 1 piece of dough at a time, gently flatten it with your hand to expel air, then reshape it into a smooth, taut ball. Pinch the bottom seam to seal.

Top Press and roll each dough ball into a 3-inch round. Arrange the dough rounds on the prepared parchment squares on the baking sheet.

Bottom left Working with 1 doughnut at a time, lift it from the baking sheet along with the parchment square. Using the edge of the parchment to assist you, carefully flip and lower the doughnut into the hot oil, peeling away and discarding the parchment. Repeat with 4 more doughnuts.

Bottom right Cook the doughnuts until golden brown on the undersides, about 90 seconds. Using a spider skimmer, flip the doughnuts and cook until the second sides are browned, about 90 seconds.

LUNCHBOX CAKE

Dosirak Cake 도시락 케이크

doh-shi-rahk cake

SARAH
세라

If any Asian auntie or uncle tastes a dessert and says, "It's not too sweet," you can rest assured that you have just received high praise. This compliment was all too familiar to me growing up, alongside its more critical Korean counterpart, "Aigoo (goodness), this is far too sweet!" which I would hear whenever my parents sampled American desserts. These reactions, typical among my parents' generation of Koreans and those preceding, reflect their upbringing in a land shaped by poverty and displacement—the results of war and conflict. Due to the scarcity they experienced in those times, sweet desserts rarely made an appearance. However, as they aged and Korea grew more prosperous economically, sweet treats became more commonplace. Despite desserts becoming more available to them, my parents' palates have remained much the same, and they still prefer desserts that are "not too sweet" to satisfy their tastes. Thus, we only ever celebrated birthdays or holidays with Imobu's not-too-sweet Korean-style cakes growing up. With a balanced sweetness that's neither overwhelming nor too subtle, his cakes were enjoyed by children and adults alike. Here's how to make a mini version of his vanilla genoise cake with whipped milk cream frosting. These giftable little "lunchbox" cakes, often presented in charming square takeout containers, have become increasingly popular in recent years in Korea and Japan. This mini cake is perfect for celebrating with a friend or a loved one!

SERVES 2 to 4   TOTAL TIME 1½ hours, plus 1¼ hours cooling and refrigerating

LEMON SYRUP
  75 grams water
  23 grams sugar
   2 (3-inch) strips lemon zest

CAKE
  10 grams unsalted butter
  15 grams milk
   1 large egg plus ½ (10 grams) large egg yolk
  35 grams sugar
  10 grams honey
  35 grams cake flour
   4 grams cornstarch
   1 gram vanilla extract

FROSTING
 350 grams heavy cream
  50 grams sugar
   5 grams sweetened condensed milk
     Liquid food coloring (optional)

1 FOR THE LEMON SYRUP Bring the water and sugar to a boil in a small saucepan. Cook, stirring constantly, until the sugar has dissolved, about 1 minute. Remove the saucepan from the heat, stir in the lemon zest, and let cool completely, about 30 minutes. Discard the lemon zest. (Refrigerate for up to 1 week; bring to room temperature before using.)

2 FOR THE CAKE Adjust an oven rack to the middle position and heat the oven to 350 degrees. Grease a 4-inch round cake pan. Microwave the butter and milk in a small bowl until the butter has melted, about 30 seconds; set aside to cool.

RECIPE CONTINUES

3 Using a stand mixer fitted with a whisk attachment, beat the egg and half yolk, sugar, and honey on medium-low speed until combined, about 30 seconds. Increase the speed to medium-high and beat until the batter is slightly thickened and ivory in color, about 3 minutes, scraping down the sides of the bowl occasionally.

4 Sift the flour and cornstarch through a fine-mesh strainer into a small bowl. Using a silicone spatula, fold the flour mixture into the egg mixture, taking care to scrape the bottom of the bowl, until no streaks of flour remain (be careful not to overmix). Add the melted butter mixture and vanilla and continue folding with a silicone spatula until thoroughly combined.

5 Transfer the batter to the prepared pan. Using a chopstick, swirl the batter to release any small air pockets, then gently tap the pan on the counter to settle the batter. Bake until the cake is golden brown, the center of the cake is firm to the touch, and a toothpick inserted in the center comes out clean, 20 to 22 minutes. Clean and dry the mixer bowl and place it in the freezer.

6 Carefully remove the cake from the oven and gently tap the pan on the counter to settle the cake. Immediately remove the cake from the pan and let cool completely on a wire rack, about 30 minutes.

7 FOR THE FROSTING Meanwhile, using a stand mixer fitted with the chilled bowl and the whisk attachment, whip the cream, sugar, and condensed milk on medium-low speed until foamy, about 1 minute. Increase the speed to medium and whip until medium-stiff peaks form, about 4 minutes (be careful not to overbeat). If desired, transfer 1½ cups frosting to a separate bowl and fold in drops of food coloring until the desired color is achieved. Cover and refrigerate the frosting(s).

8 TO ASSEMBLE THE CAKE Using a serrated knife, trim the mounded top off the cake; discard (or snack on!) the trimmings. Score 2 evenly spaced horizontal lines around the sides of the cake. Following the top scored line, cut the first layer of cake. Carefully remove the layer. Following the remaining scored line, cut the remaining cake into 2 layers. Carefully remove the top layer.

9 Lightly brush the top of the bottom cake layer with lemon syrup; transfer to a piece of parchment or wax paper cut to fit a 6-inch square takeout container. Using a mini offset spatula or large spoon, transfer 2 tablespoons white frosting to the center of the cake layer and spread it evenly over the surface. Place the second cake layer on top and press gently to adhere. Repeat brushing with syrup; spread 2 tablespoons white frosting evenly over the second layer. Place the third cake layer on top and repeat brushing with syrup; discard the remaining syrup. Frost the top and sides of the cake with ½ cup white frosting to create a thin layer, then refrigerate the cake for 15 minutes.

10 Frost the top and sides of the cake with colored frosting, if using, or the remaining white frosting. If desired, use any remaining frosting to create a decorative design on top. Wipe away any extra frosting on the parchment square. Using the edges of the parchment to assist you, carefully transfer the cake and parchment square to the takeout box. Serve immediately or store in the refrigerator for up to 24 hours.

Uncle's Baking Wisdom

You'll need a 4-inch cake pan with at least 2-inch sides. You can substitute a 16-ounce ramekin of similar dimensions; increase the baking time to 25 to 30 minutes.

To get the 10 grams of egg yolk needed for the batter, after separating the yolk from the egg white, lightly beat the yolk with a fork to break it up, then weigh it out.

For a delicate, fluffy cake, don't skip sifting the flour and cornstarch.

Because this cake's lightness comes from the air incorporated into the batter, be careful not to overmix it. Overmixing will deflate the batter, removing the air that helps it rise.

It's crucial to give the cake batter a shock by tapping it against the counter both before and immediately after baking. This will remove large air pockets without deflating the cake.

If your stand mixer is larger than 5 quarts, I suggest using a hand mixer to mix the batter and the frosting.

GINGER-JUJUBE TEA

Saenggang Daechucha 생강대추차

saeng-gahng dae-choo-cha

UMMA
엄마

On the day of Appa's cancer surgery, I remember sitting in the car feeling an immense amount of grief, uncertainty, and fear. I recall it was early February 1997 and spring was just around the corner; however, we were so preoccupied with Appa's health that we had no sense of what season of the year we were in. Truly, I didn't know if Appa would make it through, and I worried about a life without him. I couldn't imagine it—a life without him and a life without a father for our children felt like my own death. As we drove to the hospital together as a family, I looked out the window at a row of trees near the local elementary school and noticed they were beginning to bloom. Despite walking my children along this road to school every day, I never noticed those trees or how the spring season could be so pretty. It then dawned on me that it was the start of spring. The white flowers that fell from the trees were lifted from the ground and swirled in the wind as though they were dancing. In that moment, I realized I had never seen such beauty in something so mundane. Yet, despite the beauty, I felt a deep sense of sorrow—sorrow that I had only noticed something so beautiful, that had always been there for us to enjoy, at a time when I felt my life and world were coming to an end.

Umma's Kitchen Wisdom

If your jujubes are tender and have pliable skins, you can skip hydrating them in step 1.

Use the large holes of a box grater or food processor fitted with the shredding attachment to grate the ginger.

The tea base can be enjoyed after 3 days in the refrigerator, but for the best taste, let the base sit for 2 weeks.

I like to enjoy my tea strained, often adding a few jujube strips from the tea base to my brewed tea.

SARAH
세라

In our backyard, we have two tall jujube trees that Umma planted a decade ago. They stand prominently next to each other, directly within view from my bedroom window. These deciduous trees are bare during the winter months, with only their skeletal branchlets visible. As the winter thaws and the days grow longer, leaves slowly start to form along the length of each branch. Before long, vibrant young green buds and white-blossomed flowers adorn these trees. "Did you notice the flowers blossoming on the jujube trees?" Umma asks every year. "No, I didn't notice them," I reply, my response always the same. "They blossomed about two weeks ago. You'll notice their blossoms one day," Umma says year after year. Now I understand why she wants me to notice them. Every autumn, my family and I spend a few days collecting the bountiful harvest of jujubes from our trees. Appa and my brother shake the trees with their makeshift fruit pickers on their ladders, while Umma and I gather the fallen jujubes in our large kimchi basins. A handful of jujubes will occasionally fall on our heads as we work, prompting us all to break into laughter. Our dog, MayBee, joyfully zooms to and fro in our backyard in the middle of what appears to be a shower of jujubes, while Appa hums one of his favorite American classics: "Stand by Me" by Ben E. King. It's a peaceful time with my family that I look forward to every year. Once they are all collected, Umma takes on the task of meticulously sun-drying our jujubes on several canvas drop cloths. The process takes about a month, during which the jujubes transform into beautifully wrinkled, deep red dates, sweetened by the sun's warmth. Dried jujubes are reported to have numerous health benefits, including improved sleep and digestion. We enjoy using dried jujubes, honey, and ginger to make this hot tea that enhances the fruit's flavor and natural sweetness. This is, hands down, my favorite tea of all time.

MAKES 2½ cups tea base (enough for 18 servings)
TOTAL TIME 30 minutes, plus 6 days 30 minutes
soaking and fermenting

4 ounces (113 grams) dried jujubes
8 ounces (227 grams) fresh ginger, peeled, washed, and coarsely grated
1½ cups honey

1 Soak the jujubes in a bowl with 2 cups water for at least 30 minutes or up to 24 hours. (The jujubes will float to the surface, which is okay, as this is still enough to hydrate them.) Drain the jujubes and remove the pits.

2 Cut the jujubes into very thin, 1-inch-long strips. Combine the jujubes, ginger, and honey in a bowl. Transfer the tea base to a 3-cup glass jar or storage container. Cover tightly and place the container in a 50- to 70-degree location away from direct sunlight. Let sit for 3 days.

3 Transfer the tea base to the refrigerator and let sit for at least 3 days. (Refrigerate for up to 2 months; the flavor will continue to develop over time.)

4 TO MAKE 1 SERVING Stir 1 cup boiling water and 2 tablespoons tea base together in a mug. (If a particle-free tea is desired, combine the boiling water and tea base in a liquid measuring cup, then strain the tea into the mug.)

ICED CORN LATTE

Oksusu Latte 옥수수라떼

ohk-soo-soo latte

SARAH
세라

Koreans enjoy corn in various forms and preparations the way many other cultures do; however, a lesser-known way that Koreans enjoy corn is as a sweet dessert. Korean convenience stores are stocked with corn-flavored ice cream and ice pops, while café shelves are adorned with novel and charming corn-flavored pastries. One corn-infused item that has been appearing more frequently on the drink menus of these cafés is corn latte. Enjoyed with or without espresso, corn lattes unite the buttery and sweet flavors of corn with milk. In our iteration, we include a corn-flavored, sweet vanilla cold foam, which results in a smooth and creamy drink. While some may question whether corn can be enjoyed as a sweet treat, one sip of this drink will convince their taste buds otherwise! Umma and I like the convenience of store-bought vanilla syrup, but you can make your own if you want to channel your inner barista. To get about ¾ cup syrup, combine ½ cup sugar and ½ cup water in a small saucepan. Bring it to a simmer over medium heat, whisking frequently to dissolve the sugar. Remove the saucepan from the heat and stir in ½ teaspoon vanilla extract. Let cool to room temperature and refrigerate for up to 1 week. And to make this latte a real showstopper, add a caramelized corn plank as a beautiful and delicious garnish.

SERVES 2   TOTAL TIME 15 minutes

- 1 cup (250 grams) canned whole-kernel corn, rinsed and drained
- ½ cup milk, plus extra as needed
- 2 tablespoons sweetened condensed milk
- 3 tablespoons heavy cream
- 1 tablespoon vanilla syrup
- ¼ cup brewed espresso or very strong coffee, chilled, plus extra as desired
  Torched corn planks (optional)

1 Process the corn and whole milk in a blender until smooth, about 30 seconds, scraping down the sides of the blender jar as needed. Strain the corn milk through a fine-mesh strainer set over a 2-cup liquid measuring cup, pressing on the solids to extract as much liquid as possible; discard the solids. Stir in the condensed milk until fully dissolved. You should have at least 1 cup corn milk; add extra whole milk as needed to equal 1 cup. (Refrigerate for up to 3 days.)

2 Transfer 2 tablespoons corn milk to a medium bowl. Add the cream and syrup and whisk vigorously to create a dense foam, about 2 minutes. (You can also use a handheld electric milk frother; whisk for about 1 minute.)

3 Fill two 12-ounce glasses two-thirds full with ice. Divide the remaining corn milk evenly between the glasses, then top each with 2 tablespoons espresso (or more if you prefer a stronger drink). Spoon the foam over the top; garnish with 1 or 2 torched corn planks, if using; and serve.

Making Caramelized Corn Planks

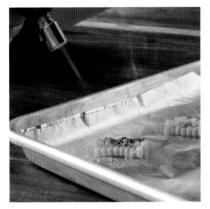

Blanch 1 (1½-inch) portion of an ear of corn, husks and silk removed, in boiling water for 2 minutes. Stabilize the corn on a cutting board by standing the ear on its cut end, then slowly slice down 1 side to remove a plank of kernels.

Using a spatula, carefully transfer the kernel plank to an aluminum foil–lined baking sheet. Repeat slicing the remaining 3 sides of the ear of corn to create 4 planks.

Sprinkle the kernel planks with 1 teaspoon brown sugar. Ignite a pastry torch and, holding the flame 4 to 5 inches from the kernels, sweep the flame over the surface to caramelize the sugar.

Sikhye 식혜

shik-hye

SARAH
세라

Sikhye, a traditional dessert drink made from rice and barley malt, is a unique and nuanced beverage that is quite fascinating. Its taste is smooth and malty while being refreshing and light. It's a drink I find myself gravitating toward throughout the day, often having multiple cups. Beyond its welcoming flavor, though, this drink offers more than meets the eye. Served as a dessert after a meal, sikhye is made by fermenting malted barley with cooked rice and sugar at a warm temperature, nowadays typically using the "keep warm" function on a rice cooker (you will need a 5½-cup or larger rice cooker to make this). During this process, a few pieces of rice rise to the surface, indicating that the malt's diastatic enzyme, amylase, has successfully converted the starch in the rice into sugar, specifically maltose. This conversion imparts a naturally derived malty sweetness to the drink, which adds a more complex flavor profile than what using only granulated sugar could provide. This fermentation process results in a beverage that's also said to aid digestion, especially after heavy, celebratory meals. For a pretty presentation, I suggest garnishing individual portions with jujube flowers.

Umma's Kitchen Wisdom

Although its texture is coarse, cracked malted barley is sometimes labeled as "flour" or "powder." Look for packages labeled "yeotgireum" (see page 21).

Adding the barley malt water to the rice while it's still warm helps activate the fermentation process.

Some people prefer to filter the sediment from the barley malt water to achieve a clear sikhye, but this is purely aesthetic. Keeping the sediment enhances the flavors, and also adds nutrition due to the presence of barley malt. (Halmeoni always kept the sediment, and so do I.)

To garnish this with grains of rice, strain out a portion of the cooked rice at the end of step 5. Rinse it well and refrigerate it in clean, cold water for up to 1 week. You can also garnish this with jujube flowers (see page 245).

SERVES 12 (makes 3½ quarts)   **TOTAL TIME** 1¼ hours, plus 5½ hours sitting, cooling, and chilling

  10 ounces (284 grams) yeotgireum (malted barley), cracked
  1½ cups (312 grams) short- or medium-grain white rice
  1½ cups (298 grams) sugar, divided
  1½ ounces (43 grams) ginger, peeled and sliced ¼ inch thick
   3 cinnamon sticks (15 grams)

1 Bundle the barley in a triple layer of cheesecloth and secure with kitchen twine. Submerge the barley bundle in 12 cups water in a large bowl; set aside.

2 Add the rice to a medium bowl and cover by 2 inches water. Using your hands, gently swish the rice to release excess starch. Carefully pour off the water, leaving the rice in the bowl. Repeat 3 times, or until the water runs almost clear. Using a fine-mesh strainer, drain the rice, then transfer to the cooking chamber of a 5½- to 6-quart electric rice cooker. Stir in 1¼ cups water, cover, and cook on the standard rice setting according to the manufacturer's directions.

3 Once the rice is finished cooking (typically indicated by the "Keep Warm" light turning on), use a moistened rice paddle or silicone spatula to gently fluff the rice (the rice should be drier than usual). Cover the cooker, still on the "Keep Warm" function, and set aside.

4 Bring 3 cups water to a boil. Add the boiling water to the bowl with the barley. Using your hands, submerge the bundle in the water and gently massage and squeeze it, rotating it occasionally, until the liquid turns milky in color, about 5 minutes. Lift the bundle above the bowl and squeeze out as much liquid as possible; discard the barley bundle.

5 Add ½ cup sugar to the rice, then stir in warm barley malt water up to the "maximum" line (about 6 cups). Break up any rice clumps. Cover the rice cooker, still on the "Keep Warm" function, and let the rice sit for 4 hours. Set aside the remaining barley malt water.

6 Transfer the rice mixture to a large, wide pot. Stir in the remaining barley malt water and any settled sediment, the ginger, cinnamon sticks, and remaining 1 cup sugar. Cover and bring the punch to a boil over medium-high heat. Reduce to a simmer and cook, stirring occasionally, for 5 minutes. Remove the punch from the heat, discard the ginger and cinnamon sticks, and let cool to room temperature. Transfer to a storage container and refrigerate until chilled, about 1 hour. Stir to recombine before serving. (Refrigerate for up to 1 week.)

Kitchen Conversation

UMMA *You know how we enjoy ice cream in the winter? Well, sikhye is what my family enjoyed in the winter. Halmeoni would chill the sikhye outside where it was very cold, and the top would become perfectly slushy.*

SARAH But it tastes so good in the summer when it's hot! I crave drinking this after walking MayBee [our dog] during the warm summer weather.

UMMA *I know. But just like how we enjoy ice cream in the winter, sikhye tastes incredible in the winter despite being a cold, refreshing drink. It's a drink we also enjoyed during Seollal [Lunar New Year] and Chuseok [Autumn Harvest Festival].*

SARAH Do you think Halmeoni made this only during the winter season because of the holidays?

UMMA *I'm not sure. I strongly associate this drink with winter only, even though it's served during any season. But to me, it just tastes better during the wintertime.*

Conversions and Equivalents

Some say cooking is a science and an art. We would say that geography has a hand in it, too. Flours and sugars manufactured in the United Kingdom and elsewhere will feel and taste different from those manufactured in the United States. So we cannot promise that the loaf of bread you bake in Canada or England will taste the same as a loaf baked in the States, but we can offer guidelines for converting weights and measures. We also recommend that you rely on your instincts when making our recipes. Refer to the visual cues provided. If the dough hasn't "come together in a ball" as described, you may need to add more flour—even if the recipe doesn't tell you to. You be the judge.

The recipes in this book were developed using standard U.S. measures following U.S. government guidelines. The charts below offer equivalents for U.S. and metric measures. All conversions are approximate and have been rounded up or down to the nearest whole number.

EXAMPLE

1 teaspoon = 4.9292 milliliters, rounded up to 5 milliliters
1 ounce = 28.3495 grams, rounded down to 28 grams

Volume Conversions

U.S.	METRIC
1 teaspoon	5 milliliters
2 teaspoons	10 milliliters
1 tablespoon	15 milliliters
2 tablespoons	30 milliliters
¼ cup	59 milliliters
⅓ cup	79 milliliters
½ cup	118 milliliters
¾ cup	177 milliliters
1 cup	237 milliliters
1¼ cups	296 milliliters
1½ cups	355 milliliters
2 cups (1 pint)	473 milliliters
2½ cups	591 milliliters
3 cups	710 milliliters
4 cups (1 quart)	0.946 liter
1.06 quarts	1 liter
4 quarts (1 gallon)	3.8 liters

Weight Conversions

OUNCES	GRAMS
½	14
¾	21
1	28
1½	43
2	57
2½	71
3	85
3½	99
4	113
4½	128
5	142
6	170
7	198
8	227
9	255
10	283
12	340
16 (1 pound)	454

Conversions for Common Baking Ingredients

Baking is an exacting science. Because measuring by weight is far more accurate than measuring by volume, and thus more likely to produce reliable results, in the baking recipes in this book we provide gram measures. Refer to the chart below to convert these measures into ounces.

INGREDIENT	OUNCES	GRAMS
Flour		
*1 cup all-purpose flour**	5	142
1 cup cake flour	4	113
1 cup whole-wheat flour	5½	156
Sugar		
1 cup granulated (white) sugar	7	198
1 cup packed brown sugar (light or dark)	7	198
1 cup confectioners' sugar	4	113
Cocoa Powder		
1 cup cocoa powder	3	85
Butter†		
4 tablespoons (½ stick or ¼ cup)	2	57
8 tablespoons (1 stick or ½ cup)	4	113
16 tablespoons (2 sticks or 1 cup)	8	227

* *U.S. all-purpose flour, the most frequently used flour in this book, does not contain leaveners, as some European flours do. These leavened flours are called self-rising or self-raising. If you are using self-rising flour, take this into consideration before adding leaveners to a recipe.*

† *In the United States, butter is sold both salted and unsalted. We generally recommend unsalted butter. If you are using salted butter, take this into consideration before adding salt to a recipe.*

Oven Temperatures

FAHRENHEIT	CELSIUS	GAS MARK
225	105	¼
250	120	½
275	135	1
300	150	2
325	165	3
350	180	4
375	190	5
400	200	6
425	220	7
450	230	8
475	245	9

Converting Temperatures from an Instant-Read Thermometer

We include doneness temperatures in many of the recipes in this book. We recommend an instant-read thermometer for the job. Refer to the table above to convert Fahrenheit degrees to Celsius. Or, for temperatures not represented in the chart, use this simple formula:

Subtract 32 degrees from the Fahrenheit reading, then divide the result by 1.8 to find the Celsius reading.

EXAMPLE
"Roast chicken until thighs register 175 degrees."

To convert:
  175°F – 32 = 143°
   143° ÷ 1.8 = 79.44°C, rounded down to 79°C

Index

NOTE Page references in *italics* indicate photographs.

C

Cabbage
Angel Hair Mixed Cold Noodles, *290,* 291
Beef Cutlets, *180,* 181–82
Cut Napa, Kimchi, *114,* 115–16, *117*
Ground Soybean Stew, *220,* 221–22
napa, about, 32
Napa, and Young Summer Radish
Kimchi, *136,* 137–39
and Radish, Soybean Paste Soup with,
226, *227*
Rolls, Rotisserie Chicken, *190,* 191–93
Steamed Thin Pork Belly with
Vegetables, 168, *169*
Whole Napa, Kimchi, *126,* 127–31
Cake, Lunchbox, *350,* 351–52, *353*
Carrots
about, 29
Banquet Noodles, 302–3, *303*
Braised Beef Ribs, 187–88, *189*
Chicken Radish, 140, *141*
cutting into matchsticks, 40
Fried Seaweed Rolls, *324,* 325–27
Fried Vegetables, 322, *323*
Mixed Rice, *262,* 263–64
Perilla Leaf Kimchi, 134–35, *135*
Rotisserie Chicken Knife-Cut Noodle
Soup, 304–5, *305*
Seasoned Acorn Jelly, 62, *63*
Seaweed Rice Rolls, *256,* 257–61
Seoul-Style Bulgogi, *184,* 185–86
Spicy Pork Bulgogi, 166–67, *167*
Steamed Thin Pork Belly with
Vegetables, 168, *169*
Stir-Fried Fish Cakes, 86–87, *87*
Stir-Fried Glass Noodles, *294,* 295–96
trimming edges of, 40
**Chadolbagi Mu Sotbap (Beef Brisket and
Radish Pot Rice), 282–83, *283***
Chamchi aek (tuna extract sauce), 14
Cheese, Kimchi Grilled, *312,* 313
Chicken
Honey-Garlic, *194,* 195
Korean Fried, 198–200, *199*
Rotisserie, Cabbage Rolls, *190,* 191–93
rotisserie, for recipes, 25
Rotisserie, Knife-Cut Noodle Soup,
304–5, *305*
Soy Sauce–Braised, 196–97, *197*
Sweet and Spicy Korean Fried, 201, *201*
-Vegetable Pickled Radish Wraps, *310,* 311
Chicken Mu (Chicken Radish), 140, *141*

Chickpeas
Multigrain Rice, 288–89, *289*
Pressure-Cooker Beans, 289
Chile(s)
Assorted Pickles, 142, *143*
Green, Pickles, 150, *151*
Green, Pickles, Spicy, 70, *71*
Seasoning Sauce for Kalguksu, 36, *36*
types of, 30
Young Summer Radish and Napa
Cabbage Kimchi, *136,* 137–39
"Chinese Restaurant Syndrome," 17
Chive(s), garlic
about, 30
Braised Marinated Pork Neck,
170–71, *171*
Seasoning Sauce, 35, *35*
Steamed Thin Pork Belly with
Vegetables, 168, *169*
Vegetable Pancakes, *313,* 314
Cho Ganjang (Vinegar Soy Sauce), 35, *35*
Chopsticks, Korean, 8
Chwinamul (aster scaber), 18
**Chwinamulbap (Aster Scaber Rice),
270, 271–72**
**Chwinamul Muchim (Seasoned Aster
Scaber), 58, *59***
Cilantro Radish Shreds, Seasoned, *78,* 79
Coffee
Iced Corn Latte, 356, *357*
Corn
caramelized planks, preparing, 357
Latte, Iced, 356, *357*
Corn syrup, 14
Costco, shopping at, 33
Crab
Spicy Raw Marinated, 202–4, *203*
trimming, 204
Crab, imitation. *See* Imitation crab
**Croaker, Pan-Fried Salted and Dried,
210, *211***
Cucumber(s)
Angel Hair Mixed Cold Noodles,
290, 291
cutting into matchsticks, 40
Kimchi, 132, *133*
Korean, about, 31
Pickles, *148,* 149
Pickles, Spicy, 68, *69*
Seasoned Acorn Jelly, 62, *63*
**Cumin Seasoning Salt, Fried Pork Ribs
with, 176, *177***

D

Daepa (jumbo Korean green onions), 31
**Daepae Samgyeopsal Yachae Jjim
(Steamed Thin Pork Belly with
Vegetables), 168, *169***
**Dakgogi Ganjang Jorim (Soy Sauce–
Braised Chicken), 196–97, *197***
Dangmyeon (Korean vermicelli), 22
**Danpatjuk (Sweet Red Bean Porridge),
246, 247–49**
Dashima, about, 18
Dasida beef stock powder, 21
Desserts
Lunchbox Cake, *350,* 351–52, *353*
Milk Cream Doughnuts, *344,* 345–49
Sweet Pancake Sandwiches, 320, *321*
Deulgae Sauce (Perilla Seed Sauce), 37, *37*
Dipori (dried large-eyed herring), 24
Distilled white vinegar, 13
Doenjang, about, 13
Doljaban, about, 18
**Doljaban Muchim (Seasoned Dried
Seaweed), 48, *49***
**Dongchimi (Radish Water Kimchi),
120–21, *121***
**Dongchimi Guksu (Radish Water
Kimchi Noodles), *298,* 299**
**Dosirak Cake (Lunchbox Cake),
350, 351–52, *353***
**Dotorimuk Muchim (Seasoned
Acorn Jelly), 62, *63***
Doughnuts, Milk Cream, *344,* 345–49
Drinks
Ginger-Jujube Tea, 354–55, *355*
Iced Corn Latte, 356, *357*
Rice Punch, 358–59, *359*
Dubu (tofu), 25
Dubu Jorim (Spicy Braised Tofu), 96, *97*
Dumplings, *156,* 157–61, *159*
Dumplings, Rice Cake Soup with, 230, *231*
Dumpling wrappers, 22
**Dwaeji Deunggalbi Kimchim Jjim
(Braised Pork Back Ribs and Kimchi),
174–75, *175***
**Dwaeji Deunggalbi Twigim (Fried Pork
Ribs with Cumin Seasoning Salt),
176, *177***
**Dwaeji Moksal Yangnyeom Gui (Braised
Marinated Pork Neck), 170–71, *171***

E

Eggplant
    about, 30
    and Squash, Seasoned, *56, 57*
Egg(s)
    Angel Hair Mixed Cold Noodles, *290,* 291
    Beef Rib Soup, 232–33, *233*
    Drop Soup, Soft Tofu, *214,* 215
    Kimchi Fried Rice, 279–80, *281*
    Kimchi Mixed Cold Noodles, *292, 293*
    Marinated Avocado and Pollack Roe
        Rice, 266, *267*
    Mixed Rice, *262,* 263–64
    Radish Water Kimchi Noodles, *298,* 299
    ribbons, creating, 42
    Rice Cake Soup with Dumplings,
        230, *231*
    Rice with Avocado, 274, *275*
    Rolled Omelet, 104–7, *105*
    Seaweed Rice Rolls, *256,* 257–61
    Soy-Braised Beef, 98, *99*
    for special occasions, 101
    Spicy Soft Tofu Stew, 242–43, *243*
    Spinach Fried Rice, *276,* 277–78
    Steamed, *102,* 103
Eomuk (fish cakes), 24
Eomuk Bokkeum (Stir-Fried Fish Cakes),
    86–87, *87*
Eomukguk (Fish Cake Soup), *236,* 237

F

Fermented vegetables, 20
Fish
    Braised Mackerel, *206,* 207–9
    dried, types of, 24, *25*
    fresh, buying, 25
    Pan-Fried Salted and Dried Croaker,
        210, *211*
    preparing whole mackerel, 209
    salted, for kimchi fermentation, 112
    see also Anchovies; Herring;
        Imitation crab
Fish Cake(s)
    about, 24
    Seaweed Rice Rolls, *256,* 257–61
    Soup, *236,* 237
    Spicy Rice Cakes, *318,* 319
    Stir-Fried, 86–87, *87*

Fish sauce
    about, 14
    for kimchi fermentation, 112
Fruit
    dried, for recipes, 18
    fresh, choosing, 29–30
    see also specific fruits

G

Gaji Aehobak Muchim (Seasoned
    Eggplant and Squash), *56, 57*
Galbi Jjim (Braised Beef Ribs), 187–88, *189*
Galbitang (Beef Rib Soup), 232–33, *233*
Gamja Bokkeum (Stir-Fried Potatoes),
    88, **89**
Ganjang Mu Jangajji (Soy Sauce Radish
    Pickles), 144, *145*
Ganjang Mu Jangajji Muchim (Seasoned
    Soy Sauce Radish Pickles), *66,* **67**
Garlic
    about, 30
    Beef Rib Soup, 232–33, *233*
    -Honey Chicken, *194,* 195
    minced, prepping, 39
    Pickled, *146, 147*
    Spicy Raw Marinated Crab, 202–4, *203*
Garlic chives. *See* **Chive(s), garlic**
Gim
    about, 18
    Fried Seaweed Rolls, *324,* 325–27
    Roasted, with Crispy Tofu, 76, *77*
    Seaweed Rice Rolls, *256,* 257–61
Gimbap (Seaweed Rice Rolls), *256,* 257–61
Gimbap, and Korean culture, 254–55
Gim Mari (Fried Seaweed Rolls),
    324, **325–27**
Ginger
    Beef Rib Soup, 232–33, *233*
    -Jujube Tea, 354–55, *355*
    Rice Punch, 358–59, *359*
Glutinous rice flour
    about, 21
    Sweet Red Bean Porridge, *246,* 247–49
Gochugaru
    about, 16
    Cut Napa Cabbage Kimchi,
        114, 115–16, *117*
    Radish Kimchi, 118–19, *119*
    Seasoning Sauce for Kalguksu, *36,* 36

Gochugaru *(cont.)*
    Spicy Raw Marinated Crab, 202–4, *203*
    Whole Napa Cabbage Kimchi,
        126, 127–31
Gochujang
    about, 13
    Angel Hair Mixed Cold Noodles, *290,* 291
    Mixed Rice, *262,* 263–64
    Mustard Sauce, 37, *37*
    Seasoned, 34, *34*
    Seasoned Spinach with, 54, *55*
    Spam Stew, 218, *219*
    Stir-Fried Anchovies with, 84, *85*
Gochu Jangajji (Green Chile Pickles),
    150, *151*
Gochu Jangajji Muchim (Spicy Green
    Chile Pickles), 70, *71*
Godeungeo Jorim (Braised Mackerel),
    206, **207–9**
Gosu Musaengchae (Seasoned Cilantro
    Radish Shreds), *78,* **79**
Green onions
    about, 31
    slicing, 40
Greens
    Green Salad, 72, *73*
    see also Spinach
Guk (soup), for Korean meals, 8
Gulbi Gui (Pan-Fried Salted and Dried
    Croaker), 210, *211*
Gul Musaengchae (Seasoned Oyster
    Radish Shreds), 80, *81*
Guun Gimgwa Dubu (Roasted Gim with
    Crispy Tofu), 76, *77*
Gyeranbap (Egg Rice with Avocado),
    274, *275*
Gyeran Jjim (Steamed Eggs), *102,* **103**
Gyeran Mari (Rolled Omelet), 104–7, *105*

H

Haitai Honey Butter Chips, 26
Haitai Matdongsan Peanut Crunch
    Snack, 26
Haitai Nougat Bar, 26
Herbs and spices, 16–17
Herring, dried large-eyed
    about, 24
    Cut Napa Cabbage Kimchi,
        114, 115–16, *117*

M

Mackerel
  Braised, *206,* 207–9
  whole, preparing, 209
Maesil cheong (plum extract syrup), 14
**Maeun Dwaejibulgogi (Spicy Pork
  Bulgogi), 166–67,** *167*
Malted barley
  about, 21
  Rice Punch, 358–59, *359*
Mandu (Dumplings), *156,* **157–61,** *159*
Mandu pi (dumpling wrappers), 22
Maneul Jangajji (Pickled Garlic), *146,* **147**
Mat Kimchi (Cut Napa Cabbage Kimchi),
  114, **115–16,** *117*
Meat. *See* Beef; Pork
Milk Bread, *332,* **333–35**
Milk Cream Doughnuts, *344,* **345–49**
Mirin (rice wine), 14
**Miwon matsogeum (MSG seasoning
  salt), 17**
Miyeok, about, 18
Miyeokguk (Seaweed Soup), **238,** *239*
Modeum Jangajji (Assorted Pickles),
  142, *143*
MSG seasoning salt, 17
MSG stigma syndrome, 17
Muchim
  Broccoli Dubu (Seasoned Broccoli Tofu),
    52, *53*
  Chwinamul (Seasoned Aster Scaber),
    58, *59*
  Doljaban (Seasoned Dried Seaweed),
    48, *49*
  Dotorimuk (Seasoned Acorn Jelly), 62, *63*
  Gaji Aehobak (Seasoned Eggplant and
    Squash), *56,* 57
  Ganjang Mu Jangajji (Seasoned Soy
    Sauce Radish Pickles), *66,* 67
  Gochu Jangajji (Spicy Green Chile
    Pickles), 70, *71*
  Jinmichae (Spicy Dried Squid), 64–65, *65*
  Kongnamul (Seasoned Soybean Sprouts),
    50, 51
  Mumallaengi (Seasoned Dried Radish),
    60, 61
  Oiji (Spicy Cucumber Pickles), 68, *69*
  Sigeumchi Gochujang (Seasoned
    Spinach with Gochujang), 54, *55*
Mumallaengi (dried radish), 18

**Mumallaengi Muchim (Seasoned Dried
  Radish),** *60, 61*
Mung bean sprouts
  Dumplings, *156,* 157–61, *159*
  Steamed Thin Pork Belly with
    Vegetables, 168, *169*
Mushrooms
  about, 32
  Mixed Rice, *262,* 263–64
  Seoul-Style Bulgogi, *184,* 185–86
  Steamed Thin Pork Belly with
    Vegetables, 168, *169*
Mustard
  Gochujang Sauce, 37, *37*
  -Honey Sauce, 36, *36*
Myeolchi (dried anchovies), 24
**Myeolchi Gochujang Bokkeum (Stir-Fried
  Anchovies with Gochujang), 84,** *85*
**Myeongranjeot (salted/seasoned
  pollack roe), 25**

N

Neutral cooking oil, 13
New sugar, 17
Nongshim Honey Twist Snack, 26
Nongshim Salt Bread Snack, 26
**Nongshim Spicy Flavor Shrimp
  Crackers, 26**
Noodle(s)
  Angel Hair Mixed Cold, *290,* 291
  Banquet, 302–3, *303*
  Beef Rib Soup, 232–33, *233*
  dried wheat, about, 22
  Dumplings, *156,* 157–61, *159*
  Fried Seaweed Rolls, *324,* 325–27
  Glass, Stir-Fried, *294,* 295–96
  Kimchi Mixed Cold, 292, *293*
  Knife-Cut, Rotisserie Chicken Soup,
    304–5, *305*
  knife-cut wheat, about, 22
  for Korean meals, 8
  Korean vermicelli, about, 22
  Radish Water Kimchi, *298,* 299
  Seoul-Style Bulgogi, *184,* 185–86
  Stir-Fried Udon with Beef Belly,
    300–301, *301*
  udon, about, 22
Nuts
  Sweet Pancake Sandwiches, 320, *321*

O

Oiji (Cucumber Pickles), *148,* **149**
**Oiji Muchim (Spicy Cucumber Pickles),
  68,** *69*
Oi Kimchi (Cucumber Kimchi), 132, *133*
Oils, 13
Oksusu Latte (Iced Corn Latte), 356, *357*
Omelet, Rolled, 104–7, *105*
Onions
  green, about, 31
  green, slicing, 40
  yellow, making fresh juice from, 41
Orion Gosomi Sweet & Salty Cracker, 26
Orion Hot & Spicy Squid Peanut Balls, 26
Orion Sweet Corn Turtle Chips, 26
Ottogi Mild Jin Ramen, 26
Oyster(s)
  Radish Shreds, Seasoned, 80, *81*
  Spicy Soft Tofu Stew, 242–43, *243*

P

Pancake mix, 21
Pancakes
  Beef, 178, *179*
  Kimchi, 316–17, *317*
  Vegetable, *313,* 314
Pasta. *See* Angel Hair
Peanut Butter Streusel Bread, *340,* **341–43**
Pear. *See* Asian pear
Peas
  Multigrain Rice, 288–89, *289*
  Steamed White Rice, 284, *285*
Peppers
  Pickled Radish Chicken-Vegetable
    Wraps, *310,* 311
  Sausage and Vegetable Stir-Fry, *164,* 165
  Soy-Braised Beef, 98, *99*
  Stir-Fried Glass Noodles, *294,* 295–96
  see also Chile(s)
Perilla leaves
  about, 32
  Perilla Leaf Kimchi, 134–35, *135*
  Seasoned Acorn Jelly, 62, *63*
  Spicy Pork Bulgogi, 166–67, *167*
  Vegetable Pancakes, *313,* 314
Perilla seeds, 17
Perilla Seed Sauce, 37, *37*
Pickled Garlic, *146,* **147**